Contents

W9-BWF-922

INTRODUCTION 4

What to see	6	Things not to miss	10
When to go	8	Itineraries	16
Author picks	9		

BASICS 18

Getting there	19	Culture and etiquette	27
Arrival	20	LGBTQ Tokyo	29
City transport	21	Kids' Tokyo	30
The media	25	Travel essentials	31
Festivals and events	25		

THE GUIDE 39

1 The Imperial Palace and around	40	7 Bayside Tokyo	86
2 Ginza and around	50	8 Akasaka and Roppongi	96
3 Akihabara and around	58	9 Ebisu and the south	106
4 Ueno and around	64	10 Harajuku, Aoyama and Shibuya	114
5 Asakusa and around	73	11 Shinjuku and the west	126
6 Ryōgoku and Kiyosumi	80	12 Ikebukuro and the north	136

LISTINGS 145

13 Accommodation	145	16 Entertainment and the arts	191
14 Eating	157	17 Shopping	197
15 Drinking and nightlife	178	18 Sport and health	210

OUT OF THE CITY

19 Around Tokyo	215

CONTEXTS 254

History	255	The arts, architecture and design	268
Books	263	Japanese	273
Film	266	Glossary	281

SMALL PRINT & INDEX 282

Introduction to
Tokyo

With its sushi and sumo, geisha and gardens, neon and noodles, it may seem that Tokyo is in danger of collapsing under the weight of its own stereotypes. Yet ticking off a bunch of travel clichés is rarely this much fun, and as you might expect of the planet's largest metropolis, there's also enough nuance here to keep you entertained for a lifetime. Ordered yet bewildering, Japan's pulsating capital will lead you a merry dance: this is Asia at its weirdest, straightest, prettiest, sleaziest and coolest, all at the same time.

Caught up in an untidy web of overhead cables, plagued by seemingly incessant noise, the concrete and steel conurbation may seem the stereotypical urban nightmare. Yet step back from the frenetic main roads and chances are you'll find yourself in tranquil backstreets, where dinky **wooden houses** are fronted by neatly clipped bonsai trees; wander beyond the high-tech emporia, and you'll discover charming fragments of the old city such as **temples** and **shrines** wreathed in wisps of smoking incense.

Centuries of organizing itself around the daily demands of millions of inhabitants have made Tokyo something of a **model metropolitan environment**. Trains run on time and to practically every corner of the city, **crime** is hardly worth worrying about, and convenience stores and vending machines provide everything you could need (and many things you never thought you did) 24 hours a day.

With so much going on, just walking the streets of this hyperactive city can be an energizing experience. It need not be an expensive one, either – you'll be pleasantly surprised by how **affordable** many things are. Cheap-and-cheerful *izakaya* – bars that serve food – and casual cafés serving noodles and rice dishes are plentiful, the metro is a bargain, and tickets for a sumo tournament or a kabuki play can be bought for the price of a few drinks.

Browsing the **shops** and marvelling at the passing parade is mesmerizing – the next best thing to having a ringside seat at the hippest of catwalk shows. The city's great wealth and relative lack of planning restrictions have given **architects** almost unparalleled freedom to

THE ROUGH GUIDE TO
TOKYO

ROUGH GUIDES

This eighth edition updated by
Martin Zatko

LEFT-FIELD TOKYO

Many visitors to Tokyo expect to see something a little quirky during their stay – here are a few places to sample the city's more intriguing facets.

Capsule hotels The rooms at capsule hotels are pretty darn small – there's no more characteristic Japanese sleeping experience (see page 153).

Robot Restaurant Seeing is believing at this zany attraction, where performances feature dozens of dancing girls and robots (see page 194).

Game centres Bash the hell out of the world's weirdest arcade machines in one of the city's many game centres (see page 91).

Oddball cafés Have your coffee served by costumed girls, fawning guys in dicky-bows, or surrounded by owls, cats or snakes (see page 173).

Golden Gai Tokyo drinking at its most atmospheric, this is a warren of minuscule bars in neon-drenched Shinjuku (see page 133).

Shibuya crossing It's amazing to see just how many people can cross a road at the same time; take in the spectacle over a coffee at *L'Occitane* (see page 175).

Standing bars Eat like a horse, standing up at one of the city's umpteen cheap and cheerful *soba-ya* or *udon-ya* (see page 162), or do likewise with alcohol at a tachinomiya (see page 179).

---

realize their wildest dreams. Likewise, in uber-chic bars, restaurants and clubs you'll see today what the rest of the world will get tomorrow. You may not figure out exactly what makes Tokyo tick – and you're sure to get a little confused while trying – but the conclusion is inescapable: Japan's powerhouse capital is a seductive and addictive experience.

What to see

One way to ease yourself into the city is by taking a relatively crowd-free turn around the **Imperial Palace** – the inviolate home of the emperor and a tangible link to the past. From here it's a quick hop to **Marunouchi** which has been busily restyling itself as a chic shopping and dining destination to rival glitzy **Ginza**.

High on your sightseeing agenda should also be Tokyo's evocative northeast quarter, where the Edo-era spirit of the city remains. **Asakusa**'s primary focus is the major Buddhist temple of **Sensō-ji**, surrounded by a plethora of traditional craft shops. The leafy precincts of **Ueno Park** contain several major museums, including the **Tokyo National Museum**. From here it's an easy stroll to the charming and tranquil districts of **Nezu**, **Sendagi** and **Yanaka**, packed with small temples, shrines and shops.

The weird, wired and wonderful **Akihabara** area – famous worldwide for its electronics stores – has recently rebooted as the focus of Tokyo's dynamic manga and anime scene; nearby you'll find the **Kanda Myōjin**, one of Tokyo's oldest shrines and host to one of the city's top three festivals, the **Kanda Matsuri**. Across the Sumida-gawa is **Ryōguku**, home to the colossal **Edo-Tokyo Museum** and the **National Sumo Stadium**.

Linked by the impressive Rainbow Bridge is **Odaiba**, a futuristic man-made island, where you'll find the **Miraikan**, Tokyo's most fascinating science museum, and the touristy, fun public **bathhouse** Ōedo Onsen Monogatari.

Roppongi's nightlife can exhaust the most committed hedonist, but save some energy to return by day to explore the **Roppongi Art Triangle** formed by the **National**

Art Center, housed in one of the city's most dazzling architectural spaces; the **Suntory Museum of Art**; and the excellent Mori Art Museum, atop the **Roppongi Hills** complex.

The southern part of central Tokyo is a slightly unwieldy mishmash of districts revolving around **Ebisu** and **Meguro**; highlights here include the calmer, boutique-filled **Daikanyama** and **Nakameguro** neighbourhoods.

Fashionistas should head towards on-trend **Shibuya** and **Harajuku**, and the super-chic, boutique-lined boulevards of **Aoyama**. When you've reached consumer saturation point, retreat to the wooded grounds of nearby **Meiji-jingū**, the city's most venerable Shinto shrine, or peruse the delicate woodblock prints and crafts and artworks in the **Nezu Museum**, the **Ōta Memorial Museum of Art** or the **Japan Folk Crafts Museum**.

Also on the west side of the city lies **Shinjuku**, bursting with towering skyscrapers, endless amounts of neon, TV screens several storeys tall, and arguably the world's most complicated railway station. Attractions here include the monumental **Tokyo Metropolitan Government Building**, the beautiful gardens of **Shinjuku Gyoen** and the lively and raffish **Kabukichō** entertainment area; the hipster paradise of **Shimokitazawa** is a short trip to the west.

In the north of Tokyo, offbeat pleasures include the rickety **Sakura Line**, the city centre's last tramway; the Frank Lloyd Wright-designed **Myonichi-kan** in Ikebukuro; and a trio of pretty Japanese **gardens**.

TOP 5 URBAN GREEN ESCAPES

Look at any map of central Tokyo and you'll quickly realize that there isn't much in the way of parkland – just 5.3 square metres of park per resident, compared to 29 square metres in New York and 26 square metres in Paris. Compounding this, two of the biggest central patches of greenery (those immediately around the Imperial Palace and the Akasaka Detached Palace) are largely off-limits to the general public. However, here are five bona fide urban green escapes; see ⓦtokyo-park.or.jp for further suggestions.

Hama Rikyū Onshi Teien Once the duck-hunting grounds of the shogun, now a beautiful bayside retreat (see page 52).

Higashi Gyoen The east garden of the Imperial Palace, an oasis of tranquillity in the heart of the city (see page 43).

Meiji-jingū Inner Garden Peaceful grounds surrounding Tokyo's most important Shinto shrine (see page 118).

National Park for Nature Study A slightly inconvenient location helps to preserve this park's natural serenity (see page 111).

Shinjuku Gyoen English, French and Japanese garden styles combine harmoniously at this spacious park (see page 133).

High-speed trains put several important sights within **day-trip** range of Tokyo, including the ancient temple and shrine towns of **Kamakura** to the south and **Nikkō** to the north. **Mount Fuji**, 100km southwest of the capital, can be climbed from July to September, while the adjoining national park area of **Hakone** offers relaxed hiking amid beautiful lakeland scenery and the chance to take a dip in an onsen – a Japanese mineral bath.

When to go

One of the best times to visit is in the spring, from April to early May. At the start of this period (known as *hanami*) flurries of falling cherry blossom give the city a soft pink hue and by the end the temperatures are pleasant. October and November are also good months to come; this is when you'll catch the fireburst of **autumn** leaves in Tokyo's parks and gardens.

Avoid the steamy height of **summer** (late July to early Sept), when the city's humidity sees its citizens scurrying from one air-conditioned haven to another. From January through to March temperatures can dip to freezing, but the crisp blue **winter** skies are rarely disturbed by rain or snow showers. Carrying an umbrella is a good idea during *tsuyu*, the rainy season in June and July, and in September, when typhoons occasionally strike the coast.

When planning your visit also check the city's calendar of **festivals** and special events (see page 25) for any that may interest you. Note also that many attractions shut for several days around New Year when Tokyo becomes oddly calm, as many people return to their family homes elsewhere in the country.

AVERAGE MONTHLY TEMPERATURES AND RAINFALL

	Jan	Feb	March	April	May	June	July	Aug	Sept	Oct	Nov	Dec
Max/min (°C)	10/1	10/1	13/4	18/10	23/15	25/18	29/22	31/24	27/20	21/14	17/8	12/3
Max/min (°F)	49/33	50/34	55/40	65/50	73/58	78/65	84/72	87/75	80/68	70/57	62/47	58/38
Rainfall (mm)	110	155	228	254	244	305	254	203	279	228	162	96

Author picks

Our intrepid author, Martin Zatko, has explored every corner of Tokyo in a quest to better understand the machinations of this fascinating city. Here are some of his favourite places and experiences.

Nakameguro This charming neighbourhood remains more popular with expats than visitors – pop by for a meal, a coffee or a stroll along the banks of the Meguro-gawa (see page 110), and see what the tourists are missing.

Sake This Japanese rice-booze is a delight to drink in all its forms: head to an *izakaya* and have it served hot, housed in a lacquered box; take your pick of the stylish range of "cup sake" jars on offer at a specialist bar like *Buri* (see page 182); or select one of the beautiful sake bottles (or even a simple carton) on sale at any convenience store.

Karaoke A Japanese invention, karaoke is a great way to bond with new friends, and many foreigners end up discovering, to their glee, that it can also provide one of the cheapest ways to get a little drunk.

Sumo This sport is often ridiculed by foreigners – until they visit a tournament for themselves, and witness the brute force and centuries-old pageantry on display. Even if you can't get to an event, it's on local TV from 4pm to 6pm during tournament time (see page 213).

Tsukemen Most foreigners have heard of soba, udon and ramen, but relatively few know about *tsukemen*, Tokyo's own creation, and just the treat during the city's steamy summer – these springy noodles are served lukewarm, to be dipped into and then slurped from a side bowl of broth (see page 160).

Ryokan breakfasts Perhaps the best thing about staying at a ryokan – a traditional Japanese inn – is the delectable breakfast usually plonked in front of you in the morning (see page 152).

Our author recommendations don't end here. We've flagged up our favourite places – a perfectly sited hotel, an atmospheric café, a special restaurant – throughout the Guide, highlighted with the ★ symbol.

MEGURO RIVER, NAKAMEGURO

A MYRIAD OF SAKE BOTTLES

15

things not to miss

It's impossible to see everything that Tokyo has to offer in one trip – and we don't suggest you try. What follows, in no particular order, is a selective and subjective taste of the city's highlights, from the most impressive museums to tranquil gardens, and the best day-trip destinations around the city. All highlights are colour-coded by chapter and have a page reference to take you straight into the Guide, where you can find out more.

1

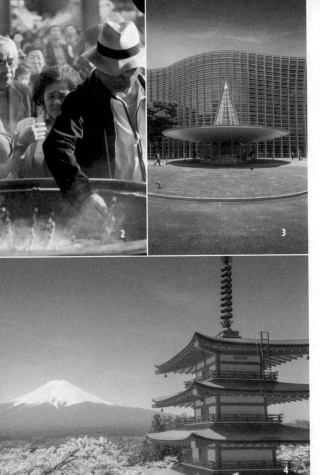

1 SUMO
See page 213
Witness the titanic clashes of wrestling giants at the National Sumo Stadium in Ryōgoku.

2 ASAKUSA
See page 74
Home to old craft shops, traditional inns and the bustling Sensō-ji.

3 NATIONAL ART CENTER
See page 102
Set aside a chunk of time to explore this enormous gallery, a highlight of the so-called Roppongi Art Triangle.

4 MOUNT FUJI
See page 228
The stunning symmetry of this Japanese icon is visible from Tokyo, if you're in luck, and it's quite possible to climb it on a day-trip from the capital.

5 TRADITIONAL PERFORMING ARTS
See page 192
Enjoy kabuki, nō and *bunraku* puppetry at the National Theatre, Kabukiza Theatre or Shimbashi Embujō.

6 SUSHI
See page 160
There are innumerable places in which to scoff delectable raw fish – don't leave without giving it a try.

7 RIKUGI-EN
See page 142
A quintessential Japanese-style garden designed to reflect scenes from ancient Japanese poetry.

8 MATSURI
See page 25
Your visit may well coincide with one of the capital's umpteen *matsuri* (traditional festivals) – a slice of quintessential Japan.

9 NIKKŌ
See page 216
The dazzling Tōshō-gū is the star turn of this quiet mountain town, surrounded by some of the most beautiful countryside in the land.

10 GOLDEN GAI
See page 133
It's amazing how many bars are squeezed into this corner of neon-soaked Kabukichō – getting to and from your seat can resemble a game of Twister.

11 HANAMI PARTIES
See page 26
Pack a picnic and sit under the cherry blossoms in Ueno Park, around the Imperial Palace moat or along the Meguro-gawa.

12 ONSEN BATHING
See page 212
Soak in an old neighbourhood bathhouse such as the resort-like spa complex of Ōedo Onsen Monogatari in Tokyo Bay.

13 MEIJI-JINGŪ
See page 118
Enjoy one of the many annual festivals or regular wedding ceremonies held at Tokyo's most venerable Shinto shrine.

14 GHIBLI MUSEUM
See page 135
Most visitors will have seen at least one Studio Ghibli anime – get behind the scenes at this imaginative museum.

15 NEZU MUSEUM
See page 120
Housed in one of Tokyo's most impressive pieces of modern architecture, this repository of Asian arts also has a magnificent garden.

13

14

15

Itineraries

The Japanese tend to holiday with their every second mapped out beforehand, but it's hard to do the same in their own capital city – it's a gigantic place whose every neighbourhood can eat up a full day of your time, if not several. If time is an issue, these itineraries will give you at least a taster of what Tokyo is all about, lassoing together some of its most spellbinding districts and enchanting sights.

THE YAMANOTE LINE

Japan Rail has an astonishing 32 separate lines crisscrossing the capital (and that's not even counting private lines, or those of the metro system), but most famous of all is the Yamanote-sen, which encircles central Tokyo and links some of its most significant neighbourhoods. The following itinerary takes you anticlockwise around the line.

Shinjuku Perhaps the most famous Tokyo neighbourhood of all, a high-rise, high-octane mishmash of pulsating neon, teeming crowds and hundreds upon hundreds of bars and restaurants. See page 127

Harajuku See the city's most colourful youngsters dressed up to the nines in outlandish attire. See page 115

Shibuya Just as madcap as Shinjuku – the sheer number of people making their way across the road when the traffic lights change outside Shibuya station is absolutely mind-boggling. See page 123

Ginza Head east from the newly revamped Tokyo station and you're in this classic shopping neighbourhood. See page 50

Akihabara Famed as the capital's capital of electronics, head here to get your fix of arcade games, maid cafés, manga-character stores and much more. See page 59

Ueno Stroll around Ueno Park's lily-filled lake, visit the zoo, experience a couple of temples and gardens, or hit a few excellent museums. See page 65

Ikebukuro Though off the regular tourist radar, there's plenty to like about Ikebukuro – nearby sights include a retro-futurist cathedral, several onsen and one of architect Frank Lloyd Wright's most famous creations. See page 137

THE BEST OF MODERN TOKYO

You only really need to walk down the street to get a handle on Tokyo's contemporary delights, but tracking down the sights on the following itinerary will give you a great introduction to the quirkiness of modern Tokyo.

Maid café Enjoy a coffee served by cartoon-character-costumed maids at *Maidreamin* in the neon-soaked mega-district of Shibuya. See page 173

Takeshita-dōri, Harajuku Kit yourself out in the latest weird and wonderful Tokyo styles along this fun, hip shopping alley. See page 115

Tokyo Metropolitan Government Building This twin-towered beast is one of the most astonishing looking buildings in the otherworldly neon craziness of Shinjuku. Head to its lofty observation decks for one of Tokyo's best sunset views. See page 129

Odaiba If Tokyo happened to be stomped to the floor by Godzilla and forced to rebuild itself from scratch, it might end up looking rather like this man-made island, which has plenty of things to see and do. See page 90

Contemporary art Top-rate galleries abound across the capital, with a particularly strong concentration of small, independent affairs in the Ginza and Roppongi neighbourhoods. See pages 56 and 101

Robot Restaurant It would spoil the surprise to describe this wacky performance venue in full. Pop along for an evening show and see what all the fuss is about. See page 194

Karaoke Japan blessed the world with this wonderful concept, so it would be a pity to leave the country without letting it hear your own crimes against music. See page 185

Jicoo Take an evening trip down to Tokyo Bay on this space-age floating bar. See page 181

THE BEST OF TRADITIONAL TOKYO

Though relentlessly modern, Tokyo wears its history and traditions with pride, and there are innumerable ways to get into the old-fashioned spirit of things – dip in and out of the following itinerary to explore the best of traditional Tokyo.

Hot springs If you're willing to bare all to total strangers, Tokyo is a great place to do it – there are several great bathhouses dotted around the city. See page 212

Sensō-ji This charming temple is the focus of the traditional Asakusa neighbourhood; try to visit it in the early evening, when the illuminations come on after sundown. See page 76

Traditional gardens A whole host of immaculately sculpted gardens keep things natural amid the all-pervasive high-rise, with Rikugi-en a particularly appealing example. See page 142

Yushima Seidō Just west of Akihabara, this black-laquered shrine receives relatively few visitors, but scores highly on the atmosphere front. See page 61

Izakaya These traditional drinking dens also function as superbly atmospheric places to eat and make new friends. Try sticks of *yakitori* or deep-fried *kushiage*, give some bubbling *oden* a go, and wash the lot down with sake or a cold beer. See page 178

Traditional theatre Pop along to Kabukiza Theatre for a spellbinding kabuki performance. See page 192

FUJI TV BUILDING

TAXI IN SHINJUKU

Basics

19 Getting there

20 Arrival

21 City transport

25 The media

25 Festivals and events

27 Culture and etiquette

29 LGBTQ Tokyo

30 Kids' Tokyo

31 Travel essentials

Getting there

If you're flying to Tokyo, note that airfares are at their highest around the Japanese holiday periods of Golden Week (early May) and the Obon festival in mid-August, as well as at Christmas and New Year, when seats are at a premium. Flying at weekends is also generally more expensive; you may end up paying more than the prices quoted below.

Tokyo isn't a difficult city for the independent traveller to negotiate, nor need it be horrendously expensive. However, if you're worried about the cost or potential language problems, a **package tour** is worth considering. Flight-and-accommodation packages can be cheaper than booking the two separately, particularly if you want to stay in the more upmarket hotels. Prices for a return flight, five nights' accommodation at a three- or four-star hotel and airport transfers begin at around £750 from the UK, US$1000 from the US and Aus$1100 from Australia, based on double occupancy.

Flights from the UK and Ireland

All Nippon Airways (ANA; Ⓦana.co.jp), British Airways (Ⓦbritishairways.com) and Japan Airlines (Ⓦjal.co.jp) all fly nonstop from **London** to Tokyo, with the trip taking about 12hr. Return fares start from around £550 direct if you're very lucky, but you'll usually have to transfer in Europe, China or the Middle East to get prices like this; fares can fall as low as £400, so it pays to shop around and be flexible with your schedule. There are no direct flights **from Dublin**; again, transferring can bring return prices under €600, though it's always worth considering a budget flight to London or mainland Europe if you can find a good deal from there.

Flights from the US and Canada

A number of airlines fly nonstop **from the US and Canada** to Tokyo, including Air Canada (Ⓦaircanada.

com), All Nippon Airways (ANA), American Airlines (Ⓦaa.com), Japan Airlines (JAL) and United (Ⓦunited.com), with connections from virtually every regional airport. Flying time is around 15hr from New York, 13hr from Chicago and 10hr from Los Angeles.

Many flights are offered at substantial discounts, so keep an eye out for special offers. In general, return fares to Tokyo start at around US$650 from Chicago or New York, US$500 from Los Angeles and Can$900 from Vancouver. However, be prepared to pay up to double these fares (especially for direct flights), and note that to get the cheapest deals you may have to transfer in China – which, unfortunately, involves looping back on yourself.

Flights from Australia, New Zealand and South Africa

Qantas (Ⓦqantas.com), Japan Airlines (JAL) and Air New Zealand (Ⓦairnewzealand.com) operate nonstop flights to Tokyo **from Australia and New Zealand, with flight times of** 10–12hr. Return fares from Australia to Tokyo sometimes go under Aus$700 with Jetstar (Ⓦjetstar.com), who fly direct from Cairns and the Gold Coast. From New Zealand direct routings cost NZ$1200 return and up, though you can lop a fair bit off this by flying with via Australia, or looking for a Fiji Airways sale via Nadi.

Flying **from South Africa**, you'll be routed through Southeast Asia or the Middle East; prices usually start in the region of R12,000, though keep an eye out for promotional deals or fight-and-hotel packages.

Flights from other Asian countries

If you're already in Asia, it can be quite cheap to fly to Tokyo with **low-cost regional carriers**. Air Asia (Ⓦairasia.com) have flights from Kuala Lumpur; Cebu Pacific (Ⓦcebupacificair.com) fly from Cebu and Manila; Eastar (Ⓦeastarjet.com), Jeju Air (Ⓦjejuair.net), Jin (Ⓦjinair.com) and T'way (Ⓦtwayair.com) each run flights from Seoul; HK Express (Ⓦhkex-

A BETTER KIND OF TRAVEL

At Rough Guides we are passionately committed to travel. We believe it helps us understand the world we live in and the people we share it with – and of course tourism is vital to many developing economies. But the scale of modern tourism has also damaged some places irreparably, and climate change is accelerated by most forms of transport, especially flying. We encourage our authors to consider the carbon footprint of the journeys they make in the course of researching our guides.

press.com) make the run from Hong Kong; and Scoot (Ⓦflyscoot.com) scoot over from Bangkok, Singapore and Taipei. Finally, Japanese operator Peach (Ⓦflypeach.com) offers flights from Seoul, Shanghai and Taipei.

Flights from within Japan

For flights to Tokyo from within Japan, the big two **domestic airlines** are All Nippon Airways (ANA; Ⓦana. co.jp) and Japan Airlines (JAL; Ⓦjal.co.jp). Both carriers offer substantial discounts for advance bookings, though there's little to choose between the two as far as prices and quality of service are concerned.

Local **low-cost airlines** have ballooned of late, providing much-needed competition to the rail operators; these include Jetstar (Ⓦjetstar.com), Peach (Ⓦflypeach.com), Skymark (Ⓦskymark.co.jp) and Solaseed Air (Ⓦsolaseedair.jp). Services are usually fine, though with the usual restrictions on baggage allowance.

AGENTS AND INTERNATIONAL TOUR OPERATORS

Japan Package Australia ☎02 9264 7384, Ⓦjapanpackage. com.au. Sydney-based agent offering a variety of Japan packages (including plenty of anime tours) as well as Japan Rail Passes.
Mitsui Travel Australia ☎02 9232 2720, Ⓦmitsuitravel.com. au. Specializing in shorter tours, including a two-day onsen stay in Tokyo and Hakone.
Travel Japan Australia ☎1800 802 552, Ⓦtraveljapan.com. au. Provides everything from flights to Tokyo to packages and customized itineraries.
Travel Wright Ⓦwrightwaytravel.org. An annual tour to Japan (usually in the autumn) focused around the work and legacy of architect Frank Lloyd Wright.

Arrival

Tokyo boasts two major international airports: Narita, the old stalwart out east; and Haneda, far more central, recently upgraded, and hosting an ever-greater range of international connections. Other access points to the city include a slew of train stations, long-distance bus terminals and ferry points, all for domestic connections only.

By plane to Narita

Narita International Airport (成田空港; ☎0476 34-8000, Ⓦwww.narita-airport.jp) is some 66km east

of the city centre. There are three terminals; T3 is a newer wing used by low-cost carriers and designed with a nod to the 2020 Olympics, while the other two both have **tourist information** and **accommodation-booking** booths. If you have a **Japan Rail Pass** (see page 23) exchange order, you can arrange to use your pass immediately (it's valid on JR services from the airport); pick it up at the JR travel agencies – not the ticket offices – in the basement, though be aware the queues can be very long. Alternatively, you can collect it later from any major JR station. Annoyingly, services into Tokyo start to dry up at 10pm, forcing many late arrivals into grabbing some sleep at the airport (see page 154 for one relatively comfortable option).

Trains to Tokyo

The fastest way into Tokyo **from Narita** is on the **Skyliner** (1–3 hourly, 7.30am–10.30pm; 41min to Ueno; ¥2470) express train operated by Keisei (Ⓦkeisei.co.jp), who also offer the cheapest train connection into town in the form of the *tokkyū* (limited express) service (every 30min; 6am–11pm; 1hr 11min to Ueno; ¥1030). Both services stop at Nippori (same prices), where it's easy to transfer to the JR Yamanote or the Keihin Tōhoku lines.

JR's **Narita Express**, also known as the **N'EX** (Ⓦwww.jreast.co.jp), runs to several city stations. The cheapest fare is ¥3020 to Tokyo station (every 30min, 7.45am–9.45pm; 1hr), and there are also frequent direct N'EX services to Shinjuku (hourly; 1hr 20min) for ¥3190. N'EX services to Ikebukuro (1hr 20min; ¥3190) and Yokohama (1hr 30min; ¥4290), both via Shinagawa, are less frequent. JR usually run some kind of **discount scheme** for foreign passport holders; at the time of writing, return tickets valid for two weeks were available to all stations (even Yokohama, making it cheaper than a single) for ¥4000. You can save some money by taking the slightly slower, but far less comfortable, JR *kaisoku* (rapid) train to Tokyo station (hourly; 1hr 25min; ¥1320).

Buses and taxis to Tokyo

The cheapest way into Tokyo is on the **Access Narita buses** (Ⓦaccessnarita.jp; 7.30am–11pm), which head to Ginza and Tokyo stations, and cost just ¥1000; departing every 15min at peak times, they even have toilets on board, but they can be prone to traffic delays. You can pay with cash on the bus; check the website for boarding points.

Alternatively, the more costly **Airport Limousine buses** (☎03 3665 7220, Ⓦwww.limousinebus.co.jp) can be useful if you're weighed down by luggage and staying at or near a major hotel. Tickets are sold in each of the arrival lobbies; the buses depart directly outside (check which platform you need) and stop at many major hotels and train stations around the city. Journeys to central Tokyo typically cost ¥3100, and take at least ninety minutes. Once you factor in the cost of a taxi from one of the train stations to your hotel, these buses can be a good deal; as with JR trains, it's worth keeping an eye out for discounts. The ¥3400 **Limousine & Metro Pass** combines a one-way bus trip from Narita to central Tokyo and a 24-hour metro pass valid on nine of Tokyo's thirteen subway lines.

Lastly, **taxis** to the city centre cost around ¥30,000, and are little faster than going by bus.

By plane to Haneda

Jutting into Tokyo Bay just 20km south of the Imperial Palace, **Haneda Airport** (羽田空港; flight information ☎03 5757 8111, ⓦhaneda-airport.jp) is where most domestic flights touch down, as well as a healthy roster of international services, including some long-haul destinations.

From Haneda Airport, it's a short monorail journey (every 5–10min, 5.20am–11.15pm; 13–19min; ¥490) to Hamamatsuchō station on the JR Yamanote line. Alternatively, you can board a Keihin Kūkō-line train to Shinagawa or Sengakuji and connect directly with other rail and subway lines. A limousine bus (☎03 3665 7220, ⓦwww.limousinebus.co.jp) to the city centre will set you back ¥1030–1230, depending upon your destination, and take around an hour; the same goes for the Keikyu services (ⓦhnd-bus. com). A taxi from Haneda to central Tokyo costs ¥4000–8000.

By train

Shinkansen trains from western Japan pull into **Tokyo station** (東京駅) and **Shinagawa station** (品川駅), around 6km southwest. Most Shinkansen services from the north arrive at Tokyo station, though a few services go only as far as **Ueno station** (上野駅), some 4km northeast of the Imperial Palace. Tokyo, Shinagawa and Ueno stations are all on the Yamanote line and are connected to several subway lines, putting them within reach of most of the capital. Other long-distance JR services stop at Tokyo and Ueno stations, Shinjuku station on Tokyo's west side and Ikebukuro station in the city's northwest corner.

Non-JR trains terminate at different stations: the Tōkyū Tōyoko line from Yokohama ends at **Shibuya Station** (渋谷駅), though some services carry on to Ikebukuro and beyond after they magically turn into the Fukutōshin subway line; the Tōbu Nikkō line runs from Nikkō to **Asakusa Station** (浅草駅), east of Ueno; and the Odakyū line from Hakone finishes at **Shinjuku Station** (新宿駅), which is also the terminus for the Seibu Shinjuku line from Kawagoe. All these stations have subway connections and (apart from Asakusa) are on the JR Yamanote rail line.

By bus

Long-distance buses pull in at several major stations around the city, making transport connections straightforward. The main overnight services from Kyoto and Ōsaka arrive at the eastern Yaesu exit of Tokyo station; other buses arrive at Ikebukuro, Shibuya, Shinagawa and Shinjuku.

By boat

The near-daily long-distance **ferries** from Tokushima (on Shikoku island; 18hr) and Kitakyūshū (on Kyūshū island; 34hr) arrive at Tokyo Port Ferry Terminal (東京港フェリーターミナル) at Ariake, on the man-made island of Odaiba (see page 90) in Tokyo Bay; for details, see Ocean Tōkyū Ferry (☎03 3528 1011, ⓦwww.otf.jp). Buses run from the port to Shin-Kiba station, from which you can catch the metro or the overland JR Keiyō line. A taxi from the port to central Tokyo costs around ¥2000.

City transport

Tokyo's public transport system is efficient, clean and safe, with trains and subways the best way of getting around; a lack of signs in English makes the bus system a lot more challenging. For short, cross-town journeys, taxis are handy and, if shared by a group of people, not all that expensive. Sightseeing tours are also worth considering if you are pushed for time or would like a guided commentary.

By subway

Its colourful map may look daunting, but Tokyo's **subway** is relatively easy to negotiate: the simple colour-coding on trains and maps, as well as clear signposts (many also in English), directional arrows and alpha-numeric station codes, make this by far

TOKYO TRANSPORT PASSES AND TRAVEL CARDS

A useful alternative to buying individual tickets is to get one of the many types of pass available, or to use a prepaid travel card.

PASSES

Both Tokyo Metro and Toei have **24-hour tickets** for use on their respective subway systems (¥600 and ¥700 respectively), with the Toei pass also covering the city's buses; depending upon your precise plans, it may work out better to get a one-day **economy pass** covering both systems (¥800).

JR has its own one-day **Tokunai Pass** (¥750), which gives unlimited travel on JR trains within the Tokyo Metropolitan District Area.

For day-use of the city's subways, JR trains and buses there's the **Tokyo Free Ticket** (¥1590), but you'd really have to be tearing all over town to get your money's worth.

PREPAID CARDS

Although they don't save you any money, the most convenient way to travel is to use a **Pasmo** (ⓦ www.pasmo.co.jp) or JR **Suica** stored-value card. Both can be used on all subways, many buses and both JR and private trains in the wider Tokyo area. The card can be recharged at ticket machines and ticket offices. To get either card (available from ticket machines in metro and JR stations), you need to spend a minimum of ¥2000, of which ¥500 is a deposit, which will be returned to you, plus any remaining value, when you cash in the card before leaving Tokyo – note that this can be done at Haneda airport, but not Narita.

the most *gaijin*-friendly form of transport. You'll have a much less crowded journey if you avoid travelling at rush hour (7.30–9am & 5–7.30pm).

There are two systems, the nine-line **Tokyo Metro** (ⓦ www.tokyometro.jp) and the slightly scruffier four-line **Toei** (ⓦ www.kotsu.metro.tokyo.jp). The systems share some stations, but unless you buy a special ticket from the vending machines that specifies your route from one system to the other, or you have a pass (see page 22), you cannot switch mid-journey between the two sets of lines without paying extra at the ticket barrier. Subways also connect to overland train lines, such as the Yamanote. A colour **map** of the subway system appears at the back of this book.

Tickets are bought at the vending machines beside the electronic ticket gates (ticket sales windows are only found at major stations). Most trips across central Tokyo cost no more than ¥200. Ticket machines generally have multi-language functions, but if you're fazed by the wide range of price buttons, either get a travel pass (see page 22), or buy the cheapest ticket (usually ¥170) and sort out the difference with the gatekeeper at the other end.

Trains run daily from around 5am to just after midnight, and during peak daytime hours as frequently as every five minutes (and at least every fifteen minutes at other times). Maps close to the ticket barriers, and often on the platforms themselves, indicate where the exits emerge.

For **planning journeys** on both subway and regular trains, the route function on Google Maps (ⓦ maps.google.com) usually works like a charm. A local alternative is Hyperdia (ⓦ www.hyperdia.com), which also offers a helpful smartphone app.

By train

Japan Railways East (ⓦ jreast.co.jp), part of the national rail network, runs the main overland services in and around Tokyo, and there are also several **private railways**, including lines run by Odakyū, Tōbu, Seibu and Tōkyū. They all have their own colour coding on maps, with the various JR lines coming in many different shades – take care not to confuse these with those of the subway network. The famous JR **Yamanote train line** (shown in green on network maps, and indicated by green flashes on the trains) loops around the city centre. Another useful JR route is the orange **Chūō line**, which starts at Tokyo station and runs west to Shinjuku and the suburbs beyond; rapid services (look for the red *kanji* characters on the side of the train, or on the platform displays) miss out some stations. JR's yellow **Sōbu line** goes from Chiba in the east to Mitaka in the west, and runs parallel to the Chūō line in the centre of Tokyo. The blue JR **Keihin Tōhoku line** runs from Ōmiya in the north through Tokyo station, and on to Yokohama and beyond. It's fine to transfer between JR lines on the same ticket.

The lowest **fare** on JR lines is ¥140. Ticket machines are easy to operate if buying single tickets, if you can find your destination on the network maps above. Both Pasmo and JR Suica prepaid cards (see page 22) work at the ticket gates.

If you're planning a lot of train travel around Japan in a short period of time, the **Japan Rail Pass** (Ⓦjapan-railpass.net) can be a good deal, though you have to buy this outside Japan; prepare for giant queues if picking it up at the airport, though note that you can also pick it up from any major JR station. JR East (Ⓦwww.jreast.co.jp) offers its own cheaper versions of the pass, covering its network in the Tokyo region and northern Japan; these can be purchased in Japan from JR ticket offices.

By monorail

Tokyo has a couple of monorail systems: the **Tokyo monorail**, which runs from Hamamatsuchō to Haneda Airport (see page 21); and the **Yurika-mome monorail**, which connects Shimbashi with Toyosu via Odaiba (see page 90). These services operate like the city's private rail lines – you buy separate tickets for journeys on them or travel using the various stored-value cards, such as Pasmo and Suica (see page 22).

By bus

Buses are a good way of cutting across the few areas of Tokyo not served by a subway or train line, though they're little used by overseas visitors. Compared to the subway there's little information in English; you may have to get used to recognizing *kanji* place names, or memorize the numbers of useful bus routes. The final destination is listed on the front of the bus, along with the route number. You pay on entry, by dropping the flat rate (¥210) into the fare box by the driver (there's a machine in the box for changing notes); travel cards are also accepted.

By bicycle

You'll see people **cycling** all over Tokyo, but despite this it's not a terribly bike-friendly city. Most locals cycle on the pavement, there being very few dedicated bike lanes, and Japanese rules of courtesy dictate that even though every bike has a bell, absolutely nobody

---

JAPANESE ADDRESSES

Japanese **addresses** are, frankly, a little bit ridiculous – when it's impossible to find the building you're looking for even when you're standing right in front of it, it's clear that there are some major system failures. This stems from the fact that in many places, including Tokyo, **few roads have names**; instead, city districts are split into numbered blocks, on which the numbers themselves are usually not visible.

Addresses start with the largest **administrative district** – in Tokyo's case it's Tōkyō-*to* (metropolis), but elsewhere most commonly it's the *ken* (prefecture) accompanied by a seven-digit postcode – for example, Saitama-ken 850-0072. Next comes the *ku* (ward; for example Shinjuku-ku), followed by the *chō* (district), then three numbers representing the *chōme* (local neighbourhood), block and individual building. Finally there might come the building name and the floor on which the business or person is located – much like the American system, 1F is the ground floor, 2F the first floor above ground, and B1F the first floor below ground.

Japanese addresses are therefore written in **reverse order** from the Western system. However, when written in English, they usually follow the Western order; this is the system we adopt in this guide. For example, the address 2-12-7 Roppongi, Minato-ku identifies building number 7, somewhere on block 12 of number 2 *chōme* in Roppongi district, in the Minato ward of Tokyo (this can also be written as 12-7 Roppongi, 2-chōme, Minato-ku). Where the block is entirely taken up by one building, the address will have only two numbers.

Actually **locating an address** on the ground can be frustrating – even Japanese people find it tough. The old-fashioned way is to have the address written down, preferably in Japanese, and then get to the nearest train or bus station; once in the neighbourhood, find a local police box (*kōban*), which will have a detailed local map. The modern-day solution is, inevitably, Google Maps, on which the results of address searches are usually accurate. If all else fails, don't be afraid to phone – often someone will come to meet you.

uses them – even if they're coming up behind you, at speed, on a narrow path, in the rain.

BIKE RENTAL

Community Cycle ⓦ docomo-cycle.jp. One of the easiest means of getting hold of a bike, with cycle docks across the city; after registering online (you pay with your bank card) and receiving a pass code, it's ¥150 for the first half-hour, then ¥100 for each subsequent one.

Inbound League ⓦ inbound-league.jp. A good option if you're looking for something in the Shinjuku area, with bikes going for ¥1000/hr or ¥3000/day.

Tokyobike ⓦ tokyobike.com. Without doubt the coolest bike store and the coolest rental spot in the city, if a little expensive; it's good if you're in the Ueno and Yanaka area (see page 65 for details).

By ferry

The Tokyo Cruise Ship Company (ⓦ suijobus.co.jp) runs several **ferry** services, known as *suijō basu* (water buses), in and around Tokyo Bay. The popular Sumida-gawa service (every 30–50min, 10am–6.30pm; 40min; ¥860) plies the route between **Hinode Pier** on Tokyo Bay and **Asakusa** to the northeast of the city centre. Some boats call at the **Hama Rikyū Teien** (see page 54), entry to which is often included with the ticket price; you can also head to Hinode from Odaiba (20min; ¥520). The ferries' large picture windows give a completely different view of the city from the one you'll get on the streets – reason enough for hopping aboard.

For a little more you can travel on the *Himiko* or the *Hotaluna*, near-identical space-age ferries that run from Asakusa to Odaiba (6 daily; ¥1720), sometimes via Hinode. Designed by Matsumoto Reiji, a famous manga artist, these silver-painted ships become floating bars at night.

Hinode Pier (close by Hinode station on the Yurikamome monorail or a 10min walk from Hamamatsuchō station on the Yamanote line) is also the jumping-off point for several good daily **cruises** around Tokyo Bay, and for ferries to various points around the island of Odaiba, or across to Kasai Rinkai-kōen on the east side of the bay.

By taxi

For short hops, **taxis** are often the best option. The basic rate is ¥410 for the first 1km, after which the meter racks up ¥80 every 237m, plus a time charge when the taxi is moving at less than 10km per hour. Between 11pm and 5am, rates are 25 percent higher.

Most taxis have a limit of four passengers. There's never any need to open or close the passenger doors, which are operated by the taxi driver – trying to do it manually can damage the mechanism, and will get your driver seething. This is just one reason why some taxis refuse to take foreigners; communication difficulties are another, bigger reason, and as such it's always a good idea to have the name and address of your destination clearly written on a piece of paper (in Japanese, if possible). If your driver doesn't know exactly where your destination is, a stop at a local police box may be necessary to locate the exact address.

When flagging down a taxi, a red light next to the driver means the cab is free; green means it's occupied. There are designated stands in the busiest parts of town; after the trains stop at night, be prepared for long queues, especially in areas such as Roppongi and Shinjuku. Major taxi firms include Hinomaru Limousine (☎03 3212 0505, ⓦ hinomaru.co.jp) and Nippon Kōtsū (☎03 3799 9220, ⓦ www.nihon-kotsu.co.jp).

Those who have sworn off licenced taxis forever will be glad to know that Uber (ⓦ uber.com) is functional in Tokyo. It's not all that much cheaper than the regular cabs (and quite often more expensive), though there are no late-night surcharges, and drivers are more likely to speak at least a little English.

Sightseeing tours

For a quick overview of Tokyo there are the usual **bus tours**, offered by operations such as Hato Bus (ⓦ www.hatobus.com), Japan Grey Line (ⓦ www.jgl.co.jp) and Sky Bus (see page 25), ranging from half-day jaunts around the central sights (around ¥4500, excluding lunch) to visits out to Kamakura, Nikkō and Hakone. If the sky's the limit on your budget, go for a spin in a **helicopter** instead: Excel Air Service (ⓦ excel-air.com) will take you for a fifteen-minute flight for around ¥24,000.

If bus tours are not your cup of tea, but you still fancy having a guide on hand, you might consider one of the various **walking** or **cycling** tours (see below), **culinary** tours and activities (see page 169) or sightseeing **ferries** (see above). Free walking tours are available on selected days of the week around the Imperial Palace (see page 41), Ueno (see page 65) and Asakusa (see page 74). Finally, there's even a go-kart tour inspired by the Mario Kart game (see page 112).

LOCAL TOUR OPERATORS

Eyexplore Tokyo ⓦ eyexploretokyo.com. Small outfit running a few photo-tours of the city (¥9900).

Haunted Tokyo Ⓦ hauntedtokyotours.com. Interesting English-language tours focusing on the spookier parts of Tokyo's history (usually 2–3hr; ¥4500).

His Go ☎ 080 4869 0514, Ⓦ www.hisgo.com. Try your hand at calligraphy, *taiko* drumming or wielding a samurai sword, or one of many other cultural experiences. Small-group and customized options available.

Sky Bus ☎ 03 3215 0008, Ⓦ skybus.jp. Offers four tours, most in open-top double-decker buses, including a route around the Imperial Palace grounds and through Ginza and Marunouchi (50min; ¥1600), and an Odaiba night tour (2hr; ¥2100). They also have three hop-on, hop-off routes (¥3500), with tickets valid for 24hr.

Sunrise Tours ☎ 03 5796 5454, Ⓦ japanican.com. Affiliated to Japan Travel Bureau (JTB), this operator has various Tokyo programmes on offer, including sumo and maid-café tours.

Tokyo Great Cycling Tour ☎ 03 4590 2995, Ⓦ tokyocycling.jp. See the capital on a series of guided bike tours (1hr 30min–6hr; ¥3000–10,000, sometimes including lunch).

The media

English newspapers and magazines are readily available, while on TV and radio there are some programmes presented in English or with an alternative English soundtrack, such as the main news bulletins on NHK. Throughout this guide we list English-language websites wherever useful; most places also have Japanese-only websites.

Newspapers and magazines

The English-language daily **newspaper** you'll most commonly find at Tokyo's newsstands is *The Japan Times* (Ⓦ japantimes.co.jp). It has comprehensive coverage of national and international news, as well as occasionally interesting features, some culled from the world's media; the online sumo coverage is good when there's a tournament on. There's also the *Daily Yomiuri* (Ⓦ yomiuri.co.jp) newspaper, as well as English-language magazines including *Time* and *The Economist*.

The free monthly **magazine** *Metropolis* (Ⓦ metropolisjapan.com) is packed with interesting features, reviews, and listings of film, music and other events, as is their website; the same can be said for *Time Out* (Ⓦ timeout.com/tokyo), whose magazine comes out every three months. The twice-yearly publication *KIE* (Kateigahō International Edition; Ⓦ int.kateigaho.com) is a gorgeous, glossy magazine covering cultural matters, with many travel features and in-depth

profiles of areas of Tokyo and other parts of Japan. Also worth a look is *Tokyo Notice Board* (Ⓦ tokyonoticeboard.co.jp), a freesheet devoted almost entirely to classifieds.

You'll find all these at the tourist information centres, larger hotels, foreign-language bookstores (see page 200) and bars or restaurants frequented by *gaijin*.

Television

Funded much like Britain's BBC, the state broadcaster **NHK** (Ⓦ nhk.or.jp) has two **TV channels** – the regular NHK, and NHK–Educational – as well as three satellite channels, and NHK World, an international channel which often veers towards nationalist propaganda. Many TV sets can access a bilingual soundtrack, and it's thus possible to tune into English-language commentary for NHK's nightly 7pm news; films and imported TV shows on both NHK and the commercial channels are also sometimes broadcast with an alternative English soundtrack. **Digital, satellite and cable** channels – not always available in hotels, even at the higher end – include BBC World, CNN and the regular entertainment channels.

Festivals and events

No matter when you visit Tokyo, chances are there'll be a religious festival (*matsuri*) taking place somewhere – fantastic fun for first-time visitors and old Tokyo hands alike. You'll find details of upcoming events online; try the official city site (Ⓦ gotokyo.org), or those of the main expat magazines (see page 25). The dates given in the festival listings here can vary according to the lunar calendar, so check ahead if you wish to attend a particular event.

Of the major events listed, by far the most important is **New Year**, when most of the city closes down for a week (roughly Dec 28–Jan 3). Tokyo also hosts three grand **sumo tournaments** each year (see page 213), as well as film, theatre and music festivals. Several non-Japanese festivals which have also caught on include **Valentine's Day** (Feb 14), when women give men gifts of chocolate; on **White Day** (March 14) men get their turn (white chocolates, of course). Later in the year, **Pocky Day** (November 11) is an even more overtly commercial

HANAMI PARTIES

With the arrival of spring in late March or early April, a pink tide of **cherry blossom** washes north over Tokyo, lasting little more than a week. The finest displays are along the moat around the Imperial Palace (particularly the section close by Yasukuni-jinja), in Ueno-kōen, Aoyama Cemetery, Shinjuku Gyoen, the riverside Sumida-kōen and on the banks of the Meguro-gawa by Nakameguro station, where every tree shelters a blossom-viewing (**hanami**) party.

affair, even by Japanese standards – people give their loved ones boxes of Pocky, sweet breadsticks whose skinny nature vaguely resembles the date (eleven-eleven). **Christmas** is also commercial, and celebrated with glee; Christmas Eve, in particular, is one of the most popular date nights of the year, and all fancy restaurants are booked solid. By contrast, **New Year's Eve** is a fairly subdued, family-oriented event, though of course there are places to go wild too.

For details of public holidays, see page 37.

JANUARY

Ganjitsu (or Gantan) January 1. The *hatsu-mōde* – the first shrine visit of the year – draws the crowds to Meiji-jingū, Hie-jinja, Kanda Myōjin and other city shrines to pray for good fortune. Performances of traditional dance and music take place at Yasukuni-jinja. National holiday.

Kōkyo Ippan Sanga January 2. Thousands of loyal Japanese – and a few curious foreigners – troop into the Imperial Palace grounds to greet the emperor. The royal family appear on the balcony several times from 9.30am to 3pm.

Dezomeshiki January 6. At Tokyo Big Sight in Odaiba, firemen in Edo-period costume pull off dazzling stunts atop long bamboo ladders.

Seijin-no-hi (Coming-of-Age Day) Second Monday in January. A colourful pageant of 20-year-old women, and a few men, visit city shrines in traditional dress to celebrate their entry into adulthood. At Meiji-jingū various ancient rituals are observed, including a ceremonial archery contest. National holiday.

FEBRUARY

Setsubun February 3 or 4. On the last day of winter by the lunar calendar, people scatter lucky beans around their homes and at shrines or temples, to drive out evil and welcome in the year's good luck. The liveliest festivities take place at Sensō-ji, Kanda Myōjin, Zōjō-ji and Hie-jinja.

MARCH

Hina Matsuri (Doll Festival) March 3. Families with young girls display beautiful dolls of the emperor, empress and their courtiers dressed in ancient costume. Department stores, hotels and museums often put on special displays at this time.

Hi Watari Second Sunday in March. A spectacular fire-walking ceremony held at the foot of Mount Takao.

Anime Japan Late March ⓦ anime-japan.jp. Three-day event during which Japan's anime industry displays its shows and films for the coming year.

Cherry Blossoms Usually late March to early April. Not a festival as such, and the precise dates are dictated by the weather, but the coming of the cherry blossoms is *huge* in Tokyo, with hordes gathering to eat, drink and be merry in picnic-like affairs known as *hanami*.

APRIL

Art Fair Tokyo Early April ⓦ artfairtokyo.com. Tokyo International Forum is the focus for Japan's largest commercial art event, with around a hundred local and national galleries participating.

Hana Matsuri April 8. The Buddha's birthday is celebrated in all Tokyo's temples with either parades or quieter celebrations, during which a small statue of Buddha is sprinkled with sweet tea.

Jibeta Matsuri Mid-April. In this celebration of fertility, an iron phallus is forged and giant wooden phalluses are paraded around Kanayama-jinja, in the southern Tokyo suburb of Kawasaki, amid dancing crowds, including a group of demure transvestites.

Kamakura Matsuri Mid-April. Kamakura's week-long festival includes traditional dances, costume parades and horseback archery.

Earth Day Tokyo Around 22 April ⓦ earthday-tokyo.org. The capital joins in global celebrations of our planet's environment with big events in Yoyogi Park and elsewhere.

MAY

Design Festa May and August ⓦ designfesta.com. Thousands of young and aspiring artists converge on Tokyo Big Sight in Odaiba for this twice-yearly weekend celebration of design.

Kodomo-no-hi (Children's Day) May 5. Families fly carp banners, symbolizing strength, outside their homes. National holiday.

Rainbow Pride Early May ⓦ tokyorainbowpride.com. The largest Pride event in the country, usually featuring a suitably colourful parade.

Kanda Matsuri Mid-May. One of the city's top three festivals, taking place in odd-numbered years at Kanda Myōjin, during which people in Heian-period costume escort eighty gilded *mikoshi* (portable shrines) through the streets.

Roppongi Art Night Late May ⓦ roppongiartnight.com. Dusk-to-dawn street performances and art events are held across Tokyo's party district.

Tōshō-gū Haru Matsuri May 17–18. Huge procession of one thousand armour-clad warriors and three *mikoshi*, commemorating the burial of Shogun Tokugawa Ieyasu in Nikkō in 1617; takes place outside the eponymous shrine (see page 67).

Sanja Matsuri Third weekend in May. Tokyo's most boisterous festival, when over one hundred *mikoshi* are jostled through the streets of Asakusa, accompanied by lion dancers, geisha and musicians.

JUNE

Sannō Matsuri Mid-June. In even-numbered years the last of the big three *matsuri* (after Kanda and Sanja) takes place, focusing on colourful processions of *mikoshi* through Akasaka.

JULY

Rainbow Reel Tokyo Mid-July ⓦ rainbowreeltokyo.com. One of the best Tokyo film festivals, dedicated to queer movies.

Fuji Rock Late July. The biggest event on the Japanese musical calendar, and a major draw for both bands and festival-goers from overseas (see page 189).

Lantern Festivals Late July and early August. Connected to O-bon (see below), this tradition sees paper lanterns floated down various waterways, including the Imperial Palace moat.

Hanabi Taikai Late July and early August. The summer skies explode with thousands of fireworks, harking back to traditional "river-opening" ceremonies to mark the start of the summer boating season. The Sumida-gawa display is the most spectacular (view it from river boats or Asakusa's Sumida-kōen on the last Sat in July), but those in Edogawa, Tamagawa, Arakawa and Harumi come close. Kamakura has its *hanabi taikai* on August 10.

AUGUST

Fukagawa Matsuri Mid-August. Every three years Tomioka Hachiman-gū, a shrine in Fukagawa (east across the Sumida River from central Tokyo), hosts the city's wettest festival, when spectators throw buckets of water over a hundred *mikoshi* being shouldered through the streets.

O-bon Mid-August. Families gather around their ancestral graves and much of Tokyo closes down, while many neighbourhoods stage dances in honour of the deceased.

Summer Sonic Mid-August ⓦ summersonic.com. Two-day rock festival (see page 189).

Asakusa Samba Carnival Last Saturday in August. Rio comes to the streets of Asakusa with this spectacular parade of sequinned and feathered dancers – it might sound a bit random, but there are over 200,000 Brazilians living in Japan.

SEPTEMBER

Tsurugaoka Hachiman-gū Matsuri September 14–16. Annual shrine festival of Tsurugaoka Hachiman-gū in Kamakura. The highlight is a demonstration of horseback archery on the final day.

Ningyō Kuyō September 25. A funeral service for unwanted dolls is held at Kiyomizu Kannon-dō in Ueno-kōen, after which they are cremated – just as sad as it sounds.

OCTOBER

Festival/Tokyo October to December ⓦ www.festival-tokyo.jp. Major theatre and performing arts events, held at various venues across the city.

Kawagoe Grand Matsuri October 14–15. One of the liveliest festivals in the Tokyo area, involving some 25 ornate floats and hundreds of costumed revellers.

Tōshō-gū Aki Matsuri October 17. Repeat of Nikkō's fabulous procession held for the spring festival, minus the horseback archery displays.

Tokyo International Film Festival Late October and early November ⓦ tiff-jp.net. Major film festival at which a slew of works from Japan and beyond are shown on screens around the city.

NOVEMBER

Daimyō Gyōretsu November 3. Re-enactment of a feudal lord's procession along the Tōkaidō (the great road linking Tokyo and Kyoto), accompanied by his doctor, accountant, tea master and road sweepers. At Sōun-ji, near Hakone-Yumoto.

Shichi-go-san-no-hi November 15. Children aged seven, five and three ("*shichi-go-san*") don traditional garb to visit the shrines, particularly Meiji-jingū, Hie-jinja and Yasukuni-jinja.

Tori-no-ichi Mid-November. Fairs selling *kumade* (bamboo rakes decorated with lucky charms) are held at shrines on "rooster days" in the zodiacal calendar. The main fair is at Ōtori-jinja (Iriya station).

Tokyo Filmex Late November ⓦ filmex.net. Film festival focusing on pieces from emerging Asian directors.

DECEMBER

Gishi-sai December 14. Costume parade in Nihombashi re-enacting the famous vendetta of the 47 *rōnin* (see page 113), followed by a memorial service for them at Sengaku-ji.

Hagoita-ichi December 17–19. The build-up to New Year begins with a battledore fair outside Asakusa's Sensō-ji.

Ōmisoka December 31. Leading up to midnight, temple bells ring out 108 times (the number of human frailties according to Buddhist thinking), while thousands gather at Meiji-jingū, Hie-jinja and other major shrines to honour the gods with the first visit of the New Year. If you don't like crowds, head for a small local shrine.

Culture and etiquette

Japan is famous for its complex web of social conventions and rules of behaviour. Fortunately, allowances are made for befuddled foreigners, but it will be greatly appreciated – and even draw gasps of astonishment – if you show a grasp of the basic principles. The two main danger

areas are to do with footwear and bathing which, if you get them wrong, can cause great offence. There are also etiquette points to bear in mind around eating (see page 158) and drinking (see page 179).

Japan is a strictly hierarchical society where men generally take precedence, so women shouldn't expect doors to be held open or seats vacated. **Sexual discrimination** remains widespread, and foreign women working in Japan can find the predominantly male business culture hard going.

Pushing and shoving on crowded trains or buses is not uncommon. Never respond by getting angry or showing **aggression**, as this is considered a complete loss of face. By the same token, don't make your **opinions** known too forcefully or contradict people outright; it's more polite to say "maybe" than a direct "no", so if you get a vague answer to a question don't push for confirmation unless it's important.

Note that it's particularly unwise to criticize any aspect of Japanese society, however small, to a local; in a land where people tend to describe themselves as a "we", it's often taken as a personal insult.

Blowing your nose in public is also considered rude – locals keep sniffing until they find somewhere private (this can continue for hours on end, which is great fun if you're sat next to a sniffler on a long train ride). An even more common agony for visitors is having to **sit on the floor** at people's houses and certain restaurants – excruciatingly uncomfortable for people who aren't used to it. If you're wearing trousers, sitting cross-legged is fine; otherwise, tuck your legs to one side.

Meetings and greetings

Some visitors to Japan complain that it's difficult to **meet local people** – the Japanese themselves famously have problems meeting each other, as evidenced by regular pay-for-company stories in the international press, and the legion of "snack" bars (where local men essentially pay to have their egos massaged). It's also true that many Japanese are shy of foreigners, mainly through a fear of being unable to communicate. A few words of Japanese will help enormously, and there are various opportunities for fairly formal contact, such as through the Goodwill Guides (see page 38). Otherwise, try popping into a local bar, a *yakitori* joint or suchlike; with everyone crammed in like sardines, and emboldened by alcohol, it's far easier to strike up a conversation.

Whenever Japanese meet, express thanks or say goodbye, there's a flurry of **bowing** – and, between friends, an energetic waving of hands. The precise depth of the bow and the length of time it's held for depend on the relative status of the two individuals; foreigners aren't expected to bow, but it's terribly infectious and you'll soon find yourself bobbing with the best of them. The usual compromise is a slight nod or a quick half-bow. Japanese more familiar with Western customs might offer you a hand to shake, in which case treat it gently – they won't be expecting a firm grip.

Japanese **names** are traditionally written with the family name first, followed by a given name, which is the practice used throughout this book (except where the Western version has become famous, such as Issey Miyake). When dealing with foreigners, however, they may well write their name the other way round. Check if you're not sure because, when **addressing people**, it's normal to use the family name plus -*san*: for example, Suzuki-san. *San* is an honorific term applied to others, so you do not use it when introducing yourself or your family. As a foreigner, you can choose whichever of your names you feel comfortable with; you'll usually have a -*san* tacked onto the end of your given name. You'll also often hear -*chan* or -*kun* as a form of address; these are diminutive suffixes reserved for very good friends, young children and pets. The suffix -*sama* is the most polite form of address.

Japanese people tend to **dress** smartly, especially in Tokyo. Tourists don't have to go overboard, but will be better received if they look neat and tidy, while for anyone hoping to do business, a snappy suit (almost always black, though blue can also be spotted these days) is *de rigueur*. It's also important to be **punctual** for social and business appointments.

An essential part of any **business meeting** is the swapping of *meishi* (**name cards**); if you're doing business here, it's a very good idea to have them printed in Japanese as well as English. Always carry a copious supply, since you'll be expected to exchange a card with everyone present. *Meishi* are offered with both hands, held so that the recipient can read the writing. It's polite to read the card and then place it on the table beside you, face up. Never write on a *meishi*, at least not in the owner's presence, and never shove it into a pocket – pop it into your wallet, a dedicated card-holder, or somewhere suitably respectful.

Hospitality, gifts and tips

Entertaining, whether it's business or purely social, usually takes place in bars and restaurants. The host generally orders and, if it's a Japanese-style meal, will keep passing you different things to try. You'll also find your glass continually topped up. It's polite to return the gesture but if you don't drink, or don't want any more, leave it full.

It's a rare honour to be invited to someone's home in Japan, and if this happens you should always take a **gift**, which should always be wrapped, using plenty of fancy paper and ribbon if possible. Most shops gift-wrap purchases automatically, and anything swathed in paper from a big department store has extra cachet.

Japanese people love giving gifts (in fact, they are more or less obliged to give souvenirs known as *omiyage* to friends and colleagues following any holiday), and you should never refuse one if offered, though it's good manners to protest at their generosity first. Again, it's polite to give and receive with both hands, and to belittle your humble donation while giving profuse thanks for the gift you receive. It's the custom not to open gifts in front of the donor, thus avoiding potential embarrassment.

Tipping is not expected in Japan. If someone's been particularly helpful, the best approach is to give a small present, or offer some money discreetly in an envelope.

Shoes and slippers

It's customary to change into **slippers** when entering a Japanese home or a ryokan, and not uncommon in traditional restaurants, temples and, occasionally, museums and art galleries. If you come across a slightly raised floor and a row of slippers, then use them; leave your shoes either on the lower floor (the *genkan*) or on the shelves (sometimes lockers) provided. Also try not to step on the *genkan* with bare or stockinged feet. Once inside, remove your slippers before stepping onto tatami (the rice-straw flooring), and remember to change into the special **toilet slippers** kept inside the bathroom when you go to the toilet.

Toilets

Although you'll still come across traditional Japanese squat-style **toilets** (*toire* or *otearai*; トイレ／お手洗い), Western sit-down toilets are becoming the norm. Look out for nifty enhancements such as a heated seat, and those that flush automatically as you walk away. Another handy device plays the sound of flushing water, ostensibly to cover embarrassing noises (though it doesn't usually work out this way, and while the sound's playing, everyone will know what you're doing in any case).

High-tech toilets, with a control panel to one side, are very common. Finding the flush button can be a challenge – they're often tiny things on wall panels, most commonly marked with the *kanji* for large (大) or small (小), used for number twos and ones respectively.

Most public toilets provide **paper** (often extremely thin), though not always soap for washing your hands. There are public toilets at most train and subway stations, department stores, and city parks. They're generally pretty clean.

Bathing

Taking a traditional Japanese **bath**, whether in an onsen, a *sentō* or a ryokan (see page 152), is a ritual that's definitely worth mastering. Everyone uses the same water, and the golden rule is to wash and rinse the soap off thoroughly before stepping into the bath – showers and bowls are provided, as well as soap and shampoo in most cases. Ryokan and the more upmarket public bathhouses provide small towels (bring your own or buy one on the door if using a cheaper *sentō*), though no one minds full nudity. Baths are typically **segregated**, so memorize the *kanji* for female (女), which looks a little like a woman; and male (男), which looks sort of like a chap running around with a box on his head.

Note that **tattoos** – which are associated with the *yakuza* in Japan – are a big issue when it comes to public bathing. Even if you look nothing like a member of the local mafia, you may be asked to cover up the offending image, or even denied access to the baths entirely. If you're intending to visit any particular bathing establishment, the best course of action is to get your accommodation (or a local tourist office) to call ahead for verification of their tattoo regulations.

LGBTQ Tokyo

LGBTQ travellers should have few concerns about visiting Tokyo and are unlikely to encounter any problems. Japan has no laws against homosexual activity and outward discrimination is very rare, including at hotels and ryokan where two people of the same sex sharing a room will hardly raise an eyebrow.

That said, marriage remains an almost essential step on the career ladder, keeping many Japanese gays in the closet, often leading double lives and/or being apathetic to concepts of gay liberation and rights.

General codes of behaviour mean that public displays of affection between any couple, gay or straight, are very rare – so don't expect a warm welcome if you walk down the street hand in hand or kiss in public. In recent times being part of the LGBTQ community has come to be seen as more acceptable – and among young people it's rarely an issue – but Tokyo has a long way to go before it can be considered truly LGBTQ-friendly.

There's a decent number of LGBTQ venues, particularly in the Shinjuku Nichōme area (see page 190).

ONLINE RESOURCES

Fridae ⓦ fridae.asia. Asia-wide site with some good Tokyo info.
Tokyo Wrestling ⓦ tokyowrestling.com. Trilingual (it's in French too) lesbian-focused website.
Utopia ⓦ utopia-asia.com. Pan-Asian site with good Japan specifics.

Kids' Tokyo

What with Japan being the land of anime, manga and a treasure chest of must-have toys and computer games, you'll have no problem selling the kids on a trip to Tokyo. It's a safe, child-friendly city that offers a vast number of ways to distract and entertain kids of every age. For families who don't mind bedding down together, a ryokan or Japanese-style room in a hotel, where you can share a big tatami room, is ideal (see page 152).

Essentials

At most attractions, school-age children get **reduced rates**, typically half the adult price. Children under 6 ride free on trains, subways and buses, while those aged 6–11 pay half fare. **Nappies**, **baby food** and pretty much anything else you may need are widely available in supermarkets and pharmacies, though not necessarily your favourite brand. While **breast-feeding** in public is generally accepted, it's best to be as discreet as possible. Most Japanese women who breast-feed use the private rooms provided in department stores and public buildings and in many shops. Only at the more upmarket Western-style hotels will you be able to arrange **babysitting**; Poppins (ⓦ poppins.co.jp) is one reputable baby-sitting service.

Sights and activities

We've listed a selection of amusement and **theme parks** (see page 195), and there's also the wonderful Ghibli Museum in Mitaka (see page 135), which is part gallery and part theme park. To give children their **animal** fix, try Tokyo Sea Life Park (see page 95) or Ueno Zoo (see page 67). The best **museums** for kids include Ueno's National Science Museum (see page 68), Odaiba's Miraikan (see page 92) and the Edo-Tokyo Museum in Ryōgoku (see page 81).

Other family-friendly outings to consider include taking a **boat trip** across Tokyo Bay (see page 90), learning how to make **paper** cranes at the Origami Kaikan (see page 61), or visiting the PUK **puppet theatre** (see page 193).

Chances are that near most hotels will be a small **playground**; if your kids need more room to burn off steam, head to the open spaces of Yoyogi-kōen (see page 119) or Shinjuku Gyoen (see page 133).

Also check out the listings for **toyshops** and those specializing in manga, anime and character product goods (see pages 198 and 208). The showrooms for products by Sony (see page 52) and Panasonic (see page 91) will be appealing to **teenagers**, as will spending time exploring electronic, anime and manga hotspot Akihabara (see page 59).

Finally, you'll find local-authority-managed **children's halls** (*jidokan*) throughout the city, which are free to long-term Tokyo residents and provide a whole range of activities and classes for school-age kids and younger.

Dining

The hazy situation with regard to **smoking** in Tokyo restaurants (many still allow it), combined with uncommon dishes and Japanese-language menus,

---

GRUTT PASS

One of the best deals on offer in Tokyo is the **Grutt Pass**. For ¥2200 you get a ticket booklet which allows free or discounted entry to seventy attractions, including all major museums. Valid for two months after first being used, the ticket can be bought at participating venues and at the Tokyo Metropolitan Government tourist information centre in Shinjuku (see page 127), among other outlets.

will provide parents trying to feed fussy kids with certain challenges. One solution is to ask your hotel to point you in the direction of the nearest **"family restaurant" chain**, such as *Denny's*, *Royal Host* or *Jonathan's*; all have children's menus including Western and Japanese dishes with pictures of each dish, as well as non-smoking sections. Tokyo's **vegetarian** cafés and restaurants (see page 168) are another option.

Travel essentials

Costs

Despite its reputation as an outrageously expensive city, prices in Tokyo have dropped or at least stabilized in recent years, and with a little planning it is a manageable destination even for those on a fairly modest budget. The key is to do what the majority of Japanese do: eat in local restaurants, avoid the ritzier bars and take advantage of any available discounts. There's also a surprising amount you can do in Tokyo without spending any money at all (see page 32).

By staying in hostels and eating in the cheapest local restaurants, the absolute minimum **daily budget** for food and accommodation is ¥4000–7000. By the time you've added in some transport costs, a few entry tickets, meals in classier restaurants and one or two nights in a ryokan or business hotel, you'll be reaching an expenditure of at least ¥15,000 per day.

Holders of the **International Student Identity Card** (ISIC; Ⓦisic.org) are eligible for discounts on some transport and admission fees, as are children.

Crime and personal safety

Tokyo boasts one of the lowest crime rates in the world. On the whole, the Japanese are honest and law-abiding; there's little theft, and drug-related crimes are relatively rare. Nonetheless, it always pays to be careful in crowds, and to keep money and important documents stowed in an inside pocket or money belt, or in your hotel safe.

The presence of **police boxes** (*kōban*) in every neighbourhood helps to discourage petty crime, and the local police seem to spend the majority of their time dealing with stolen bikes and helping bemused visitors – Japanese and foreigners – find addresses. In theory, you should carry your **passport** or ID at all times; the police have the right

---

EMERGENCY NUMBERS

Police Ⓣ110
Fire or ambulance Ⓣ119

---

to arrest anyone who fails to do so. In practice they rarely stop foreigners, but if you're found without ID, you may well be escorted back to your hotel or apartment to collect it. Anyone found with **drugs** will be treated less leniently; if you're lucky, you'll simply be fined and deported, rather than sent to prison.

The generally low status of women in Japan is reflected in the amount of **groping** that still goes on in crowded commuter trains. If you do have the misfortune to be groped, the best solution is to grab the offending hand, yank it high in the air and embarrass the guy as much as possible. Fortunately, more violent **sexual attacks** are rare, though harassment, stalking and rape are under-reported. Women should exercise the same caution about being alone with a man as they would anywhere – violent crimes against women are rare, but they do occur. Tokyo Metropolitan Police run an **English-language hotline** (Ⓣ03 3503 8484; Mon–Fri 8.30am–5.15pm). Another useful option is **Tokyo English Language Lifeline** (TELL; Ⓣ03 5774 0992, Ⓦtelljp.com; daily 9am–11pm).

Earthquakes

Japan is home to one-tenth of the world's active volcanoes; it's also the site of one-tenth of its major earthquakes (over magnitude 7 on the Richter scale). At least one quake is recorded every day somewhere in the country (see Ⓦwww.jma.go.jp/en/quake for details of the most recent), though fortunately the vast majority consist of **minor tremors** that you probably won't even notice. One that the whole world noticed occurred off the country's east coast in March 2011 (see page 261). The fourth most powerful earthquake in recorded history, it unleashed a **tsunami** of prodigious force; the combined effect killed almost 16,000 people, and caused a meltdown at the nuclear power plant in Fukushima, where the effects will be felt for decades. Do note, however, that since the 1980s buildings have been designed to withstand even the most powerful 'quakes. Tokyo is equipped with some of the world's most **sophisticated sensors**, and architects employ mind-boggling techniques to try to ensure the city's high-rises remain upright.

TOKYO FOR FREE

Bear in mind that many of the best things to do in Tokyo are absolutely **free**. Some of the top places in town – in a very literal sense – won't set you back a single yen; most popular are the **observatories** at the Tokyo Metropolitan Government Building (see page 129), while those heading to the restaurant levels in the Caretta Building in Shidome (home to *Hibiki*; see page 161) or Ebisu Garden Place (home to *Longrain*; page 166) will get an eyeful even if they're not eating. The majority of **temples and shrines** are free, as are many **museums and galleries** – and a whole bunch more become so if you invest in a Grutt Pass (see page 30). Lastly, there are free **walking tours** around Asakusa (see page 74), Ueno (see page 65) and the Imperial City area (see page 41).

If you do have the misfortune to experience more than a minor rumble, follow the **safety procedures** listed below:

• Extinguish any fires and turn off electrical appliances.
• Open any doors leading out of the room, as they can get jammed shut, blocking your exit.
• Stay away from windows, to avoid the danger of splintering glass. If you have time, draw the curtains to contain the glass.
• Don't rush outside (many people are injured by falling masonry), but get under something solid, such as a ground-floor doorway, or a desk.
• If you are outside when the quake hits, beware of falling objects and head for the nearest park or other open space.
• If the earthquake occurs at night, make sure you've got a torch (all hotels and ryokan provide flashlights in the rooms).
• When the tremors have died down, go to the nearest park, playing field or open space, taking your documents and other valuables with you. If available, take a cushion or pillow to protect your head against falling glass.
• Eventually, make your way to the designated neighbourhood emergency centre for information, food and shelter.
• Ultimately, get in touch with your embassy.

Beware of aftershocks, which may go on for a long time and can topple structures that are already weakened; also note that most casualties are caused by fire and traffic accidents, rather than collapsing buildings. In the aftermath of a major earthquake, it may be impossible to contact friends and relatives for a while, since the phone lines are likely to be down or reserved for emergency services, while internet servers may be hit by power cuts.

Climate

The **summer** months in Tokyo are hot and humid, while **winters** are cold but drier; the rainy season –

known as *tsuyu* – is in June and July, but rain can fall at any time, especially between March and October. The most pleasant seasons to visit are **spring** (April to early May) and **autumn** (Oct and Nov). There's more advice on the best time to visit the city, as well as information on average temperatures and rainfall, in the Introduction (see page 8).

Electricity

Mains **electricity** in Tokyo is 100V, 50Hz AC. Japanese plugs have two flat pins or, less commonly, three pins (two flat and one rounded, earth pin). If you are arriving from North America or Canada, the voltage difference should cause no problems with computers, digital cameras, cell phones and the like. Appliances such as hair dryers, curling irons and travel kettles should also work, but not quite as efficiently, in which case you may need a converter. Large hotels can often provide voltage converters and adaptors.

Entry requirements

All visitors to Japan must have a passport valid for the duration of their stay. Citizens of Ireland, the UK and certain other European countries can stay in Japan for up to ninety days without a visa provided they are visiting for tourism or business purposes; this stay can be **extended** for another three months (see below). Citizens of Australia, Canada, New Zealand and the US can also stay for up to ninety days without a visa, though this is not extendable and you are required to be in possession of a return air ticket. Anyone from these countries wishing to stay longer will have to leave Japan and then re-enter.

Citizens of certain other countries must apply for a **visa** in advance in their own country. Visas are usually free, though in certain circumstances you may be charged a fee of around ¥3000 for a single-entry visa. The rules on visas do change from time to time, so check first with the nearest Japanese embassy or consulate, or on the Japanese Ministry of Foreign Affairs website ⓦ www.mofa.go.jp.

To get a **visa extension** you'll need to fill in two copies of an "Application for Extension of Stay", available from the **Tokyo Regional Immigration Bureau** at 5-5-30 Kōnan, Minato-ku (Mon–Fri 9am–noon & 1–4pm; ☎ 03 5796 7111, ⓦ www.immi-moj. go.jp), a short walk from Tennozu Isle station. Go early in the day, since the process takes forever; note that your application may not be confirmed for two weeks. Bring along passport photos (and your passport, of course), a letter explaining your reasons for wanting to extend your stay, and a fee of ¥4000. In addition, you may be asked to show proof of **sufficient funds** to support your stay, and a valid onward ticket out of the country. If you're not a national of one of the few countries with six-month reciprocal visa exemptions (these include Ireland and the UK), expect a thorough grilling from the immigration officials. An easier option – and the only alternative available to nationals of those countries who are not eligible for an extension – may be a short trip out of the country, say to South Korea or Hong Kong, though you may still have to run the gauntlet of immigration officials on your return.

Citizens of the UK, Ireland, Canada, Australia and New Zealand, among other countries, can apply for a **working holiday visa** if they are aged between 18 and 30 (officially up to 25 for Canadians and Australians, though there are often ways around this if you're under 30); this grants a stay of up to one year and entitles the holder to take paid employment so long as your stay is "primarily deemed to be a holiday". Full details of the scheme can be found at ⓦ mofa.go.jp.

British nationals are also eligible for the **volunteer visa scheme**, which allows holders to undertake voluntary work for charitable organizations in Japan for up to one year. Your application must include a letter from the host organization confirming details of the voluntary work to be undertaken and the treatment the volunteer will receive (pocket money and board and lodging are allowed, but formal remuneration is not). You must also be able to show evidence of sufficient funds for your stay in Japan. Contact your local embassy or consulate to check the current details of the scheme.

Foreigners legally allowed to stay in Japan for more than ninety days – basically those with legal employment or married to a Japanese citizen – must obtain **residency status** before their first ninety days is up. Resident cards can be issued, with prior arrangement, at the main international airports, though most people end up applying at their local government office. The resident cards (Zairyū kādo; 在留カード) include your photograph and must (legally speaking) be carried at all times, though they're rarely checked.

In addition, if you're on any sort of working visa and you leave Japan temporarily, you must get a **re-entry visa** before you leave if you wish to continue working on your return. Re-entry visas are available from local immigration bureaus.

EMBASSIES IN TOKYO

Australia 2-1-14 Mita, Minato-ku ☎ 03 5232 4111, ⓦ japan. embassy.gov.au.
Canada 7-3-38 Akasaka, Minato-ku ☎ 03 5412 6200, ⓦ japan. gc.ca.
China 3-4-33 Moto-Azabu, Minato-ku ☎ 03 3403 3064, ⓦ www. china-embassy.or.jp.
Ireland 2-10-7 Kōjimachi, Chiyoda-ku ☎ 03 3263 0695, ⓦ irishembassy.jp.
New Zealand 20-40 Kamiyamachō, Shibuya-ku ☎ 03 3467 2271, ⓦ nzembassy.com/japan.
Russian Federation 2-1-1 Azabudai, Minato-ku ☎ 03 3583 4445, ⓦ tokyo.mid.ru.
South Africa 4F 1-4 Kojimachi, Chiyoda-ku ☎ 03 3265 3366, ⓦ sajapan.org.
South Korea 1-2-5 Minami-Azabu, Minato-ku ☎ 03 3452 7611.
UK 1 Ichibanchō, Chiyoda-ku ☎ 03 5211 1100, ⓦ ukinjapan.fco. gov.uk.
USA 1-10-5 Akasaka, Minato-ku ☎ 03 3224 5000, ⓦ jp.usembassy. gov.

JAPANESE EMBASSIES AND CONSULATES ABROAD

You'll find a full list on ⓦ www.mofa.go.jp.
Australia 112 Empire Circuit, Yarralumla, Canberra ☎ 02 6273 3244, ⓦ www.au.emb-japan.go.jp.
Canada 255 Sussex Drive, Ottawa ☎ 613 241 8541, ⓦ www. ca.emb-japan.go.jp.
China 1 Liangmaqiao Dongjie, Chaoyang, Beijing ☎ 010 8531 9800, ⓦ www.cn.emb-japan.go.jp.
Ireland Nutley Building, Merrion Centre, Nutley Lane, Dublin ☎ 01 202 8300, ⓦ www.ie.emb-japan.go.jp.
New Zealand Level 18, Majestic Centre, 100 Willis St, Wellington ☎ 04 473 1540, ⓦ www.nz.emb-japan.go.jp.
Singapore 16 Nassim Rd ☎ 65 235 8855, ⓦ www.sg.emb-japan. go.jp.
South Africa 259 Baines St, Groenkloof, Pretoria ☎ 012 452 1500, ⓦ www.za.emb-japan.go.jp.
South Korea 6 Yulgok-ro, Jongno-gu, Seoul ☎ 02 2170 5200, ⓦ www.kr.emb-japan.go.jp.
UK 101–104 Piccadilly, London ☎ 020 7465 6500, ⓦ www. uk.emb-japan.go.jp; 2 Melville Crescent, Edinburgh ☎ 0131 225 4777, ⓦ www.edinburgh.uk.emb-japan.go.jp.

ROUGH GUIDES TRAVEL INSURANCE

Rough Guides has teamed up with WorldNomads.com to offer great travel insurance deals. Policies are available to residents of over 150 countries, with cover for a wide range of adventure sports, 24hr emergency assistance, high levels of medical and evacuation cover and a stream of travel safety information. Roughguides.com users can take advantage of their policies online 24/7, from anywhere in the world – even if you're already travelling. And since plans often change when you're on the road, you can extend your policy and even claim online. Roughguides.com users who buy travel insurance with WorldNomads.com can also leave a positive footprint and donate to a community development project. For more information, go to ⓦ roughguides.com/travel-insurance.

US 2520 Massachusetts Ave NW, Washington DC ☎ 202 238 6700, ⓦ www.us.emb-japan.go.jp.

Health

To find an English-speaking doctor and the hospital or clinic best suited to your needs, contact the **Tokyo Medical Information Service** (Mon–Fri 9am–8pm; ☎ 03 5285 8181, ⓦ www.himawari.metro. tokyo.jp); they can also provide emergency medical translation services over the phone. Major hotels usually stock a limited array of common medicines. You should find English-speaking staff at the establishments below.

Note that certain medications that are commonplace outside Japan are actually **illegal** here – some of the more prominent prescription drugs on the no-no list are codeine (beyond a certain amount) and some ADHD medication. The health ministry website (ⓦ www.mhlw.go.jp) has more specific details on these, and the forms you'll need to fill in if you're to bring these meds into Japan legally.

HOSPITALS, CLINICS AND PHARMACIES

American Pharmacy Marunouchi Building, 2-4-1 Marunouchi, Chiyoda-ku ☎ 03 5220 7716; Tokyo station. Has English-speaking pharmacists and a good range of drugs and general medical supplies. Mon–Fri 9am–9pm, Sat 10am–9pm, Sun 10am–8pm.

National Azabu Pharmacy Above the National Azabu supermarket ☎ 03 3442 3495; Hiro-o station.

St Luke's International Hospital 9-1 Akashichō, Chūō-ku ☎ 03 3541 5151, ⓦ hospital.luke.or.jp. Reception desk open Mon–Fri 8.30–11am for non-emergency cases.

Tokyo Adventist Hospital 3-17-3 Amanuma, Suginami-ku ☎ 03 3392 6151. Open 24hr for emergencies.

Tokyo Medical and Surgical Clinic 32 Shiba-kōen Building, 3-4-30 Shiba-kōen, Minato-ku ☎ 03 3436 3028, ⓦ tmsc.jp. Mon–Fri 8.30am–5.30pm, Sat 8.30am–noon, by appointment only.

Insurance

It's essential to take out a good **travel insurance** policy (see page 34), particularly one with comprehensive medical coverage, due to the high cost of hospital treatment in Japan.

Internet access

Many visitors soon realize that Japan doesn't quite live up to its tech-savvy reputation. A fair few local websites (including those of some expensive hotels and restaurants) are laughably bad; with italicized Times New Roman fonts and copious Clipart characters, many seem to have been imported directly from the mid-1990s.

However, things are finally starting to improve, and **wi-fi** access is becoming more widespread. Most big-city **cafés** offer it for free (though at some you have to register), and it's par for the course at privately run **hostels**, though at **hotels** you still can't be sure; at the top end, you may well have to pay a daily fee (typically ¥1000). Some hotels also offer free broadband in the rooms, and should be able to supply a cable if necessary. Others may provide terminals in the lobby or business centre (generally also for free), and rental laptops (usually ¥1000 or so).

Wi-fi has now been rolled out in most **subway stations** and **convenience stores** – you have to register once, with a fake email address if necessary, then log in each time. At the time of writing, 7-Eleven stores were by far the easiest at which to get online; you may well find your device connecting automatically each time you pass one.

Laundry

All hotels provide either a laundry service or coin-operated machines. These typically cost ¥200–300 for a wash (powder ¥30–50) and ¥100–200 for ten minutes in the drier. Failing that, neighbourhood laundromats are everywhere.

Left luggage

Most hotels will keep luggage for a few days. The baggage room (daily 7.30am–8.30pm) at Tokyo station can hold bags for the day for ¥600; the station information desks will point the way. Coin lockers can be found in many metro stations (¥400–800, depending on size), but can only be used for a maximum of three days.

Living and working in Tokyo

Employment opportunities for foreigners have shrunk since the Japanese economy took a nosedive, though finding employment is far from impossible, especially if you have the right qualifications (a degree is often essential) and appropriate visa.

Unless you take part in the **working holiday visa** programme (see page 32), foreigners working in Japan must apply for a **work visa** *outside* the country, for which the proper sponsorship papers from your prospective employer will be necessary. Work visas do not need to be obtained in your home country, so if you get offered a job, it's possible to sort out the paperwork in South Korea, for example. A few employers may be willing to hire you before the proper papers are sorted, but you shouldn't rely on this, and if you arrive without a job make sure you have plenty of funds to live on until you find one. Anyone staying in Japan more than ninety days must also apply for residency status (see page 32).

The most common job available to foreigners is **teaching English**. Some of the smaller schools are far from professional operations (and even the big ones get lots of complaints), so before signing any contract it's a good idea to talk to other teachers and, if possible, attend a class and find out what will be expected of you. If you have a professional teaching qualification, plus experience, or if you also speak another language such as French or Italian, your chances of getting one of the better jobs will be higher.

Another option is to get a place on the government-run **Japan Exchange and Teaching Programme** (JET; Ⓦ jetprogramme.org), aimed at improving foreign-language teaching in schools and promoting international understanding. The scheme is open to graduates aged 40 and under, preferably holding some sort of language-teaching qualification. Benefits include a decent-enough salary, help with accommodation, return air travel to Japan and paid holidays. Applying for the JET programme is a lengthy process for which you need to be well prepared. Application forms for the following year's quota are available from late September, and the deadline for submission is early December. Interviews are held in January and February, with decisions made in March. After health checks and orientation meetings, JETs head off to their posts in late July on year-long contracts, which can be renewed for up to two more years by mutual consent.

Whatever work you're looking for – or if you're doing any sort of business in Japan – a smart set of clothes will give you an advantage, as will following other general rules of social etiquette (see page 27).

EMPLOYMENT RESOURCES

Apart from the websites listed below the main places to look for job adverts are the free magazines *Metropolis* and *Tokyo Notice Board* (see page 25).

Daijob Ⓦ daijob.com. Japan's largest bilingual jobs website – and a great pun to boot (*daijobu* means "no problem").
GaijinPot Ⓦ gaijinpot.com. Classifieds focused on English-language teaching.
Japan Association for Working Holiday Makers Ⓦ jawhm. or.jp. Job referrals for people on working holiday visas.
Jobs in Japan Ⓦ jobsinjapan.com. Broad range of classified ads.

Studying Japanese language and culture

Tokyo offers all sorts of opportunities to study Japanese language and culture. In order to get a student or **cultural visa**, you'll need various documents from the institution where you plan to study and proof that you have sufficient funds to support yourself, among other things. Full-time courses are expensive, but once you have your visa you may be allowed to undertake a minimal amount of paid work.

Japan's Ministry of Education, Culture, Sports, Science and Technology (MEXT; Ⓦ www.mext.go.jp) offers various **scholarships** to foreign students wishing to further their knowledge of Japanese or Japanese studies, or to enrol at a Japanese university. You'll find further information on the informative Study in Japan website (Ⓦ www.study-japan.go.jp), run by the Ministry of Foreign Affairs, or by contacting your nearest Japanese embassy or consulate.

Tokyo has numerous **Japanese language schools** offering intensive and part-time courses. Among the most established are Berlitz (Ⓦ berlitz. co.jp), with over thirty schools in central Tokyo; GenkiJACS (Ⓦ genkijacs.com), whose Shinjuku branch is particularly popular with younger European students; and Tokyo Kogakuin Japanese Language School (5-30-16 Sendagaya, Shibuya-ku; ☎03 3352 3851, Ⓦ technos-jpschool.ac.jp). The monthly bilingual magazine *Hiragana Times* (Ⓦ hira-

EXCHANGE RATES

Exchange rates at the time of writing are as follows:

£1 = ¥136
€1 = ¥121
US$1 = ¥108
Can$1 = ¥81
Aus$1 = ¥74
NZ$1 = ¥71

For current exchange rates see ⓦxe.com.

ganatimes.com) and the magazines *Metropolis* and *Tokyo Journal* (see page 25) also carry adverts for schools, or check out the Association for the Promotion of Japanese Language Education (2F Ishiyama Bldg, 1-58-1 Yoyogi, Shinjuku-ku; ☎03 4304 7815, ⓦwww.nisshinkyo.org), whose website lists accredited institutions.

Mail

Japan's **mail** service is highly efficient and fast, with thousands of post offices, easily identified by their red-and-white signs showing a T with a parallel bar across the top (the same symbol that you'll find on the red letterboxes) scattered across the capital. All post can be addressed in Western script (*rōmaji*), provided that it's clearly printed.

Major post offices that are open 24/7 include the **Central Post Office**, on the west side of Tokyo station, as well as ones in Shinjuku (see map on page 128), Shibuya (see map on page 116) and other city areas.

If you need to send bulkier items or **parcels** back home, you can buy reasonably priced special envelopes and boxes for packaging from any post office. The maximum weight for an overseas parcel is 30kg (less for some destinations). A good compromise between expensive air mail and slow sea mail is Surface Air Lifted (SAL) mail, which costs somewhere between the two, and takes around three weeks to reach most destinations. For English-language information about postal services, including postal fees, see the Post Office website (ⓦpost.japanpost.jp).

Maps

Decent free **maps** of the city are available from any of the tourist information centres (see page 38). Bilingual maps on public notice boards outside the main exits to most subway and train stations are handy for getting your immediate bearings – these are usually oriented the way you are facing, so if you're facing southeast, for example, the top of the map will be southeast and the bottom northwest.

There are also decent maps **online**. Google's is typically excellent, while with a little hunting you'll be able to find apps offering offline-friendly maps of the city (ⓦmaps.me is a good one). Perhaps equally useful are maps portraying the Tokyo subway network, since such maps are not visible anywhere once you're on the trains themselves – there is, of course, one in this guide.

Money

The **Japanese currency** is the **yen** (*en* in Japanese). Notes are available in denominations of ¥1000, ¥2000 (rarely seen), ¥5000 and ¥10,000, while coins come in values of ¥1, ¥5, ¥10, ¥50, ¥100 and ¥500. Apart from the ¥5 piece, a copper-coloured coin with a hole in the centre, all other notes and coins indicate their value in Western numerals.

Though **credit and debit cards** are far more widely accepted than they were a few years ago, Japan is still very much a cash society. The most useful cards to carry are Visa and American Express, followed closely by MasterCard, then Diners Club; you should be able to use these in hotels, restaurants, shops and travel agencies accustomed to serving foreigners. However, some retailers only accept locally issued cards, and many will only take cash.

ATMs

The simplest way of obtaining cash in Japan is by making an **ATM** withdrawal on a credit or debit card. Both the **post office** and Seven Bank (whose machines are located in **7-Eleven** stores) operate ATMs that accept foreign-issued cards. Post office machines accept Visa, PLUS, MasterCard, Maestro, Cirrus and American Express, with instructions

CONSUMPTION TAX

A **consumption tax** (*shōhizei*) is levied on virtually all goods and services in Japan, including restaurant meals and accommodation. At the time of writing, the rate was eight percent, though it's set to rise to ten percent from October 2019. Tax is supposed to be included in the advertised price, though you'll come across plenty of shops, hotels, restaurants and bars which haven't quite got around to it; double-check to be on the safe side.

provided in English; 7-Eleven ATMs accept all of these, too, and their hours of use are longer (often round the clock). Withdrawal limits will depend on the card issuer and your credit limit – if the machine doesn't allow you to withdraw money in the first instance, try again with a smaller amount.

You'll also find post office ATMs not only in post offices, but also in stations, department stores and the like throughout the city – they're identified with a sticker saying "International ATM Service". Their ATMs have more **restricted hours** than the Seven Bank machines, but the ones in major post offices can be accessed at weekends and after the counters have closed, though none are open round the clock.

Changing money

You can change cash at the **exchange counters** (*ryōgae-jo*; 両替所) of main post offices and certain banks – the bigger branches of Tokyo-Mitsubishi UFJ (Ⓦbk.mufg.jp/english) and SMBC (Sumitomo Mitsubishi Banking Corporation; Ⓦwww.smbcgroup.com) are your best bet. The post office handles cash in six major currencies, including American, Canadian and Australian dollars, sterling and euros. **Hotels** are only supposed to change money for guests, but some might be persuaded to help in an emergency. Remember to take your passport along in case it's needed, and allow plenty of time, since even a simple transaction can take twenty minutes or more.

Opening hours and public holidays

Business hours are generally Monday to Friday 9am to 5pm, though private companies often close much later in the evening and may also open on Saturday mornings. Department stores and bigger **shops** tend to open around 10am and shut at 7 or 8pm. Local shops, however, will generally stay open later, while most convenience stores stay open 24 hours. Most shops take one day off a week, but not necessarily on a Sunday.

The majority of **museums** close on a Monday, but stay open on Sundays and national holidays; last entry is normally thirty minutes before closing. Most museums and department stores stay open on **national holidays** and take the following day off instead. However, during the New Year festival (January 1–3), Golden Week (April 29–May 5) and O-bon (the week around August 15), almost everything shuts down. Around these periods transport and accommodation can get booked out weeks in advance, and all major tourist spots get overrun.

PUBLIC HOLIDAYS

If one of the holidays listed below falls on a Sunday, then the Monday is also a holiday.
New Year's Day Jan 1
Coming-of-Age Day Second Mon in Jan
National Foundation Day Feb 11
Emperor's Birthday Feb 23 (date subject to change if there is a succession)
Spring Equinox March 20/21
Shōwa Day April 29
Constitution Memorial Day May 3
Green Day May 4
Children's Day May 5
Mountain Day May 11
Marine Day Third Mon in July
Respect-the-Aged Day Third Mon in Sept
Autumn Equinox Sept 23/24
Health and Sports Day Second Mon in Oct
Culture Day Nov 3
Labour Thanksgiving Day Nov 23

Phones

You're rarely far from a payphone in Tokyo. The vast majority take both coins (¥10 and ¥100) and **phonecards**; they don't give change but do return unused coins, so for local calls use ¥10 rather than ¥100 coins.

Everywhere in Japan has an **area code** (Tokyo's is Ⓣ030), which can be omitted if the call is a local one. All toll-free numbers begin with either Ⓣ0120 or Ⓣ0088. In a few cases you may come across codes such as Ⓣ0570, which are not region-specific and thus should always be dialled wherever in Japan you're calling from. Numbers starting with Ⓣ080 or Ⓣ090 belong to mobiles.

Mobile phones

Practically everyone in Japan has a **mobile phone** (*keitai-denwa*, sometimes shortened to *keitai*), many of which can be used like a prepaid travel card on trains, subways and in shops.

Most foreign **models** will work in Japan – contact your mobile phone service provider before leaving your home country. Another solution for short-term visitors is to **rent** a phone (buying a prepaid phone in Japan generally requires you to show proof of local residency) at the airport, in Tokyo or online; options include B-Mobile (Ⓦwww.bmobile.ne.jp/english), who also rent out data cards for internet access on your laptop. Other mobile phone operators include the predominant **DoCoMo** (Ⓦwww.nttdocomo.co.jp), and **Softbank** (Ⓦsoftbank.jp/en), both of which have rental booths at Narita Airport.

Alternatively, around all major stations (especially those on the Yamanote line) you'll be able to track down outlets selling pocket wi-fi "eggs"; plans with a decent amount of data tend to cost ¥750 per day, up to ¥10,000 for a month (check online at Ⓦ en.wifi-rent-al-store.jp, or Ⓦ pupuruwifi.com).

Phoning abroad from Japan

The main companies in Japan offering **international phone calls** are KDDI (Ⓣ001), Softbank Telecom (Ⓣ010) and NTT (Ⓣ0033). If you want to call abroad from Japan from any type of phone, choose a company (there's little difference between them all as far as rates are concerned) and dial the relevant access code, then the country code (UK Ⓣ44; Ireland Ⓣ353; US and Canada Ⓣ01; Australia Ⓣ61; New Zealand Ⓣ64; South Africa Ⓣ27), then the area code minus the initial zero, then the number. You can make international operator-assisted calls by calling Ⓣ0051 via KDDI.

Phoning Japan from abroad

To **call Japan** from abroad, dial your international access code (UK and Ireland Ⓣ00; US Ⓣ011; Canada Ⓣ011; Australia Ⓣ0011; New Zealand Ⓣ00; South Africa Ⓣ09), plus the country code Ⓣ81, then the area code minus the initial zero, then the number.

Smoking

Smoking laws in Japan verge on the ridiculous – the practice is banned in public spaces but not inside bars and restaurants, so while you'll see smokers huddled like penguins in dedicated zones on the street, you'll regularly find people lighting up next to you over your meal, coffee or beer. Tighter restrictions have been mooted, but in this conservative land these things take serious time – and, it has to be said, the Japanese are serious smokers.

Time

Tokyo is nine hours ahead of Greenwich Mean Time, fourteen hours ahead of New York, seventeen hours ahead of Los Angeles and two hours behind Sydney. There is no daylight saving time, so during British Summer Time, for example, the difference drops to eight hours.

Tourist information

Other than the resources below, **Goodwill Guides** (Ⓦ www.jnto.go.jp) can provide English-language information. These **volunteers** offer their services free – although you're expected to pay for their transport, entry tickets and any meals you have together. Their language abilities vary, but they do provide a great opportunity to learn more about Japanese culture and to visit local restaurants, shops and so forth with a Japanese-speaker. You can contact members through the JNTO and Asakusa information offices.

TOURIST INFORMATION RESOURCES

Asakusa Culture and Sightseeing Centre Ⓣ 03 3842 5566. Near Asakusa station, and housed in a highly distinctive building designed by Kengo Kuma. Daily 9am–8pm.

Japan National Tourism Organization Ⓦ jnto.go.jp. The JNTO maintains a number of overseas offices – see the website for a full list of locations. They have tourist information kiosks in the arrivals halls at Narita and Haneda airports.

Tokyo City i B1F Kitte Building, 2-7-2 Marunouchi Ⓦ en. tokyocity-i.jp; Tokyo station. The city's best tourist information centre, with multilingual staff, accommodation- and tour-booking facilities, and good general advice. Daily 8am–8pm.

Tokyo Tourist Information Centre 1F Tokyo Metropolitan Government No. 1 Building, 2-8-1 Nishi-Shinjuku Ⓣ 03 5321 3077, Ⓦ gotokyo.org; Tochōmae station. Another excellent tourist information centre (TIC), though it's a little bit out of the way unless you're visiting the Tokyo Metropolitan Government Building (see page 129). Daily 9.30am–6.30pm.

Travellers with disabilities

Disability has always been something of an uncomfortable topic in Japan, with disabled people generally hidden from public view. In recent years, however, there has been a certain shift in public opinion, particularly in the wake of the bestseller *No One's Perfect* by Ototake Hirotada, the upbeat, forthright autobiography of a 23-year-old student born without arms or legs. Hopefully, Tokyo's hosting of the 2020 Paralympics will provide a further push in the right direction.

The government is spearheading a drive to provide more accessible hotels and other facilities (referred to as "barrier-free" in Japan). All train and subway **stations** now have an extra-wide manned ticket gate and an increasing number have escalators or lifts. Some **trains**, such as the Narita Express, have spaces for wheelchair users, but you should reserve well in advance. For travelling short distances, **taxis** are an obvious solution, though they are not adapted to take wheelchairs, and few drivers will offer help getting in or out of the car.

Hotels are required to provide accessible facilities. Your best bet is one of the international chains or modern Western-style business hotels, which are most likely to provide fully adapted rooms, ramps and lifts; check ahead to ensure the facilities meet your requirements. Similarly, most modern shopping complexes, museums and other public buildings are equipped with ramps, wide doors and accessible toilets.

While things are improving, Tokyo is not an easy place to get around for anyone using a wheelchair, or for those who find it difficult to negotiate stairs or walk long distances. Although it's usually possible to organize assistance at stations, you'll need a Japanese-speaker to phone ahead and make the arrangements. For further information and help, contact the **Japanese Red Cross Society** (1-1-3 Shiba Daimon, Minato-ku, Tokyo 105-8521). You'll find useful information on their website (W accessible.jp.org).

FUJIMI-YAGURA, THE IMPERIAL PALACE

The Imperial Palace and around

Wrapped round with moats and broad avenues, the enigmatic Imperial Palace lies at the city's geographical and spiritual heart. The palace itself – home to the emperor and his family since 1868 – is closed to the public, but the surrounding parks are a natural place to start any exploration of Tokyo. The most attractive is Higashi Gyoen, where remnants of the old Edo Castle still stand amid formal gardens; to its north lies Kitanomaru-kōen, a more natural park containing the excellent National Museum of Modern Art. Look east from the Imperial Palace area and you'll see that the flat parkland on its periphery is, almost immediately, punctuated by a wall of high-rise – this is Marunouchi (literally meaning "inside the circle"), whose crowded streets are transformed at dusk into neon-lit canyons, lined with many of Tokyo's swankiest places to eat, drink and sleep.

> **BEST OF THE IMPERIAL PALACE AREA**
> **Higashi Gyoen** Wonder "am I really in the middle of the world's biggest city?" in this peaceful palace park (see page 43)
> **Intermediatheque** Explore one of the city's most popular new museums (see page 48)
> **Hoshinoya** Check in at a five-star hotel with ryokan-like sensibilities – the perfect combination (see page 147)
> **The Oyster Shack** Slurp down some molluscs beneath the train tracks (see page 159)
> **Old Imperial Bar** Enjoy a "Mount Fuji" cocktail (see page 179)

Marunouchi has enjoyed a stylish reinvention of late, with the opening of several new shopping and restaurant complexes, and the recent redevelopment of **Tokyo station** and its environs. The adjoining **Yūrakuchō** district to the south is – like Marunouchi – home to theatres, airline offices, banks and corporate headquarters, as well as the dramatic modern architecture of the multipurpose **Tokyo International Forum**. Head south from Yūrakuchō and you'll soon be in the **Hibiya district**, highlight of which is its Western-style **park**, a refreshing oasis of greenery.

GETTING AROUND AND INFORMATION　　　　**THE IMPERIAL PALACE AND AROUND**

By foot The maze of tunnels in this area is truly spectacular in scope: from Ōte-mon (the main gate to Higashi Gyoen) in the north, you'll be able to walk to Hibiya-kōen down south, without once popping your head above ground, with this underground lattice linking the subway stations on both east and west sides of the railway tracks – very handy if it's rainy or too hot out. In addition, with the aid of over-road walkways, you'll be able to walk on pedestrian-only paths pretty much all the way to Yasukuni-jinja too.

Tokyo City i B1F Kitte Building, 2-7-2 Marunouchi ⓦ en.tokyocity-i.jp; Tokyo station. An excellent tourist information centre with English-speaking staff. Daily 8am–8pm.

The Imperial Palace

皇居, Kōkyo

The site of the **Imperial Palace** is as old as Tokyo itself. Edo Castle was built here by Tokugawa Ieyasu in 1497 (see page 257), and its boundaries fluctuated through the following centuries; at its greatest extent, the castle walls also surrounded what is now Tokyo station, as well as parts of present-day Marunouchi. The main citadel, however, lay in today's **Higashi Gyoen**, or East Garden, and this was surrounded by moats, watchtowers and ramparts spreading over several kilometres. Little remains today, save for three fortified towers and some massive stone walls.

The present-day incarnation of the palace is a long, sleek, 1960s structure, built to replace the nineteenth-century Meiji palace building, which burnt down in the 1945 bombing raids. The actual imperial **residences**, built in the early 1990s, are tucked away out of sight in the thickly wooded western section of the **palace grounds**, which cover 284 acres, surrounded by a protective moat. Further defence against attack was afforded in earlier times by the large, windswept island now known as the **Imperial Plaza**, where the shogunate's most trusted followers were allowed to build their mansions; after 1899 these were razed to make way for today's austere expanse of spruce lawns and manicured pine trees.

The palace grounds

Entrance off Uchibori-dōri • Access by official tour only; apply online and bring your passport • Tues–Sat 10am & 1.30pm • 75min • Free • ☎ 03 3213 1111, ⓦ sankan.kunaicho.go.jp • Sakuradamon or Nijūbashimae stations

Except for the two days a year when Nijūbashi is open to the general public (see below), admission to the **palace grounds** is only on prearranged **official tours**, some

1

of which have been conducted in English since 2018. They are a bit of a hassle to get on, but there is a certain fascination in taking a peek inside this secret world, and the pre-tour video shows tantalizing glimpses of vast function rooms and esoteric court rituals.

Nijūbashi
二重橋

The primary reason to follow the groups of tourists straggling across the broad avenues is to view one of the palace's most photogenic corners, **Nijūbashi**, where two bridges span the moat and a jaunty little watchtower perches on its grey stone pedestal beyond. Though this double bridge is a late nineteenth-century embellishment, the tower dates back to the seventeenth century and is one of the castle's few original structures. Twice a year (on Dec 23, the emperor's official birthday, and on Jan 2) thousands of well-

DESCENDANTS OF THE SUN GODDESS

Emperor Akihito, the 125th incumbent of the Chrysanthemum Throne, traces his ancestry back to 660 BC and Emperor Jimmu, great-great-grandson of the mythological Sun Goddess Amaterasu. Most scholars, however, acknowledge that the first emperor for whom there is any historical evidence is the fifth-century Emperor Ojin.

Until the twentieth century, emperors were regarded as living deities whom ordinary folk were forbidden to set eyes on, or even hear. Japan's defeat in World War II ended all that and today the emperor is a symbolic figure, a head of state with no governmental power. While he was crown prince, **Emperor Akihito** had an American tutor and studied at Tokyo's elite Gakushūin University, followed by a stint at Oxford University. In 1959 he broke further with tradition by marrying a commoner, **Shōda Michiko**.

Akihito's son, **Naruhito**, followed in his father's footsteps in 1993 by marrying high-flying, Harvard-educated diplomat Owada Masako. Current Japanese law prohibits a female succession, and as such the couple came under intense media scrutiny when failing to produce a male heir; the crown princess gave birth to a baby girl, **Aiko**, in 2001, but a constitutional amendment was averted when Naruhito's younger brother Akishino gave birth to a boy, Hisahito, in 2006.

In August 2016, Akihito gave only his second-ever televised address, mentioning his health problems and advancing age, and hinting at an extremely rare Japanese abdication. This duly came to pass in 2019, when he handed over the Chrysanthemum Throne to its 126th incumbent, eldest son Naruhito, thus ushering in the **Reiwa period**.

wishers file across Nijūbashi to greet the royal family, lined up behind bulletproof glass, with a rousing cheer of "*Banzai!*" ("May you live 10,000 years!").

Higashi Gyoen

東御苑 • East entrance off Uchibori-dōri, north entrance opposite National Museum of Modern Art • Tues–Thurs, Sat & Sun 9am–4pm (closed occasionally for court functions) • Free tokens issued at park entrance; hand back on exit • Ōtemachi or Takebashi stations

Hemmed in by moats, the **Higashi Gyoen**, or East Garden, was opened to the public in 1968 to commemorate the completion of the new Imperial Palace, and is a good place for a stroll. The towering granite walls, as well as several formidable gates, hint at the grandeur of the shogunate's Edo Castle, part of which stood here until being consumed by a catastrophic fire in the seventeenth century.

Ōte-mon

大手門 • Museum Tues–Thurs, Sat & Sun 9am–3.45pm • Free

The main gate to the former Edo Castle – and, today, to the garden – is **Ōte-mon**, an austere, moat-side construction whose bottom half is made up of charmingly wonky cubes of rock. Much of it was destroyed in 1945, but it has been lovingly restored since. The first building ahead on the right is a small **museum**, exhibiting a tiny fraction of the eight thousand artworks in the imperial collection, and worth a quick look.

Fujimi-yagura

富士見櫓

The finest of the fortress's remaining watchtowers is the three-tiered **Fujimi-yagura**, built in 1659 to protect the main citadel's southern flank. These days it rises above the Higashi Gyoen like a miniature version of the old castle itself, standing clear above the trees to the north of the Imperial Plaza.

Shiomizaka and Honmaru

Retrace your steps from Fujimi-yagura and bank to the left; by following the gentle uphill path you'll soon be beneath the walls of the main Edo Castle citadel. The path

1

then climbs more steeply towards **Shiomizaka**, the Tide-Viewing Slope, from where it was once possible to gaze out over Edo Bay rather than the concrete blocks of Ōtemachi. You emerge on a flat, grassy area which is a real rarity in Tokyo – in clement weather, it's all too tempting to walk barefoot. The stone foundations of **Honmaru** (the "inner citadel") rise from here, providing fine views from the top. Elsewhere are a scattering of modern edifices, among them the bizarre, mosaic-clad **Imperial Music Hall**; designed by Imai Kenji, the hall commemorates the sixtieth birthday of the then empress in 1963, and is used for occasional performances of court music.

Kitanomaru-kōen

北の丸公園 • North entrance off Yasukuni-dōri • 24hr • Free • Kudanshita or Takebashi stations

Edo Castle's old northern citadel is now occupied by the park of **Kitanomaru-kōen**. With its ninety-odd cherry trees, it's a popular viewing spot come *hanami* time, while rowing boats can be rented in warmer months on **Chidoriga-fuchi**, an ancient pond once incorporated into Edo Castle's moat. These natural pleasures aside, the park is also home to a couple of interesting museums: the **National Museum of Modern Art** to the south, and the **Crafts Gallery** to the west.

National Museum of Modern Art

国立近代美術館, Kokuritsu Kindai Bijutsukan • Tues–Sun 10am–5pm, Fri & Sat 10am–8pm • ¥500, or ¥300 after 5pm Fri & Sat; extra fees apply for special exhibitions • ☎ 03 5777 8600, ⓦ momat.go.jp

Located on the southern perimeter of the park is the **National Museum of Modern Art**. Strewn over three large levels, its excellent permanent collection showcases Japanese art since 1900, as well as a few pieces of work from overseas; the former includes Gyokudo Kawai's magnificent screen painting *Parting Spring* and works by Kishida Ryūsei, Fujita Tsuguharu and postwar artists such as Yoshihara Jiro. On the fourth floor you'll find the earliest works, as well as a resting area with fantastic views over the moat and palace grounds; the third floor contains perhaps the most interesting section, featuring art made either during wartime or its aftermath.

Crafts Gallery

工芸館, Kōgeikan • Tues–Sun 10am–5pm • ¥210; usually ¥900 for special exhibitions • ☎ 03 5777 8600, ⓦ momat.go.jp

Tucked away on the west side of Kitanomaru-kōen, the **Crafts Gallery** exhibits a selection of top-quality traditional Japanese craft works, many by modern masters.

MASAKADO AND THE TOKYO CURSE

Hidden away just east of the Imperial Palace stands a small gravestone, located in a little garden. Humble though it may sound, some consider this gravestone the most important in Tokyo, and believe that its occupant continues to demonise the city.

The grave belongs to **Masakado** of the Taira clan, who is often referred to as the "first samurai". In 939, he led a rebellion against the ruling powers out west in Kyoto – some consider him the "first samurai". After proclaiming himself emperor, a bounty was put on his head, which was duly lopped off by one of his cousins and taken to Kyoto. However, the authorities had been spooked, and it wasn't long before myths and legends became attributed to Masakado; his head was hung from a tree in the marketplace, though it apparently howled through the night, and eventually flew off. Bad luck continued to strike the small fishing village where it came to rest; once given a gravestone and relocated to Tokyo, it was blamed for anything and everything, including the 1927 earthquake, a 1940 lightning strike which destroyed a row of nearby offices, and a spate of curious and untimely deaths.

However, Masakado's continuing influence was not completely spiritual in nature – the rebels he inspired eventually succeeded in bringing an end to Kyoto's rule, and proclaimed their own capital in Edo, a small hamlet which eventually blossomed into the Tokyo we know today.

Erected in 1910 as the headquarters of the Imperial Guards, this neo-Gothic red-brick pile is one of very few Tokyo buildings dating from before the Great Earthquake of 1923 – it looks like the kind of place Harry Potter would have gone to school, had he been Japanese.

Budōkan
武道館

The **Budōkan** was built in 1964 to host Olympic judo events and was chosen for the same purpose for the 2020 Olympics (this time including karate). The design, with its graceful, curving roof and gold topknot, pays homage to a famous octagonal hall at Hōryū-ji in Nara, near Kyoto, though the shape is also supposedly inspired by that of Mount Fuji. Today the huge arena is used for sports meetings, graduation ceremonies and, most famously, big-name rock concerts – the Beatles were first to play here.

Ichigaya
市ヶ谷

When you're done with the regal gardens, the area around **Ichigaya** station – just northwest of the palace – has a few more sights, including two pertaining to World War II: a museum, and a shrine to the war dead.

Shōwa-kan
昭和館 • Off Yasukuni-dōri • Tues–Sun 10am–5.30pm • ¥300; English-language audio-guides free • ☎ 03 3222 2577, ⓦ www.showakan.go.jp • Kudanshita station

There is something more than a little creepy about the **Shōwa-kan**, a museum devoted to life in Japan during and after World War II. It's almost as if the designers of this windowless corrugated building were acknowledging the secrecy that surrounds what really happened in those years – take a look at the exhibits and you'll see scarcely a mention of bombs or destruction. To be fair, the government originally wanted the museum to document the war's origins but ran into bitter opposition from pacifists, insistent on tackling the hot-potato issue of responsibility, and from a right-wing lobby opposed to any hint that Japan was an aggressor during the conflict. The resultant compromise sticks to a sanitized portrayal of the hardships suffered by wives and children left behind. However, there's some interesting material concerning life during the occupation in the sixth- and seventh-floor exhibition rooms, including empty hacky sacks from which starving children ate the dried beans used as stuffing.

Yasukuni-jinja
靖国神社 • Entrance off Yasukuni-dōri • Daily: March–Oct 6am–6pm, Nov–Feb 6am–5pm • Free • ⓦ yasukuni.or.jp • Kudanshita or Ichigaya stations

A monumental red steel *torii*, claimed to be Japan's tallest, marks the entrance to **Yasukuni-jinja**. This shrine, whose name means "for the repose of the country", was founded in 1869 to worship supporters of the emperor killed in the run-up to the Meiji Restoration. Since then it has expanded to include the legions sacrificed in subsequent wars, in total nearly 2.5 million souls, of whom some two million died in the Pacific War alone; the parting words of kamikaze pilots were said to be "see you at Yasukuni". Every year some eight million Japanese visit this shrine, which controversially includes several war criminals (see page 46); security has been tight since a minor explosion here in late 2015.

Standing at the end of a long avenue lined with cherry and ginkgo trees and accessed through a simple wooden gate, the architecture is classic Shinto styling, solid and

1

THE PROBLEM WITH YASUKUNI

Ever since its foundation as part of a Shinto revival promoting the new emperor, **Yasukuni-jinja** has been a place of high controversy. In its early years the shrine became a natural focus for the increasingly aggressive nationalism that ultimately took Japan to war in 1941. Then, in 1978, General Tōjō, prime minister during World War II, and thirteen other "Class A" war criminals were enshrined here, to be honoured along with all the other military dead. Japan's neighbours, still smarting from their treatment by the Japanese during the war, were outraged.

This has not stopped top politicians from visiting Yasukuni on the anniversary of Japan's defeat in World War II (August 15). Because Japan's postwar constitution requires the separation of state and religion, ministers have usually maintained that they attend as private individuals, but in 1985 Nakasone, in typically uncompromising mood, caused uproar when he signed the visitors' book as "Prime Minister". Recent PMs have continued to visit Yasukuni – always in an "unofficial" capacity – despite continued protests both at home and abroad.

unadorned except for two gold imperial chrysanthemums embossed on the main doors. If this is all surprisingly unassuming, the same cannot be said for a couple of menacing metal lanterns near the entrance, whose distinctive Rising Sun-like patterns are most evident at dusk.

Yūshūkan

遊就館 • Daily 9am–4.30pm • ¥1000 • ☎ 03 3261 8326

To the right of the Inner Shrine you'll find the **Yūshūkan**, a military museum established in 1882. The displays are well presented, with plentiful information in English, but the problem is as much what is left out as what is included. Events such as the Nanking Massacre ("Incident" in Japanese) and other atrocities by Japanese troops are glossed over, while the Pacific War is presented as a war of liberation, freeing the peoples of Southeast Asia from Western colonialism. The most moving displays are the ranks of faded photographs and the "bride dolls" donated by the families of young soldiers who died before they were married. You exit through a hall full of military hardware, including a replica of the gliders used by kamikaze pilots on their suicide missions, its nose elongated to carry a 1200-kilo bomb, while a spine-chilling black *kaiten* (manned torpedo) looms to one side.

The garden

Before leaving the complex, walk through the little Japanese **garden** behind the shrine buildings. The sunken enclosure next door is the venue for a sumo tournament (not one of the official ones; see page 213) during the shrine's spring festival, when wrestlers perform under trees laden with cherry blossom. In early July the shrine also hosts a lively *matsuri*, when the precincts are illuminated by thousands of paper lanterns and there's dancing, parades and music nightly.

Ichigaya Kamegaoka Hachimangū

市谷亀岡八幡宮 • 15 Ichigaya Hachiman--chō, Shijuku-ku • Daily 24hr • Free • Ichigaya station

On the face of things, **Ichigaya Kamegaoka Hachimangū** is just another neighbourhood shrine. However, look a little harder at the statues and plaques and you'll notice many of them feature animals. This place is, in fact, a semiofficial shrine for locals to pray with their pets; this usually happens around New Year, but you'll still see the occasional dog, cat or tortoise getting into the Shinto spirit of things. Even if you're out of luck,

1

you can take a look at the wooden *ema* plaques on which petitioners write their wishes, all of which feature some animal or other in picture form.

Marunouchi

丸の内

Squeezed between the Imperial Palace and Tokyo station, the business-focused **Marunouchi** district has been broadening its appeal with a raft of sleek, multistorey developments combining offices, hotels, shopping plazas and all manner of restaurants and cafés. Completed in 2002, the 36-storey **Marunouchi Building**, affectionately (or, perhaps, lazily) known as the "Maru Biru", was first off the blocks, followed by the **Oazo** complex, and the **Shin-Marunouchi Building**, with a seventh-floor upscale dining and drinking area (see page 179), and an outdoor terrace that offers terrific views. Then there's **Tokyo station** itself, whose red-brick entrance dates to the station's 1914 opening, and was inspired by the design of Amsterdam's Centraal station. The **Mitsubishi Ichigokan Museum**, meanwhile, fronts Marunouchi Brick Square, where shops and restaurants overlook a lovely landscaped garden.

Mitsubishi Ichigokan Museum

三菱一号館美術館 • 2-6-2 Marunouchi, Chiyoda-ku • Daily 10am–6pm, Fri and final week of each exhibition until 9pm • Price depends on exhibition – usually ¥1700, with ¥200 discount to foreign tourists with ID • ☎ 03 5405 8686, ⓦ mimt.jp • Tokyo or Nijūbashimae stations

Worth a look for its design as much as its contents, the **Mitsubishi Ichigokan Museum** is housed in a meticulous reconstruction of a red-brick office block designed by British architect Josiah Conder (see page 62); the original was erected on the same site in 1894, only to be demolished in 1968. Exhibitions rotate every four months or so, and almost exclusively focus on nineteenth-century European art, usually of a pretty high calibre.

Meiji Seimei-kan

明治生命館 • 2-1-1 Marunouchi, Chiyoda-ku • Sat & Sun 11am–5pm • Free • Nijūbashimae or Yūrakuchō stations

A block west of Brick Square, the 1934 **Meiji Seimei-kan**, part of the newer My Plaza building, is home to the Meiji Yasuda life insurance company. On weekends you're allowed in to admire the highly polished marble floors and plaster detailing. Upstairs is a parquet-floored conference room, where the Allied Council of Japan met in the aftermath of World War II, and a dining room complete with dumbwaiters.

Intermediatheque

インターメディアテク • 2–3F Kitte Building, 2-7-2 Marunouchi, Chiyoda-ku • Mon–Thurs & Sun 11am–6pm; Fri & Sat 11am–8pm; closed a few days per month • Free • ☎ 03 5777 8600, ⓦ intermediatheque.jp • Tokyo station

The double-level **Intermediatheque** is, without doubt, one of the most intriguing museum spaces in the city, hosting exhibitions that are sharply curated and pieced together with a rare attention to aesthetic detail. The permanent exhibition is a well-presented mishmash of various objects of scientific and cultural heritage accumulated by the Tokyo University (see page 69); the animal skeletons are the most eye-catching exhibits, but poke around and you'll find everything from Central American headwear to objects damaged by the nuclear explosions in Nagasaki. There's a pleasing range to the temporary exhibitions, which can feature anything from photography to international objets d'art, via documentary work. Before you leave the building, check out the garden up on the roof.

Yūrakuchō

有楽町

South of Marunouchi lies **Yūrakuchō**, a high-rise district that's home to yet more giant pieces of urban furniture. Most notable is the arresting **Tokyo International Forum**, a stunning creation by American architect Rafael Viñoly, which hosts concerts and conventions, plus the Ōedo Antique Market (see page 201); it was chosen to host the weightlifting events in the 2020 Olympics (see page 123). Its boat-shaped main hall consists of a 60m-high atrium sheathed in 2600 sheets of earthquake-resistant glass, with a ceiling ribbed like a ship's hull – it looks magical at night.

Idemitsu Museum of Arts

出光美術館, Idemitsu Bijutsukan • 9F Teigeki Building, 3-1-1 Marunouchi, Chiyoda-ku • Tues–Sun 10am–5pm, Fri until 7pm • ¥1000 • ☎ 03 5777 8600, Ⓦ idemitsu-museum.or.jp • Hibiya or Yūrakuchō stations

Sitting above the Imperial Theatre, the **Idemitsu Museum of Arts** houses a magnificent assortment of mostly Japanese art, though only a tiny proportion is on show at any one time. The collection includes many historically important pieces, ranging from fine examples of early Jōmon (10,000 BC–300 BC) pottery to Zen Buddhist calligraphy, hand-painted scrolls, richly gilded folding screens and elegant, late seventeenth-century *ukiyo-e* paintings. The museum also owns valuable collections of Chinese and Korean ceramics.

Hibiya

日比谷

The area south of where Edo Castle once stood was occupied by the Tokugawa shogunate's less favoured *daimyō*. The land was cleared after 1868, but was too waterlogged to support modern buildings, so in 1903 **Hibiya-kōen** (日比谷公園), Tokyo's first European-style park, came into being. These days the tree-filled park is a popular lunchtime spot for office workers and courting couples, and makes a very pleasant escape from the bustle of the nearby skyscraper districts.

Imperial Hotel

1-1-1 Uchisaiwai-chō, Chiyoda-ku • Hibiya station

Across the road from Hibiya-kōen is the celebrated **Imperial Hotel**, Tokyo's first Western-style hotel when it opened in 1890 (see page 147). The original building was subsequently replaced by a stunning creation from American architect Frank Lloyd Wright: part Art Deco, part Aztec palace, it famously withstood both the Great Kantō Earthquake (which struck the city on September 1, 1923, the day after the hotel's formal opening) and World War II. After all this, Wright's building was replaced in the 1960s by the looming tower you see today. Still, a hint of Wright's style exists in the *Old Imperial Bar* (see page 179), which incorporates some of the original brickwork.

TOKYO SKYLINE WITH VIEWS OVER TOKYO BAY

Ginza and around

Ginza, the "place where silver is minted", took its name after Shogun Tokugawa Ieyasu started making coins here in the early 1600s. It turned into a happy association: one street, Chūō-dōri, soon grew to become Japan's most stylish shopping thoroughfare. Although now a couple of decades past its heyday, the glut of luxury malls and flagship stores here remains the envy of Tokyo, while various bars, restaurants and cafés still reverberate with distinct echoes of the "bubble period", a time in which Tokyo itself was the envy of the rest of the world. This slice of quintessential modern-day Japan is fascinating enough, but add a sprinkling of great museums and galleries, and you're set for the day, especially when you factor in the sights of the neighbouring districts of Nihombashi and Shiodome, which bookend Ginza to north and south.

> **BEST OF GINZA**
>
> **Hama Rikyū Onshi Teien** Go for a stroll in this beautiful park (see page 54)
> **Kabukiza Theatre** Catch a traditional play (see page 51)
> **Komparu-yu** Soak away the city grime at an old-fashioned bathhouse (see page 52)
> **Hibiki** Get a cheap, filling lunch on the 46th floor (see page 161)
> **Tea** Ginza is home to some of Tokyo's most appealing teahouses (see page 175)
> **Dover Street Market** Peruse clothing from Japan's top designers (see page 204)
> **Tamiya Plamodel Factory** Relive your childhood at this model-kit emporium (see page 209)

2

Snaking above ground to the west of these areas is Tokyo's most important section of rail line: this carries the JR Yamanote line, with some tracks also designed to bear the famed Shinkansen bullet trains – you'll see these gleaming, high-speed beasts purring past every few minutes. There are some wonderfully atmospheric places to eat and drink lurking under the **railway arches**, also accessible from the western side of the tracks.

South of Ginza is **Shiodome**, where a clutch of sparkling skyscrapers harbour hotels, restaurants and a few bona fide tourist sights, the best of which is **ADMT**, a museum dedicated to advertising. North of Shiodome is **Ginza** itself; bar the revamped Kabukiza Theatre, there are no must-see sights here, but it's a compact area worth exploring, especially since even the most anonymous building can yield a speciality store or avant-garde gallery. North again you'll find the high-finance district of **Nihombashi**, once the heart of boisterous, low-town Edo but now the preserve of blue-suited bankers; it's home to the original **Mitsukoshi** department store, and a couple of fine art museums.

Ginza

銀座

Although cutting-edge fashion has moved elsewhere in Tokyo, **Ginza** retains much of its elegance and its undoubted snob appeal. Here you'll find the city's greatest concentration of exclusive shops and restaurants, the most theatres and cinemas, major department stores, and a fair number of art galleries (see page 56).

The area is packed into a compact rectangular grid enclosed by the Shuto Expressway. Three broad avenues run from north to south, **Chūō-dōri** being the main shopping street, while **Harumi-dōri** cuts across the centre from the east. The two roads meet at a famed intersection known as **Ginza Yon-chōme crossing**, which marks the heart of Ginza: awesome at rush hour, this spot often features in films and documentaries as the epitome of this overcrowded yet totally efficient city.

One could argue, however, that it's in the smaller lanes where the "Ginza feel" is most palpable, in hidey-hole shops and restaurants – and a fair few "bubble-era" buildings still patiently awaiting the wrecking ball.

Kabukiza Theatre

歌舞伎座 • 4-12-15 Ginza, Chūō-ku • Gallery open daily 11am–7pm • Free • ⓦ kabuki-za.co.jp • Higashi-Ginza station

Tokyo rejoiced when the famed **Kabukiza Theatre**, one of Ginza's most iconic buildings, reopened its doors in early 2013. First opened in 1889, the theatre has been rebuilt several times, a victim of fires and war damage. The architect behind its most recent incarnation is Kengo Kuma (see page 270), who reinstated the elaborate facade of the original, which burned down in 1921; backed by a modern 29-storey office block, this

2

GINZA GLITZ

Much of the credit for **Ginza**'s unusually regular pattern of streets can go to British architect Thomas Waters, who was given the task of creating a less combustible city after a fire in 1872 destroyed virtually all of old, wooden Ginza. His "Bricktown", as it soon became known, proved an instant local tourist attraction, with its rows of two-storey brick houses, tree-lined avenues, gaslights and brick pavements.

Most of the first businesses here dealt in foreign wares, and in no time Ginza became the centre of all that was modern and Western – and, by extension, fashionable. Bricktown itself fell down in the Great Earthquake of 1923, but by then Ginza's status was well established. In the 1930s the height of sophistication was simply to stroll around Ginza, and the practice still continues, particularly on Sunday afternoons, when Chūō-dōri is closed to traffic and everyone turns out for a spot of window-shopping.

It's still possible to hunt down some of Ginza's older establishments. A number of venerable emporia cluster round the **Ginza Yon-chōme** junction. **Wakō**, now an exclusive department store, started life over a century ago as the stall of a young, enterprising watchmaker who developed a line called Seikō (meaning "precision"); its clock tower, built in 1894, is one of Ginza's most enduring landmarks, and the little watch company is now world famous. Immediately north of Wakō on Chūō-dōri, **Kimuraya bakery** was founded in 1874, while **Mikimoto** (see page 204) opened next door a couple of decades later. South of the crossing, just beyond the cylindrical, glass San'ai Building, **Kyūkyodō** (see page 199) has been selling traditional paper, calligraphy brushes and inkstones since 1800.

---

is classic "city of contrasts" territory. Catch a play (see page 192) or simply check out the fifth-floor gallery, with its wonderful display of kabuki costumes.

Ginza Sony Park

銀座ソニーパーク • 5-3-1 Ginza, Chūō-ku • Daily 24hr • Free • Ⓦ www.ginzasonypark.jp • Ginza station

A technophile's dream for decades, Ginza's iconic **Sony Building** was brought down in 2017. Its replacement is due to open in 2022, but until then you'll have to content yourself with the **Ginza Sony Park**, a "three-dimensional" public space hosting occasional events, plus a few places to eat and drink.

Komparu-yu

金春湯 • 8-7-5 Ginza, Chūō-ku • Mon–Sat 2–10pm • ¥460, plus ¥130 for a towel • Ginza station

One of the most central bathhouses in Tokyo, little Komparu-yu is a great little place to stop off for a scrub while touring Ginza. It's cheap, and suits the area nicely (as it should, having been here since 1863), with the decor featuring the near-obligatory Mount Fuji mural as well as other tiling depicting flowers, animals and the like. All in all, it's a lovely experience.

Shiodome

汐留

Shiodome was once most notable as the site of the Japan Railways freight terminal. While echoes of this history survive, most pertinently in the form of the **Railway History Exhibition Hall**, what now draws your gaze is a clutch of ultra-modern skyscrapers known collectively as **Shiodome Sio-Site** (汐留シオサイト); the towers are home to major companies, including Nippon TV and Kyodo News. The most interesting sight in this alienating concrete environment – one which can prove rather hard to traverse for newbie pedestrians – is the high-tech Advertising Museum Tokyo, or **ADMT**. From Shiodome, it's an easy walk to the **Hama Rikyū Onshi Teien** traditional

GINZA AND AROUND

0   200
metres

N

Higashi Gyoen

Fujimi-yagura

Museum

Ôte-mon

Masakado grave

Ôtemachi Ⓢ

Coredo

Mitsui Memorial Museum

Mitsukoshimae Ⓢ

Mitsukoshi Department Store

Mitsukoshimae Ⓢ

Nihombashi Bridge

Nihombashi

Kite Museum Ⓢ

NIHOMBASHI

EITAI-DÔRI

YAESU-DÔRI

YAESU-DÔRI

Bridgestone Museum of Art

Kyōbashi Ⓢ

National Film Archive

Takarachô

Shintomicho Ⓢ

Oazo

Shin-Marunouchi Building

IMPERIAL PLAZA

Marunouchi Building

Nijūbashimae Ⓢ

Mitsubishi Ichigokan Museum

Meiji Seimei-kan

Tokyo Ⓢ

Tokyo Station

JP Tower, Kitte & Intermediatheque ⓘ

MARUNOUCHI

Shin-Tokyo Building

Idemitsu Museum of Arts

Tokyo International Forum

Ôedo Antique Market

Yūrakuchô Ⓢ

YŪRAKUCHÔ

Hibiya Ⓢ

Hibiya-kōen

HIBIYA

Takarazuka Theatre

Imperial Hotel

UCHISAIWAICHÔ

Uchisaiwaichô Ⓢ

Sony Building

Tokyu Plaza

Maison Hermès

Yūrakuchô Station

Ginza Itchome Ⓢ

GINZA

Design Gallery

Ginza

Wakō

Kimuraya

GINZA YON-CHÔME CROSSING

Ginza Graphic Gallery

Komparu-yu

Shiseidō Gallery

Creation Gallery G8

Shimbashi Ⓢ

Shimbashi Station

Tokyo Gallery +BTAP

Shiodome City Centre

Railway History Exhibition Hall

Nakagin Capsule Tower

Shimbashi Station (Yurikamome)

SHIODOME

Shiodome

Entrance

Caretta Shiodome & Advertising Museum Tokyo

Entrance

Hama Rikyū Onshi Teien

Higashi-Ginza Ⓢ

Kabukiza Theatre

Shinbashi Enbujō

Tsukiji Ⓢ

Tsukiji Hongan-ji

Jōgai-shijō

Tsukijishijō Ⓢ

Jōnai-shijō

Babasaki Moat

Hibiya Moat

Hibiya Moat

UCHIBORI-DÔRI

HIBIYA-DÔRI

SOTOBORI-DÔRI

HIBIYA-DÔRI

UCHIBORI-DÔRI

HARUMI-DÔRI

CHÛÔ-DÔRI

SHÔWA-DÔRI

HARUMI-DÔRI

SHIN-ÔHASHI-DÔRI

INNER CIRCULAR ROUTE

TÔHOKU-JÔETSU LINE

YAMANOTE LINE

INNER CIRCULAR ROUTE

CHÛÔ-DÔRI

SHÔWA-DÔRI

EITAI-DÔRI

TOKYO EXPRESSWAY

SHUTO EXPRESSWAY 4

SHÔWA-DÔRI

HIBIYA-DÔRI

SOTOBORI-DÔRI

HIBIYA-DÔRI

TOKYO EXPRESSWAY

🍴 EATING

RESTAURANTS

Aoki	11
Dhaba India	2
Ginza Hirai	12
Hibiki	16
Little Okinawa	13
Old Thailand	15
Sakyō Higashiyama	7
Taimeiken	1
Torigin Honten	10
Ume-no-hana	4

CAFÉS

Café de l'Ambre	14
Henri Charpentier	5
Kiriko Lounge	6

TEAHOUSES

Cha Ginza	9
Higashiya Ginza	3
Sabō Nonohana	8

🏨 ACCOMMODATION

HOTELS

Conrad Tokyo	9
Four Seasons	3
Mandarin Oriental Tokyo	1
Mitsui Garden Ginza	8
Muji Hotel	5
Ryūmeikan Tokyo	2
Sunroute Ginza	4

CAPSULE HOTEL

Ginza Bay Hotel	7

HOSTEL

Imano Tokyo Ginza	6

🛍 SHOPPING

Dover Street Market	10
Ginza Natsuno	9
Haibara	2
Hakuhinkan Toy Park	14
Itô-ya	6
Kyūkyodō	8
Mikimoto	4
Mitsukoshi	1
Muji	5
S Watanabe	13
Shimizu Camera	7
Shiseidō	12
Takashimaya	3
Tamiya Plamodel Factory	15
Uniqlo	11

🍸 DRINKING AND NIGHTLIFE

BARS

300 Bar	2
Dry Dock	4
Lion	3
Marugin	1

garden or Tsukiji; you can also pick up the monorail to Odaiba from here (see page 90).

Advertising Museum Tokyo

広告とマーケティングの資料館, Kōkoku to Māketingu no Shiryōkan • B1 Caretta Shiodome, Minato-ku • Tues–Sat 11am–6pm • Free • ⊕ 03 62182500, ⊕ admt.jp • Shiodome station

In the basement of the **Caretta Shiodome** skyscraper – the sleek headquarters of the Dentsu ad agency – you'll find **Advertising Museum Tokyo (ADMT)**, a small permanent exhibition providing a fascinating flick through some of the twentieth century's most arresting commercial images, including a decade-by-decade look at Japanese product design and advertising. Afterwards, zip up in the glass-fronted lifts to the restaurants on the 46th and 47th floors for a free panoramic view across Tokyo Bay and the Hama Rikyū Teien; *Hibiki* (see page 161) is the pick of several great restaurants occupying this lofty space.

Railway History Exhibition Hall

旧新橋停車場, Kyūshinbashi Teishajō • 1-5-3 Shiodome, Minato-ku • Tues–Sun 10am–5pm • Free • ☎ 03 3572 1872 • Shiodome or Shimbashi stations

Immediately west of Caretta Shiodome is Shiodome's second major tower complex, **Shiodome City Centre**. Back in 1872, this was the site of the original Shimbashi station, the terminus of Japan's first railway line. A faithful reproduction of the station building, designed by American architect R.P. Bridgens, now rests incongruously at the foot of the tower and contains the **Railway History Exhibition Hall**. Part of the foundations of the original building, uncovered during excavations on the site, have been preserved, and you can also see some engaging videos (in English) about Japan's early railways, as well as woodblock prints and old photos of how the area once looked.

Nakagin Capsule Tower

中銀カプセルタワー • 8-16-10 Ginza, Chūō-ku • Shiodome or Shimbashi stations

If you're in the area and have any interest in architecture, it's worth tracking down the **Nakagin Capsule Tower**, a true oddity brushing up against the expressway junction. Built in 1972, it's made up of 140 capsules, each a self-contained, ten-square-metre housing unit boasting a retro-futuristic circular window), and designed to be removable from the central body (though none ever have been). Initially constructed as a sort of architectural guinea pig, the concept never took off, and the building is falling into disrepair – at the time of writing, fewer than a quarter of the capsules were inhabited, with the rest either empty or used as storage space. You can occasionally find some listed as accommodation on Airbnb, though often at extortionate prices.

Hama Rikyū Onshi Teien

浜離宮恩賜庭園 • 1-1 Hamarikyūteien, Chūō-ku • Daily 9am–4.30pm • ¥300; tea ¥510 • Shiodome station

The beautifully designed traditional garden of **Hama Rikyū Onshi Teien** once belonged to the shogunate, who hunted ducks here. These days the ducks are protected inside the garden's nature reserve, and no longer used for target practice. Next to the entrance is a sprawling, 300-year-old pine tree and a manicured lawn dotted with sculpted, stunted trees. There are three ponds, the largest spanned by a trellis-covered bridge that leads to a floating teahouse, *Nakajima-no-Chaya*; in early spring lilac wisteria hangs in fluffy bunches from trellises around the central pond. From the Tokyo Bay side of the garden, there's a view across to the Rainbow Bridge (see page 94), and you can see

2

ON THE ART TRAIL IN GINZA

Though a little short on tourist sights, Ginza is the bastion of Tokyo's commercial galleries – there are enough of them here to keep you busy for a full day.

Ginza Graphic Gallery 7-7-2 Ginza, Chūō-ku ☎03 3571 5206, ⓦwww.dnp.co.jp/gallery/ggg; Ginza station. Single-room space hosting monthly exhibitions that cover – for the most part – graphic design work from the best of Japan's creators. Closes for a few days between shows. Mon–Fri 11am–7pm, Sat 11am–6pm.

Maison Hermès 8F 5-4-1 Ginza, Chūō-ku ☎03 3569 3611, ⓦmaisonhermes.jp/ginza; Ginza station. Possibly the most charming gallery space in all Tokyo, set at the top of the Renzo Piano-designed "bubble-wrap" building that's home to the high-end fashion behemoth's Tokyo boutique. Worth a look whatever the exhibit – the gallery usually hosts themed shows of Japanese and international art. Daily 11am–7pm.

Shiseidō Gallery B1F 8-8-3 Ginza, Chūō-ku ☎03 3572 3901, ⓦshiseidogroup.jp/gallery; Shimbashi or Ginza stations. Located in the distinctive red showroom of the eponymous Japanese cosmetics giant, this small basement gallery hosts group and solo shows – some well worth a look, others merely so-so. Tues–Sat 11am–7pm, Sun 11am–6pm.

Tokyo Gallery + BTAP 7F 8-10-5 Ginza, Chūō-ku ☎03 3571 1808, ⓦtokyo-gallery.com; Shimbashi station. Dating back to 1950, Tokyo Gallery shows cutting-edge work from the Chinese and Korean contemporary art scenes (they have a branch in Beijing). Tues–Fri 11am–7pm, Sat 11am–5pm.

the floodgate which regulates how much sea water flows in and out of the ponds with the tides.

By far the nicest way of approaching the gardens is to take a ferry from Asakusa, down the Sumida-gawa (see page 74); often the entry price is included with the ticket.

Nihombashi

日本橋

North of Ginza, **Nihombashi** (also Romanized as "Nihonbashi") was once the heart of Edo's teeming Shitamachi (see page 77), growing from a cluster of early seventeenth-century riverside markets to become the city's chief financial district; the early warehouses and moneylenders evolved into the banks, brokers and trading companies you'll see here today. The area takes its name from the **Nihombashi**, literally the "Bridge of Japan", which marks the point from which all distances from Tokyo are measured (look for the small disc in the middle of the road on the bridge). The original arched, red-lacquer-coated bridge was built in 1603, and was long a favourite of *ukiyo-e* artists; the current stone incarnation, erected in 1911 and now with the Shuto Expressway passing over it, hardly bears comparison. Recent years have seen whole chunks of the area ripped up for ambitious rebuilding projects, of which the most interesting to date are the various shopping, dining and office wings of **Coredo**, one of which is located opposite the Mitsui Memorial Museum.

Artizon Museum of Art

ブリヂストン美術館, Burijisuton Bijutsukan • 1-7-2 Kyōbashi, Chūō-ku • ☎03 3563 0241, ⓦartizon.museum• Tokyo, Kyōbashi or Nihombashi stations

The Bridgestone Museum of Art was renamed the **Artizon Museum of Art** and is due to reopen in January 2020. The museum is home to an impressive collection of paintings by Van Gogh, Renoir, Degas, Monet, Manet, Miró, Picasso and other heavyweights, as well as Meiji-era Japanese paintings in Western style – it's well worth swinging by.

Kite Museum

凧の博物館, Tako-no Hakubutsukan • 5F 1-12-10 Nihombashi, Chūō-ku • Mon–Sat 11am–5pm • ¥200 • ☎ 03 3271 2465, ⓦ tako.gr.jp • Nihombashi station

There's no English sign for the cluttered little **Kite Museum,** but it's on the fifth floor above *Taimeiken* restaurant (see page 161). Since 1977 the restaurant's former owner has amassed over three hundred kites of every shape and size, from one no bigger than a postage stamp to a monster 18m square. If you have kids in tow, they can try making their own from bamboo and *washi* paper.

Mitsui Memorial Museum

三井記念美術館, Mitsui Kinen Bijutsukan • 7F Mitsui Main Building, 2-1-1 Nihombashi Muromachi, Chūō-ku • Tues–Sun 10am–5pm • ¥1000, or ¥1300 for special exhibitions • ☎ 03 5777 8600, ⓦ mitsui-museum.jp • Mitsukoshimae station

Just north of the main branch of the Mitsukoshi department store (see page 202), wood-panelled lifts rise to the seventh-floor **Mitsui Memorial Museum,** where a superb collection spanning three hundred years of Japanese and Asian art is on display. Put together by the Mitsui family (behind the eponymous, enormously successful trading dynasty), changing exhibitions follow a seasonal theme, and are mostly aimed at the connoisseur – you'll often see older Tokyoites purring with pleasure at the pottery, calligraphy, jades or jewellery before them.

2

Akihabara and around

Up the tracks from the Ginza area, a blaze of adverts and a cacophony of competing audio systems announce Akihabara. "Akiba", as it's popularly known, is Tokyo's foremost discount shopping area for electrical and electronic goods of all kinds, but these days it has also become a hotspot for fans of anime and manga, and is famed as the spawning ground for the decidedly surreal "maid cafés" (see page 61). Though Akiba's buzzing, neon-lit streets are almost entirely dedicated to technological wizardry and pop culture, there are sights of a different nature to the west, including the lively Shinto shrine of Kanda Myōjin, and an austere monument to Confucius at Yushima Seidō.

> **BEST OF AKIHABARA**
>
> **3331 Arts Chiyoda** Check out cutting-edge contemporary art (see page 59)
> **Super Potato** Go all retro by pumping coins into some Nintendo arcade games (see page 61)
> **Origami Kaikan** Purchase perfectly made origami souvenirs (see page 61)
> **Yushima Seidō** Savour the atmosphere at this peaceful shrine (see page 61)
> **Hachimaki** Wolf down some of Tokyo's best *tendon* (tempura on rice) (see page 161)
> **Maid cafés** Sup a coffee at *gaijin*-friendly *Maidreamin* or *Mai:lish* (see page 61)
> **Pop Life Department M's** Perhaps the world's only sex-toy department store (see page 61)

There's yet more to see in the wide area south of the Kanda-gawa (神田川), a small river skirting the southern flank of Akihabara station. To the west, **Ochanomizu** has become rather trendy of late due to the opening of some stylish new shopping and eating complexes, while older sights such as the Nikolai Cathedral are also worthy of attention. To the east is **Bakurochō**, a notably artistic quarter.

Akihabara

秋葉原

The bulk of **Akihabara**'s attractions lie north of the small Kanda river, with Akihabara station the best starting point. The station's surroundings are excellent photo-fodder – an audiovisual cacophony of neon and teeming humanity, crisscrossed by elevated rail tracks. It's best to swing by on a Sunday, when much of the main drag, Chūō-dōri, is closed to traffic. Although the area can seem a little bewildering, it's surprisingly easy to get your fix of the anime, computer games and other facets of **contemporary culture** that Akihabara is known for (see page 61). For all this, Akihabara does actually have a few bona-fide sights: within easy walking distance you'll find the superb **3331 Arts Chiyoda** centre, the **Kanda Myōjin** Shinto shrine and the brooding **Yushima Seidō**.

3331 Arts Chiyoda

３３３１アーツ千代田 • 6-11-14 Sotokanda, Chiyoda-ku • Daily (except Tues) noon–7pm • Usually free, though charges apply for some special exhibitions • ☎ 03 6803 2441, ⓦ 3331.jp • Suehirochō station

Down a side street a little north of Suehirochō subway station is the landscaped entrance to the large **3331 Arts Chiyoda** complex. Based inside a renovated school, the centre hosts close to twenty galleries; although some spaces tend towards the twee, a handful of prominent artists have cut their teeth here, and all in all it usually makes for an absorbing look at the Japanese art scene. Stroll around and you'll find a revolving mix of exhibitions, interactive installations and workshops; there's also an on-site café-restaurant.

Kanda Myōjin

神田明神 • 2-16-2 Sotokanda, Shiyoda-ku • Daily 9am–4pm • Free • Ochanomizu station

A vermilion gate marks the entrance to **Kanda Myōjin**, one of the city's oldest shrines and host to one of its top three festivals, the **Kanda Matsuri** (see page 26). Founded in 730 AD, the shrine originally stood in front of Edo Castle, where it was dedicated to the gods of farming and fishing (Daikoku and Ebisu). Later, the tenth-century rebel Taira no Masakado was also enshrined here. When Shogun Tokugawa Ieyasu was strengthening the castle's fortifications in 1616, he took the opportunity to move the shrine, but mollified Masakado's supporters by declaring him a guardian deity of the city. Poke around to the west of the main shrine, and you'll find charming *Imasa*, an almost otherworldly café (see page 172).

AKIHABARA AND AROUND

■ ACCOMMODATION	
HOTELS	
Akihabara Washington	4
Hilltop	3
Juraku	2
CAPSULE HOTEL	
Glansit Akihabara	1
HOSTEL	
Citan	5

● SHOPPING	
Comic Tora-no-ana	2
Kitazawa Book Store	8
Laox	6
Mandarake	3
Origami Kaikan	7
Radio Kaikan	5
Tsukumo Robot Kingdom	9
Yodobashi Camera	4

● EATING	
RESTAURANTS	
Botan	7
Go Go Curry	6
Hachimaki	9
Kagawa Ippuku	10
Toritsune Shizendo	1
CAFÉS	
Gundam Café	5
Imasa	3
Maidreamin	4
Maiiish	2
Sabōru	8

● DRINKING AND NIGHTLIFE	
BAR	
Hitachino Brewing Lab	1

TAKING THE PULSE OF AKIHABARA

There are few other Tokyo districts in which so many travellers actually avoid the sights: instead, **contemporary culture** is Akihabara's main, or even exclusive, drawcard. Here are a few ways in which to enjoy the more modern delights of Akiba.

Anime Part of a city-wide chain, *Mandarake* (see page 198) is a good bet for figurines, films, anime-related clothing, and pretty much everything in between.

Capsule toys Small as it may be, **Gachapon Hall** (ガチャポン会館; 3-15-5 Sotokanda; daily 11am–8pm) is stuffed with over 500 coin-operated capsule toy machines; it's hard to say whether it's adults or children that constitute the bulk of customers.

Electronics Akihabara's electronic stores are descendants of a postwar black market in radios and radio parts that took place beneath the train tracks around Akihabara station. You can recapture some of the atmosphere in the **Tōkyō Radio Depāto** (東京ラジオデパート; 1-10-11 Sotokanda; daily 11am–7pm) – four floors stuffed with plugs, wires, boards and tools for making or repairing audiovisual equipment.

Games If you want to see "crazy" Japan, **Taito Station** (タイトー自慢; 4-2-2 Sotokanda; daily 10am–midnight) is a pretty good place to start. Around the complex you'll see Tokyoites – and not just the young ones – perfecting their moves on dance machines, thrashing the hell out of computerized drum kits, playing all sorts of screen-whacking games, and using grabbing cranes to pluck teddies for their dates.

Maid cafés The whole area is riddled with maid cafés (see page 173), which come in many different guises, from cosplay and sailor to kimono and many more. You'll see a bunch of cafés clamouring for custom on the road outside *Super Potato* (see below); two safe bets are *Mai-lish* (see page 173) and *Maidreamin* (see page 173) – the latter is on the second floor of the Zeniya Building, which boasts seven full levels of maid cafés, and nothing else.

Robots You'd have to bring quite a bit of cash to purchase the equipment necessary to put together a full robot at **Tsukumo Robot Kingdom** (see page 202), but this store carries a large amount of such goodies, and is well worth a peek even if you're not a roboteer. Smaller toys are available for purchase, as are DVDs of robot battles.

Sex toys The **Pop Life Department M's** (1-15-13 Sotokanda; daily 10am–11pm) is essentially a department store full of sex toys and equipment, and soft-core pornography – seven whole floors of the stuff.

Video games Head on up to the fifth floor of **Super Potato** (スーパーポテト; 1-11-2 Sotokanda; daily 11am–8pm), which has a whole bunch of old-school arcade games including Bomberman, Mario (the NES version) and several iterations of Street Fighter II. If that sounds a little Nintendo-focused, try **Club Sega** (クラブセガ; 1-11-1 Sotokanda; daily 10am–11.30pm), which has two floors of arcade games and one of interactive music machines atop its six levels.

3

Origami Kaikan

おりがみ会館 • 1-7-14 Yushima, Bunkyō-ku • Mon–Sat 9.30am–6pm • ☎ 03 3811 4025 • Ochanomizu station

The six-storey **Origami Kaikan** is considered one of the "Six Cultural Treasures" of the Bunkyo Ward. This outpost for the production and dyeing of *washi* (Japanese paper) was founded in 1859, and to this day they continue to sell it on the premises (see page 199) – there's also an exhibition hall on the second floor. It's possible to take lessons (some free) in the art of paper folding here, although English instruction is unlikely.

Yushima Seidō

湯島聖堂 • 1-4-25 Yushima, Bunkyō-ku • Daily: May–Oct 9.30am–5pm; Nov–April 9.30am–4pm • Free • Ochanomizu station

A copse of woodland hides the distinctive shrine of **Yushima Seidō**, dedicated to the Chinese sage Confucius. The Seidō (Sacred Hall) was founded in 1632 as an academy for the study of the ancient classics at a time when the Tokugawa were promoting Confucianism as the state's ethical foundation. In 1691 the hall was moved to its present location, where it became an elite school for the sons of samurai and high-ranking officials, though most of these buildings were lost in the fires of 1923. Today, the quiet compound contains an eighteenth-century wooden gate and, at the top of broad steps, the imposing, black-lacquered Taisen-den, or "Hall of Accomplishments", where the shrine to Confucius is located. There are rarely many people here, and the place actually looks at its best in the rain or at dusk – darkness seems to show these brooding buildings in their best light.

Ochanomizu

御茶ノ水

The small Kanda-gawa runs between the JR and Tokyo Metro **Ochanomizu** stations. The name of the area (literally, "the water for the tea") dates back to the Edo period when water from the river was used to make the shogun's tea, though nowadays it's the stream itself that's usually tea-like in pigment; however, with trains appearing all over the place – crossing a bridge here, emerging from a tunnel there – it's all quite photogenic. The **rail arches** east of the JR station have also been subject to fairly major refurbishment of late, and within the confusingly named mAAch-Ecute mini-mall you'll find the *Hitachino* brew-pub (see page 180).

Trains aside, the area boasts a relaxed air and a modest collection of interesting sights, including a pretty **cathedral** (wonderfully incongruous in its mid-Tokyo location), the city's prime **bookshop** area, and prestigious **Meiji University**, home to a diverting **museum**. In addition, just to the west, the lively student centre of **Jimbōchō** is home to dozens of secondhand **bookshops**, where racks of dog-eared novels and textbooks sit outside shops stacked high with dusty tomes; most are in Japanese, but some specialize in English-language books: try *Kitazawa Shoten* (see page 200).

Nikolai Cathedral

ニコライ堂, Nikorai-jō • 4-1-3 Kanda Surugadai, Chiyoda-ku • Tues–Sun: April–Sept 1–4pm; Oct–March 1–3.30pm • Suggested donation ¥300 • ☎ 03 3295 6879 • Shin-Ochanomizu station

If you're in the area in the afternoon, pay a visit to the Russian Orthodox **Nikolai Cathedral**. Founded by Archbishop Nikolai Kasatkin, who came to Japan in 1861 as chaplain to the Russian consulate in Hokkaidō, the cathedral took seven years to complete (1884–91). The plans were sent from Russia, but British architect Josiah Conder (see page 62) gets most of the credit.

JOSIAH CONDER

Of the many Western architects invited by the Meiji government to Japan to help it modernize, **Josiah Conder** had the greatest impact. When he arrived in 1877, a freshly graduated 25-year-old, his position was to teach architecture at what would become the Faculty of Engineering at Tokyo University. By the time he died in Tokyo in 1920 he had designed over fifty major buildings including the original **Imperial Museum** at Ueno, and the **Nikolai Cathedral** in Ochanomizu (see page 62). His crowning glory was generally considered to be the **Rokumeikan** reception hall in Hibiya, a synthesis of Japanese and Western architectural styles. This was torn down in 1940, but a model can be seen in the Edo-Tokyo Museum (see page 81). His students Tatsuno Kingo and Katayama Tōkuma went on, respectively, to design Tokyo station and the Akasaka Detached Palace.

In the West, Conder is perhaps best known for his study of Japanese **gardens** and his 1893 book *Landscape Gardens in Japan*. Buildings he designed can be seen in Kyū Iwasaki-tei in Ueno (see page 69) and Kyū Furukawa near Komagome (see page 142), gardens which are both open to the public. His Mitsubishi Ichigokan building (see page 48) has also been resurrected in recent years.

Meiji University Museum

明治大学博物館, Meiji Daigaku Hakubutsukan • 1-1 Kanda Surugadai, Chiyoda-ku • Daily 10am–5pm, sometimes closed weekends in summer • Free • ☎ 03 3296 4448, ⓦ www.meiji.ac.jp/museum • Jimbōchō station

The **Meiji University Museum** sits off Meidai-dōri in the basement of the university's Academy Common Building. The most interesting – and spine-chilling – exhibits are to be found in the "criminal zone", and come courtesy of the university's original 1881 incarnation as a law school. After breaking you in gently with examples of Edo-era laws and edicts, the displays move on to the tools used by police to arrest miscreants: goads, the U-shaped "military fork" and the delightfully named "sleeve entangler". Then it's a rapid descent into prints showing instruments of torture and methods of punishment, including some truly gruesome ways of carrying out the death penalty. The other two zones cover archeology and traditional crafts, and overall there's a fair amount of information in English.

Bakurochō

馬喰町

There are some quirky galleries east of Akihabara station in the district of **Bakurochō**, accessible via the subway station of the same name. The **Agata-Takezawa** building, a run-down office block which houses the **Taro Nasu Gallery**, is the hub of this up-and-coming arty neighbourhood: it also includes a nonprofit, university-funded exhibition space, and an interesting bunch of arts, crafts and fashion tenants.

Taro Nasu Gallery

タロウナスギャラリー, Tarō Nasu Gyarerī • 1-2-11 Higashi-Kanda, Chiyoda-ku • Tues–Sat 11am–7pm • Free • ☎ 03 5856 5713, ⓦ taronasugallery.com • Bakurochō station

The respected **Taro Nasu Gallery** acts as an anchor of sorts to the trendy Agata-Takezawa building, having moved here in 2009 from their Ōsaka base. They have ten or so exhibitions per year, mainly of Japanese artists, mixed in with a few from Europe.

AMEYOKOCHŌ MARKET

Ueno and around

Directly north of Akihabara is Ueno, another of Tokyo's teeming mega-neighbourhoods. Around the area's main park, Ueno Kōen, you'll find a host of good museums, as well as a few relics from the vast temple complex at Kan'ei-ji, built on this hilltop in 1624 by the second shogun, Tokugawa Hidetada, to protect his castle's northeast quarter. The prestigious Tokyo National Museum alone could easily fill a day, but there's also the entertaining Museum of Nature and Science, the Museum of Western Art and the endearing Shitamachi Museum, which harks back to Ueno's proletarian past. Much of downtown Ueno, meanwhile, has a rough-and-ready feel, especially around the station and bustling Ameyokochō Market. Further west, there's a more sedate atmosphere in and around the ivory towers of Tokyo University.

BEST OF UENO AND AROUND

Shinobazu Pond Take a stroll along the causeway (see page 65)
Ueno Zoo Visit at feeding times to see the animals at their liveliest (see page 67)
National Museum of Nature and Science See Japan's hero mutt, Hachikō, in stuffed form (see page 68)
Tokyo University Mingle with Japan's future leaders (see page 69)
Sasa-no-yuki Purr over some of Tokyo's best tofu (see page 163)
Yukikage Characterful one-stop shop for ramen, shōchū and IPA (see page 163)
Jūsan-ya Pick up some wonderful wooden combs (see page 199)

North of the university campus are **Nezu** and **Yanaka**, two of Tokyo's most charmingly old-fashioned neighbourhoods and a world away from the usual hustle and bustle of the city. Along with **Sendagi** they form an area referred to as **Yanasen**, where you can experience a slower and more relaxed side of Tokyo. One draw is the historic and tranquil shrine of **Nezu-jinja**, but the whole area is strewn with small temples, craft shops and other attractions, such as the picturesque and historic **Yanaka Cemetery** and the old-style shopping street of **Yanaka Ginza**. There are also a couple of good traditional Japanese-style hotels around here (see page 152) for those who really want to soak up the atmosphere of Shitamachi (literally "low town") – the area's former incarnation (see page 77).

GETTING AROUND   **UENO AND AROUND**

Tours Free walking tours of the Ueno area (ⓦtokyosgg.jp; Wed, Fri, Sat & Sun 10.30am & 1.30pm), with English-speaking guides, start from the park-side exit of Ueno station (see map page 66).
Bike rental If you're planning to be in the Yanaka area for much of the day, consider renting a bike from the young team at Tokyobike (Wed–Sun 10am–7pm; ¥2500 for the day, ¥1500 for any subsequent days; ☎03 5809 0980, ⓦtokyobike.com; see map page 66).

Ueno

上野

The **Ueno** district sprawls south and east of the eponymous **train station**, a real whopper that has the honour of hosting high-speed services – one of only three stations in Tokyo to do so. The atmosphere is completely different on the west side of the tracks, with much of the immediate area taken up by **Ueno Kōen**, a wide park with absolutely stacks of things to see and do.

Ueno Kōen

上野公園 • Various entrances; information desk by east gate • Ueno station
Although it's far from being the city's most attractive park, all of Tokyo seems to flock to **Ueno Kōen** during spring's cherry blossom season. Outside this brief period, however, the park only really gets busy at weekends, and during the week it can be a pleasant place for a stroll, particularly around Shinobazu Pond. At the top of the steps leading up to the park from Ueno station you'll find a bronze statue of **Saigō Takamori**, the great leader of the Restoration army, which helped bring Emperor Meiji to power – his life story was the inspiration for the Tom Cruise movie *The Last Samurai*.

Shinobazu Pond

不忍池, Shinobazu-no Ike • Rowboats and pedaloes March–Oct daily 10am–6pm, ¥600–700 • Ueno station
Much of the park's southwest is taken up by **Shinobazu Pond**, whose western banks are lined with ancient cherry trees. Once an inlet of Tokyo Bay, the pond is now a

wildlife protection area and hosts a permanent colony of wild black cormorants as well as temporary populations of migrating waterfowl. A causeway leads out across its reeds and lotus beds to a small, leafy island occupied by an octagonal-roofed temple, **Benten-dō**, dedicated to the goddess of good fortune, water and music (among other things). Inside the dimly lit worship hall you can just make out Benten's eight arms, each clutching a holy weapon, while the ceiling sports a snarling dragon.

Kiyomizu Kannon-dō
清水観音堂 · Daily 7am–5pm · Free

UENO AND AROUND

ACCOMMODATION
HOTELS
Coco Grand Ueno Shinobazu	6
Graphy Nezu	4
Hanare	1
Nohga	5

RYOKAN & MINSHUKU
Ryokan Katsutarō	3
Ryokan Sawanoya	2

EATING
RESTAURANTS
Hantei	4
Izuei	5
Musashino	6
Sasa-no-yuki	2
Yukikage	3

CAFÉ
Hagiso	1

DRINKING AND NIGHTLIFE
BARS
Echigoya Honten	1
Kadokura	3
Sumire	2
Warrior Celt	4

SHOPPING
Jūsan-ya	2
Matsuzakaya	3
Yanaka Matsunoya	1

Built out over the hillside, the red-lacquered **Kiyomizu Kannon-dō** temple, dating from 1631, is a smaller, less impressive version of Kyoto's famous Kiyomizu temple, but it has the rare distinction of being one of the last parts of the Kan'ei-ji complex still standing. The temple is dedicated to **Senju Kannon** (the thousand-armed Kannon), whose image is displayed only in February, although the second-rank **Kosodate Kannon** receives more visitors as the Bodhisattva in charge of conception. Hopeful women leave dolls at the altar during the year, following which the dolls are all burnt at a rather sad memorial service on September 25.

Ueno Zoo

上野動物園, Ueno Dōbutsuen • 9-83 Ueno Kōen, Taitō-ku • Tues–Sun 9.30am–4pm • ¥600, free for children 12 and under; monorail ¥150 • ☎ 03 3828 5171, ⓦ tokyo-zoo.net

Considering the fact that **Ueno Zoo** is over a century old, it's less depressing than might be feared; there's plenty of vegetation around, including some magnificent, corkscrewing lianas. Among the animals here are rare gorillas and pygmy hippos, as well as a couple of pandas – make a note of the feeding time when you enter the zoo, as they tend to spend the rest of the day doing very little at all. The macaques, particularly the younger ones, seem to have a whale of a time on the rocky crag they call home; the same cannot be said of the bears and big cats, who tend to pace around small corners of their pens. The east and west parts of the zoo are connected by monorail, though walking is just as pleasant; on your way around, you can brush up on some basic Japanese adjectives, since you'll hear the words "kawaii" (cute) and "sugoi" (great) several hundred times.

4

Shitamachi Museum

下町風俗資料館, Shitamachi Fūzoku Shiryōkan • 2-1 Ueno Kōen, Taitō-ku • Tues–Sun 9.30am–5.30pm • ¥300 • ☎ 03 3823 7451, ⓦ www.taitocity.net/taito/shitamachi • Ueno or Ueno-Hirokōji stations

At the far southern end of the park, the interesting **Shitamachi Museum** is set in a distinctive, partly traditional-style building beside Shinobazu Pond. The museum opened in 1980 to preserve something of the working-class Shitamachi of old (see page 77), while it was still within living memory. The ground floor is made up of a reconstructed merchant's shophouse and a 1920s tenement row, complete with sweet shop and coppersmith's workroom. The upper floor is devoted to rotating exhibitions focusing on articles of daily life – old photos, toys, advertisements and artisans' tools, with all exhibits donated by local residents. There's plenty of information in English and it's possible to handle most items, but be sure to take off your shoes before exploring the shop interiors.

Tōshō-gū

東照宮 • 9-88 Ueno, Taitō-ku • Daily 9am–sunset • ¥200 • Ueno or Nezu stations

A tree-lined avenue marks the approach to Tokugawa Ieyasu's shrine, **Tōshō-gū**. Ieyasu died in 1616 and is buried in Nikkō, but this was his main shrine in Tokyo, founded in 1627 and rebuilt on a grander scale in 1651. For once it's possible to penetrate beyond the screened entrance and enclosing walls to take a closer look inside. A path leads from the ticket gate clockwise round the polychrome halls and into the worship hall, whose faded decorative work contrasts sharply with the burnished black and gold of Ieyasu's shrine room behind. Before leaving, take a look at the ornate, Chinese-style front gate, where two golden dragons carved in 1651 by Hidari Jingorō – he of Nikkō's sleeping cat fame (see page 220) – attract much attention. So realistic is the carving that, according to local tradition, the pair sneak off at midnight to drink in Shinobazu Pond. The seventeenth-century, five-storey pagoda rising above the trees to the north of Tōshō-gū is actually marooned inside Ueno Zoo (see page 67).

National Museum of Western Art

国立西洋美術館, Kokuritsu Seiyō Bijutsukan • 7-7 Ueno Kōen, Taitō-ku • Tues–Sun 9.30am–5.30pm, Fri until 8pm • ¥500, or more for special exhibitions • ☎ 03 3828 5131, ⓦ nmwa.go.jp • Ueno station

The **National Museum of Western Art** is instantly recognizable from the Rodin statues on the forecourt. The museum, designed by Le Corbusier, was erected in 1959 to house the mostly French Impressionist paintings left to the nation by Kawasaki shipping magnate Matsukata Kōjirō. Since then, works by Rubens, Tintoretto, Max Ernst and Jackson Pollock have broadened the scope of this impressive collection.

National Museum of Nature and Science

国立科学博物館, Kokuritsu Kagaku Hakubutsukan • 7-20 Ueno Kōen, Taitō-ku • Tues–Sun 9am–5pm, Fri until 8pm • ¥620 • ☎ 03 5777 8600, ⓦ www.kahaku.go.jp • Ueno station

The **National Museum of Nature and Science** offers lots of videos and interactive displays, and was recently expanded to include new, slightly fancier, wings on most floors. Six floors of displays cover natural history as well as science and technology. In the "exploration space" on the second floor, pendulums, magnets, mirrors and hand-powered generators provide entertainment for the mainly school-age audience, while down in the basement there's an aquarium and a dinosaur skeleton. One interesting highlight is on the second floor: sitting amid other stuffed animals, with surprisingly little fanfare, is Hachikō, Japan's canine hero (see page 125). Almost all visitors, even the locals, walk past without a second glance – a rather sad end for the country's most famous hound.

Tokyo National Museum

東京国立博物, Tokyo Kokuritsu Hakubutsukan • 13-9 Ueno Kōen, Taitō-ku • Tues–Sun 9.30am–5pm, though often later (see website) • ¥620 • ☎ 03 5405 8686, ⓦ www.tnm.jp • Ueno station

Dominating the northern reaches of Ueno Park is the **Tokyo National Museum**, containing the world's largest collection of Japanese art, plus an extensive collection of eastern antiquities. The museum style tends to old-fashioned reverential dryness, but among such a vast collection there's something to excite everyone's imagination. Displays are rotated every few months from a collection of around 110,000 pieces, and the special exhibitions are usually worth seeing if you can stand the crowds.

Japanese Gallery

It's best to start with the **Japanese Gallery**, the central building, which presents the sweep of Japanese art from Jōmon-period pottery (pre-fourth century BC) to paintings from the Edo period. On your way around you'll most likely spy theatrical costume for kabuki, nō and *bunraku*, as well as colourful Buddhist mandalas, *ukiyo-e* prints, samurai swords, exquisite lacquerware and even seventeenth-century Christian art from southern Japan. There's a decent shop by the entrance (good for souvenirs), and a beautiful garden out back (good for green-tea ice cream).

Japanese Archeology Gallery

In the building's northwest corner, look out for a passage leading to the **Heisei-kan** building, on the ground level of which is the splendid **Japanese Archeology Gallery**, containing important recent finds. Some of the ground it covers is the same as at the larger Japanese Gallery, but modern presentation really brings the objects to life; highlights are the chunky, flame-shaped Jōmon pots and a collection of super-heated Sue stoneware, made using a technique introduced from Korea in the fifth century. Look out, too, for the bug-eyed, curvaceous clay figures (*dogū*) of the Jōmon period, and the funerary *haniwa* from the fourth to sixth centuries AD – these terracotta representations of houses, animals, musicians and stocky little warriors were placed on

AMEYOKOCHŌ

The bustling **market** area south of Ueno station, **Ameyokochō** (アメ横丁), extends nearly half a kilometre along the west side of the elevated JR train lines down to Okachimachi station. The name – an abbreviation of "Ameya Yokochō", or "Candy Sellers' Alley" – dates from the immediate postwar days when sweets were a luxury and the hundreds of stalls here mostly peddled sweet potatoes coated in sugar syrup (*daigakuimo*). Since **rationing** was in force, black marketeers joined the candy sellers, dealing in rice and other foodstuffs, household goods and personal items. Later, American imports found their way from army stores onto the streets here, especially during the Korean War in the early 1950s, which is also when the market was legalized. Ameyokochō still retains a flavour of those early days: stalls specializing in everything from bulk tea and coffee to jewellery and fish line the street, gruff men with sandpaper voices shout out their wares, and there's a clutch of *yakitori* bars under the arches.

burial mounds to protect the deceased lord in the afterlife. The upper level hosts special exhibitions – usually very well curated.

Gallery of Hōryū-ji Treasures

In the southwest corner of the compound, behind the copper-domed Hyōkei-kan of 1908 (sadly closed off, but used for occasional talks and exhibitions), lurks the **Gallery of Hōryū-ji Treasures**. This sleek gallery contains a selection of priceless artefacts donated over the centuries to the Hōryū-ji in Nara, many dating back as far as the seventh century. Exhibits are rotated occasionally, but keep your fingers crossed for an eye-catching display of gilt-bronze Buddhist statues. The upper level has separate rooms for wooden and lacquered material, metalwork and painting.

Asian Gallery

The **Asian Gallery** houses a delightful hotchpotch of antiquities, with Javanese textiles and nineteenth-century Indian prints rubbing shoulders with Egyptian mummies (not quite Asian, but evidently close enough) and a wonderful collection of Southeast Asian bronze Buddhas. The Chinese and, particularly, the Korean collections are also interesting for their obvious parallels with Japanese art.

Tokyo University and around

東京大学, Tōkyō Daigaku

The west side of central Ueno is dominated by seedy love hotels and dubious bars. Take a short walk past Yushima subway station, however, and you'll discover a remnant of a much more genteel past. Founded in 1869, **Tokyo University** – or Tōdai, as it's commonly known – is the nation's top-ranking establishment, and its graduates fill the corridors of power. The university occupies the former estate of the wealthy Maeda lords, though there's little sign of their mansion beyond a pond and the one-storey, red-lacquer gate, **Aka-mon**, which forms the front (west) entrance into the sleepy, pleasant campus. Passing through Aka-mon and immediately turning left brings you to **Fukutake Hall**, a concrete-lined piece of industrial chic designed by renowned architect Andō Tadao. In the area around the university, you'll find some sculpted **gardens** and a charming **shrine**.

Kyū Iwasaki-tei Gardens

旧岩崎邸庭園, Kyū Iwasaki-tei Teien · 1-3-45 Ikenohata, Taito-ku · Daily 9am–5pm · ¥400; tea ¥500 · ☏ 03 3823 8340 · Yushima station

Off the southeastern corner of Tokyo University, the **Kyū Iwasaki-tei Gardens** date from 1896 and surround an elegant **house**, designed by British architect Josiah Conder (see page 62), which combines a *café au lait*-painted, Western-style two-storey mansion with a traditional single-storey Japanese residence. The wooden Jacobean- and Moorish-influenced arabesque interiors of the mansion are in fantastic condition, in stark contrast to the severely faded screen paintings of the Japanese section. The lack of furniture in both houses makes them a little lifeless, but it's nonetheless an impressive artefact in a city where such buildings are increasingly rare. You can take **tea** in the Japanese section or sit outside and admire the gardens, which also combine Eastern and Western influences.

Yushima Tenjin

湯島天神・3-30-1 Yushima, Bunkyō-ku・24hr・Free・Yushima station

Yushima Tenjin (also known as Yushima Tenmangū) is a shrine dedicated to Tenjin, the god of scholarship. The best time to visit is in late February when the plum trees are in blossom and candidates for university entrance exams leave mountains of *ema* (wooden votive tablets) inscribed with their requirements. At other times of year it's still worth a visit, with the tree-covered south end of the complex a lovely place to relax.

Nezu

根津

The old Tokyo district of **Nezu-jinja**, meaning "Water's Edge", is north of Tokyo University, a short walk west of Ueno Park. The area has become highly popular with foreign visitors in recent years, mainly due to a recent spike in decent, affordable accommodation. Its main sight is **Nezu-jinja**, a venerable, cedar-shaded shrine; while you're in the neighbourhood you may also want to visit *Hantei*, a traditional *kushiage* restaurant (see page 162).

Nezu-jinja

根津神社・1-28-9 Nezu, Bunkyō-ku・Daily 7am–sunset・Free・Nezu station

The cracking **Nezu** shrine dates from the early eighteenth century when it was built in honour of the sixth Tokugawa shogun, Ienobu. Ornate and colourfully decorated, it is notable for its corridor of vermilion *torii* (you may have to stoop to get under them) and a hillside bedecked with some three thousand azalea bushes which bloom in a profusion of pinks and reds during late April and early May, attracting throngs of camera-toting visitors. At other times the shrine is serene and peaceful.

Yanaka

谷中

After the Long Sleeves Fire of 1657 (see page 258), many temples relocated to the higher ground of **Yanaka**, where they remain today, alongside old wooden buildings that seem to have miraculously escaped the ensuing centuries' various calamities. It's a charming area to explore on foot, and you could spend many hours rambling through its narrow, quiet streets, discovering small temples, shrines and traditional craft shops.

Yanaka Ginza

谷中銀座・Sendagi station

The focal point of Yanaka, for many, is the pedestrianized shopping street known as **Yanaka Ginza**, an appealing shopping promenade lined with small family businesses

selling *geta* (wooden sandals), baskets, tea, *sembei* (rice crackers) and suchlike; recent years have seen it take a turn for the cheesy, but it's still worth a look.

Yanaka Cemetery

谷中霊園, Yanaka Reien • 24hr • Free • Nippori station

The Yanaka area is dominated by **Yanaka Cemetery**, one of Tokyo's oldest and largest graveyards. A couple of minutes' walk south of the Nippori entrance to the cemetery (there are several), you'll find one of the area's most attractive temples, **Tennō-ji** (天王寺), beside which stands a large copper Buddha dating from 1690. Head southwest down the cemetery's main avenue from here to reach the **graveyard offices**, opposite the public toilet, around which are Japanese maps locating the graves of various notables, including the last Tokugawa shogun, Yoshinobu, who is buried in a large plot on the southern edge of the cemetery.

Asakura Museum of Sculpture

朝倉彫塑館, Asakura Chōsokan • 7-18-10 Yanaka, Taitō-ku • Tues–Thurs, Sat & Sun 9.30am–4.30pm • ¥500 • Nippori station

The **Asakura Museum of Sculpture**, the lovely former home, studio and gardens of sculptor Asakura Fumio (1883–1964), is one of Yanaka's many gems. It's filled with examples of his work, the largest of which are presented in airy rooms with soaring ceilings.

Oguraya

小倉屋 • 7-6-8 Yanaka, Taitō-ku • Thurs–Sun 10.30am–4.30pm • Free • ☎ 03 3828 0562 • Nippori station

Off the western flank of Yanaka cemetery, and sitting on an attractive residential street, is **Oguraya**, a pawnbroker's shop dating from 1847. It's now a gallery-cum-shop whose lofty interior is often filled with traditional paintings; also of interest is the black-painted, three-storey wooden *dozō* (storehouse), which is worth popping inside just to see this lovingly preserved and increasingly rare type of architecture.

Kyū Yoshidaya Sake-ten

旧吉田屋酒店 • 10-6 Ueno-Sakuragi 2-chōme, Taitō-ku • Tues–Sun 9.30am–4.30pm • Free • ☎ 03 3823 4408 • Nezu station

Just south of Yanaka cemetery, a five-minute walk from Nezu station along the major road Kototoi-dōri, is **Kyū Yoshidaya Sake-ten**, an early twentieth-century sake store which was moved here in 1987 and is an annexe of the Shitamachi Museum (see page 67). It is worth a quick glimpse to check out the giant glass bottles, china barrels and other accoutrements of the trade.

SCAI The Bathhouse

スカイザバスハウス • 6-1-23 Yanaka, Taitō-ku • Tues–Sat noon–6pm • Free • ☎ 03 3821 1144, ⓦ scaithebathhouse.com • Nippori or Nezu stations

A bizarre little contemporary art gallery, **SCAI The Bathhouse** occupies a 200-year-old public bath west of Yanaka Cemetery. It's best known for bringing younger local artists greater international attention, though its own exhibits are often sourced from abroad – this successful East–West interplay resulted in both Anish Kapoor and Julian Opie finding Japanese inspiration. The gallery also hosts a range of lectures and performance art.

SENSŌ-JI TEMPLE

Asakusa and around

Tokyo boasts many wonderful neighbourhoods, but few score as highly as Asakusa for sheer charm. With its historic buildings, craft shops and ryokan, the area wears its tradition gallantly, though it conceals a surprisingly seedy heart – here you'll find vivid reminders of Edo's Shitamachi (see page 77), and the popular culture it spawned. Asakusa is best known as the site of Tokyo's most venerable Buddhist temple, Sensō-ji, whose towering worship hall is filled with a continual throng of petitioners and tourists. Stalls before the temple cater to the crowds, peddling trinkets and keepsakes as they have done for centuries, while all around is the inevitable array of restaurants, drinking places and fast-food stands. This infectious, carnival atmosphere changes abruptly just to the west of the temple, where the Rokku area has long been a byword for sleaze and vice.

5

BEST OF ASAKUSA

Himiko Float down the Sumida-gawa in style on a spaceship-like ferry (see page 24)
Sensō-ji Stroll along Nakamise-dōri to this wonderful temple (see page 76)
Tokyo Skytree Gaze down over the city from the world's second-tallest structure (see page 78)
Andon Ryokan Take in tradition with a twist at a friendly ryokan (see page 152)
Bunka Hostel Sup sake in the bar – or stay overnight – at this stylish hostel (see page 154)
Sometarō Stuff yourself with quality *okonomiyaki* (see page 164)

Though you can easily get to Asakusa by subway, it's more fun to arrive (or depart) by **ferry** along the Sumida-gawa (see below). The ferry station is beside the Azuma-bashi, a bridge that also makes a great viewing site for a couple of Tokyo's most striking pieces of modern architecture: dominating the horizon is the city's newest mega-structure, the soaring **Tokyo Skytree** telecommunications tower (see page 78); closer to the bridge is the Philippe Starck-designed Asahi Beer Hall, replete with what's supposed to be a stylized flame, but is known to all and sundry as the "Golden Turd" (金のうんこ, *kin-no-unko*).

ARRIVAL AND GETTING AROUND
ASAKUSA AND AROUND

By ferry Floating down the Sumida-gawa is by far the best way of getting to or from Asakusa. The Sumida-gawa service (see page 24) runs between Hinode Pier (every 30–50min, 10am–6.30pm; 40min; ¥860) and the jetty at Asakusa, by the bridge just east of the subway station. Alternatively, the space-age *Himoko* and *Hotaruna* ferries (see page 24) connect Odaiba with Asakusa, usually via Hinode (6–8 daily; ¥1720).

Tours You can join free walking tours (ⓦ tokyosgg.jp; Mon, Thurs, Sat & Sun 10.30am & 1.15pm) of the area with English-speaking guides, starting from the tourist information office (see below).

Rickshaw rides You'll see plenty of *jin-riki-sha* (the Japanese term which begat the bastardized English one) hawking for business opposite the tourist office; some speak English, including the Ebisuya team (ⓦ ebisuya.com). Figure on ¥4000 for a ten-minute ride for two, up to ¥17,000 for an hour.

Bike rental Sumida-kōen bicycle park is underground beside the bridge (daily 6am–8pm; ¥200 for 4hr, ¥300 for a day, ¥1200 for the week; ☎ 03 5246 1305), although they only have a limited number of bikes available.

INFORMATION

Tourist information The Asakusa Culture and Sightseeing Centre is in front of Sensō-ji's main gate, Kaminari-mon (daily 9am–8pm; ☎ 03 3842 5566), and provides English-language information on local festivals, tours and so on; staff here give better ferry information than the staff in the ferry terminal itself, and can also advise on places to eat. The office almost counts as a sight in itself – designed by Kengo Kuma (see page 270), the interior is rather striking, and it's also possible to take the lift up to the eighth floor for spectacular views out over the Asakusa area.

Asakusa

浅草

Many of Tokyo's backpackers call **Asakusa** home during their stay in the capital, and they're in the right place: it's full of pep and vigour, great things to see, and suitably earthy places in which to eat, drink and be merry. South of Sensō-ji are hundreds of small shops and stands, some of which have been around for centuries; west of the temple things take a turn for the seedier, and many a traveller has got sozzled along a small lane known as "**Hoppy-dōri**" (named after Hoppy, a beer-like drink).

When kabuki and *bunraku* were banished from central Edo in the 1840s, they settled in the area known as **Rokku** ("Block 6"), between Sensō-ji and today's Kokusai-dōri. Over the next century almost every fad and fashion in Japanese popular entertainment started life here, from cinema to cabaret and striptease. Today a handful of the old venues survive, most famously **Rock-za**, with its daily strip shows, and there are loads of cinemas, pachinko parlours (see page 132), gambling halls and drinking dives. It's not all lowbrow, though: several small theatres in the area, such as Asakusa Engei Hall,

ASAKUSA AND AROUND

■ ACCOMMODATION

HOTEL

Asakusa Central	12

RYOKAN & MINSHUKU

Andon Ryokan	2
New Koyo	3
Ryokan Kamogawa	10
Ryokan Shigetsu	9
Sukeroku-no-yado	4
Sadachiyo	8
Tokyo Ryokan	1

HOSTELS

1980 Hostel	11
Bunka Hostel	5
Khaosan Tokyo Origami	7
Retrometro Backpackers	7
Sakura Hostel	6

■ EATING

RESTAURANTS

320 Ramen	4
Amisei	11
Bon	1
Chin-ya	10
Hatsuogawa	14
La Sora Seed	13
Maguro Bito	8
Matsunami	6
Nakae	2
Otafuku	9
Sometarō	7

CAFÉ

Gallery éf	12

TEAROOMS

Suzukien	3
Umezono	5

● DRINKING AND NIGHTLIFE

BARS

Bunka Hostel	4
Campion Ale	3
Gin Maku Roku	2
Ichimon	1
Kamiya	5

● SHOPPING

Bengara	5
Bunsendō	7
Ganso Sample-ya	3
Fujiya	8
Kanesō	9
Kurodaya	2
Sakura	6
Takahisa	1
Yonoya Kushiho	4

5

ASAKUSA, KING OF FESTIVALS

Taking place annually on the third weekend in May, and centred on Asakusa, the **Sanja Matsuri** is Tokyo's biggest festival, attracting up to two million spectators. The climax comes on the second day, when over one hundred *mikoshi* (portable shrines) are paraded through the seething crowds, among them the three *mikoshi* of Asakusa-jinja, each weighing around 1000kg and carried by at least seventy men.

There are numerous other festivals held in Asakusa throughout the year, including the **Samba Carnival** at the end of August. East of the Amuse Museum, alongside narrow **Sumida-kōen** (隅田公園) park, the river provides the stage for one of the city's great summer **firework displays** (*hanabi taikai*), held on the last Saturday in July.

---

still stage *rakugo*, a centuries-old form of comic monologue in which familiar jokes and stories are mixed with modern satire.

Sensō-ji

浅草寺 • North end of Nakamise-dōri • Grounds daily 24hr; main hall 6am–5pm • Free • Asakusa station

Walking west from the river or Asakusa subway station, you can't miss the solid red-lacquer Kaminari-mon gate, with its enormous paper lantern, that marks the southern entrance to **Sensō-ji**. This magnificent temple, also known as Asakusa Kannon, was founded in the mid-seventh century to enshrine a tiny golden image of Kannon, the goddess of mercy, which had turned up in the nets of two local fishermen. Most of the present buildings are postwar concrete reconstructions, and recent renovation work has seen the roof of the main structure completely covered in titanium tiles, to improve earthquake resistance.

Kaminari-mon

The main temple approach starts under **Kaminari-mon**, or "Thunder Gate", which shelters statues of the guardian gods of Thunder and Wind (named Raijin and Fūjin). More notable, and photogenic, is the gate's gigantic red paper lantern – four metres in height, it weighs in at a whopping 670kg. On your way to the temple you'll proceed along **Nakamise-dōri**, a colourful parade of small shops packed with gaudy souvenirs, tiny traditional dolls, kimono accessories and sweet-scented piles of *sembei* rice crackers.

Hōzō-mon

A double-storeyed treasure gate, **Hōzō-mon** stands astride the entrance to the main temple complex. The treasures themselves, fourteenth-century Chinese sutras, are locked away on the upper floor. The gate's two protective Niō – the traditional guardians of Buddhist temples – are even more imposing than those at Kaminari-mon; look out for their enormous rice-straw sandals slung on the gate's rear wall.

The main hall

Drum ceremonies daily 6.30am, 10am & 2pm

Beyond Hōzō-mon there's a constant crowd clustered around a large, bronze incense bowl where people waft the pungent smoke over themselves: considered the breath of the gods, it is supposed to have curative powers. There's nothing much to see inside the temple itself, since the little Kannon – said to be just 7.5cm tall – is a *hibutsu* or hidden image, considered too holy to be put on view. The **hall**, however, is full of life, with the rattle of coins being tossed into a huge wooden coffer, the swirling plumes of incense smoke and the constant bustle of people coming to pray, buy charms and fortune papers or to attend a service. Three times a day, drums echo through the hall into the courtyard as priests chant sutras beneath the altar's gilded canopy.

Asakusa-jinja

浅草神社・Ⓦasakusajinja.jp
Like many Buddhist temples, Sensō-ji accommodates Shinto shrines in its grounds, the most important being **Asakusa-jinja**, dedicated to the two fishermen brothers who netted the Kannon image, and their overlord. The shrine was founded in the mid-seventeenth century by Tokugawa Iemitsu and the original building still survives, though it's hard to tell under all the restored paintwork. More popularly known as Sanja-sama, "Shrine of the Three Guardians", this is the focus of the tumultuous **Sanja Matsuri** (see page 76).

Niten-mon

Sensō-ji's eastern entrance is guarded by the attractively aged **Niten-mon**. Originally built in 1618, this gate is all that remains of a shrine honouring Tokugawa Ieyasu, which was relocated to Ueno in 1651 after a series of fires. Niten-mon has since been rededicated and now houses two seventeenth-century Buddhist guardians of the south and east.

Asakusa Hanayashiki

浅草花やしき・2-28-1 Asakusa, Taitō-ku・Daily 10am–6pm・Adult ¥1000, child aged 7–12 ¥500, under-7s free; ride tickets ¥100; free pass adults ¥2300, children ¥2000・☎ 03 3842 8780, Ⓦhanayashiki.net・Asakusa station
Japan's oldest amusement park, dating back to 1853, **Asakusa Hanayashiki** seems a little incongruous in the refined Asakusa area – it's really more in keeping with the hedonistic Rokku district to the west. The park features rickety roller-coasters (rickety but safe – this *is* Japan) and vintage funfair rides and attractions, including a haunted house.

Edo Taito Traditional Crafts Center

江戸たいとう伝統工芸館, Edo Shitamachi Dentō-kōgei-kan・2F 2-22-13 Asakusa, Taitō-ku・Daily 10am–8pm・Free・☎ 03 3842 1990・Asakusa station
At the top end of Hisago-dōri, a covered arcade stretching north of Rokku, is the **Edo Taiti Traditional Crafts Center**, whose modest collection of traditional implements won't detain you for more than ten minutes, though it's still worth popping by. At weekends a variety of artisans can be seen at work, and there are occasional video presentations about crafts production. There's also a selection of crafts on sale in the ground-floor lobby.

SHITAMACHI

Although the Tokyo of today is a city made up of umpteen mega-districts, under Tokugawa rule (1603–1867) things were a little different. Edo, as Tokyo was known in those times, was essentially divided by caste: the *daimyō* (feudal lords) and samurai resided in the high city, known as **Yamanote** ("the hand of the mountains"), while merchants, artesans and other elements of the working class lived down in cramped **Shitamachi** ("under-town"), an area which resembled a shantytown, its wooden buildings often going up in flames.

While Yamanote is today best-known as the name of the JR line that encircles central Tokyo, elements of Shitamachi have survived through the intervening centuries, especially in the areas around Ueno and Asakusa (and, indeed, all the way up to Kita-Senju). Some original wooden buildings still stand, and the packed layout of yore is evident in countless meandering alleyways. Many elements of culture now thought of as quintessentially Japanese can trace their lineage back to Shitamachi, too – sumo, kabuki and all manner of arts and crafts started life as subcultures spawned by Shitamachi's unique combination of deprivation and artistic creation.

5

Drum Museum

宮本卯之助西浅草店, 2-1-1 Nishi-Asakusa • Wed–Sun 10am–5pm; shop daily 9am–6pm • ¥500 • ☎03 3842 5622, ⓦmiyamoto-unosuke.co.jp • Asakusa station

Easily identifiable from the elaborate *mikoshi* (portable shrines) in the window, the **Miyamoto Unosuke Store** is an Aladdin's cave of traditional Japanese percussion instruments and festival paraphernalia: masks, shortened kimono-style *happi* coats, flutes, cymbals and, of course, all kinds of *mikoshi*, the largest with a price tag of over ¥3 million. Since 1861, however, the family passion has been drums, resulting in an impressive collection from around the world – one that now fills the fourth-floor **Drum Museum**. There's every type imaginable here and, best of all, you're allowed to have a go on some. A red dot on the name card indicates those not to be touched; blue dots mean you can tap lightly, just with your hands; and the rest have the appropriate drumsticks ready and waiting for you to pelt away.

Kitchenware Town

かっぱ橋道具街, Kappabashi Dōgu-gai • Many shops closed on Sun • ⓦkappabashi.or.jp • Asakusa station

Just west of the Rokku area is the main road of **Kappabashi Dōgu-gai**, flanked with covered walkways and signs from the "bubble period". Locally known as **Kappabashi**, or "**Kitchenware Town**", the surrounding area is essentially a wholesale market where you can kit out a whole restaurant. You don't have to be a bulk buyer, however, and this is a great place to pick up unusual souvenirs, such as the **plastic food** displayed outside restaurants to tempt the customer. This practice, which originally used wax instead of plastic, dates from the nineteenth century but came into its own about forty years ago when foreign foods were being introduced to a puzzled Japanese market.

Sumida

墨田

On the opposite side of the Sumida-gawa from Asakusa, the district of **Sumida** is utterly dominated by the **Tokyo Skytree**, a whopper built to replace the comparatively puny Tokyo Tower (see page 104) as the city's digital broadcasting beacon. The sightseeing potential of the Skytree has been fully exploited, with the city's highest public **observatory** – a dizzying 450m above the ground – as the main draw, as well as an **aquarium** and **planetarium** at the tower's base, plus tourist shops, restaurants and landscaped public spaces.

Tokyo Skytree

東京スカイツリー • 1-1-2 Oshiage, Sumida-ku • ☎03 6658 8012, ⓦtokyo-skytree.jp • Oshiage or Tokyo Skytree stations

At 634m, the **Tokyo Skytree** is, for now, the world's second-tallest structure after Dubai's mighty Burj Khalifa (830m). Popular though it is as a tourist attraction, the tower divides opinion. Sited close to Asakusa, one of Tokyo's most proudly traditional areas, attempts were made to give the Skytree an appropriate feel – note the Japanese design motifs in the lobby and lifts. Yet some of it comes across as rather forced – it's hard, after all, to paint ancient tradition over something shaped like a gigantic hypodermic needle. Though the shape isn't terribly pleasing, it's now part and parcel of the Tokyo skyline.

Triangular at the base, its pale-blue, latticed sides gently morph towards a circular shape before hitting the lower observation deck; the second deck is another 100m up, with the super-skinny transmitting antenna protruding another 184m beyond.

The observation decks

Daily 8am–10pm • 350m deck ¥2100/2300 weekdays/weekends; 450m deck ¥1000/1100 extra weekdays/weekends • Foreign visitors with ID can also purchase a special "Fast Skytree" ticket, which beats the queues: 350m deck ¥3200, both decks ¥4200

There's a certain tingly excitement to be had in watching the numbers on the lift panel getting higher and higher – even the **lower deck** is marked as "Floor 350", which is a little ridiculous, since "floors" of buildings are rarely one metre high. The views from here are, predictably, fantastic: giant touch-screen displays show precisely what you're looking at, and also let you see how the view would appear at night (or by day, if you're visiting in the evening). Mount Fuji is, in theory, within visible range, but the unfortunate reality is that mist often blocks the view even in sunny weather, and it's usually only visible a couple of times per month.

Those who choose to head on to the **upper deck** will see more or less the same thing, although its space-age interior design is rather lovely – the inclined walkway wraps around the building, giving you the impression that you're climbing to the top. There's a pricey **restaurant** on the upper deck, and a cheaper **café** on the lower one, though there's far more choice on the 30th and 31st floors of the adjacent Solamachi building, from where you can actually see the tower.

Note that there's a lot of queuing involved, especially on weekends and holidays – first to buy the ticket, then for the lift up, and again for the lift to the upper level. Foreign visitors with valid ID can beat the queues for a small premium, and most find it worth the extra investment.

Sumida aquarium

すみだ水族館, Sumida Suizokukan • 5F and 6F Tokyo Solamachi West Yard • Daily 9am–9pm • ¥2050 • ☏ 03 5619 1821, ⓦ sumida-aquarium.com

Every major tower in Tokyo seems to have an aquarium attached, and the Skytree is no exception. The **Sumida aquarium** is a pretty good one, though, with a 350,000-litre tank (the largest in Japan) at its centre; clever design of the glass walls mean that you can see the whole tank from almost any angle. Most visitors make a beeline for the seals and penguins, but the jellyfish display is worth tracking down too.

Konica Minolta planetarium

コニカミノルタプラネタリウム • 7F Tokyo Solamachi East Yard • Hourly shows daily 11am–9pm • ¥1500 • ☏ 03 5610 3043

At the **Konica Minolta planetarium** – part planetarium, part 4D cinema – the delights of the cosmos are relayed, for the sake of superfluous technology, in glorious smell-o-vision. Science has yet to capture the true scent of the stars, and though it's probably fair to assume that Finnish forests and Asian aromatherapy oils might be a bit wide of the mark, it's a fun experience nonetheless.

SUMO WRESTLERS

Ryōgoku and Kiyosumi

There's a surprise in store just down the Sumida-gawa from touristy Asakusa: Ryōgoku is a sort of sumo town, where shops sell outsize clothes and restaurants serve flavourful tureens of *chanko-nabe*, the wrestlers' traditional body-building hotpot. The area is also home to the absorbing, ultra-modern Edo-Tokyo Museum. A short train ride south, and all within walking distance of each other in the Kiyosumi area, are Kiyosumi Teien, a pleasant Meiji-era garden; the delightful Fukagawa Edo Museum, an atmospheric re-creation of a mid-nineteenth-century Shitamachi neighbourhood; and the Museum of Contemporary Art, gathering together the best of post-1945 Japanese art in one spacious, top-class venue.

BEST OF RYŌGOKU AND KIYOSUMI

National Sumo Stadium Watch gargantuan fighters in action (see page 81)
Edo-Tokyo Museum Spend an hour or two wandering around this museum's huge collection (see page 81)
Tokyo Museum of Contemporary Art Admire the talents of some of Japan's most prominent contemporary artists (see page 84)
Kiyosumi Teien Stroll through some enchanting gardens (see page 84)
Fukagawa Fudō-dō Watch the noisy ceremonies – involving fire – at this quirky temple (see page 84)
Tomoegata Eat like a sumo wrestler (see page 164)

6

Ryōgoku

両国

The **Ryōgoku** area has just two sights, and one of those is only accessible for a few weeks of the year. But even if your visit doesn't coincide with a tournament at the **National Sumo Stadium**, it's still worth coming along to visit a sumo training "**stable**" (see page 213) or to see the fantastic **Edo-Tokyo Museum** – or even just to take a stroll down the banks of the Sumida-gawa.

National Sumo Stadium

両国国技館, Ryōgoku Kokugikan • 1-3-28 Yokoami, Sumida-ku • See page 213 for details of tickets for tournaments • Ryōgoku station

For a fortnight each January, May and September, major sumo tournaments fill the **National Sumo Stadium** with a pageant of thigh-slapping, foot-stamping and arcane ritual (see pages 213 and 82). The streets south of the stadium were, until recently, home to many of the major "**stables**" where wrestlers lived and trained. Though rising land prices have forced most of them out, a fair few remain, and there's still a good chance of bumping into some junior wrestlers, with slicked-back hair, wearing *yukata* (loose dressing gowns) and *geta* (wooden sandals), popping out for a quick snack of *chanko-nabe*. If you're feeling peckish yourself, try either the *Yoshiba* or *Tomoegata* restaurants (see page 164), two of the best places to sample the hearty stew.

Edo-Tokyo Museum

江戸東京博物館, Edo-Tōkyō Hakubutsukan • 1-4-1 Yokoami, Sumida-ku • Tues–Fri & Sun 9.30am–5.30pm, Sat 9.30am–7.30pm • ¥600 • ☎ 03 3626 9974, ⓦ edo-tokyo-museum.or.jp • Ryōgoku station

You'll need plenty of stamina for the extensive **Edo-Tokyo Museum**, housed in a colossal building (supposedly modelled on a *geta*) behind the Sumo Stadium, although the ticket lasts a whole day so you can come and go. With plenty of information in English, including a free audio-guide, the museum tells the history of Tokyo from the days of the Tokugawa shogunate to postwar reconstruction, using life-size replicas, models and holograms, as well as more conventional screen paintings, ancient maps and documents.

The museum starts on the sixth floor, where a bridge (a replica of the original Nihombashi; see page 56) takes you over the roofs of some mock Edo landmarks – a kabuki theatre, *daimyō* residence and Western-style newspaper office – on the main exhibition floor below. The displays then run roughly chronologically, with a particularly strong treatment of life in Edo's Shitamachi, with its pleasure quarters, festivals and vibrant popular culture, and on the giddy days after 1868, when Japan opened up to the outside world.

6

SUMO: THE BORN-IN-MONGOLIA SUPREMACY

Japan's national sport, **sumo**, developed out of the divination rites performed at Shinto shrines, and its religious roots are still apparent in the various rituals which form an integral part of a *basho*, or **tournament**. These take place in odd-numbered months: Tokyo's are in January, May and September (see page 213), with other tournaments taking place in Ōsaka, Nagoya and Fukuoka. Starting on the second Sunday of the month, and lasting for fifteen days, the fights run from 9am to 6pm, although the top competitors only appear after 4pm or so. The bouts involve two huge wrestlers, each weighing 170 kilos on average and wearing nothing but a hefty loincloth, facing off in a small ring of hard-packed clay. The loser is the first to step outside the rope or touch the ground with any part of the body except the feet – the contest is often over in seconds, but the **pageantry** and ritual make for a wonderfully absorbing spectacle. The top two divisions of wrestlers fight every day, and the top-division fighter with the most wins out of fifteen – with play-offs if necessary – is declared champion.

In recent years, champions have been almost exclusively **Mongolian** in origin. The Japanese veteran **Kotoshogiku**'s victory in January 2016 came ten long years after the previous win by a Japanese-born wrestler, with Mongolian fighters scooping an incredible 57 of the 59 intervening tournaments (the other two were won by Kotooshu from Bulgaria, and Estonia's Baruto). The Mongolian run started in 2002 with the great **Asashōryū**, a pantomime villain who stirred up controversy on a regular basis before being ushered out of the sport in 2010. By then he had developed a tremendous rivalry with his closest challenger, fellow-Mongolian **Hakuhō**, who had broken his most-wins-in-a-year record by winning 86 out of 90 bouts in 2009. These two great fighters both became *yokozuna*; the very top level of wrestler, this is a lifelong rank and does not necessarily signify the most recent champion. Shortly after Asashōryū's retirement, Hakuhō was joined as *yokozuna* by **Harumafuji** and **Kakuryū**, two fellow Mongolians; at the time of writing, both Hakuhō and Kakuryū were still going strong, with the former having become the most decorated wrestler in centuries of sumo history. However, a clutch of Japanese pups are vying to become the new heroes, led by power-pusher **Takakeishō** who, in 2018, became champion in just his 12th top-level tournament.

Sword Museum

刀剣博物館, Tōken Hakubutsukan • 1-12-9 Yokoami, Sumida-ku • Tues–Thurs & Sat–Sun 9.30am–5pm (last admission 4.30pm) • ¥1000; under 15s free • ☎ 03 6284 1000, ⓦ touken.or.jp • Ryōgoku station

Fans of swashbuckling samurai dramas will love the **Sword Museum**, recently relocated here from Shinjuku. Even if you're determinedly anti-violence it's hard not to admire the incredible decorative detail on the blades, handles and sheaths of the lethal weapons displayed. However, some find it a long way to go to one smallish hall – for a bit more variety, try the Samurai Museum east of Shinjuku station (see page 132).

Sumida Hokusai Museum

北斎美術館, Hokusai Bijutsukan • 2-7-2 Kamezawa, Sumida-ku • Daily (except Mon) 9.30am–5.30pm • ¥400 • ☎ 03 6658 8936, ⓦ hokusai-museum.jp • Ryōgoku station

One of the newest sights in the area is the **Sumida Hokusai Museum**, devoted to the Japanese artist most familiar to the Western world – even if you don't know the name, you've probably seen "The Great Wave off Kanagawa", his most famous painting. Unfortunately, the museum is still finding its feet, and there's not all that much to get your teeth into here yet, bar the splendid structure it's set in – a little like a smaller, friendlier version of Beijing's CCTV building, pushed onto its side.

Kiyosumi

The district of **Kiyosumi** gets even fewer travellers than Ryōgoku, but there's actually more to see, with the beautiful **Kiyosumi Teien**, the excellent **Fukagawa Edo Museum**

RYŌGOKU AND KIYOSUMI

N

0 — 200
metres

EDO-DŌRI

Ⓢ **Kuramae**

KURAMAE BASHI-DŌRI

KURAMAE BASHI-DŌRI

KURAMAE BASHI-DŌRI

MITSUME-DŌRI

SHUTO EXPRESSWAY 6

Sumida-gawa

EDO-DŌRI

Ⓢ **Asakushabashi**

**Asakushabashi
Station**

**National
Sumo
Stadium**

**Edo-Tokyo
Museum**

Ⓢ **Ryōgoku**

**Ryōgoku
Station**

YASUKUNI-DŌRI

KEIYŌ-DŌRI

KEIYŌ-DŌRI

KIYOSUMI-DŌRI

MITSUME-DŌRI

■ **Tokitsukaze-beya**

RYŌGOKU

■ **Kasugano-beya**

■ **Dewanoumi-beya**

SHUTO EXPRESSWAY 7

SHUTO EXPRESSWAY 7

■ **Studio Geisha Café**

Ⓢ *Hamachō*

Morishita Ⓢ

SHIN-ŌHASHI-DŌRI

Ⓢ **Kikukawa**

KIYOSUMI-DŌRI

MITSUME-DŌRI

Ⓢ *Suitengumae*

Ⓢ **Kiyosumi-shirakawa**

KIYOSU-BASHI-DŌRI

KIYOSUMI

**Fukagawa
Edo Museum**

🏠 🏠

**Museum of
Contemporary
Art**

*Kiyosumi
Teien*

🏠

🏠

Ⓢ

Kiba Park

**Fukagawa
Fudō-dō**

KASAIBASHI-DŌRI

**Botanical
Garden**

Monzennakacho Ⓢ

⛩ **Tomioka Hachiman-gū**

● **SHOPPING**
Merikoti   **1**

● **EATING**
RESTAURANTS
Ryōgoku Terrace   **3**
Tomoegata   **4**
Yoshiba   **2**
CAFÉS
Allpress   **5**
Cielo y Rio   **1**

■ **ACCOMMODATION**
HOSTELS
Anne Hostel   **3**
K's House Tokyo   **1**
Nui Hostel & Bar Lounge **2**

and the **Tokyo Museum of Contemporary Art** all vying for your attention. Getting here from Ryōgoku is easy by subway, though it's more pleasurable to walk down the pedestrianized banks of the Sumida-gawa, then cut east along the banks of a tributary which runs just to the north of the sights listed here. The Kiyosumi area also has more temples than you could count – whichever one you pop into, you're likely to see no other visitors. This is unlikely to be the case at pyromaniacal **Fukagawa Fudō-dō**, located a short way south, near the shrine where sumo was born. All these sights are a little distant from each other, but walking between them can be pleasant, especially along the many canals that criss-cross the area.

Kiyosumi Teien

清澄庭園 • 3-9 Kiyosumi, Kōtō-ku • Daily 9am–5pm • ¥150 • ☎ 03 3641 5892 • Kiyosumi-shirakawa station

A beautiful Edo-era garden surrounding a large pond, **Kiyosumi Teien** counts as a must-see if you're in the area. Originally the property of a merchant, the gardens were landscaped to within an inch of their life upon their acquisition by a local feudal lord; the stones that you'll see around the grounds come from all over Japan. The gardens are particularly worth visiting in spring for their cherry blossom and azaleas.

Fukagawa Edo Museum

深川江戸資料館, Fukagawa Edo Shiryōkan • 1-3-28 Shirakawa, Kōtō-ku • Daily 9.30am–5pm, closed second & fourth Mon of the month • ¥400 • ☎ 03 3630 8625 • Kiyosumi-shirakawa station

Located down a charming neighbourhood shopping street is the captivating **Fukagawa Edo Museum**, which re-creates a Shitamachi neighbourhood (see page 77). The museum's large, subterranean exhibition hall could be a film set for nineteenth-century Edo, and contains seven complete buildings: the homes of various artisans and labourers, a watchtower and storehouses. As you walk by the rooms, all furnished with the clutter of daily life, you're accompanied by the cries of street vendors and birdsong, while the lighting shifts from dawn through to a soft dusk – a bit cheesy, but pleasant nonetheless.

Tokyo Museum of Contemporary Art

東京都現代美術館, Tōkyō-to Gendai Bijutsukan • 4-1-1 Miyoshi, Kōtō-ku • Daily (except Mon) 10am–6pm • ¥500, more for special exhibitions • ☎ 03 5245 4111, ⊕ mot-art-museum.jp • 15min walk north of Kiba station

A severe glass-and-grey-steel building houses Tokyo's premier modern art venue, the **Tokyo Museum of Contemporary Art**. The vast spaces inside provide the perfect setting for a fine collection of works by various artists from the post-1945 avant-garde through the 1950s abstract revolution to pop art, minimalism and beyond; most are Japanese in origin (keep an eye out for the work of Nakazono Koji, which bears some similarity to Picasso and Miró), but you'll see works from prominent Western artists too (notably Roy Lichtenstein). Some of the exhibitions in the main halls are interesting enough, but it's often worth splashing out a bit more for the well-curated special exhibitions.

Fukagawa Fudō-dō

深川不動堂 • 1-17-3 Tomioka, Kōtō-ku • ☎ 03 3641 8288 • Fire rituals 9am, 11am, 1pm, 3pm & 5pm • Monzennakachō station

Just south of the main Kiyosumi sights, and reached via an unusually blocky *torii*, the **Fukagawa Fudō-dō** is certainly up there with Tokyo's most interesting temples. It belongs to the Shingon sect, also known as the "Japanese Esoteric" offshoot; however, the casual observer is more likely to be interested in the temple's liberal use of fire – rituals involving objects being passed over flames take place at least five times daily, with drums and sutra-chanting providing atmospheric backing tracks. Don't miss the stunning prayer corridor, in which almost 10,000 crystal Buddha statues glow in the dark; in theory you're not supposed to take photos, but in practice it's a little hard to resist.

Tomioka Hachiman-gū

富岡八幡宮 • 1-20-3 Tomioka, Kōtō-ku • ☎ 03 3642 1315 • Monzennakachō station

It may look like just another shrine, but **Tomioka Hachiman-gū** has an interesting claim to fame: less than six decades after its founding in 1627, it became the birthplace of the style of sumo used today. Around the back of the main hall you'll find the *yokozuna* stones, onto which the names of those who've reached the eponymous level of grand champion (see page 82) are engraved; at the time of writing these numbered 72 (plus an ancient fighter known as Raiden, who was never promoted to *yokozuna*, but was considered pretty good anyway). *Yokozuna* promotions are rare events (every two or three years, on average), but the official unveilings always take place at this shrine – you'd have to be very, very lucky to see one.

6

ODAIBA ISLAND, OVERLOOKING RAINBOW BRIDGE

Bayside Tokyo

So thoroughly urban is Tokyo that it can seem surprising to discover that the city is actually beside the sea. Yet many of the *ukiyo-e* masterpieces of Hokusai and Hiroshige depict waterside scenes around Tokyo Bay, and several of the city's prime attractions are to be found here, not least the vast Toyosu fish market, whose relocation from Tsukiji in 2018 became a major controversy. Across the bay to the south lies Odaiba, built on vast islands of reclaimed land; its principal sights are a couple of excellent museums and a raucous onsen complex, as well as some of Tokyo's most striking and distinctive architecture.

BEST OF BAYSIDE TOKYO

Toyosu Watch the world-famous tuna auctions (see page 89)
Panasonic Center Tokyo Try out Nintendo's latest gadgets (see page 91)
Mega Web Take a virtual Toyota for a spin (see page 91)
Tokyo Leisureland Hone your Dance Dance Revolution moves (see page 91)
Ramen Kokugikan Enjoy twinkly night-time bay views and some great noodles (see page 164)
Sushibun Indulge in some of the finest sushi on the planet (see page 164)
Ageha Throw some shapes at one of Asia's biggest nightclubs (see page 187)

Tsukiji

築地

The bayside area of **Tsukiji** dates back to 1657, when Tokugawa Ieyasu had the debris from the **Fire of the Long Sleeves** (see page 258) shovelled into the marshes at the edge of Ginza, thus creating "reclaimed land", or "*tsukiji*". The area was long famed for its huge, almost otherworldly fish market, which was finally shifted **east** to Tosoyu, after years of delays (see page 89) , and no small amount of controversy. Most of the area's prime sushi shops have also relocated, but Tsukiji still boasts a distinctive atmosphere, and a lovely temple.

7

Tsukiji Hongan-ji

築地本願寺 • 3-15-1 Tsukiji • Free • ⓦ tsukijihongwanji.jp • Tsukiji station

If you're in the area, it's worth a quick visit to **Tsukiji Hongan-ji**, one of the largest and most Indian-looking of Tokyo's Buddhist temples. From the outside, it looks a little like a European bank topped with a South Asian roof; inside it's more traditional, with an intricately carved golden altar and cavernous interior, and room for a thousand worshippers.

Tsukudashima

佃島

Across the Sumida-gawa from Tsukiji is **Tsukudashima** (meaning "island of rice fields"), a tiny enclave of wooden houses and shops clustered around a backwater spanned by a dinky red bridge. Sheltering in the shadow of the modern River City 21 residential tower blocks, the area has a history stretching back to 1613, when a group of Ōsaka fishermen were settled on the island by the shogun.

Tsukudashima is famous for several types of **food**: *tsukudani*, preserved seaweed and fish best bought at *Tenyasu Honten* (see page 206); and the savoury pancakes known as *okonomiyaki* and *monjayaki* (see page 160), served in restaurants lining Monja-dōri, a colourful shopping street a short walk southwest from Tsukishima station – try *Kondo* (see page 164).

Sumiyoshi-jinja

住吉神社 • Shrine building open daily 8am–4pm • Free • Tsukishima station

In addition to providing food for the castle, the island's founding fishermen were expected to report on any suspicious comings and goings in the bay. For their spiritual protection, they built themselves the delightful **Sumiyoshi-jinja**, a shrine dedicated to the god of the sea. The roof of the well beside the shrine's *torii* has eaves decorated with exquisite carvings of scenes from the fishermen's lives. Every three years, on the first weekend in August, the shrine hosts the Sumiyoshi Matsuri, during which a special

mikoshi (portable shrine) is doused in water as it is paraded through the streets; this is symbolic of the real dunking it would once have had in the river.

Jōgai-shijō and around

場外市場 • Tsukiji or Tsukijishijō stations

While Tsukiji's old inner market has shifted out to Toyosu, the **Jōgai-shijō** (outer market) has largely stayed put. Arrayed around a dense grid of streets, it exudes an atmosphere now totally drained from the new place in Toyosu, heaving with grocers, pottery merchants, kitchenware sellers, and even a few holdout fishmongers.

Toyosu

豊洲

Just over 2km down the bay from Tsukiji, **Toyosu** finally became the venue of the new wholesale **fish market** in 2018 – the buildings had been there for years, but environmental concerns (see page 89) saw the issue become a political hot-potato. With these problems now fading into the past, Toyosu has suddenly become an extremely popular tourist spot, with thousands of visitors arriving every day to sample top-quality sushi – or, for those able to wake up pre-dawn, to witness the famous tuna auctions.

7

Wholesale Fish Market

水産卸売場棟; Suisan Oroshiuri-ba-tō • Daily (except Sun) 5am–5pm; auctions daily (except Sun) 5.30–6.30am • Free • Ⓦ shijo.metro.tokyo.jp • Shijo-mae monorail; also walkable from Toyosu station

Out with the old, in with the new. Toyosu's modern **Wholesale Fish Market** is almost the polar opposite of its predecessor in Tsukiji – much of the chaotic air has disappeared, though so too has most of the charm. The three new, interconnected buildings that constitute the present market have been designed to keep visitors at arm's length from the action, restricted to walkways overlooking the wholesale fish section; while not as "fun", this has significantly reduced the danger element for visitors, and made life easier for those working here. Eels from Taiwan, salmon from Santiago and tuna from Tasmania are among the 480 different types of seafood – two thousand tonnes of it – that come under the hammer here daily. Most famed are the tuna, which are auctioned off each day – frozen rock-solid, they look rather like steel torpedoes, and are all labelled with yellow stickers indicating their weight and country of origin.

SOMETHING FISHY: TROUBLES AT THE MARKET

It was dubbed the "fish market at the centre of the world" for its influence on world seafood prices. Generating almost **¥2 billion** (£14m/US$17.5m) in sales daily, Tsukiji's Wholesale Food Market was massive business, but things stalled somewhat when the Tokyo Metropolitan Government made plans to shift the market to **Toyosu**, 2km across the bay. The planned site had previously been used by Tokyo Gas, and its highly toxic ground was cleaned up before construction started on the new complex, which cost around ¥590bn (then £4.2bn/US$5.2bn) to build. The stalls were all supposed to move out to Toyosu in November 2016, but surveys conducted in the months before showed that the new site's levels of mercury, benzene, arsenic and cyanide – slightly worrying substances, even away from raw fish – were all above government standards. Because of these concerns over **toxins**, ones echoed by many of the marketfolk themselves, Tokyo governor Yuriko Koike brought a sudden halt to proceedings just before the move. Things were delayed for almost two years before the go-ahead was finally given in 2018; in October of that year, more than 600 merchants made the move along the bay to their new base of operations.

The headline **tuna auctions** are a lot harder to get on than was the case in Tsukiji; only 120 visitors per day are allowed in (follow links from the website given above), with lottery-like applications usually closing more than a month ahead, and each successful applicant given a ten-minute viewing slot. Those without a slot can still witness some of the action from a rather pathetic viewing area on the third floor.

Many of the esteemed **sushi restaurants** which once flanked the market in Tsukiji have also moved to Toyosu, but again, it's a far more sterile experience than before; *Sushibun* (see page 164) is recommended, though as with all of the in-house sushi restaurants here, come armed with cash, and be prepared to queue.

KidZania Tokyo

キッザニア東京 • Urban Dock LaLaport Toyosu, 2-4-9 Toyosu, Kōtō-ku • Daily 9am–3pm & 4–9pm • Adults ¥1850, children ¥2950–4800 depending upon age and visiting time • ☎ 0120 924901, ⓦ www.kidzania.jp • Toyosu station or monorail

Set inside a giant shopping mall, **KidZania Tokyo** is an imaginative mini theme-park where kids run all the various shops and services. It's designed for children aged 2 to 12, and although everything is in Japanese it's possible for non-Japanese-speaking children to join in the fun. Prices vary depending upon the day of the week, what time you arrive and so on – see the website for details.

Odaiba

お台場

Odaiba is an island of reclaimed land, sitting pretty in Tokyo Bay. The name means "cannon emplacements", referring to the defences set up in the bay by the shogun in 1853 to protect the city from Commodore Perry's threatening Black Ships (see page 258). The remains of the two cannon emplacements, one now a public park, are these days dwarfed by the huge landfill site Rinkai Fukutoshin, of which Odaiba is a part. Here the Metropolitan Government set about constructing a brand-new urban development, fit for the twenty-first century, in 1988. The subsequent economic slump and spiralling development costs slowed the project down and, when the **Rainbow Bridge** linking Odaiba to the city opened in 1993, the area was still a series of empty lots.

More than two decades on, Odaiba has blossomed into one of the most popular spots in the city for locals, who love its seaside location and sense of space – so rare in most parts of Tokyo. At night, the illuminated Rainbow Bridge, giant technicolour Ferris wheel and twinkling towers of the Tokyo skyline make Odaiba a romantic spot – you'll see plenty of canoodling couples staring wistfully at the glittering panorama.

ARRIVAL AND GETTING AROUND
ODAIBA

By monorail The simplest way of getting to Odaiba is to hop on the Yurikamome monorail (ⓦyurikamome. co.jp), which starts at Shimbashi station and arcs up to the Rainbow Bridge on a splendid circular line, stopping at all the area's major sites before terminating at Toyosu, also a subway stop; single tickets here from the "mainland" are ¥250–380, and you can buy a day pass for ¥820.
By train Trains on the Rinkai line, linked to the JR Saikyō line and the Yūrakuchō subway line, run to the central Tokyo-Teleport station on Odaiba; if you're coming to the area on JR trains, this usually works out cheaper than the monorail, and there are direct services from Ikebukuro, Shinjuku, Shibuya and Ebisu, among other places.

By bus Buses from Shinagawa station, southwest of the bay, cross the Rainbow Bridge and run as far as the Maritime Museum, stopping at Odaiba Kaihin-kōen on the way. Once you're on Odaiba, you can make use of the free Tokyo Bay Shuttle bus services, which depart on a loop every 20min or so.
By ferry Ferries shuttle from the pier at Hinode (日の出) to either Odaiba Seaside Park or Palette Town; some also stop next to Tokyo Big Sight. The journey costs from just ¥520, and doubles as a Tokyo Bay cruise. The space-age *Himoko* and *Hotaruna* ferries (see page 24) also connect Odaiba with Asakusa, sometimes via Hinode (6–8 daily; ¥1720), and there are also ferries to Kasai Rinkai-kōen, 7km east, home to an excellent aquarium (see page 95).

Panasonic Center Tokyo

パナソニックセンター東京 • 3-5-1 Ariake, Kōtō-ku • Tues–Sun 10am–6pm • Free; RiSuPia ¥500 • ☎ 03 3599 2600, ⓦ panasonic.
com/global • Ariake or Kokusai Tenjijō Seimon monorail stations

Less than a minute's walk from Ariake station is **Panasonic Center Tokyo**, the
electronics group's showcase. Here you can try out the latest Nintendo games on
a large-screen plasma display or high-resolution projector, as well as check out
the company's technologies of tomorrow. The centre includes the fun "digital
network museum" **RiSuPia**, at which you're issued with an electronic tag upon
entering; as you learn about science and mathematics from the computer games
and simulations within the high-tech display hall, the tag keeps track of how well
you're doing.

Tokyo Big Sight

東京ビッグサイト • 3-11-1 Ariake, Kōtō-ku • ☎ 03 5530 1111, ⓦ bigsight.jp • Kokusai Tenjijō Seimon monorail station

Outside Kokusai Tenjijō Seimon station, you can't fail to see the Tokyo International
Exhibition Centre, better known as the **Tokyo Big Sight**. This is one of Japan's largest
venues for business fairs and exhibitions, with an entrance composed of four huge
inverted pyramids; also look out for a 15.5m-high sculpture of a saw, sticking out of
the ground as if left behind by some absent-minded giant. Events held here include
vast antique fairs, the twice-yearly Design Festa (see page 26) and Comiket manga
events, as well as the Tokyo Anime Fair in March.

Palette Town

パレットタウン • 1-3-15 Aomi, Kōtō-ku • Aomi monorail station

Aomi station is the stop for the vast **Palette Town** shopping and entertainment
complex, which offers something for almost everyone: test-drive a Toyota, go for a spin
on a giant Ferris wheel, see Tokyo at its wackiest in Tokyo Leisureland, or sip coffee on
a faux Italian piazza at Venus Fort. Outside Harajuku and Akihabara, this is the most
popular place in Tokyo for *cosplay* costume-wearing youngsters.

Mega Web

メガウェブ • Daily 11am–9pm • Entry and simulations free, vehicle rental at Ride Studio ¥200–300 • ☎ 03 3599 0808, ⓦ megaweb.gr.jp

On Palette Town's east side, **Mega Web** is a design showcase for Toyota's range of cars.
For the casual visitor, it's most interesting as a glimpse into the future of the company,
and by extension the automotive industry in general. It's often possible to pilot some
kind of futuristic electric vehicle along the pleasing blue track that swoops around
the building; consult the website for information, and note that you'll probably need
to show an international driving licence. VR "rides" are available through the day,
though you may need to queue for a while; kids (and adults with zero shame) can take
an extremely slow spin around the Ride Studio, housed in a separate building just to
the east.

Wonder Wheel

ワンダーウィール • Daily 10am–10pm • ¥1000

Just behind the Mega Web showroom are some more high-tech diversions, the best
of which is the **Wonder Wheel**, a candy-coloured, 115m-diameter Ferris wheel, which
takes sixteen minutes to make a full circuit. If heights hold no fear then plump for one
of the wheel's four fully transparent gondolas, which enable you to see down through
the floor; they cost no extra, though you may have to queue.

Mori Digital Art Museum

Mon–Fri 10am–7pm, Sat & Sun 10am–9pm, closed second & fourth Tues of month • ¥3200 • ⓦ borderless.teamlab.art

Odaiba's newest and most fabulous attraction is the **Mori Digital Art Museum**, which currently also goes by the name of **teamLAB Borderless**; while this doesn't exactly trip off the tongue (and the full one is even longer), it's a real winner. The whizkid group known as teamLAB have been staging high-profile exhibitions outside Japan for years, but this is their biggest home project to date. "Borderless" is a good way to describe some of the exhibits, some of which flow between rooms; visitors are encouraged to touch, disrupt or enhance a few of them, meaning that the "art" itself continues to morph. As such, it's a little hard to explain what the experience will be like during your own visit – expect things like mirror-filled infinity rooms, forests of dangling lamps, projected flowers or giant balloons, and a very, very strange teahouse.

Venus Fort

ヴィナスフォート • Daily 11am–9pm • ⓦ www.venusfort.co.jp
The west side of Palette Town is dominated by **Venus Fort**, one of Tokyo's most original shopping and factory outlet malls. It's partly designed as a mock Italian city, complete with piazza, fountains and Roman-style statues – even the ceiling is painted and lit to resemble a perfect Mediterranean sky from dawn to dusk – and is worth swinging through if only to gawk at the sheer lunacy of it all. The on-site *Starbucks* (see page 174) is located on a particularly charming "piazza".

Ōedo Onsen Monogatari

大江戸温泉物語 • 2-6-3 Aomi, Kōtō-ku • Daily 11am–9am (next day) • Mon–Fri ¥2720 (¥2180 after 6pm), Sat & Sun ¥2940 (¥2400 after 6pm), ¥2160 surcharge 1am–6am • ⓦ daiba.ooedoonsen.jp • Telecom Center monorail station, or free shuttle buses from Shinagawa, Tokyo and Tokyo Teleport stations
More of a theme park than a bathhouse, the giant **Ōedo Onsen Monogatari** goes in for nostalgic kitsch in a big way. Extra fees are charged for massages, hot sand and stone baths and a separate footbath in which tiny fish nibble the dead skin from your feet – more pleasant than it sounds. Free shuttle buses head here, so if you're planning to hit the onsen you can save some money on your trip to Odaiba.

Miraikan

日本科学未来館, Nihon Kakagu Miraikan • 2-3-6 Aomi, Kōtō-ku • Daily (except Tues) 10am–5pm • ¥620, Dome Theater ¥300 • ☎ 03 3570 9151, ⓦ www.miraikan.jst.go.jp • Telecom Center monorail station
West of Palette Town is Tokyo's best science museum, the **National Museum of Emerging Science and Innovation**, also known as the **Miraikan**. Here you can learn about the latest in robot technology, superconductivity (including Maglev trains), space exploration, earthquakes and much more, as well as check out the weather around the world by looking up at a giant sphere covered with one million light-emitting diodes showing the globe as it appears from space that day. For an extra fee you can catch a science flick in the spherical Dome Theater.

Museum of Maritime Science

船の科学館, Fune-no Kagakukan • 3-1 Higashiyashio, Shinagawa-ku • *Sōya* daily 10am–5pm • Free • ⓦ funenokagakukan.or.jp • Fune-no-kagakukan monorail station
The **Museum of Maritime Science**, housed in a concrete reproduction of a cruise ship, was undergoing substantial renovation at the time of writing; check the website for the latest developments. Until its reopening, you'll have to be content with poking around a real boat instead: the *Sōya*, which undertook scientific missions to the South Pole, is moored outside.

Shiokaze-kōen

潮風公園 • 2 Higashiyashio, Shinagawa-ku • 24hr • Daiba monorail station

Over on the western side of Odaiba island is **Shiokaze-kōen**, a pleasant park where families come to use the outdoor barbecue pits in good weather. It provides a ringside seat to watch the action across the bay at the container port, where lines of red cranes look like giraffes at feeding time.

Odaiba beach

お台場浜, Odaiba-hama • Daiba monorail station

On the north side of the island, Odaiba's man-made **beach** – part of **Odaiba Seaside Park** – boasts a fantastic view of the Rainbow Bridge (see page 94), as well as an unexpected scale copy of the Statue of Liberty. It's a wonderful place to be in the evening, looking at the bridge and twinkly lights beyond, especially if you take off your shoes and dip your feet into the water.

Joypolis

ジョイポリス • 1-6-1 Daiba, Minato-ku • Daily 10am–10pm • Adult ¥800, child aged 7–17 ¥500; passport for unlimited rides (day/evening) adult ¥4500/3500, child ¥3500/2500 • ☏ 03 5500 1801, ⓦ tokyo-joypolis.com • Odaiba-Kaihin-kōen monorail station

Fronting the beach are a couple of linked shopping malls, **Aqua City** and **Decks Tokyo Beach**. Apart from plenty of shops and restaurants, the former includes the Mediage multiplex cinema, while the latter has **Joypolis**, a three-floor, high-tech amusement park packed with the latest in Sega's arcade video and computer games, as well as extreme thrill rides such as a spinning roller-coaster.

Fuji TV Building

富士テレビビル, Fuji Terebi Biru • 2-4-8 Daiba, Minato-ku • Viewing platform Tues–Sun 10am–6pm • ¥700 • Daiba monorail

A surreal, sci-fi aura hangs over Tange Kenzō's **Fuji TV Building** – with a huge metal sphere suspended in its middle, it looks as if it's been made from a giant Meccano set. You can head up to the free rooftop "garden" on the seventh floor (just be warned that there's not much greenery), or pay to visit the 25th-floor **viewing platform**; alternatively, save the cash for a drink in the *Sky Lounge* at the top of the neighbouring *Grand Pacific Le Daiba* hotel, where spectacular views are thrown in for free.

Rainbow Bridge

レインボーブリッジ • Observation rooms and promenade daily: Jan–March, Nov & Dec 10am–6pm; April–Oct 9am–9pm • Free • Shibaura Futō monorail station

From Odaiba you can cross back to mainland Tokyo along the **Rainbow Bridge**, a 918m-long, single-span suspension bridge in two levels: the lower bears the waterfront road and the monorail, the upper the Metropolitan Expressway. On both sides is a pedestrian **promenade** linking the **observation rooms** in the anchorages at either end of the bridge. The walk along the bridge takes about half an hour and provides good views across the bay, even as far as Mount Fuji if the sky is clear.

East of Odaiba

An enjoyable way to experience Tokyo Bay is to head out to **Kasai Rinkai-kōen** (葛西臨海公園), some 7km east of Odaiba. The park's biggest draw is its superb aquarium, the **Tokyo Sea Life Park**, but it's also a favourite weekend spot for many families who visit to picnic, cycle or paddle off its small, crescent-shaped beach. Bird enthusiasts also come to ogle water birds and waders in the well-designed sanctuary. Just to the east is Tokyo's own take on the **Disney** mega-park theme.

Tokyo Sea Life Park

葛西臨海水族館, Kasai Rinkai Suizokukan • 6-2-3 Rinkai-chō, Edogawa-ku • Daily except Wed 9.30am–5pm, last entry 4pm • ¥700, children free • ☎ 03 3869 5152, ⓦ tokyo-zoo.net • Ferry from Odaiba Seaside Park; 50min; ¥1130 one way, ¥1650 return; last boat back around 5pm • Kasai Rinkai-kōen station; from Odaiba, take the Rinkai line and transfer to JR Keiyo line at Shin-Kiba

The highlight of the **Tokyo Sea Life Park**, set under a glass-and-steel dome overlooking the sea, is a pair of vast tanks filled with tuna and sharks, where silver shoals race round you at dizzying speeds. Smaller tanks elsewhere showcase sea life from around the world, from flashy tropical butterfly fish and paper-thin seahorses to the lumpy mudskippers of Tokyo Bay.

Tokyo Disney Resort

東京ディズニーリゾート • 1-1 Maihama, Urayasu-shi, Chiba • Generally open 8/9am–10pm; call to check times beforehand • One-day passport for Tokyo Disneyland or Tokyo DisneySea adult ¥7400, child aged 12–17 ¥6400, child aged 4–11 ¥4800; two-day passport for both parks ¥13,200/11,600/8600 respectively; discount passports available from 3pm • ☎ 0570-008632, ⓦ tokyodisneyresort.jp • Maihama station

This big daddy of Tokyo's theme parks, **Tokyo Disney Resort**, is made up of two main sections: **Tokyo Disneyland**, a close copy of the Californian original; and **Tokyo DisneySea**, a water- and world travel-themed area. With an average of over 30,000 visitors per day (many more over weekends and holidays), expect queues.

7

Akasaka and Roppongi

At one time, Akasaka and Roppongi were pretty much all about nightlife – the former a nocturnal playground for bureaucrats and politicians, the latter an even more boozy place aimed at younger Japanese and *gaijin*. In recent years, with the opening of complexes such as Tokyo Midtown, the emphasis has shifted to daytime activity. Roppongi is styling itself as Tokyo's arts hub, home to the National Art Center, Suntory Museum of Art and Mori Art Museum, the last of which sits atop the area's other mega-development, Roppongi Hills. Both districts have old-established attractions, too, such as Akasaka's premier shrine, Hie-jinja; Zōjō-ji, near Roppongi, once the temple of the Tokugawa clan; and some pretty Japanese gardens. And while Tokyo Tower is no longer the city's most elevated viewing spot, it remains an iconic landmark.

BEST OF AKASAKA AND ROPPONGI

Hie-jinja Explore one of the city's finest Shinto shrines (see page 97)
Tokyo Midtown and Roppongi Hills Take the pulse of modern Tokyo at these huge developments (see pages 102 and 104)
Mori Art Museum and Tokyo City View See some top-notch art, then head one floor up for a killer view (see page 104)
Gonpachi Get your *Kill Bill* fix (see page 165)
Kurosawa Satisfy your *Yojimbo* cravings over a bowl of soba (see page 165)
Cask Strength Savour some rare Japanese whiskies (see page 181)
Art & Design Store Stock up on products from some of Japan's most famous designers (see page 200)

Akasaka

赤坂

Lying southwest of the Imperial Palace, **Akasaka** was once an agricultural area where plants producing a red dye were farmed – hence the locality's name, which means "red slope". Akasaka developed as an entertainment district in the late nineteenth century, when *ryōtei* restaurants, staffed with performing geisha, began to cater for the modern breed of politicians and bureaucrats. The area still has its fair share of exclusive establishments, shielded from the hoi polloi by high walls and even higher prices, and their presence lends Akasaka a certain cachet.

8

Hie-jinja

日枝神社 • 2-10-15 Nagatachō, Chiyoda-ku • 24hr • Free • Akasaka, Akasaka-mitsuke or Tameike-sannō stations

At the southern end of Akasaka's main thoroughfare, Sotobori-dōri, stands a huge stone *torii*, beyond which is a picturesque avenue of red *torii* leading up the hill to **Hie-jinja**, a Shinto shrine dedicated to the god Ōyamakui-no-kami, who is believed to protect against evil. Hie-jinja's history stretches back to 830 AD, when it was first established on the outskirts of what would become Edo. The shrine's location shifted a couple more times before Shogun Tokugawa Ietsuna placed it here in the seventeenth century as a source of protection for his castle (now the site of the Imperial Palace); the current buildings date from the 1950s.

From the main entrance through the large stone *torii* on the east side of the hill, 51 steps lead up to a spacious enclosed courtyard. To the left of the main shrine, look for the carving of a female monkey cradling her baby, a symbol that has come to signify protection for pregnant women. In June, Hie-jinja hosts one of Tokyo's most important festivals, the **Sannō Matsuri** (see page 27).

National Diet Building

国会議事堂, Kokkai Gijidō • 1-7-1 Nagatachō, Chiyoda-ku • Tours of House of Councillors Mon–Fri 9am–4pm unless in session • Free • ☎ 03 5521 7445, ⓦ www.sangiin.go.jp • Kokkai-gijidō-mae station

The squat, three-storey **National Diet Building** is dominated by a central tower block decorated with pillars and a pyramid-shaped roof. On the left stands the House of Representatives, the main body of government; on the right is the House of Councillors, which is similar to Britain's House of Lords and open for hour-long **tours**.

There's an Edwardian-style grandeur to the Diet's interior, especially in the carved-wood debating chamber and the central reception hall, which is decorated with paintings reflecting the seasons, and bronze statues of significant statesmen. The room the emperor uses when he visits the Diet is predictably ornate, with detailing picked

AKASAKA AND ROPPONGI

CHŪŌ LINE Shinanomachi Station

New Ōtani Hotel

Edo Ise Katagai Museum

SHUTO EXPRESSWAY 4

Benkei-bashi

Akasaka Detached Palace

Meiji Memorial Picture Gallery

Meiji Kinenkan

Meiji-jingū
Outer Garden

Toyokawa Inari Tokyo Betsuin

Akasaka-mitsuke

SOTOBORI-DŌRI

AOYAMA-DŌRI

Jingū Baseball Stadium

Rugby Ground

Aoyama-itchome

Canada Embassy

Sogetsu Foundation

AKASAKA

Akasaka

Aoyama-itchome

GAIEN-HIGASHI-DŌRI

AOYAMA-DŌRI

Gaienmae

Nogi-jinja

21_21 Design Sight

MINATO-KU

Gallery MA

Nogizaka

Suntory Museum of Art

Hinokichō-kōen

Aoyama Reien

GAIEN-NISHI-DŌRI

GAIEN-HIGASHI-DŌRI

National Art Center, Tokyo

Billboard Live Tokyo

Midtown Tower

Fujifilm Square

TOKYO MIDTOWN

SHUTO EXPRESSWAY 3

N

AOYAMA

Roppongi

ROPPONGI

Kaguwa

Kingyo

Nezu Museum

Roppongi

SHUTO EXPRESSWAY 3

Striped House Gallery

GAIEN-NISHI-DŌRI

Toho Cinema

Mori Art Museum & Tower

ROPPONGI HILLS

INNER CIRCULAR ROUTE

ACCOMMODATION

HOTELS
ANA InterContinental Tokyo	2
Andaz	3
The b Roppongi	6
The Glanz	8
Grand Hyatt Tokyo	7
Ōkura	4
The Ritz-Carlton	5

HOSTEL
Kaisu	1

NISHI-AZABU

0   200
metres

Azabu-jūban

AZABU-JŪBAN

MOTO-AZABU

Take-no-yu

SHOPPING
Art & Design Store	7
Asa-no-ha	8
Blue & White	9
The Cover Nippon	3
Don Quijote	5
Fukumitsuya	4
Japan Traditional Craft Centre	2
Nuno	6
Toraya	1

DRINKING AND NIGHTLIFE
BARS	
BrewDog	5
Cask Strength	2
Gen Yamamoto	11
Hobgoblin	6
Pink Cow	1
Public Six	9
Warayakiya	7
CLUBS	
Alife	8
Esprit	4
Jumanji 55	3
Muse	10

EATING
RESTAURANTS	
Felafel Brothers	7
Gold Scorpion	11
Gonpachi	9
Kurosawa	2
L'Atelier de Joël Robuchon	8
Nobu Tokyo	4
Nodaiwa	12
Shunjū	3
Sukiyabashi Jiro	10
Suzunami	5
Tōfuya-Ukai	13
CAFÉS	
Bluebottle Coffee	6
Gelateria Marghera	14
TEAROOM	
Toraya	1

out in real gold. The tour finishes at the Diet's front garden, planted with native trees and plants from all of Japan's 47 prefectures.

Hotel New Ōtani and garden

4-1 Kiyoichō, Chiyoda-ku • Daily 6am–10pm • Free • Kojimachi, Akasaka-mitsuke or Nagatachō stations

Near Benkei-bashi, the bridge that spans what was once the outer moat of the shogun's castle, you'll find the **Hotel New Ōtani** – you may recognize the place from Bond film *You Only Live Twice*, where it functioned as Blofeld's Tokyo base. Within its grounds is a traditional Japanese **garden**, originally designed for the *daimyō* Katō Kiyomasa, lord of Kumamoto in Kyūshū over four hundred years ago. It's actually one of the most spectacular in the whole city, with a vermillion bridge overlooking a miniature waterfall. Those visiting in the shoulder seasons may get to see cheery pink flowers or fiery autumnal leaves, though it's a pretty place at any time of the year.

Toyokawa Inari Tokyo Betsuin

豊川稲荷東京別院 • 1-4-7 Motoakasaka, Minato-ku • 24hr • Free • Akasaka-mitsuke station

The colourful **Toyokawa Inari Tokyo Betsuin**, also known as Toyokawa Inari, is a combined temple and shrine. Such holy places were much more common across Japan before the Meiji government forcibly separated Shinto and Buddhist places of worship. The temple's compact precincts are decked with red lanterns and banners, while the main hall is guarded by statues of pointy-eared foxes wearing red bibs: messengers of the Shinto god Inari, they are found at all Inari shrines.

Akasaka Detached Palace

迎賓館, Geihinkan • 2-1-1 Motoakasaka, Minato-ku • Entry by lottery; opening days irregular but usually Thurs–Tues • Main building (or annexe) and garden ¥1500, garden only ¥300; reserve online • ⓦ www.geihinkan.go.jp • Yotsuya station

Sitting amid extensive grounds, the grand, European-style **Akasaka Detached Palace** serves as the official State Guesthouse. When it was completed in 1909, this vast building, modelled on Buckingham Palace on the outside and Versailles on the inside, had only one bathroom in the basement, and the empress's apartments were in a separate wing from her husband's (an arrangement that suited the emperor fine, since he was in the habit of taking his nightly pick from the ladies-in-waiting). The palace is not open all year, with entry limited to 50 people per group. It's sometimes possible to gain entry on the spot; even if you're out of luck, the front gardens are free to enter on the days the palace is open, and count as a consolation prize. At other times of year you can peek through the main gates, close to Yotsuya station.

Sōgetsu Foundation

草月会館, Sōgetsu Kaikan • 7-2-21 Akasaka, Minato-ku • Hour-long trial classes ¥3240; reserve online • ☎ 03 3408 1209, ⓦ sogetsu. or.jp • Aoyama-itchōme station

Founded in 1927, the **Sōgetsu Foundation** is a famous school of *ikebana* – traditional Japanese flower-arranging – and holds classes in English. It is housed in a glass-fronted building designed by influential architect Tange Kenzō (see page 270), and the lobby features strikingly contemporary *ikebana* displays, as well as sculptures by the renowned American-Japanese artist Isamu Noguchi.

Toranomon

虎ノ門

As with Roppongi before it, **Toranomon** has seen its stock rise in recent years with the opening of a mammoth new development: **Toranomon Hills**. While not as flashy or as interesting to the casual tourist as its near namesake, Roppongi Hills, it's still worth an amble around if you're in the area; it's topped by the fancy *Andaz Tokyo* hotel (see page 149), and tailed by a rather predictable clutch of shops and restaurants. It will be interesting to see what effect this development has on the rest of the area, but for now Toranomon's only real draw is the excellent **Musée Tomo** gallery.

Musée Tomo

智美術館, Tomo Bijutsukan • 4-1-35 Toranomon, Minato-ku • Daily (except Mon) 11am–6pm • Most exhibitions ¥1000 • ☎ 03 5733 5131, Ⓦ musee-tomo.or.jp • Roppongi-itchōme, Kamiyachō or Toranomon stations

Home to the outstanding contemporary Japanese ceramics collection of Tomo Kikuchi, the classy **Musée Tomo** gallery is as elegant as its exhibits – fifty-odd pieces carefully spotlit as objets d'art. Inside is a stunning stairwell with a barley-sugar-like banister and slivers of *washi* paper decorating the walls, while out the front is the old Kikuchi family home, an incongruous Taishō-era villa. From the museum's fancy French café and restaurant, there's a lovely view on to the old home's tranquil garden.

Roppongi

六本木

Its name meaning "six trees", **Roppongi** was once reputed to be home to six *daimyō*, all of whom coincidentally had the Chinese character for "tree" in their names. From the Meiji era onwards, the area was a military stamping ground, first for the imperial troops and then, during the American Occupation, for US forces. Thus the *gaijin* community started hanging out here, and today's entertainment district was born. Roppongi is still principally a party town, but three major developments – Roppongi Hills, the National Art Center and Tokyo Midtown – have recast the area in a more refined light, and today it's increasingly known for its galleries and arts scene (see page 101). Roppongi subway station is the principal access point for the area, although you can also use Nogizaka for the National Art Center and Kamiyachō for Tokyo Tower.

8

ROPPONGI GALLERIES

Those bumping and grinding in Roppongi's clubs would likely scoff at you for suggesting so, but the area is now almost as notable for its excellent **art scene** as it is for drinking – there are **galleries** dotted all over the place, all the way south to Azabu-Jūban. As well as those listed here, there's excellent art on display at Musée Tomo in Toranomon (see above), the Suntory Museum of Art (see page 102) and 21_21 Design Sight (see page 102) in Tokyo Midtown, the lofty Mori Art Museum atop Roppongi Hills (see page 104) and the National Art Center (see page 102).

Gallery MA 8-11-27 Akasaka, Minato-ku ☎ 03 3402 1010; Nogizaka station. Across the road from the Nogi-jinja (see page 102), there's often an interesting exhibition at Gallery MA, on the third floor of the TOTO Nogizaka building (which belongs to Japan's largest manufacturer of toilets). The gallery specializes in interior design and architecture, both from Japan and overseas, and has an excellent bookstore. Tues–Thurs & Sat 11am–6pm, Fri 11am–7pm.

Striped House Gallery 5-10-33 Roppongi, Minato-ku ☎ 03 3405 8108, Ⓦ striped-house.com; Roppongi station. Taking its name from the striped brick building in which it's based, this gallery has an eclectic range of exhibitions, almost all of which focus on young, adventurous local artists. Daily 11am–6.30pm.

Take Ninagawa 2-12-4 Higashi-Azabu, Minato-ku ☎ 03 5571 5844, Ⓦ takeninagawa.com; Azabu-Jūban station. Representing mixed media artists such as Ohtake Shinrō and Misaki Kawai, it's worth swinging by to see what's on at this space for up-and-coming local artists. Wed–Sun 11am–7pm.

Tokyo Midtown

東京ミッドタウン • 9-7-1 Akasaka, Minato-ku • ⓦ www.tokyo-midtown.com • Roppongi or Nogizaka station

Tokyo Midtown is an enormous mixed-use complex of offices, shops, apartments, a convention centre, two museums and other public facilities, plus the small park Hinokichō-kōen, all revolving around the 248m-high **Midtown Tower**. Completed in 2007, this was Tokyo's tallest building until the Skytree came along; oddly, there's no viewing deck. With its slightly bulbous middle, the tower's design was inspired by an Isamu Noguchi sculpture; in keeping with a general theme of traditional motifs, the pattern of the tower's windows is reminiscent of a woven bamboo fence.

Suntory Museum of Art

サントリー美術館, Santorii Bijutsukan • 3F Galleria, Tokyo Midtown • Mon & Sun 10am–6pm, Wed–Sat 10am–8pm • Entry price varies by exhibition, usually around ¥1000 • ☎ 03 3470 1073, ⓦ suntory.co.jp/sma

Landscaped gardens planted with 140 trees nestle behind and along the west side of the Tokyo Midtown complex, where you'll find the **Suntory Museum of Art**. This elegant Kuma Kengo-designed building hosts changing exhibitions of ceramics, lacquerware, paintings and textiles. There's also an on-site café serving tasty nibbles from Kanazawa, the capital of Ishikawa prefecture.

21_21 Design Sight

9-7-6 Akasaka, Minato-ku • Daily 10am–7pm • ¥1100 • ☎ 03 3475 2121, ⓦ 2121designsight.jp

Two giant triangular planes of steel, concrete and glass peeking out of a green lawn are part of the **21_21 Design Sight**, a fascinating collaboration between architect Andō Tadao and fashion designer Issey Miyake. The building's seamless shape was inspired by Miyake's A-POC ("A Piece Of Cloth") line, and the main gallery digs one floor into the ground to provide an elevated, airy space in which to view the various design exhibitions.

Fujifilm Square

フジフイルムスクエア • 1F Midtown West, Tokyo Midtown • Daily 10am–7pm • Free • ⓦ fujifilmsquare.jp

At the front of the Midtown complex, facing Gaien-Higashi-dōri, is **Fujifilm Square**, with photography exhibitions changing on a monthly basis, and a permanent display showcasing the history of cameras, from the relatively ancient to the modern day. There's also a shop selling fine photographic prints.

National Art Center

国立新美術館, Kokuritsu Shin Bijutsukan • 7-22-2 Roppongi, Minato-ku • Daily (except Tues) 10am–6pm, Fri 10am–8pm • Entrance fee varies with exhibition • ☎ 03 6812 9900, ⓦ www.nact.jp • Nogizaka or Roppongi station

The stunning **National Art Center** is one of the three principal points on the **Roppongi Art Triangle**, which also includes the Suntory Museum of Art (see page 102) and Mori Art Museum (see page 104). A billowing wave of pale green glass ripples across the facade of the Kurokawa Kisha-designed building which, at 48,000 square metres, is Japan's largest such museum, the huge halls allowing for some very ambitious works to be displayed. Of the twelve exhibition rooms, two are devoted to shows curated by the museum (the centre has no collection of its own); the rest of the rooms are organized by various art associations from across Japan, with the sum total making for a very eclectic mix. While you are here, linger in the main atrium to admire the conical pods that soar up three storeys, and explore the excellent museum shop.

Nogi-jinja

乃木神社 • 8-11-27 Akasaka, Minato-ku • 24hr • Free • Nogizaka station

The small shrine and terraced garden of **Nogi-jinja** honour the Meiji-era **General Nogi Maresuke**, a hero in both the Sino-Japanese and Russo-Japanese wars. When the Emperor Meiji died, Nogi and his wife followed the samurai tradition and committed suicide in his house within the shrine grounds.

There's a good **antique flea market** here, while the interesting Gallery MA (see page 101) sits just on the other side of the main road.

Roppongi Hills

六本木ヒルズ • 8-11-27 Akasaka, Minato-ku • ⓦ roppongihills.com • Roppongi station

Originally billed as an "Urban New Deal" for Tokyo, **Roppongi Hills** is the development that spearheaded Roppongi's partial evolution from sleaze to sophistication. The overhead utility cables that plague the rest of Tokyo have been banished here, and there's a good dose of open space and greenery, so unusual in this land-starved city. A Japanese garden and pond, a liberal sprinkling of funky street sculptures, an open-air arena for free performances, several roof gardens and even a rice paddy on the roof above the multiplex cinema are all part of the mix. Louise Bourgeois' **Maman**, a giant bronze, stainless steel and marble spider, squats at the base of the 54-storey, Kohn Pedersen Fox-designed **Mori Tower**, home to the Mori Art Museum and the Tokyo City View observation deck.

Mori Art Museum

森美術館, Mori Bijutsukan • 53F Mori Tower, Roppongi Hills • Wed–Mon 10am–10pm, Tues 10am–5pm • ¥1800, including Tokyo City View • ☎ 03 6406 6100, ⓦ mori.art.museum

The "Museum Cone", a glass structure enclosing a swirling staircase, forms the entrance to the **Mori Art Museum**, more than fifty storeys overhead. This large gallery space, which occupies the prime top floors of the Mori Tower, puts on large and adventurous exhibitions, with a particular focus on Asian artists – they're generally extremely well-curated affairs, even down to themed menu items at the on-site café.

Tokyo City View

東京シティビュー • 54F Mori Tower, Roppongi Hills • Daily 9am–1am, last entry midnight • ¥1800, including Mori Art Museum; Skydeck ¥500 extra • ⓦ tcv.roppongihills.com

In the same tower as the Mori Art Museum (see page 104), one floor up, the **Tokyo City View** observation deck is one of the best viewpoints in the city. If the weather is fine, it's possible to get out on to the rooftop **Skydeck** for an alfresco view that's particularly enchanting during and after sunset.

Azabu-Jūban and around

麻布十番

Of the many expats and moneyed Japanese you'll see traipsing their kids around Roppongi's various shops and cafés, a fairly high proportion actually live just to the southeast in **Azabu-Jūban**. There's little of note for the traveller in this rather grey area, bar the giant **matsuri** which takes place in August – up there with the busiest summer festivals in Tokyo – when most streets become absolutely rammed with food stalls and beer-toting visitors. However, just to the east of Azabu-Jūban is one of the city's most prominent sights: **Tokyo Tower**, flanked on its eastern side by a large park, **Shiba-kōen**, and **Zōjō-ji**.

Tokyo Tower

東京タワー • 4-2-8 Shiba-kōen • Daily 9am–11pm • Main observatory ¥900, top observatory ¥1900 extra • ☎ 03 3433 5111, ⓦ tokyotower.co.jp • Akabanebashi or Kamiyachō stations

You can't miss **Tokyo Tower**, a distinctive red-and-white structure rising high above the wider Roppongi area. Built during an era when Japan was becoming famous for producing cheap copies of foreign goods, this 333m-high replica of the Eiffel Tower, opened in 1958, manages to top its Parisian role model by several metres. At the tower's base a plethora of the usual souvenir shops, restaurants and other minor attractions have been added over the years, most incurring additional fees and none really worth seeing in their own right. There are good views of Tokyo Bay from the uppermost observation deck but, at 250m, it's no longer the city's highest viewpoint – you can get 20m higher at the nearby Tokyo City View (see page 104), while the Tokyo Skytree (see page 78) rises to a vertiginous 450m.

Zōjō-ji

增上寺 • 4-7-35 Shiba-kōen • 24hr • Free • Akabanebashi, Onarimon or Shiba-kōen stations

The main point of interest at **Shiba-kōen** (芝公園) is **Zōjō-ji**, the family temple of the Tokugawa clan. Dating from 1393, Zōjō-ji was moved to this site in 1598 by Tokugawa Ieyasu (the first Tokugawa shogun) in order to protect southeast Edo spiritually and provide a waystation for pilgrims approaching the capital from the Tōkaidō road. This was once the city's largest holy site, with 48 sub-temples and over a hundred other buildings. Since the fall of the Tokugawa, however, Zōjō-ji has been razed to the ground by fire three times, and virtually all the current buildings date from the mid-1970s; some find it all rather lacking in charm.

San-gadatsu-mon

One ancient element still standing at the temple is its imposing **San-gadatsu-mon**, a 21m-high gateway dating from 1612 – it is the oldest wooden structure in Tokyo and designated one of Japan's Important Cultural Properties. The name translates as "Three Deliverances Gate" (Buddhism is supposed to save believers from the evils of anger, greed and stupidity). As you pass through, look out for the tower with a large bell, said to have been made from melted metal hairpins donated by the ladies of the shogun's court, and for the pair of Himalayan cedar trees, one planted by US President Grant when he visited the temple in 1879 and the other by the then Vice President George Bush in 1982. Ahead lies the **Taiden** (Great Main Hall), while to the right are ranks of *jizō* statues, capped with red bonnets and decorated with plastic flowers and colourful windmills that twirl in the breeze. Amid this army of mini-guardians lie the remains of six shogun, behind a wrought-iron gate decorated with dragons.

Take-no-yu

竹の湯 • 1-15-12 Minami-Azabu, Minato-ku • Tues–Thurs, Sat & Sun 3.30–11.30pm • ¥460 • Azabu-Jūban station

A short walk south of Azabu-Jūban, the **Take-no-yu** baths are somewhat different to most other Tokyo establishments for one major reason: the water in these parts comes out brown, and is so prized for its medical properties that locals pay to take it away by the litre. The experience of bathing here is a little like being steeped in tea – or being a dirty plate in a sink full of dirty dishwater.

8

SAKURA SEASON IN NAKAMEGURO

Ebisu and the south

The area immediately to the south of Shibuya has, of late, become one of the most fashionable in the city – a maze of chic cafés, tiny clothing boutiques, and lunchtime specials of foreign and fusion cuisine. Like Shibuya, Ebisu is best visited at night, when its many bars and restaurants are at their liveliest. The district is also home to the former Yebisu brewery (the old transliteration of Ebisu lives on in the name of the beer), now developed into the Yebisu Garden Place complex, where you'll find the excellent Tokyo Photographic Art Museum. Head uphill to the west of Ebisu and you'll hit Daikanyama, one of Tokyo's most upscale districts and a great place to chill out at a pavement café or browse boutiques. Dip downhill again to explore a rather more down-to-earth version of the same in Nakameguro, whose cherry tree-lined river banks are prime strolling territory, especially during sakura season.

BEST OF EBISU AND THE SOUTH
Tokyo Photographic Art Museum Ogle world-class images (see page 107)
Nakameguro Stroll the river banks or have a *hanami* party in this delightful district (see page 110)
Hillside Terrace Take your pick of one of the countless cafés (see page 110)
Iroha Scoff a super-cheap, yet very high quality sushi set (see page 166)
Buri Sample an expertly curated – and near-frozen – range of boutique cup-sake at this great little bar (see page 182)
Meguro Cinema Go retro with an old film (see page 196)

South along the Meguro River from here is **Meguro**, site of the tranquil **National Park for Nature Study** and the serene gardens of **Happōen**. Near the transport and hotel hub of **Shinagawa**, east of Meguro, you'll find the historic temple **Sengaku-ji**, a key location in Tokyo's bloodiest true-life samurai saga, and the **Hara Museum of Contemporary Art**, which houses an interesting collection of modern art and a lovely café.

Ebisu

恵比寿

The main focus of **Ebisu** (named after the Shinto god of good fortune) is **Yebisu Garden Place**, a sprawling shopping, office and entertainment development, built on the site of the nineteenth-century brewery that was once the source of the area's fortunes. The brewery is now a small **museum** dedicated to Yebisu beer, while the worthy **Tokyo Photographic Art Museum** also lies within the wider complex. The excellent **Yamatane Museum of Art**, due northeast of Ebisu station, is another artsy sight to tick off in the area.

Yebisu Garden Place

恵比寿ガーデンプレイス • 4-20 Ebisu, Shibuya-ku • Ebisu station

Slated as an architectural cock-up, the **Yebisu Garden Place** complex – connected to Ebisu station by a series of moving walkways – includes the glitzy *Westin Hotel*, a cinema, a performance hall and a mock French château housing a Joël Robuchon restaurant. Rising up above it all is the 39-storey **Yebisu Tower**, from the top floor of which you can take in some spectacular free city views; there are plenty of restaurants taking advantage of these lofty surroundings, with *Hokkaido* recommended for its cheap-ish seafood.

Tokyo Photographic Art Museum

東京都写真美術館, Tōkyō-to Shashin Bijutsukan • Yebisu Garden Place • Tues–Sun 10am–6pm, Thurs & Fri until 8pm • Admission charges vary • ☎ 03 3280 0031, ⓦ topmuseum.jp

The best sight in the Ebisu area is the **Tokyo Photographic Museum** – also known as the **TOP Museum** – which was fully remodelled in 2016 and hosts excellent exhibitions by major Japanese and Western photographers. There are three full floors of exhibitions (two above ground, one below), with a café on the entrance floor; exhibitions can last anything from two weeks to three months, but there's usually a good spread of themes at any one time.

Museum of Yebisu Beer

エビスビール記念館, Yebisu Biiru Kinenkan • B1 west side of Yebisu Garden Place complex, best accessed through Mitsukoshi mall • Tues–Sun 11am–7pm • Free; beer samples ¥400 • ☎ 03 5423 7255, ⓦ sapporobeer.jp/yebisu/museum

Beer drinkers may care to visit the **Museum of Yebisu Beer** to find out about the history of the Yebisu brand – now owned by the Sapporo Brewery, though still sold under its

■ ACCOMMODATION

HOTELS
Claska	3
Dormy Inn	1
The Strings	6
Tōyoko Inn Takanawaguchi	4

RYOKAN AND MINSHUKU
Akimoto	2
Ryokan Sansuisō	5

Yamatane
Museum of Art

Log Road

DAIKANYAMA

Hillside Terrace

Daikan'yama

Liquid Room

Yogajaya

Container
Gallery

Ebisu

Ebisu
Station

EBISU

KOMAZAWA-DŌRI

Nakameguro

Yebisu
Garden
Cinema

Museum of
Yebisu Beer

Yebisu
Tower

NAKAMEGURO

Tokyo Photographic
Art Museum

Yebisu
Garden
Place

Yutenji

CHIBA-ZAKA

Meguro-gawa

Meguro
Cinema

Blues Alley Japan

MEGURO

MEGURO-DŌRI

KOMAZAWA-DŌRI

MEGURO-DŌRI

YAMATE-DŌRI

CENTRAL CIRCULAR ROUTE

Fudomae

TOKYŪ MEGURO LINE

● SHOPPING

Bonjour Records	7
Do	9
Evisu	8
Jun Ashida	2
Kamawanu	4
National Azabu	1
Okura	3
Tsutaya	5
Yamada Heiandō	6

0   200
metres

EBISU AND THE SOUTH

DRINKING AND NIGHTLIFE
BARS
Baja	6
Buri	3
Footnik	5
Nakameguro Taproom	7
Spring Valley Brewery	1
Xex	2
CLUB	
Unit	4

EATING
CAFÉ
Mocha Coffee	2
RESTAURANTS	
Chano-ma	10
Ebisu Yokochō	4
Futatsume	11
Higashiyama	7
Iroha Sushi	9
Ivy Place	1
Jasmine	3
Kosyu Ichiba	6
Longrain	12
Pizzeria da Isa	5
Tonki	13
TEAROOM	
Ganchabō	8

HIRO-O

Hiro-o Ⓢ

SHUTO EXPRESSWAY 2

MEIJI-DORI

GAIEN-NISHI-DORI

SHIROKANE

Shirokane-Takanawa

Westin Hotel

SHUTO EXPRESSWAY 2

SAKURADA DORI

MEGURO-DORI

GAIEN-NISHI-DORI

National Park for Nature Study

Shirokanedai Ⓢ

Happóen

Sengaku-ji

Sengaku-ji

Tokyo Metropolitan Teien Art Museum

Entrance
Entrance
MEGURO-DORI

SHIROKANEDAI

YAMANOTE LINE

Meguro Station

Ⓢ Meguro

Hatakeyama Memorial Museum of Fine Art

Takanawadai Ⓢ

SHINAGAWA

KEIKYU LINE

Aqua Park

Shingawa Station

SHUTO EXPRESSWAY 2

SAKURADA DORI

Ⓢ

Gotanda
Gotanda Station

TOKYU IKEGAMI LINE

Hara Museum of Contemporary Art (300m)

9

old label – and of the brewery that used to be here. There's not all that much to see, bar a display of how the company's beer bottles have become progressively uglier over the years, but thanks to relatively late opening hours, the tasting room is a great place to sample some of Sapporo's beers.

Yamatane Museum of Art

山種美術館, Yamatane Bijutsukan • 3-12-36 Hiro-o, Shibuya-ku • Tues–Sun 10am–5pm • ¥1000 • ☎ 03 5777 8600, ⓦ www.yamatane-museum.or.jp • 10min walk northeast of Ebisu station

Art lovers should consider dropping by the refined **Yamatane Museum of Art**. The museum's focus is Japanese paintings from the Meiji Era, of which it has an impressive collection – over 1800 works. There are usually six or seven different exhibitions a year, all arranged around a particular genre, era or artist.

Daikanyama

代官山

The classy residential suburb of **Daikanyama** has a village-like atmosphere that provides a refreshing break from the frenzy of nearby Shibuya, just one stop away on the Tōkyū Tōyoko line (or a nice half-hour walk). It's also possible to get here from Ebisu station, by taking a ten-minute stroll uphill heading west along Komazawa-dōri. The area is most notable for its many boutiques (see page 108) and cafés (see page 108), but even if you're not in the market for clothing or caffeine it's worth visiting for the relaxed air. Major developments here include **Hillside Terrace**, a one-stop area for drinking, dining and shopping; and the even newer **Log Road** complex, a relatively small affair bookended by craft-beer pubs.

Hillside Terrace

Off Kyū-yamate-dōri • ⓦ hillsideterrace.com • Daikanyama station

Daikanyama's contemporary style has been defined by the **Hillside Terrace** shopping and dining complex, designed by Maki Fumihiko, recipient of the 1993 Pritzker Prize for architecture. Strung along leafy Kyū-yamate-dōri, the various stages of Hillside Terrace were developed over nearly a quarter-century, its courtyards and vistas paying homage to ancient Japanese and Buddhist concepts of space. Poke around and you'll find plenty of appealing boutiques and ritzy restaurants and cafés. It's impossible to miss the huge *Tsutaya* book store (see page 200), while the **Hillside Gallery** (Tues–Sun 10am–5pm; free), opposite the Danish Embassy, has interesting modern art exhibitions.

Nakameguro

中目黒

Immediately to the southwest of Daikanyama is **Nakameguro**, one of Tokyo's trendiest areas, with a laidback, boho feel and a liberal sprinkling of eclectic boutiques (see page 108), restaurants (see page 108) and bars (see page 108). The district hugs the banks of the Meguro-gawa and is a particularly lovely spot to head during *hanami* season, thanks to its generous number of cherry trees. This is also one of the less sweltering places in Tokyo come high summer, with evaporation from the languid waterway providing some natural air conditioning. Another thing in Nakameguro's favour is convenience: as people from all over Tokyo will attest with envy, the area is directly accessible from almost all major parts of the city.

The Container Gallery

ザコンテナギャラリー • 1F Hills Daikanyama, 1-8-30 Kamimeguro, Meguro-ku • Mon & Wed–Fri 11am–9pm, Sat & Sun 10am–8pm • Free • ⓦ the-container.com • Nakameguro station

One of the smallest galleries in the city – the clue's in the name – the **Container Gallery** is set inside a shipping container, itself set inside a hair salon; exhibitions change every couple of months, and showcase a mix of young Japanese and international talent.

Meguro

目黒

Within walking distance of Nakameguro and Ebisu, **Meguro** is decidedly less appealing than its neighbouring areas – the atmosphere here is rather more city than village. Nevertheless, there are a few interesting things to see, even if they're frustratingly spread out.

Tokyo Metropolitan Teien Art Museum

東京都庭園美術館, Tōkyō-to Teien Bijutsukan • 5-21-9 Shirokanedai, Meguro-ku • **Museum** Daily 10am–6pm, closed second & fourth Wed of the month • Entry varies by exhibitions, usually ¥1000 • **Garden** Daily 10am–9pm • Entry included with museum ticket, otherwise ¥200 • ☎ 03 3443 0201, ⓦ www.teien-art-museum.ne.jp • Meguro or Shirokanedai stations

The Art Deco building housing the elegant **Tokyo Metropolitan Teien Art Museum** is the former home of Prince Asaka Yasuhiko, Emperor Hirohito's uncle, who lived in Paris for three years during the 1920s, where he developed a taste for the European style. It's worth popping in to admire the gorgeous interior decoration (particularly in the octagonal study room upstairs) and tranquil surrounding Japanese gardens; the exhibitions themselves tend to be curated along similarly genteel lines.

National Park for Nature Study

自然教育園, Shizen Kyōiku-en • 5-21-5 Shirokanedai, Meguro-ku • Tues–Sun 9am–4.30pm, May–Aug until 5pm • ¥310 • ⓦ www.ins. kahaku.go.jp • Meguro or Shirokanedai station

The spacious **National Park for Nature Study** is a worthy attempt to preserve the original natural features of the countryside before Edo was settled and developed into Tokyo. Among the eight thousand trees in the park are some that have been growing for five hundred years, while frogs can be heard croaking amid the grass beside the marshy ponds. The whole place is a bird-spotter's paradise, and it's also one of the few areas in Tokyo where you can really escape the crowds; the entrance is a stone's throw to the east of the Teien Art Museum (see above).

Happōen

八芳園 • 1-1-1 Shirokanedai, Meguro-ku • **Garden** Daily 10am–5pm • Free • **Teahouse** Daily 11am–5pm • ¥800 • Shirokanedai station

Shirokanedai subway station is the handiest jumping-off point for the lovely **Happōen**. The garden's name means "beautiful from any angle" and, despite the addition of a modern wedding hall on one side, this is still true. A renowned adviser to the shogunate, Hikozaemon Okubo, lived here during the early seventeenth century, but most of the garden's design dates from the early twentieth century, when a business tycoon bought up the land, built a classical Japanese villa (still standing by the garden's entrance) and gave the garden its present name. Take a turn through its twisting pathways and you'll pass two bonsai trees, each more than a hundred years old, a stone lantern said to have been carved eight hundred years ago by the Heike warrior Taira-no Munekiyo, and a central pond. Nestling amid the trees is the delightful **teahouse**, where ladies in kimono will serve you *matcha* and *okashi*. At weekends many smartly dressed wedding parties line up for group photos against the verdant backdrop.

9

Hatakeyama Memorial Museum of Fine Art

畠山記念館, Hatakeyama Kinenkan • 2-20-12 Shirokanedai, Meguro-ku • Tues–Sun: April–Sept 10am–5pm; Oct–March
10am–4.30pm • ¥700; tea ¥500 • ☏ 03 3447 5787 • Takanawadai station

Devoted to the art of the tea ceremony, the **Hatakeyama Memorial Museum of Fine
Art** is situated in the midst of a quiet residential area, overlooking a pretty Japanese
garden. This compact but appealing museum houses the collection of business magnate
Hatakeyama Issei, who made his fortune manufacturing waste incinerators and pumps.
Hatakeyama had exquisite taste and his collection contains many lovely works of art;
he also designed the building, which reflects the structure of a traditional teahouse,
albeit on a much larger scale. Tea is served in the exhibition hall.

Shinagawa

品川

The transport and hotel hub of **Shinagawa** was once the location of one of the original
checkpoints on the Tōkaidō, the major highway into Edo during the reign of the
shoguns. These days, most travellers who find themselves in Shinagawa are merely
changing trains or passing through on one of the many train lines snaking through the
area, but those with a little time to spare have a few sights to choose from, including
the eclectic **Hara Museum of Contemporary Art**.

Aqua Park

アクアパーク • 4-30-10 Takanawa, Shinagawa-ku • Daily 10am–10pm • Adult ¥2200, child aged 7–15 ¥1200, child under 7 ¥700 •
☏ 03 5421 1111, ⊛ aqua-park.jp • Shinagawa station

There are some three hundred different species of marine life on display at the
aquarium in the large **Aqua Park** entertainment complex, sitting behind the *Shinagawa
Prince* hotel. It also offers dolphin and sea lion shows, amusement rides and a range of
themed restaurants.

Hara Museum of Contemporary Art

原美術館, Hara Bijutsukan • 4-7-25 Kitashinagawa, Shinagawa-ku • Tues–Sun 11am–5pm, Wed until 8pm • ¥1100 • ☏ 03 3445 0651,
⊛ www.haramuseum.or.jp • Shinagawa station

In a quiet residential area around 800m south of Shinagawa station, the **Hara Museum
of Contemporary Art** has a small permanent collection including quirky installations,

---

REAL-LIFE MARIO KART

While walking around certain parts of Tokyo, you may well see foreigners dressed as
superheroes dashing around the city streets in tiny go-karts. This is no marketing stunt, but
an activity that you can actually take part in yourself. Whizzing about in a costume, and most
likely unable to remove the cartoonish grin from your face, this is about the best fun you can
have in Tokyo; the only disappointment is that thanks to pressure from Nintendo, the team
had to stop dressing their customers up as Mario, Luigi, Toad, Yoshi and other characters from
classic game **Super Mario Kart** (though this is still possible if you can rent your own costume
somewhere else).

The **Street Kart** team (☏ 03 6712 8275, ⊛ kart.st) run three separate courses from their
office in Shinagawa; all of them take in Tokyo Tower and Roppongi, with Shibuya and Odaiba
also options, and prices start at ¥10,000 (reduced to ¥8500 if you give a positive social media
review immediately after your ride). You'll need to be in possession of a foreign or international
driving licence (full details are on the website); note that you'll be driving on real roads, and
unlike in the game, you only have one life.

THE 47 RŌNIN

Celebrated in kabuki and *bunraku* plays, as well as on film, **Chūshingura** is a true story of honour, revenge and loyalty. In 1701, a young *daimyō*, Asano Takumi, became embroiled in a fatal argument in the shogun's court with his teacher and fellow lord Kira Yoshinaka. Asano had lost face in his performance of court rituals and, blaming his mentor for his lax tuition, drew his sword within the castle walls and attacked Kira. Although Kira survived, the shogun, on hearing of this breach of etiquette, ordered Asano to commit *seppuku*, the traditional form of suicide, which he did.

Their lord having been disgraced, Asano's loyal retainers, the **rōnin** – or masterless samurai – vowed revenge. On December 14, 1702, the 47 *rōnin*, lead by **Oishi Kuranosuke**, stormed Kira's villa, cut off his head and paraded it through Edo in triumph before placing it on Asano's grave in Sengaku-ji. The shogun ordered the *rōnin's* deaths, but instead all 47 committed *seppuku* on February 14, 1703, including Oishi's 15-year-old son. They were buried with Asano in Sengaku-ji, and today their graves are still wreathed in the smoke from the bundles of incense placed by their gravestones.

---

such as *Rondo*, by Morimura Yasumasa, whose self-portrait occupies the downstairs toilet. The building itself, a 1938 Bauhaus-style house designed by Watanabe Jin, the architect responsible for Ueno's Tokyo National Museum and the Wakō department store in Ginza, is worth a look, as are the tranquil sculpture gardens overlooked by the museum's pleasant café.

Sengaku-ji

泉岳寺 • 2-11-1 Akanawa, Minato-ku • **Temple** Daily: April–Sept 7am–6pm; Oct–March 7am–5pm • Free • ☎ 03 3441 5560, ⓦ sengakuji.or.jp • **Museum** Daily: April–Sept 9am–4.30pm; Oct–March 9am–4pm • ¥500 • Sengaku-ji station

Around a kilometre north of Shinagawa is **Sengaku-ji**, home to the graves of **Asano Takumi** and his **47 rōnin** (see page 113). Most of what you see now was rebuilt after World War II, but a striking gate decorated with a metalwork dragon dates back to 1836. The graves of the 47 *rōnin* are in the temple grounds (it's hard to resist the temptation to count them all), as well as the statue and grave of **Oishi Kuranosuke**, their avenging leader; a **museum** to the left of the main building contains their personal belongings, as well as a receipt for the severed head of Kira. The entrance is on the eastern side of the complex, which is a little tricky to track down.

DECORA HARAJUKU STYLE

Harajuku, Aoyama and Shibuya

If it's "wacky" Japan you're after, Harajuku should be neighbourhood number one on your list. Much of Tokyo's youth culture starts here, on streets which often resemble densely-populated catwalks, complete with zany clothing, hairstyles and accessories; in the surrounding soup of quirky boutiques and cafés, you'll be able to kit yourself out and dine in much the same manner as the local fashionistas. Shibuya, just south of Harajuku, is almost absurdly busy – a neon-drenched, *kanji*-splattered, high-rise jungle second only to Shinjuku for sheer eye-popping madness. East of Harajuku, those with gilt-edged credit cards will feel more at home among the antique shops of Aoyama and the big brand boutiques along Omotesandō, the area's key tree-lined boulevard, often referred to as Tokyo's Champs-Elysées.

BEST OF HARAJUKU, AOYAMA AND SHIBUYA

Harajuku station Gawp at some of Japan's craziest fashion (see page 115)
Meiji-jingū Wander the paths of the richly forested Inner Garden (see page 118)
Nezu Museum Enjoy the captivating gardens at this superbly designed museum (see page 120)
The Millennials Shibuya Bed down for the night at this excellent example of Tokyo's new breed of capsule hotels (see page 154)
Commune 2nd A great outdoor hub for snacks or craft beer (see page 168)
Shibuya Crossing Watching hordes crossing a road is rarely this much fun; do it over a coffee at *L'Occitane* (see page 175)
Karaoke-kan Do your very best Lady Gaga or Bill Murray impression (see page 185)
Omotesandō Check out the fashion flagships (see page 120)

10

Traditional sights take a bit of a back seat in these areas, and yet there is plenty to take in, the best being the verdant grounds of the city's most venerable shrine, **Meiji-jingū**, which merge into the greenery of **Yoyogi-kōen** to the south, one of the most pleasant parks in Tokyo, and often full of picnickers on sunny afternoons. Just off Omotesandō are several interesting **galleries**, including the **Nezu Museum** with its beautiful garden; the **Ōta Memorial Museum of Art**, dedicated to *ukiyo-e* prints; and the anarchic **Design Festa Gallery**.

Harajuku

原宿

Crammed with places to eat, drink and shop, the **Harajuku** area is bisected by **Omotesandō**, an elegant, ginkgo-tree-lined boulevard which leads from the main entrance of **Meiji-jingū** to the cluster of contemporary designer boutiques on the other side of Aoyama-dōri. On either side are dense networks of streets, packed with funky little boutiques, restaurants and bars.

The hungry mouth of the **Takeshita-dōri** shopping alley gobbles up teenage fashion victims as they swarm out of the north exit of Harajuku station, and spits them out the other end on Meiji-dōri, minus their cash. Selling every kind of tat imaginable, the shops here are hugely enjoyable to root around in and provide an intriguing window on Japanese teen fashion.

The hip, independent Harajuku style is very much in evidence south of Omotesandō on **Cat Street**, a curvy pathway lined with cafés, small restaurants and eclectic emporia.

HARAJUKU STYLE

With its name immortalized in several Western songs, Harajuku is better known abroad for its zany **youth culture** than it is for shopping, and with very good reason. Swing by the Harajuku station area on a weekend and you'll see crowds of youngsters, mainly female, dressed up to the nines in a series of bizarre costumes; the epicentre is Jingū-bashi, a small bridge heading towards Meiji-Jingū (see page 118) from Harajuku station.

Of the styles to look out for, **Cosplay** is probably the most familiar to outsiders: it involves dressing up as an anime, manga or game character, with occasionally startling results.

Also easy to spot is **Gothic Lolita**, a mix of the gothic and the girlie; this itself is split into subgenres including punk, black, white (as in the hues) and country style. There are plenty more, including a whole host of smaller genres: **Visual Kei** adherents go for crazy make-up and hairstyles; **Decora** is a bright, flamboyant style often featuring myriad toys, pieces of jewellery and other accessories; **Kawaii**, which means "cute" in Japanese, usually involves clothing more appropriate to children. More styles are born every year, of course.

Shinjuku
Park Tower

NTT
Intercommunication
Centre
Tokyo
Opera City
New
National
Theatre

Minami-Shinjuku

Yoyogi
Station

Yoyogi

Hatsudai

Sword Museum

Sangubashi

Black
Stripe Theater

Honden

Meiji-jingū
Inner Garden

Kita-mon

Jingū Naien

Yoyogi-kōen

Harajuku
Station

Ōta
Memorial
Museum
of Art

Ō-torii

Yoyogihachiman

Yoyogi-kōen

Yoyogi
National
Gymnasium

SEE 'SHIBUYA' MAP FOR DETAIL

NHK Hall

Kanze
Nō-gakudō

Uplink

Toguri
Museum
of Art

Bunkamura
(Theatre
Cocoon &
Orchard Hall)

SHIBUYA

Japan Folk
Crafts Musuem

Komaba-Tōdaimae

109 Building

DŌGENZAKA

Shibuya

Hachiko

Shibuya

Shibuya
Station

Shibuya
Hikarie

Myth of
Tomorrow

Shinsen

ACCOMMODATION
HOTEL
Tōkyū Stay Aoyama   1
HOSTEL
Turntable Hostel   2

EATING
RESTAURANTS
Florilège   1
Royal Garden Café   2

SHOPPING
Arts & Science   4
Beniya   6
Cibone   1
Francfranc   2
Isehan Honten   5
Sou Sou   3

DRINKING AND NIGHTLIFE
BARS
Forest Beer Garden   1
Sekirei   2
CLUB
Bonobo   3

N

ODAKYU ODAWARA LINE

SHUTO EXPRESSWAY 4

SHUTO EXPRESSWAY 4

CENTRAL CIRCULAR ROUTE

CENTRAL CIRCULAR ROUTE

YAMANOTE LINE

MEIJI-DŌRI

MEIJI-DŌRI

SHUTO EXPRESSWAY 3

0   500
metres

HARAJUKU, AOYAMA AND SHIBUYA

Shinjuku Gyoen

CHŪŌ LINE   Sendagaya

SHUTO EXPRESSWAY 4

Shinanomachi
Station

National Nō
Theatre

National
Metropolitan
Gymnasium

Tokyo

Ⓢ Kokuritsu-kyōgijō

Kitasando

Ⓢ

Akasaka
Detached
Palace

Meiji Memorial
Picture Gallery

National
Stadium

Ⓘ

Meiji
Kinenkan

Jingū Batting Dome

Ⓔ

Meiji-jingū
Outer Garden

Sōgetsu
Foundation

Jingū
Baseball
Stadium

Ⓔ Canada
Embassy

Ⓔ

Ⓔ

Rugby
Ground

Aoyama-Itchōme Ⓢ

Ⓔ

AOYAMA-DŌRI

SEE 'OMOTESANDŌ' MAP FOR DETAIL

HARAJUKU

Gaienmae Ⓢ

Design Festa
Gallery

JINGŪMAE

Nogi-jinja
⛩

Laforet

Ⓐ
Ⓐ Ⓐ

Ⓢ Meiji-jingūmae

Omotesandō
Hills

Gallery MA

Aoyama
Reien

Ⓢ Nogizaka

Foreigners' Area

Ⓢ Omotesandō

OMOTESANDŌ-DŌRI

AOYAMA

National Art
Center, Tokyo

Nezu Museum

Okamoto Tarō
Memorial Museum

Ⓔ

Blue Note

Ⓔ
Ⓔ

Mori Art
Museum

Red Shoes

SHUTO EXPRESSWAY 3

SHUTO EXPRESSWAY 3

Konnō
Hachimangū
⛩

NISHI-AZABU

10

FESTIVALS AT MEIJI-JINGŪ

The most popular of the many festivals held at Meiji-jingū is **Hatsu-mōde** (literally, "first shrine visit of the year"), held on January 1 and attracting three million visitors – traffic lights are set up within the shrine grounds to control the crowds on the day.

On **Seijin-no-hi** (Adults' Day), the second Monday in January, 20-year-olds attend the shrine to celebrate their coming of age and to seek blessings from the gods; the women often dress in elaborate long-sleeved kimono, with fur stoles wrapped around their necks, while Meiji-jingū's gravel approach is lined with ice sculptures and there's a colourful display of traditional *momoteshiki* archery by costumed archers.

From April 29 to May 3 and November 1 to 3, **bugaku** (court music and dances) are performed on a stage erected in the shrine's main courtyard, while **Shichi-go-san-no-hi** (Seven-Five-Three Day), on November 15, provides an opportunity to see children of these ages dressed in mini-kimono.

Shadowing the course of the old Shibuya river (now built over), it provides a far more pleasant walking route to Shibuya than the busy main roads.

Meiji-jingū

明治神宮 • Daily sunrise–sunset • Free • ⓦ meijijingu.or.jp

Covering parts of both Aoyama and Harajuku are the grounds of **Meiji-jingū**, Tokyo's premier Shinto shrine, a memorial to Emperor Meiji and his empress Shōken. Together with the neighbouring shrines to General Nogi and Admiral Tōgō, Meiji-jingū was created as a symbol of imperial power and Japanese racial superiority. Rebuilt in 1958 after being destroyed during World War II, the shrine is the focus of several annual **festivals** (see page 118). Apart from the festivals, Meiji-jingū is best visited midweek, when its calm serenity can be appreciated without the crowds.

The **Inner Garden**, beside Harajuku station, includes the emperor's shrine, the empress's iris gardens, the Treasure House and extensive wooded grounds. The less important **Outer Garden** (see page 122), 1km east, south of Sendagaya and Shinanomachi stations, contains the Meiji Memorial Picture Gallery and several sporting arenas.

Inner Garden

御苑 • Daily sunrise–sunset • Free • Harajuku or Meiji-jingumae stations

The best approach to the **Inner Garden** is through the southern gate next to Jingū-bashi, the bridge that crosses over from Harajuku's toytown-like station, complete with mock-Tudor clock tower. From the gateway, a wide gravel path runs through densely forested grounds to the 12m-high **Ō-torii**, the largest Myōjin-style gate in Japan, made from 1500-year-old Taiwanese cypress pine trees.

Signed paths make it simple to push on a little further to the picturesque **Jingū Naien** (see below). From here, the gravel path turns right and passes through a second wooden *torii*, **Kita-mon** (north gate), leading to the impressive **Honden** (central hall). With their Japanese cypress wood and green copper roofs, the Honden and its surrounding buildings are a fine example of how Shinto architecture can blend seamlessly with nature. There are exits from the courtyard in front of the central hall; alternatively, follow either of the paths northwards through the woods to arrive at pleasant grassy slopes and a pond.

Jingū Naien

神宮内苑 • Daily 8.30am–5pm • ¥500

To the left of the Ō-torii is one entrance to the **Jingū Naien**, a traditional garden said to have been designed by the Emperor Meiji for his wife; if this entrance is closed then use the one a further ten minutes up the path. The garden is at its most beautiful in June, when over one hundred varieties of **iris** pepper the greenery with their purple and white blooms.

Yoyogi-kōen

代々木公園 • Daily 24hr • Free • Tandem bike rental: daily (except Mon) 9am–4.30pm; ¥210 for first hour, then ¥100 for each 30min • Harajuku, Yoyogi-kōen or Meiji-jingumae stations

Tokyo's largest park, **Yoyogi-kōen**, is a favourite spot for joggers and bonneted groups of kindergarten kids with their minders. Once an imperial army training ground, the park was dubbed "Washington Heights" after World War II, when it housed US military personnel. In 1964 the land was given over to the Olympic athletes' village, after which it became Yoyogi-kōen. Two of the stadia, built for those Olympics and also used to host events in the 2020 Olympics (see page 123), remain the area's most famous architectural features: the boat-shaped steel suspension roof of Tange Kenzō's **Yoyogi National Gymnasium** was a structural engineering marvel at the time; the smaller stadium, in the shape of a giant swirling seashell, is used for basketball.

10

Ōta Memorial Museum of Art

太田記念美術館, Ōta Kinen Bijutsukan • 1-10-10 Jingūmae, Shibuya-ku • Daily (except Mon) 10.30am–5.30pm • Usually ¥700 for regular exhibitions, ¥1000 for special exhibitions • ☎ 03 3403 0880, ⓦ ukiyoe-ota-muse.jp • Harajuku or Meiji-jingumae stations

Just off Omotesandō, behind the trendy boutique complex **Laforet**, is the excellent **Ōta Memorial Museum of Art**. Put on slippers to wander the small galleries on two levels, which feature *ukiyo-e* paintings and prints from the private collection of the late

OMOTESANDŌ

■ **DRINKING AND NIGHTLIFE**
BARS
Commune 2nd — 2
Montoak — 1

● **EATING**
CAFÉS
Crisscross — 13
Koffee Mameya — 3
La Fée Délice — 8
Streamer Coffee Company — 12
Tokyo Snake Center — 5
RESTAURANTS
Bepokah — 1
Commune 2nd — 9
Harajuku Gyōzaro — 7
Maisen — 4
Sakuratei — 2
Two Rooms — 11
TEAROOMS
Aoyama Flower Market — 10
The Alley Lujiaoxiang — 6

● **SHOPPING**
6% Dokidoki — 6
Bapexclusive — 19
Billionaire Boys Club — 3
Chicago — 5
Comme des Garçons — 16
Gallery Kawano — 12
Hakusan — 23
Hysterics — 18
Issey Miyake — 15
Kiddyland — 9
Kura Chika Yoshida — 14
Laforet — 4
Musubi — 1
Omotesando Hills — 10
Onitsuka Tiger — 7
Oriental Bazaar — 11
Prada — 17
Ragtag — 13
Solakzade — 8
Tsumori Chisato — 20
UnderCover — 21
United Arrows — 2
Yohji Yamamoto — 22

■ **ACCOMMODATION**
Caravan Tokyo — 1
Trunk — 2

Ōta Seizō, an insurance tycoon. The art displayed comes from a collection of twelve thousand pieces, including masterpieces by Utamaro, Hokusai and Hiroshige.

Design Festa Gallery

デザイン・フェスタ・ギャラリー・3-20-18 Jingūmae, Shibuya-ku • Daily 11am–8pm • Free • ☎ 03 3479 1442, Ⓦ designfesta.com • Harajuku or Meiji-jingumae stations

An anything-goes arts space sprouting out of Harajuku's backstreets, the **Design Festa Gallery** is an offshoot of the Design Festa, Japan's biggest art and design event (see page 26). Behind the day-glo paintings, graffiti, sculptures and red scaffolding swarming over the building's front like some alien metal creeper, the interior features eclectic displays ranging from quirky sculpture to video installations – even the toilet is plastered from floor to ceiling with artwork. Many spaces are rented by the week – or even the day – and they are often presided over by the artists themselves.

Omotesandō Hills

4-12-10 Jingūmae, Shibuya-ku • Meiji-jingūmae or Omotesandō stations

The Andō Tadao-designed **Omotesandō Hills** is a glitzy complex of upmarket designer shops, restaurants and residences. At the southeastern corner Andō re-created part of the Dojunkai Aoyama Apartments, as an homage to the much-loved housing block that once stood on the site. In their later years, the crumbling apartments were occupied by artists and small boutiques, and many felt that something of the district's bohemian spirit had been lost when they were destroyed to make way for Omotesandō Hills.

Aoyama

青山

Harajuku's chaotic creativity finally gives way to Aoyama's sleek sophistication, as Omotesandō crosses Aoyama-dōri and narrows to a two-lane street lined with the boutiques of many of Japan's top designers (see page 119). The most striking building of all is the glass bubble designed by Herzog & de Meuron for Prada (see page 205), though others come close, notably the main shrine to Issey Miyake (see page 205).

Okamoto Tarō Memorial Museum

岡本太郎記念館, Okamoto Tarō Kinenkan • 6-1-19 Minami-aoyama, Minato-ku • Daily (except Tues) 10am–6pm • ¥620 • Ⓦ taro-okamoto.or.jp • Omotesandō station

The quirky **Okamoto Tarō Memorial Museum** once functioned as the studio of the avant-garde artist (see page 122); it now houses examples of his intriguing, often whimsical work, as well as a pleasant café. If this has whetted your appetite, you might consider heading to the far larger Okamoto Tarō Museum of Art in Kawasaki, between Tokyo and Yokohama.

Nezu Museum

根津美術館 • 6-5-1 Minami-aoyama, Minato-ku • Daily except Mon 10am–5pm • ¥1100 • ☎ 03 3400 2536, Ⓦ www.nezu-muse.or.jp • Omotesandō or Nogizaka stations

The prestigious **Nezu Museum** sits at the far eastern end of Omotesandō, in an elegant building designed by Kengo Kuma (see page 270). The museum houses a classy collection of Oriental treasures, including the celebrated *Irises* screens, traditionally

displayed for a month from the end of each April – expect big crowds for this popular exhibition. The museum's best feature, enjoyable any time of year and fully justifying the entrance fee, is its extensive garden, which slopes gently away around an ornamental pond. Dotted through it are several traditional teahouses, and mossy stone and bronze sculptures.

Aoyama Reien

10

青山霊園 • 2-32-2 Minami-aoyama, Minato-ku • Aoyama-itchōme, Gaienmae or Nogizaka stations

Tokyo's most important graveyard is officially entitled **Aoyama Reien**, but most know it as **Aoyama Bochi**. Everyone who was anyone is buried here, and the graves, many decorated with elaborate calligraphy, are interesting to browse – hunt around and you may find the grave of Ueno Hidesaburō, the scientist who found posthumous fame through his faithful hound, Hachikō (see page 125). Easier to spot is the section where foreigners are buried: their tombstones provide a history of early *gaijin* involvement in Japan. One quirk of this cemetery is that locals enjoy partying here during the *hanami* season, under the candyfloss bunches of pink cherry blossoms.

Meiji-jingū Outer Garden

外苑, Gaien • ⓦ www.meijijingugaien.jp • Shinanomachi, Aoyama-itchōme or Kokuritsu-kyōgijō stations

A pretty, ginkgo-tree-lined approach road heads to the south entrance of the **Outer Garden** – a dazzling, golden sight in the autumn. You'll spy the the wedding hall complex **Meiji Kinenkan** to your right, and several sporting stadiums and grounds on your left, including one of Japan's most famous sporting arenas, the **National Stadium**, which was rebuilt for the 2020 Olympic Games (see page 123).

Meiji Memorial Picture Gallery

聖徳記念絵画館, Seitoku Kinen Kaigakan • 1-1 Kasumigaokamachi, Shinjuku-ku • Daily 9am–5pm • ¥500

At the northern end of the Outer Garden's ginkgo-lined entrance road is the **Meiji Memorial Picture Gallery**, built in a similar Western style to the National Diet Building (see page 97) with a marble-clad entrance hall that soars up to a central dome. Inside are forty paintings depicting the life story of Emperor Meiji, of interest more for their scenes of Japan emerging from its feudal past than for their artistic merits.

Tokyo Metropolitan Gymnasium

ⓦ www.tef.or.jp

On the western side of the National Stadium – and best viewed from outside Sendagaya station – is the Outer Garden's most striking feature, the **Tokyo Metropolitan Gymnasium**, designed by Pritzker Prize-winning architect Maki Fumihiko. At first the building looks like a giant spacecraft, though on closer examination it becomes obvious that the inspiration is a traditional samurai helmet. The corrugated stainless-steel-roofed building houses the main arena, while to the right, crowned with a glass pyramid roof,

---

ART IS AN EXPLOSION

One of Japan's most famous post-World War II artists, **Okamoto Tarō** (1911–96) was born in Kawasaki and worked for part of his career in Aoyama, where his old studio is now a museum – **Aoyama Reien** (see page 120). His *Tower of the Sun* sculpture was the symbol of Ōsaka's Expo in 1970. In Tokyo, Okamoto's bizarre, cartoon-like sculptures can be seen next to the Toshiba Building in Ginza

Together with his enormous mural *Myth of Tomorrow* in Shibuya station (see page 123), his sculptures neatly encapsulate the artist's dictum that "art is an explosion".

THE 2020 OLYMPICS

At the time of writing, Tokyo was gearing up to host the **2020 Olympic and Paralympic Games** (Ⓦtokyo2020.jp), becoming the first Asian city to host the Games twice. The opening ceremony is set for 24 July, 2020, at the **National Stadium** in Meiji-jingū Outer Garden. The original stadium, built for the 1964 Olympics, was demolished in 2015 as part of preparations for the Games, and even clockwork-efficient Japan failed to escape the Olympic curses of funding and planning. In late 2012, it was announced that a design by the late British-Iraqi architect **Zaha Hadid** had been selected by the Sport Council, but her plans drew a raft of criticism, notably from Japanese architects ("turtle-like" and "rather vaginal" were among the most cutting descriptions), and city politicians worried about the cost. Said costs started to spiral, with Hadid's team blaming a lack of competition among contractors; by the time her plans were finally ditched in 2015, the estimates had risen to ¥252 billion (£1.82bn/$2.43bn). A cheaper, more visually pleasing design by **Kengo Kuma** (see page 270) was selected as the alternative, and chosen to host athletics events and the football final.

Mercifully, two of Tokyo's most iconic venues changed little for the 2020 Games: the superlative **Tokyo Metropolitan Gymnasium** (see page 122) and the **Yoyogi National Gymnasium** (see page 119), each a design classic built for the 1964 event, and selected to host the table tennis and handball. Other notable venues include the **Budōkan** (see page 45) for judo and karate; the **Tokyo International Forum** (see page 49) for the weightlifting; and the **National Sumo Stadium** (see page 81), temporarily switching focus from sumo slaps to boxers' punches.

are public swimming pools and a subterranean gym. Unlike the National Stadium, this venue was not changed too greatly for the 2020 Olympic Games (see page 123).

Shibuya

渋谷

As a mind-blowing introduction to contemporary Tokyo, it's hard to beat **Shibuya**, birthplace of a million-and-one consumer crazes, and best visited at night when the neon signs of restaurants, bars and cinemas battle it out with five-storey TV screens for the attention of passers-by. This blaze of lights doesn't get much brighter than around the plaza on the northwest side of Shibuya station, where you'll also find one of the most famous **pedestrian crossings** in the world outside London's Abbey Road – its stock only rose further following its depiction in the film *Lost in Translation*. One perch from which to view the crowds of people swarming across is the bridge corridor linking the JR station with Shibuya Mark City complex. This space has been put to excellent use as the gallery for Okamoto Tarō's fourteen-panel painting **Myth of Tomorrow** (*Asu-no-shinwa*), a 30m-long mural depicting the moment the atomic bomb exploded in Hiroshima. Originally created in 1969 for a luxury hotel in Mexico, then lost for decades, this powerful work seldom seems to stop the rushing commuters in their tracks.

East of Shibuya station you'll spy the tall **Shibuya Hikarie** building, while immediately west of the crossing, the **109 Building** stands at the apex of Bunkamura-dōri and Dōgenzaka, the latter leading up to **Dōgenzaka** (道玄坂), one of Tokyo's most famous love-hotel districts. This area is named after Owada Dōgen, a thirteenth-century highwayman who robbed travellers on their way through the then-isolated valley. Running parallel to the north of Bunkamura-dōri is the pedestrianized **Centre Gai** (セ ンター街), always packed with trend-obsessed Tokyoites gathering to create or spot the latest look.

Shibuya Hikarie building

渋谷ヒカリエ・2-21-1 Shibuya, Shibuya-ku・Creative Space 8 daily 11am–8pm・Ⓦ hikarie.jp・Shibuya station

A 34-storey tower just east of Shibuya station, **Shibuya Hikarie** is one of the area's more inventive recent constructions. Designed like a stack of mismatching building blocks, this complex contains offices, shops, restaurants and various cultural facilities, including a 2000-seat theatre whose lobby provides a sweeping view of the skyline. The prime attraction is **Creative Space 8** on the eighth floor, a quirky mix of gallery and shops.

10 Konnō Hachimangū

金王八幡宮 • 3-5-12 Shibuya, Shibuya-ku • Daily 24hr; buildings open 6am–5pm; ceremony daily 9am • Free • Shibuya station

One of the few bona fide sights in the Shibuya station area, the modest **Konnō Hachimangū** is of major importance. First established in 1092, though rebuilt many times since, the shrine was used as a place of worship by the Shibuya clan, who gave the area its present name. Their castle was once adjacent to the shrine, though only a couple of pieces of fortress stone are preserved on the site. Nevertheless, it's a pleasant escape from the noise of modern-day Shibuya; pop by for the morning ceremonies, if possible.

Toguri Museum of Art

戸栗美術館, Toguri Bijutsukan • 1-11-3 Shōto, Shibuya-ku • Tues–Sun 10am–5pm; English-language tours 2pm • ¥1000 including tour; check website for discount admission coupons • ☎ 03 3465 0070, ⓦ www.toguri-museum.or.jp • Shibuya station

A little to the west of central Shibuya, the superb **Toguri Museum of Art** displays Edo-era and Chinese Ming-dynasty (1368–1644) ceramics. The small but exquisitely

HACHIKŌ

A statue outside Shibuya station marks the waiting spot of **Hachikō** (1923–35), an Akita dog who would come to greet his master every day as he returned home from work – a practice that continued for almost a decade after the professor's death, with the dog arriving on time every day to greet the train. Locals were so touched by Hachikō's devotion that a **bronze statue** was cast of the dog. During World War II, the original Hachikō statue was melted down for weapons, but a replacement was reinstated beside the station in 1948 – it remains one of Tokyo's most famous rendezvous spots. You can see the real Hachikō in the National Science Museum, where he lives on in stuffed form (see page 68), and there's a memorial by his master's grave in Aoyama Cemetery (see page 122).

10

displayed exhibition, comprising selections from a collection of some 6000 pieces, is a must for those interested in pottery. Carefully positioned mirrors enable you to inspect the fine detail of work on the underside of displayed plates and bowls, and there's a pretty garden beside the lobby.

Japan Folk Crafts Museum

日本民芸館, Nihon Mingeikan • Tues–Sun 10am–5pm • ¥1100 • ☎ 03 3467 4527, ⓦ mingeikan.or.jp • Komaba-Tōdaimae station

Two stops down the Keiō Inokashira line from Shibuya station is the outstanding **Japan Folk Crafts Museum**. Set in a handsome stone-and-stucco building five minutes' walk northwest of the station, the museum is a must-see for Japanese-craft fans, with an excellent collection of pottery, textiles and lacquerware. The gift shop is a fine source of souvenirs, and an annual competition and sale of new works is held every December.

Opposite the museum stands a nineteenth-century **nagayamon** (long gate house), brought here from Tochigi-ken prefecture in northern Honshū by the museum's founder, Yanagi Soetsu, father of the famous designer Yanagi Sori; it's opened up for a couple of days each month (see website for details).

Shinjuku and the west

No Tokyo neighbourhood has as evocative a name as Shinjuku, the very mention of which will conjure images of buzzing neon, teeming masses and drunken debauchery to anybody with more than a superficial knowledge of the city. Only 4km due west of the leafy tranquillity of the Imperial Palace, Shinjuku has a long and illustrious history of pandering to the more basic of human desires. This action-packed district has it all, from the love hotels and hostess bars of Kabukichō to shop-till-you-drop department stores and dazzlingly designed skyscrapers. Throw in robot performances, two-hour all-you-can-drink specials, Tokyo's main gay bar stretch and teeming covered arcades, and you've still only just scratched the surface.

BEST OF SHINJUKU AND THE WEST

Shinjuku station Take in the mind-boggling madness at rush hour (see page 129)
Tokyo Metropolitan Government Building Catch a spectacular sunset from the observation decks (see page 129)
Omoide Yokochō Grab a pre-drink bite in crowded "Piss Alley" (see page 130)
Kabukichō Sneak a peek at the red lights and *yakuza* (see page 132)
Golden Gai Head for this cluster of minuscule bars (see page 133)
Shinjuku Gyoen Escape the area's neon insanity in a beautifully landscaped garden (see page 133)
Shimokitazawa Hang out with hipsters in this boho enclave (see page 134)
Suginami Animation Museum & Ghibli Museum Get a handle on anime culture (see pages 135 and 135)
Robot Restaurant Go goggle-eyed over a jaw-dropping performance (see page 194)
Shinjuku Nichōme See Japanese LGBTQ culture in full swing (see page 190)

11

Shinjuku is split in two by a thick band of train tracks. The western half, **Nishi-Shinjuku**, with its soaring towers, including the monumental **Tokyo Metropolitan Government Building**, is a showcase for contemporary architecture; the raunchier eastern side, **Higashi-Shinjuku**, is a nonstop red-light and shopping district – though it's also home to one of Tokyo's most attractive parks, **Shinjuku Gyoen**. As you head west from the station, the JR Chūō line will transport you to two must-see sights for anime fans: the **Suginami Animation Museum** and the **Ghibli Museum** at Mitaka. Also out this way is **Shimokitazawa**, once dubbed one of the world's coolest neighbourhoods by *Vogue*.

Brief history

The district takes its name from the "new lodgings" (*shin juku*) which were set up here in the seventeenth century for travellers en route to Edo. It eventually evolved into one of the city's six **licensed quarters**, catering mainly to the lower classes. By the late nineteenth century, Shinjuku – nicknamed "Tokyo's anus", due to the transportation of human waste through its streets to the countryside – had the most prostitutes of any area in the city.

A turning point came in 1885 when the opening of the railway encouraged people to move out of the city into the western suburbs. The commuters made Shinjuku the ideal location for the department stores which sprang up here during the early twentieth century. In the immediate postwar decades Shinjuku's seediness attracted a bohemian population of writers, students and radical intellectuals, who hung out in its jazz bars and coffee shops.

The area's first **skyscraper**, the 47-storey *Keiō Plaza Hotel*, opened in 1971 and was swiftly followed by several more earthquake-defying towers, while Tange Kenzō's **Tokyo Metropolitan Government Building** set the modernist seal on the area two decades later.

INFORMATION   SHINJUKU

Tourist information The excellent Tokyo Tourist Information Centre is on the ground floor of the Tokyo Metropolitan Government Building No. 1 (daily 9.30am– 6.30pm; ☎ 03 5321 3077).

Nishi-Shinjuku

西新宿

West of the station, **Nishi-Shinjuku** is dominated by skyscrapers; the biggest of these is the futuristic Tokyo Metropolitan Government Building complex, from which the city is administered. Several skyscrapers have free observation rooms on their upper floors,

MAKING SENSE OF SHINJUKU STATION

Shinjuku station is the busiest in the world, with an average of around 3.7 million people (more than the population of Uruguay) passing through its gates every single day. Many visitors to Tokyo erroneously assume that rail staff are employed to squeeze people onto crowded train carriages – in fact, this only happens at rush-hour in very few stations, but Shinjuku is certainly one of them. The station also features 36 platforms, and more than two hundred exits, so if you find yourself lost and a little bewildered, nobody would blame you – unless you happen to be in their way.

The station is, in fact, comprised of three overland terminals (the main **JR station**, plus the **Keiō** and **Odakyū** stations beside their respective department stores on the area's west side) and three connecting subway lines. There's also the separate **Seibu-Shinjuku station**, northeast of the JR station. The rivers of people constantly flowing along the many underground passages only add to the confusion. It's easy to get lost; if this happens, head immediately for street level and get your bearings from the skyscrapers to the west. If you're good with maps you will also be able to work out your location from the ones located next to most exits.

11

along with a wide selection of restaurants and bars with good views. Collectively, their impact is striking, mainly because their scale, coupled with the spaciousness of the surroundings, is so unusual for Tokyo – despite the recent boom of high-rise buildings across Asia, this remains predominantly a low-rise city.

Tokyo Metropolitan Government Building

東京都庁, Tōkyō Tochō • 2-8-1 Nishi-shinjuku, Shinjuku-ku; both observation rooms 45F • South observation room daily 9.30am–5.30pm; north observation room daily 9am–11pm; each observation room is closed a couple of days per month • Free; free tours Mon–Fri 10am–3pm • Tochōmae station

Some 13,000 city bureaucrats clock in each day at the Gotham City-like **Tokyo Metropolitan Government Building** (TMGB), a 400,000-square-metre complex designed by Tange Kenzō. The complex includes twin 48-storey towers, an adjacent tower block, the Metropolitan Assembly Hall (where the city's councillors meet) and a sweeping, statue-lined and colonnaded plaza. Kenzō's inspiration was Paris's Notre Dame, and there's certainly something of that cathedral's design in the shape of the twin towers. But the building is also unmistakeably Japanese, with the dense crisscross pattern of its glass and granite facade reminiscent of both traditional architecture and the circuitry of an enormous computer chip.

Free **tours** of the complex depart from the tourist office on the ground floor (see page 127). Both the towers have **observation rooms**: the southern one is quieter, more open and has a pleasant café, while the northern one is open later, and features a shopping area and overpriced restaurant. It's worth timing your visit for dusk, so you can see Shinjuku's multicoloured lights spark into action; alternatively, if you want a good view of the buildings themselves, try the lofty lobby level of the nearby Park Hyatt (see page 151).

Shinjuku Park Tower

新宿パークタワー • 3-7-1 Nishi-shinjuku, Shinjuku-ku • Tochōmae or Hatsudai stations; free shuttle bus from opposite Odakyū department store to south side of tower

On the south side of Shinjuku Chūō-kōen, a rather dull park, lies **Shinjuku Park Tower**, another building that bears Kenzō's confident modernist signature. Comprising three linked towers, all topped with glass pyramids, the style credentials of this complex are vouched for by the presence of the luxurious *Park Hyatt* hotel, which occupies the building's loftiest floors (see page 151).

NTT Intercommunication Centre

NTT インターコミュニケーションセンター • 3-20-2 Nishi-Shinjuku, Shinjuku-ku • Tues–Sun 11am–6pm • Free, although usually ¥500 for special exhibitions • ☎ 03 5353 0900, ⓦ www.ntticc.or.jp • Hatsudai station

A ten-minute walk west of the Shinjuku Park Tower is **Tokyo Opera City** (東京オペラシティ) with 54 floors of offices, shops, restaurants and a major concert hall (see page 195). On the fourth floor you'll find the invariably fascinating **NTT Intercommunication Centre** (better known as the ICC), an innovative interactive exhibition space that seeks to encourage a dialogue between technology and the arts: past displays of high-tech art have included a soundproof room where you listen to your own heartbeat, and light-sensitive robots you can control with your brain waves. The free regular exhibitions change annually; the special exhibitions usually rotate monthly. On your way up, check out the Antony Gormley-designed statue, standing alone on the second floor.

Seiji Tōgō Memorial Sompo Japan Museum of Art

損保ジャパン東郷青児美術館, Sompo Japan Tōgō Seiji Bijutsukan • 42F Sompo Japan Building, 1-26-1 Nishi-Shinjuku, Shinjuku-ku • Tues–Sun 10am–6pm • Fee varies by exhibition • ⓦ sjnk-museum.org • Shinjuku, Nishi-Shinjuku or Shinjuku-nishiguchi stations

On the 42nd floor of the Sompo Japan Building you'll find the **Seiji Tōgō Memorial Sompo Japan Museum of Art**, home to one in the series of *Sunflowers* paintings by Vincent van Gogh, flanked by other top-drawer Impressionist pieces by Cézanne and Gauguin. The *Sunflowers* canvas, dating from 1888, was bought for the astronomical sum of ¥5 billion (a shade under $40m) during the height of Japan's "bubble economy" years. More interesting and unusual is the collection of over two hundred pieces by Tōgō Seiji, a popular Japanese artist best known for his soft, contoured depictions of women.

The dazzling 50-storey crosshatched structure next to the Sompo Japan Building is known as **Mode Gakuen Cocoon Tower**, home to a fashion and computer studies college. Sadly, none of the cafés or restaurants in the lower levels give any real feel for the building's striking design.

Omoide Yokochō

思い出横丁

Squashed up against the train tracks running north from the Odakyū department store is **Omoide Yokochō**, commonly known as Memories Alley. Lit by hundreds of *akachochin* (red lanterns), it's also known as Shomben Yokochō (しょんべん横丁, Piss Alley), a reference to the time when patrons of the area's many cramped *yakitori* joints and bars relieved themselves in the street, for want of other facilities. Don't be put off: the alley remains a cheap and atmospheric place to eat and drink (and there are toilets these days). Enjoy it while you can, too, as there's regular talk of redeveloping the area. A pedestrian tunnel at the southern end of the alleys, just to the right of the cheap clothes outlets, provides a short cut to the east side of Shinjuku station.

Higashi-Shinjuku

東新宿

Some days it seems as if all of Tokyo is waiting at Shinjuku's favourite meeting spot, beneath the huge TV screen on the **Studio Alta** building on the east side of the JR station. This area and neighbouring Kabukichō is best visited in the evening when the neon sparks into action and legions of Tokyoites descend to shop and party.

11

THE BIG BUSINESS OF PACHINKO

Japan's economy may have been going through tough times for a couple of decades, but one industry that continues to rake it in – to the tune of ¥23 trillion (£155bn/$205bn) a year – is **pachinko**. This pinball gambling game is one of Japan's top pastimes, and Tokyo has thousands of pachinko parlours, plenty of them in Shinjuku. They're easy to spot since they look like mini Las Vegas casinos on steroids, all flashing lights and big neon signs. Inside, the atmosphere is no less in-your-face, and the inevitable smoke considerably more so. The noise of thousands of steel balls clattering through the upright electronic bagatelles is deafening, yet rows of players sit mesmerized as they control the speed with which balls fall through the machine – though the game requires only limited skill and a fair amount of luck.

The aim is to make the balls drop into the right holes so that more balls can be won. These are traded in for tokens, or **prizes** such as cigarette lighters and calculators; although it's illegal for the parlours to pay out cash, there's always a cubby-hole close by where prizes can be exchanged for money, a charade that the authorities have long turned a blind eye to. For all the noise, pachinko is a mind-numbingly tedious pastime; the most fun visitors can have is to simply open the parlour doors and allow the exhilarating cascade of noise and smoke to pour out into the street. If you'd like to indulge in the mechanized mayhem yourself, the initial cost can be as little as ¥100 for 25 ball bearings – just remember to take your earplugs.

Kabukichō

歌舞伎町

The lively red-light district of **Kabukichō** was named after a never-built kabuki theatre that was planned for the area in the aftermath of World War II. Although there have been plans for redevelopment, the myriad host and hostess bars, girly shows, sex venues and love hotels are well entrenched. For casual strollers it's all pretty safe, thanks to street security cameras. Take a wander in the grid of streets around Hanamichi-dōri and you can't miss the peacock-preening young Japanese male touts who hook women into the male host bars, and the notably less primped gents who do likewise for hostess bars – the *yakuza* who run the show are there, too, though generally keeping a much lower profile.

Samurai Museum

サムライミュージアム • 2-25-6 Kabukichō, Shinjuku-ku • Daily 10.30am–9pm • ¥1900, plus ¥500 to dress up in samurai clothing • Ⓦ samuraimuseum.jp • Shinjuku or Seibu-Shinjuku stations

The **Samurai Museum** is a funky new addition to the Shinjuku area, and one likely to please a different type of visitor to the more refined displays on the other side of the tracks at the Sword Museum (see below). Here you can check out displays of samurai costumes and helmets, and if you're willing to shell out more on top of the already-hefty ticket price you can don similar togs yourself. If you time it right, there are four daily "shows" in which a genuine samurai actor comes by to show off his sword-wielding prowess.

Hanazono-jinja

花園神社 • 5-17-3 Shinjuku, Shinjuku-ku • 24hr • Free • Shinjuku, Seibu-shinjuku, Higashi-shinjuku or Shinjuku-sanchōme stations

Set in grounds studded with vermillion *torii*, the attractive **Hanazono-jinja** predates the founding of Edo by the Tokugawa, but the current granite buildings are modern re-creations – the shrine was originally sited where the department store Isetan now is. At night spotlights give the shrine a special ambience and every Sunday there's a flea market in its grounds (see page 201).

Golden Gai
ゴールデン街

Just west of the Hanazono-jinja is **Golden Gai**, one of Tokyo's most atmospheric (and seedy) bar quarters. Since just after World War II, intellectuals and artists have rubbed shoulders with Kabukichō's demimonde in the tiny bars here. For decades this hugely atmospheric warren of around 150 drinking dens was teetering on the brink of oblivion, the cinderblock buildings under threat from both property developers and from their own shoddy construction. However, Golden Gai has since undergone a mini-renaissance, with a younger generation of bar masters and mistresses taking over – or at least presiding over – some of the shoebox establishments. Many bars continue to welcome regulars only (and charge exorbitant prices to newcomers), but *gaijin* visitors no longer risk being fleeced rotten, since most places now post their table and drink charges outside the door (see page 184 for a few recommendations).

Shinjuku Gyoen

新宿御苑 • 11 Naitomachi, Shinjuku-ku • **Garden** Tues–Sun 9am–4.30pm, last entry 4pm; villa second & fourth Sat of month 10am–3pm • ¥500 • **Rakū-tei** Tues–Sun 10am–4pm • Tea ¥700 • Main entrance Shinjuku-gyoenmae station; west gate Sendagaya station

The largest garden in Tokyo, and arguably the most beautiful, is **Shinjuku Gyoen**. Its grounds, which once held the mansion of Lord Naitō, the *daimyō* of Tsuruga on the Sea of Japan coast, became the property of the Imperial Household in 1868, and the garden was opened to the public after World War II.

Apart from spaciousness, the garden's most notable feature is the variety of design. The southern half is traditionally Japanese, with winding paths, stone lanterns, artificial hills and islands in ponds linked by zigzag bridges, and is home to *Rakū-tei*, a pleasant **teahouse**. At the northern end are formal, French-style gardens, with neat rows of tall birch trees and hedge-lined flowerbeds. Clipped, broad lawns dominate the middle of the grounds, modelled on English landscape design. On the eastern flank, next to the large greenhouse, there's a replica of an imperial wooden **villa** from 1869. In spring, the garden bursts with pink and white cherry blossoms, while in early November kaleidoscopic chrysanthemum displays and golden autumn leaves are the main attractions.

There are several **cafés** within the garden where you can grab a reasonable lunch for around ¥1000, but it's much nicer to bring a picnic and relax in the tranquil surroundings.

11

Western Tokyo

Tokyo sprawls for quite some way west of Shinjuku, and there are some very fashionable neighbourhoods dotted around this densely populated but relatively low-level jigsaw of suburbs. By far the most interesting for shorter-term visitors to Japan is **Shimokitazawa**, Tokyo's own little hipster paradise. Heading even further out, but still easily accessible by train, the **Suginami** area has long been associated with the animation industry; it's the location for several production houses, and home to many key artists; but of more interest to the traveller is the immensely popular **Ghibli Museum**. Even further out, there's another great draw at the **Edo-Tokyo Open Air Architectural Museum**, which inspired at least one anime "set".

Shimokitazawa

下北沢 · Shimokitazawa station, 4 stops west of Shibuya on the Keio-Inokashira line, or 6 stops southwest of Shinjuku on the Odakyū line

Small, cute and quirky, **Shimokitazawa** – known as **Shimokita** for short – is a prime draw for young, bohemian sorts, and a nice escape from "regular" Tokyo; gone are the high-rise blocks and incessant noise of Shinjuku, just 5km to the east, replaced here with narrow, relatively traffic-free lanes, and a general air of calm. The charms of Shimokita are essentially the same as most hipster areas around the world: vintage clothing stores, record shops, galleries, live music bars, and independent cafés serving flat whites to people writing blogs on their Macs. However, here they come overlaid with a double-thick slice of Japan (both the regular and the quirky), and the resultant cocktail is quite potent. There's not all that much in the way of sights here, bar a couple of tucked-away shrines, but you'll find plenty of shops, cafés and bars (see map page 134) at which to while away the time.

Kōenji

高円寺 · Kōenji station, 4 stops west of Shinjuku on the JR line

While westerners tend to go for Shimokitazawa, the local lists that matter usually rank **Kōenji**, just west of Shinjuku, as Tokyo's trendiest neighbourhood. On arrival, it may be a little hard to see why, but as you walk around you'll most likely see a fair few locals sporting some rather out-there attire, from retro Sixties to vintage 1920s. Like Shimokitazawa, the live music scene is pretty good, and there are vintage clothing stores absolutely everywhere – all in all, it's not a bad little stop on your way back from the museums out west.

SHIMOKITAZAWA

0   100
metres

N

Bear Pond

KITAZAWA

CHAZAWA-DORI

ODAKYU ODAWARA LINE

Shimokitazawa Station

CHAZAWA-DORI

Shelter

KEIO INOKASHIRA LINE

● **SHOPPING**
Disk Union   2
New York Joe   1

● **EATING**
CAFÉ
Ballon d'Essai   1
RESTAURANT
Nanban-tei   2

█ **DRINKING AND NIGHTLIFE**
BAR
Shisha   1

Suginami Animation Museum

杉並アニメーションミュージアム・3-29-5 Kamiogi, Suginami-ku・Daily (except Mon) 10am–6pm・Free・Ⓦ sam.or.jp・20min walk or 5min bus ride (platform 0 or 1; ¥220) from Ogikubo station on the JR lines or Marunouchi subway line

Astroboy, Gundam and many other anime characters are all present and correct at the well-organized **Suginami Animation Museum**, situated atop a retro-looking function hall. Colourful displays trace the development of animation in Japan, from the simple black-and-white 1917 feature *Genkanban-no-maki* (The Gatekeepers) to digital escapades such as *Blood: The Last Vampire*. Videos with English subtitles explain how anime are made, while interactive computer games allow you to create your own animations. You can watch anime screenings in the small theatre, and there's also a library packed with manga and DVDs (some with English subtitles).

Ghibli Museum

ジブリ美術館, Jiburi Bijutsukan・1-1-83 Shimorenjaku, Mitaka-ku・Daily except Tues 10am–6pm・¥1000; advance bookings only (museum can be booked out for weeks at a time); 2400 tickets per day are available (see website for details)・☎ 0570 055777, Ⓦ ghibli-museum.jp・Short walk (follow signs) or bus ride (¥210) from south exit of Mitaka station, on JR Chūō line; or walkable from Kichijōji station, also on JR Chūō line

A few stops west of the Suginami Animation Museum is the utterly beguiling **Ghibli Museum**, one of Tokyo's top draws for international visitors – and an essential one for those interested in anime. It's very popular, so reserve tickets well ahead of time. Though it needs little introduction, the Ghibli animation studio was responsible for blockbuster movies including *My Neighbour Totoro*, *Princess Mononoke* and the Oscar-winning *Spirited Away*. Visiting the museum is a little like climbing inside the mind of famed Ghibli director Hayao Miyazaki: walls are plastered with initial sketches of the characters that would eventually garner worldwide fame; a giant clock is bisected by a winding staircase; and – of course – there's the grinning cat-bus from *Totoro*. There's also a small movie theatre where original short animated features, exclusive to the museum, are screened. All in all, it's a guaranteed fun day out for all, that will probably have you scurrying to watch the films later.

Ghibli Museum sits inside pretty **Inokashira Park** (井の頭公園, Inokashira Kōen); from Kichijoji station, it's a pleasant fifteen-minute stroll through the park's tree-shaded walks to the museum, past a pleasant carp-filled lake and a small zoo. A favourite haunt of courting couples, the park is mobbed by everyone during *hanami* season, when it explodes in a profusion of pink blossoms.

Edo-Tokyo Open Air Architectural Museum

江戸東京たてもの園, Edo-Tōkyō Tatemono-en・3-7-8 Sakura-chō, Koganei・Daily (except Mon): April–Sept 9.30am–5.30pm; Oct–March 9.30am–4.30pm・¥400・Ⓦ tatemonoen.jp・5min bus ride (¥200) from Musashi-Koganei station, on JR Chūō line

A kind of retirement home for old Japanese buildings, the **Edo-Tokyo Open Air Architectural Museum** was the inspiration for the abandoned theme park in Studio Ghibli's *Spirited Away*. Some 35 buildings of varying degrees of interest are gathered within the parkland of Koganei-kōen, plus an exhibition hall with archeological artefacts and folk crafts.

On the west side of the sprawling complex, check out the grand **Mitsue Residence**, an 1852 mansion moved from Kyoto and furnished with painted screens, lacquered shrines and chandeliers. There are also several thatched farmhouses. On the east side, there's a reconstructed **Shitamachi** street (see page 77), including a tailor's shop and stationer's, plus kitchenware and flower stores. The **public bathhouse** here is a veritable palace of ablutions, with magnificent Chinese-style gables and a lakeside view of Fuji painted on the tiled wall inside. Also look out for the **Uemura-tei**, a 1927 shophouse, its copper cladding pocked by shrapnel from World War II bombings.

SHOHEI OTANI AT TOKYO DOME, THE CITY'S MAJOR BASEBALL VENUE

Ikebukuro and the north

Little more than marshland until the dawn of the twentieth century, Ikebukuro is a real product of the train age; eight lines now connect the area with central Tokyo and the low-cost dormitory suburbs to the north and east, meaning that its primary function is as a sort of commuter gateway to the city. It's not as trendy or hip as Shinjuku or Shibuya, and the area is also something of a byword for Tokyo sleaze, with its glut of "soaplands" (a particularly peculiar breed of brothels). However, stick around long enough and you'll find some of the city's best noodles, classic gardens to stroll in, a handful of butler cafés (see page 173) and some truly fascinating pieces of architecture. All in all, Ikebukuro and its environs provide a good window in which to see Tokyo simply being Tokyo.

BEST OF IKEBUKURO AND THE NORTH

Ding-ding train Ride Tokyo's last remaining tramline (see page 141)
St Mary's Cathedral Check out the stunning interior of this retro-futurist cathedral (see page 141)
Gardens Take it easy at Rikugi-en, Kyū Furukawa or Koishikawa-Kōrakuen (see page 145)
Tokyo Dome Get a handle on the Japanese baseball obsession (see page 143)
Spa LaQua Dip into the exquisite onsen waters (see page 143)
Mutekiya Join the queues for tasty ramen (see page 172)
Assist Wig Try on a colourful wig or two (see page 206)

Garden lovers should head to **Komagome** to visit **Rikugi-en**, one of the city's most attractive Edo-period gardens, as well as the nearby and equally lovely **Kyū Furukawa Gardens**, combining Western and Japanese styles of horticulture. Follow this with a stop in **Mejirodai** for **Chinzan-so**, a classic garden; **Suidōbashi**, home to the Tokyo Dome and yet more gardens; and **Kagurazaka**, a trendy, Frenchified area still home to a clutch of geisha.

Ikebukuro

池袋

Around 2.5 million passengers pass through **Ikebukuro** station every day – worldwide it's third only to Shinjuku (see page 127) and Shibuya in numbers – and its warren of connecting passages, shopping arcades and countless exits is notoriously difficult to negotiate; in addition, the place seems to have been designed in order to make people crash into each other at right angles.

Ikebukuro has had distinct east and west sides longer than American hip-hop. Two of the largest department stores in Japan, Tōbu and Seibu, square off against each other from opposite sides of the tracks; weirdly, "Tōbu" means east but is located west of the tracks, while "Seibu" means west, yet lies to the east. It's the western area, **Nishi-Ikebukuro**, which is the more interesting to explore; it's also surprisingly nice to stroll around, particularly the wedge of streets spreading out towards the attractive **Rikkyō University** campus, which boasts a plethora of bars, restaurants and good, old-fashioned sleaze. Over on the east side of Ikebukuro station is **Higashi-Ikebukuro**, the main shopping area, which has even more going on – all the way to Sunshine City, a complex featuring the area's tallest tower. Pressing on east again, you can hop on Tokyo's last **tramway**, the Toden-Arakawa Line (see page 141).

Myonichi-kan

明日館 • 2-31-3 Nishi-Ikebukuro, Toshima-ku • Tues–Sun 10am–4pm, closed during functions • ¥400, or ¥600 including coffee or Japanese tea and sweets • ☎ 03 3971 7535, ⊕ jiyu.jp • Ikebukuro station

Fans of the American architect Frank Lloyd Wright should track down one of his lesser-known but still very distinctive buildings, the **Myonichi-kan**, or "House of Tomorrow". While working on the *Imperial Hotel* (see page 147), Wright and his assistant Endo Arata also designed this complex to house the Jiyū Gakuen school. The geometric windows and low-slung roofs are trademark Wright features, but the buildings are best appreciated from inside, where you get the full effect of the clean, bold lines, echoed in the hexagonal chairs, light fittings and other original furnishings.

Rikkyō University

立教大学 • Nishi-Ikebukuro, Toshima-ku • Ikebukuro station

12

IKEBUKURO AND THE NORTH

EATING

RESTAURANTS

Canal Café	5
Hanagakura	3
Hansarang	4
Le Bretagne	2
Saemaeul Sikdang	6

TEAROOM

Saryō	1

Kōshinzuka Station

Kyū Furukawa Gardens

Somei
Onsen Sakura

KOMAGOME

Komagome

Komagome
Station

Sugamo Shinden

Sugamo Ⓢ

Sugamo
Station

Rikugi-en

Ⓢ Otsuka
Station

Otsukaekimae

SUGAMO

Mukohara

Sengoku Ⓢ

Ⓢ Shinotsuka

Honkomagome Ⓢ

Hakusan Ⓢ

Ⓢ Gokokuji

Myogadani Ⓢ

Myogadani
Station

SHUTO EXPRESSWAY 5

St Mary's
Cathedral

3

Kasuga

Edogawabashi Ⓢ

Japan Karate
Association

Korakuen
Station

Kodōkan

Ⓢ

Spa LaQua

Koishikawa-
Kōrakuen

Baseball Hall
of Fame &
Museum

Tokyo
Dome

Entrance ⊠

Tokyo
Dome City

4

⛩ Akagi-jinja

Suidōbashi Ⓢ

Kagurazaka Ⓢ

KAGURAZAKA

1 2

3

Iidabashi Ⓢ

Suidōbashi
Station

SUIDŌBASHI

Ushigome-kagurazaka Ⓢ

Iidabashi
Station

Ⓢ Ushigome-yanagichō

3

ACCOMMODATION

HOTEL
OMO5   2

CAPSULE HOTEL
Capsule Inn Komagome   1

RYOKAN AND MINSHUKU
Hōmeikan Daimachi Bekkan   3

HOSTEL
Unplan   4

0   400
metres

N

1

2

Fronted by a square, red-brick gateway, **Rikkyō University** was founded as St Paul's School in 1874 by an American Episcopalian missionary. Through the gateway, the old university courtyard has an incongruous Ivy League touch in its vine-covered halls, white windows and grassy quadrangle, making it a favourite venue for film crews. Originally located in Tsukiji, the university moved to Ikebukuro in 1918 and weathered the 1923 earthquake with minimal damage except for one toppled gate tower. The lopsided look was retained, so it's said, as a memorial to those who died, but a deciding factor was perhaps the sheer lack of bricks.

Sunshine City

サンシャインシティ・3-1 Higashi-Ikebukuro, Toshima-ku • Observation deck daily 10am–10pm • ¥1800 • ☎ 03 3989 3455, Ⓦ www. sunshinecity.co.jp • Higashi-Ikebukuro station

Heading east from Ikebukuro station, you can't miss the monstrous sixty storeys of the **Sunshine 60 Tower**, which at 240m was Japan's tallest building until it was pipped by Yokohama's Landmark Tower in 1993. An underground passage at the end of Sunshine 60-dōri leads into the tower, just one of four buildings comprising the **Sunshine City** complex of shops, offices, a hotel and various cultural centres. Compared to the city's newer developments it all looks rather dowdy, bar the freshly renovated (and overpriced) **observation deck** on the top floor, and the excellent aquarium (see below).

Sunshine Aquarium

サンシャイン水族館, Sanshain Suizokukan • Daily 9am–9pm • Adult/child ¥2200/1200 • ☎ 03 5950 0765, Ⓦ sunshinecity.jp/aquarium

IKEBUKURO

● **SHOPPING**
| Assist Wig | 1 |
| Seibu | 2 |

■ **DRINKING AND NIGHTLIFE**
BARS
Hub	1
Tachinomiya Kippei	3
Torikizoku	2

● **EATING**
CAFÉS
Fukuroshosabo	5
Nekorobi	7
Swallowtail Café	1
RESTAURANTS
Akiyoshi	2
Bakudan	4
Isomaru Suisan	6
Malaychan	3
Mutekiya	8
Taishōken	9

■ **ACCOMMODATION**
HOTELS
| Metropolitan | 3 |
| Zebra | 2 |
RYOKAN AND MINSHUKU
| Kimi Ryokan | 1 |

Kimi Information Center

TOKIWA-DŌRI

NISHIGUCHI KAISEI-DŌRI

TŌBU TŌJŌ LINE

YAMANOTE LINE

Shin-Bungei-za

MEIJI-DŌRI

SHUTO EXPRESSWAY 5

KASUGA-DŌRI

RIKKYŌ-DŌRI

Rikkyō University

Tōbu Department Store

Seibu Department Store

Ikebukuro Station

Ikebukuro

GREEN-DŌRI

SUNSHINE 60-DŌRI

Sunshine 60 Tower

Sunshine City

NISHI-IKEBUKURO

YAMANOTE LINE

SAIKYŌ LINE

HIGASHI-IKEBUKURO

N

Myonichi-kan

SEIBU IKEBUKURO LINE

MEIJI-DŌRI

Higashi-Ikebukuro

Higashi-Ikebukuro

SAKURA TRAM

Todenzoshigaya

| 0 | 200 |
metres

The wonderful **Sunshine Aquarium** is by far the best in Tokyo, with its rather high ticket price justified by inventive attractions, best of which are the "Sunshine Aqua Ring", where you'll be able to see sea-lions torpedoing around above your head, and the magical "Jellyfish Tunnel". Performances take place through the day.

Namco Namja Town

ナムコナンジャタウン • Daily 10am–10pm • Adult/child ¥500/300; passport adult/child ¥3500/2800 • ☎ 03 5950 0765, Ⓦ event. bandainamco-am.co.jp

Part of the Sunshine City complex, **Namco Namja Town** is a noisy indoor amusement centre based around a couple of cat characters. It's notable for its various themed eating areas, including sections specializing in *gyōza* (Chinese-style fried and steamed dumplings), ice cream (flavours have, in the past, included squid and shark), and desserts from around Japan. The passport allows unlimited access to fourteen of the attractions, which include a mosquito-zapping gun game, a fishing challenge and a zombie-hunting video game.

12

Mejirodai

目白台

Riding the Toden-Arakawa line (see page 141) to Waseda station will bring you to the edge of the hilly **Mejirodai** area. The top attraction here is a stroll along the **Kanda River** (神田川), where the pathways explode in cherry blossom pink at the end of March and early April.

Chinzan-sō

椿山荘 • 2-10-8 Sekiguchi, Bunkyō-ku • Daily 9am–8pm • Free • Ⓦ www.chinzanso.com • Waseda station (Sakura Tram line)

The area's prime sight is the **Chinzan-sō**, a beautiful, expansive nineteenth-century garden set around a small pond. Though sandwiched between a wedding hall complex and the *Hotel Chinzansō*, it's surprisingly easy to ignore those two ugly buildings, and concentrate on the greener delights of the garden. St Mary's Cathedral (see below) is just across the road from the north entrance; if you swing by the south entrance after lunch, you may get to see Rick, a giant horned tortoise out for a walk.

St Mary's Cathedral

東京カテドラル聖マリア大聖堂, Tōkyō Katedoraru Sei Maria Daiseidō • 3-16-15 Sekiguchi, Bunkyō-ku • Daily 9am–5pm • Ⓦ tokyo.catholic.jp • Waseda station (Toden-Arakawa line) or Gokokuji station

St Mary's Cathedral has been the centre of Tokyo's Catholic community for well over a century, with congregations a mix of foreigners and Japanese. The original Gothic structure was built in 1899, but burned down in the World War II air raids; the present building, designed by Tange Kenzō (see page 270), was completed in 1964. Steel-clad and shaped like a giant cross, it's rather iconic, almost enough to count as a Tokyo must-see. Be sure to take a peek at the dramatic interior; dominated by a massive pipe organ at one end and a retro-futurist cross at the other, it brings to mind scenes from Fritz Lang's *Metropolis*.

Komagome

駒込

There are a couple of wonderful natural spots in the Komagome area, easily accessible from Ikebukuro station, just three stops to the west. The top sight here is **Rikugi-en**, a sculpted garden redolent of old Edo; just to the north, you'll find more of the same at the gorgeous **Kyū Furukawa Gardens**.

Rikugi-en

六義園 • 6 Honkomagome, Bunkyō-ku • Daily: Gardens 9am–5pm; tearooms noon–4.30pm; closed Dec 29th to Jan 1st • Gardens ¥300; teahouse ¥300 (for tea), or ¥600 with a sweet • Entrance on Hongō-dōri, 5min south of Komagome station

Komagome's most appealing sight is **Rikugi-en**, Tokyo's best surviving example of a classical Edo-period stroll garden. In 1695 the fifth shogun granted one of his high-ranking feudal lords, Yanagisawa Yoshiyasu, a tract of farmland to the north of Edo. Yanagisawa was both a perfectionist and a literary scholar: he took seven years to design his celebrated garden – with its 88 allusions to famous scenes, real or imaginary, from ancient Japanese poetry – and then named it Rikugi-en, "garden of the six principles of poetry", in reference to the rules for composing *waka* (poems of 31 syllables). After Yanagisawa's death, Rikugi-en fell into disrepair until Iwasaki Yatarō, founder of Mitsubishi, bought the land in 1877 and restored it as part of his luxury villa. The family donated the garden to the Tokyo city authorities in 1938, since when it has been a public park.

Unsurprisingly, few of the 88 landscapes have survived – the guide map issued at the entrance identifies a mere eighteen. Nevertheless, Rikugi-en still retains its beauty, and is large enough to be relatively undisturbed by surrounding buildings and traffic noise; most take the opportunity to sample *matcha* and traditional Japanese sweets in the teahouse overlooking the lake from the west.

Kyū Furukawa Gardens

旧古河庭園, Kyū Furukawa Teien • 1-27-39 Nishigahara, Kita-ku • Daily 9am–5pm • ¥150, museum ¥800 • Entrance 5min uphill from Komagome station

Designed by Ogawa Jihei, a famed gardener from Kyoto, the **Kyū Furukawa Gardens** combine delightful Japanese-style grounds with an Italian-style terrace of rose beds and artfully shaped azalea bushes. The gardens cascade down the hill from the **Otani Museum**, set in a mansion designed in 1914 by British architect Josiah Conder (see page 62), who was also responsible for the similar Kyū Iwasaki-tei house and gardens in Ueno (see page 69). It's possible to take tea and cake in the mansion and to go on a tour of the empty (and frankly boring) rooms. The best times to visit are in late April, when the azaleas bloom, and in mid-May, when the roses are out in full force.

Somei Onsen Sakura

染井温泉桜 • 5-4-24 Komagome, Toshima-ku • Daily 10am–11pm • ¥1300 • Komagome station

Most of Tokyo's bathhouses are either small, bare-bones establishments costing next to nothing, or over-the-top mega-complexes costing way too much and giving little in the way of a traditional feel. Hooray, then, for the **Somei Onsen Sakura**, which strikes a nice halfway-house vibe: pleasantly "regular" in feel, it's a great example of the Japanese onsen experience. As you may have inferred from the name, it's best visited during cherry-blossom season, when the trees surrounding the site (though not actually visible from the baths) are cloaked with fluffy pink petals.

Suidōbashi

水道橋

Some way southeast of Ikebukuro, on the way back towards the Imperial Palace, the district of **Suidōbashi** has a handful of minor attractions including an upmarket spa complex, an amusement park and a classic seventeenth-century garden, all revolving around **Tokyo Dome City**, one of the city's most important sports complexes. The centrepiece here is the plump, white-roofed **Tokyo Dome**, Tokyo's major baseball venue, popularly known as the "Big Egg".

Tokyo Dome City Attractions

東京ドームシティ アトラクションズ • 1-3-61 Kōraku, Bunkyō-ku • Daily 10am–10pm • Individual rides ¥420–1030; passport with unlimited rides adult ¥4200, child aged 12–17 ¥3700, child aged 6–11 ¥2800, child aged 3–5 ¥2100, discounts after 5pm • ☎ 03 5800 9999, ⓦ at-raku.com • Suidōbashi or Kōrakuen stations

The best rides at the large **Tokyo Dome City Attractions** amusement park, part of the Tokyo Dome complex, are those in the LaQua section, where the highlight is Thunder Dolphin, a high-speed roller coaster guaranteed to get you screaming (for ages 8 and older). If you haven't got the stomach for that, try the Big O, the world's first hub-less and spoke-less Ferris wheel (it's spun by the two supports below), which provides a gentler ride and plenty of time to take a photo of the passing view. Tiny tots will enjoy Toys Kingdom, a space packed with playthings.

Spa LaQua

6F 1-1-1 Kasuga, Bunkyō-ku • Daily 11am–9am (next day) • Mon–Fri ¥2850, Sat & Sun ¥3170; ¥1940 surcharge 1am–6am; access to Healing Baden set of special therapeutic saunas ¥865 extra • ⓦ www.laqua.jp • Suidōbashi or Kōrakuen stations

Spread over five floors, and part of the Dome City complex, **Spa LaQua** is by far the most sophisticated of Tokyo's bathing establishments (not to mention one of the most expensive), and is fed by onsen water pumped from 1700m underground.

Baseball Hall of Fame and Museum

Gate 21, Tokyo Dome • Tues–Sun: March–Sept 10am–6pm; Oct–Feb 10am–5pm • ¥600 • ☎ 03 3811 3600, ⓦ baseball-museum.or.jp • Suidōbashi or Kōrakuen stations

Tokyo Dome is most famed for being the home of the Yomiuri Giants baseball team (see page 211). Its **Baseball Hall of Fame and Museum** is really for die-hard fans only; as well as footage of early games, there's all sorts of baseball memorabilia here, including one of Babe Ruth's jackets.

Koishikawa-Kōrakuen

小石川後楽園 • 1-6-6 Kōraku, Bunkyō-ku; entrance in southwest corner of garden • Daily 9am–5pm; English-language tours Sat 10am & 1pm • ¥300 • ☎ 03 3811 3015, ⓦ tokyo-park.or.jp • Iidabashi station

Immediately to the west of Tokyo Dome is **Koishikawa-Kōrakuen**, a fine, early seventeenth-century stroll garden. Winding paths take you past waterfalls, ponds and stone lanterns, down to the shores of a small lake draped with gnarled pines and over

12

daintily humped bridges, where each view replicates a famous beauty spot. Zhu Shun Shui, a refugee scholar from Ming China, advised on the design, so Chinese as well as Japanese landscapes feature, the most obvious being the Full Moon Bridge, echoing the ancient stone bridges of western China, and Seiko Lake, modelled on the famed West Lake in Hangzhou, a major city near China's eastern seaboard. The garden attracts few visitors, though occasional squeals and rattles from the Tokyo Dome fairground rides, peeking up over the trees, mean it's not always totally peaceful.

Kagurazaka

神楽坂

Just west of Iidabashi station, the district of **Kagurazaka** has become a popular spot of late with Tokyoites young and old. Chic restaurants, cafés and shops line Kagarazaka-dōri, the area's main drag, and there are plenty more dotting the genteel alleyways to the north. If you're in luck, you'll spot a geisha or two tripping along the lanes – some still work hereabouts, remnants of the area's history as an entertainment quarter.

Akagi-jinja

赤城神社 • 1-10 Akagi-Motomachi, Shinjuku-ku • Daily 24hr • Free • Iidabashi station

For something a little out of the ordinary, take a trip to **Akagi-jinja**, a shrine remodelled in 2010 by star architect Kengo Kuma (see page 270). Most Japanese shrines come across as somewhat brooding and secretive, but this one is effectively ensconced in a sort of giant glass box, approached by a small run of steps and flanked by a modern apartment block. It's perhaps more interesting than truly beautiful, but most find it worth the effort to get here.

12

IMPERIAL HOTEL

Accommodation

Japan's reputation for being an extremely expensive place to visit is a little outdated in many fields, but it's certainly justified as far as accommodation goes. However, the quality of accommodation in Tokyo is generally very high at all levels, from luxury hotels to budget dorms; security and cleanliness are top-notch; and except at the bottom end of the scale, you'll usually find someone who speaks at least a smattering of English. While there are few bargains, if you look hard you'll find plenty of affordable places. You'll often find the best value – along with plenty of atmosphere – at a traditional ryokan or a family-run minshuku, the Japanese equivalent of a B&B. The cheapest beds are provided by privately run hostels, mainly in the city's northern districts. Capsule hotels are a little more expensive but certainly worth trying once, if only for the experience.

13

WHICH AREA?

With Tokyo the size it is, and with each district boasting its own character, it's important to consider which part of the city to use as your base.

Imperial Palace and around There are a fair few high-end establishments dotted between the palace and the train tracks.

Ginza Highly central area with plenty to see and shopping opportunities galore. Most hotels here are, however, rather expensive.

Akihabara Tokyo's electro-capital makes a great base for those in the mood to see maid cafés, robot shops and other quirky facets of the city. There are plenty of cheap business hotels here.

Ueno There are lots of sights in and around this northern area, whose accommodation options previously centred around the squad of hotels and love hotels south of the park; in recent years, plenty of quirky mid-range options have opened up, and the area is now a prime target for foreign visitors.

Asakusa One of Tokyo's most characterful areas, and the de facto choice for backpackers thanks to its large concentration of hostels. There are also some great ryokan choices here.

Ryōgoku and Kiyosumi A few of the hostels in the wider Asakusa area fall under the extent of this chapter in our guide.

Bayside Tokyo The city's bayside area is quite beautiful, especially when seen from the upper floors of one of its upscale hotels.

Akasaka and Roppongi Roppongi is famed for its nightlife, and boasts some of Tokyo's best hotels. Neighbouring Akasaka is somewhat earthier, and correspondingly cheaper.

Ebisu, Meguro and the south Few choose to stay way down south in Ebisu, though nearby neighbourhoods such as charming Nakameguro are surprisingly convenient for the city's sights.

Harajuku, Aoyama and Shibuya There's so much to see in this wide area, both historical and contemporary, that you're unlikely to get bored. Most places are rather expensive, bar the huge cluster of love hotels in Shibuya.

Shinjuku For many visitors, Shinjuku represents the *real* Tokyo, though there are precious few budget places in this neon paradise.

Ikebukuro Not terribly interesting, few visitors use Ikebukuro as a base, though it has some good cheap options, including several ryokan.

Whatever your budget, it's wise to **reserve** your first few nights' accommodation before arrival. This is especially true of the cheaper places, which tend to fill up quickly, particularly over national holidays and in late February, when thousands of students head to Tokyo for the university entrance exams. Rooms are also in short supply during holiday periods, as well as during the cherry-blossom season in late March and early April. Good deals can be found **online** via hotel websites and general booking engines (see below), and it's always worth asking if there are any promotions on offer.

ESSENTIALS

Prices Staying in Tokyo will cost you from around ¥2500 for a hostel dorm bed, or ¥4000 for the very cheapest private rooms. You'll be looking at upwards of ¥10,000 for a more comfortable en-suite double in a business hotel. Mid-range hotels start in the region of ¥15,000, while top-end hotels charge at least twice that and often many times more. Rates in the text are given for high season (see page 147).

Taxes All hotel rates include a 10 percent consumption tax, on top of which top-end hotels levy a service charge, which is typically also 10 percent. If your room costs over ¥10,000 per person per night, there's also a Tokyo Metropolitan Government tax of ¥100 per person per night (¥200 if the room costs over ¥15,000).

Reservations The international standbys have plenty of Tokyo options: try ⓦ trivago.com or ⓦ booking.com for hotels, or ⓦ hostelworld.com for hostels. Locals usually use ⓦ travel.rakuten.com, which has an English site (though you'll need to register). Also worth checking out is ⓦ ryokan.or.jp/English, which lists good places to stay, mostly ryokan, in Tokyo and beyond, though it has no booking mechanism.

Internet Connectivity has certainly improved in Tokyo's hotels and hostels. Free wi-fi is almost always provided for free in the latter (exceptions have been noted in the reviews), though in hotels and ryokan you may be charged for the service; in addition, some places still have LAN cables rather than wi-fi.

ROOM RATES

Unless otherwise stated, the rates listed are for the cheapest **double or twin room** (inclusive of taxes) in high season (summer); typically these rates rise during peak holiday periods, in particular around Christmas and New Year, the Golden Week (April 29–May 5) and O-bon (the week around August 15). Single rates are typically a third less than for doubles; at **ryokan** the difference can show greater variation, so both single and double prices have been given in our reviews. For **dormitory** accommodation and **capsule hotels**, the price per person is listed.

Breakfast Breakfast tends to come as standard in ryokan (though you can usually forgo it to get a cheaper rate) but rarely features in hostels. At hotels it usually costs extra, from ¥700–3000 per person, essentially depending upon room price; usually you can add or forgo breakfast when booking. Establishments offering free breakfast as standard have been noted in the listings.

HOTELS

There are a few discrete stripes of **hotel** in Tokyo. Running the gamut from budget to luxury, they all feature Western-style rooms with en-suite bathrooms, TV, phone and a/c as standard; a few of the larger ones also offer tatami (traditional straw mat flooring) rooms, which tend to be a little more expensive. Many fit into the category of **business hotels**: cheap, functional places aimed at salarymen, with rooms that may be super-small but are always clean, and feature everything needed for a night's rest. Lastly, there are **love hotels**, which cater for couples seeking the privacy often not available in a small Japanese apartment (see page 150).

THE IMPERIAL PALACE AND AROUND
SEE MAP PAGE 42

★**Hoshinoya** 星のや 1-9-1 Ōtemachi, Chiyoda-ku ☎050 3786 1144, ⊛hoshinoyatokyo.com; Ōtemachi station. Though it may seen an obvious idea, this is actually quite unique in Tokyo: a top-end hotel with ryokan-like elements to its decor and service. As such, despite being seventeen floors high, it all feels rather intimate; the scent of flowers and incense wafts through the common areas, and rooms manage to exude a traditional yet contemporary air. The private *ochomoma* lounge is a grand place for tea, or even sake. ¥80,000

Imperial Hotel 帝国ホテル 1-1-1 Uchisaiwai-chō, Chiyoda-ku ☎03 3504 1111, ⊛imperialhotel.co.jp; Hibiya station. Facing the Imperial Palace, this is still one of Tokyo's most prestigious addresses, despite increasingly stiff competition. Best are the three exclusive "Imperial" floors, with butler service and the latest technological wizardry. You'll find no fewer than thirteen top-class restaurants, as well as three bars (including the *Old Imperial Bar*, page 179). ¥50,000

The Peninsula ザ ペニンシュラ東京 1-8-1 Yūrakuchō, Chiyoda-ku ☎03 6270 2288, ⊛peninsula.com; Tokyo or Yūrakuchō stations, Hibiya station. Elegantly designed luxury hotel with an unbeatable location – offering views right across to the emperor's pad – and some of the city's most spacious rooms; pleasingly decorated along earth-tone lines, they almost feel more like a home than a hotel. There's also an opulent spa, and a chic rooftop restaurant and bar. ¥76,000

Tokyo Station 東京ステーションホテル 1-9-1 Marunouchi, Chiyoda-ku ☎03 5220 1111, ⊛www.thetokyostationhotel.jp; Tokyo station. It has been great to see this grand old dame back in business – this hotel, set within Tokyo station itself, first opened for business in 1915, but was closed throughout the station's mammoth refurb. Following the template set by the hotel renovations at London's St Pancras, designers have plumped for dainty Euro-chic in the rooms, and set chandeliers all over the place. ¥47,000

GINZA AND AROUND
SEE MAP PAGE 53

★**Conrad Tokyo** コンラッド東京 1-9-1 Higashi-Shinbashi, Minato-ku ☎03 6388 8000, ⊛conradtokyo.co.jp; Shiodome station. This luxury hotel easily holds its own when it comes to cutting-edge contemporary design and five-star facilities. But it's the views that really steal the show – from the lobby and bayside rooms feast your eyes on what are arguably the best vistas in Tokyo, taking in Hama Rikyū Teien, Odaiba and the Rainbow Bridge. It's absolutely magical at night. ¥64,000

Four Seasons フォーシーズンズホテル丸の内 Pacific Century Place, 1-11-1 Marunouchi, Chiyoda-ku ☎03 5222 7222, ⊛fourseasons.com/tokyo; Tokyo station. Chic interior design and superb service are two pluses for this luxury hotel. With only 57 rooms, there's a personal touch – let them know your arrival time and someone will be there on the platform to greet you at nearby Tokyo station. Facilities include a spa, fitness centre, and a stylish bar and French restaurant. ¥82,000

Mandarin Oriental Tokyo マンダリンオリエンタル東京 2-1-1 Nihombashi-Muromachi, Chūō-ku ☎03 3270 8800, ⊛mandarinoriental.com/tokyo; Mitsukoshi-mae station. No expense has been spared here, from the

13

TOKYO'S BEST PLACES TO STAY

Best for views *Conrad Tokyo* (see page 147)
Best for glamping *Caravan Tokyo* (see page 150)
Best modern-style ryokan *Andon Ryokan* (see page 152)
Best for cocktails *Imperial Hotel* (see page 147)
Best for Godzilla fans *Gracery Shinjuku* (see page 151)
Best for luxury *Hoshinoya* (see page 147)
Best old-school ryokan *Sukeroku-no-yado Sadachiyo* (see page 153)
Best love hotel *J-Mex* (see page 151)
Best hostel *Bunka Hostel* (see page 154)
Best for weirdness *Capsule hotels* (see page 153)

---

dramatic 37th-floor lobby to some of the biggest standard-size rooms in Tokyo, where picture windows make the most of the stunning cityscapes. There's no pool, but guests can take advantage of a fabulous (and very pricey) spa, a fitness centre and seven restaurants. **¥85,000**

★ **Mitsui Garden Ginza** 三井ガーデンホテル銀座 8-13-1 Ginza, Chūō-ku ☎03 3543 1131, ⓦwww.gardenhotels.co.jp; Shimbashi station. Italian designer Piero Rissoni's chic design for Mitsui's flagship hotel helps it stand out from the crowd. Rooms are decorated in earthy tones with great attention to detail, but it's the bird's-eye views of the city and bay that grab the attention – quite spectacular from each and every room. **¥27,500**

Muji Hotel 無印ホテル 3-3-5 Ginza, Chūō-ku ☎03 3538 6101, ⓦhotel.muji.com; Ginza station. The homeware behemoth made its first foray into the Japanese accommodation market in 2019, and its rooms – sleek, accordingly minimalist and leaning on Japanese traditional design – were booked solid for months on end. Some rooms are absolutely huge, though you'll be paying a lot more for these; there are, however, few facilities to speak of, bar the giant Muji store downstairs (see page 207). **¥27,000**

Ryūmeikan Tokyo ホテル龍名館東京 1-3-22 Yaesu, Chūō-ku ☎03 3271 0971, ⓦryumeikan-tokyo.jp; Tokyo station. This long-standing traditional inn has transformed into a stylish hotel, each room mixing Western comfort with attractive Japanese touches, accented in Edo-period purple (*edomurasaki*). Big discounts on offer for those who book in advance, and there's usually a free breakfast too. **¥37,000**

★ **Sunroute Ginza** ホテルサンルート銀座 1-15-11 Ginza, Chūō-ku ☎03 5579 9733, ⓦsunroute.jp; Ginza-itchōme station. This business hotel is one of the cheaper options in fancy Ginza (especially if you book online), and just a few minutes' walk from several metro stations. Rooms are stylish and well equipped, and surprisingly large for the price and location. **¥21,000**

AKIHABARA AND AROUND
SEE MAP PAGE 60

Akihabara Washington ワシントンホテル秋葉原 1-8-3 Kanda-Sakumachō, Chiyoda-ku ☎03 3255 3311, ⓦakihabara.washington-hotels.jp; Akihabara station. A branch of the Washington chain of business hotels, with simple, clean rooms – including one single room that comes with its own train track – and a handy location right next to Akihabara station. Solo travellers often get big discounts (with the exception of the train room). The hotel also includes a nice café that opens for breakfast and turns into a bar at night. **¥15,000**

Hilltop 山の上ホテル 1-1 Kanda-Surugadai, Chiyoda-ku ☎03 3293 2311, ⓦyamanoue-hotel.co.jp; Ochanomizu station. Perched on a small rise above Meiji University, this small 1930s hotel was formerly the commissioned officers' quarters during the Occupation, and then became the haunt of famous writers, notably Mishima (see page 264). Its rooms are far from Tokyo's grandest, but there are Art Deco touches and a friendly welcome; oxygen and supposedly refreshing negative ions are pumped around the premises. Note that you can often lop up to 50 percent off the inflated rack rate. **¥24,000**

Juraku ホテルジュラク 2-9 Kanda-Awajichō, Chiyoda-ku ☎03 3271 7222, ⓦhotel-juraku.co.jp/ocha; Ochanomizu or Akihabara stations. Now, this is a super little place. On entry, it comes across as something like a four-star, with a quirky, faux-industrial facade and a smart, honey-toned lobby. The rooms (some female-only) are superbly designed too. Throw in a convenient location and cheery staff, and you can't really go wrong. **¥17,000**

UENO AND AROUND
SEE MAP PAGE 66

Coco Grand Ueno Shinobazu ココグラン上野不忍ホテル 2-12-14 Ueno, Taitō-ku ☎03 3834 6221, ⓦcocogrand.co.jp/uenoshinobazu; Yushima station. Reliable hotel with friendly staff and a choice of Western- or Japanese-style accommodation, the latter quite spacious but a bit more expensive. Many rooms have great views across Shinobazu pond. **¥19,000**

★ **Graphy Nezu** グラフィ根津 4-5-10 Ikenohata, Taitō-ku ☎03 3828 7377, ⓦhotel-graphy.com; Nezu station. Converted from a small apartment block, this is the best of the many good-value options which have proliferated around Nezu and Yakata in recent years, with winning, English-speaking staff, communal kitchen facilities, and well-appointed rooms (though you'll have to pay a little more for an en suite). Locals often pop by to mingle with guests in the café-bar. **¥11,000**

Hanare ホテルパークサイド 3-10-25 Yanaka, Taitō-ku ☏ 03 5834 7301, ⊛ hanare.hagiso.jp; Sendagi station. Although marketing itself as a hotel, this is more like a ryokan in nature, with only five old-school tatami rooms. Tucked into the quirky Yanaka area, staff are happy to advise guests regarding things to see and places to eat, and there's an excellent adjoining café (Hagiso; see page 173). **¥10,500**

★ **Nohga** ノーガホテル 2-21-10 Higashi-Ueno, Taitō-ku ☏ 03 5816 0211, ⊛ nohgahotel.com; Ueno station. There's plenty of competition at this price level in Ueno, but this boutique hotel stands out for its artistic leanings – many of the pieces you'll see around the hotel rotate in the manner of gallery exhibitions, and if you're here at the right time you may get to see one of their many collaborations with local artisans. Rooms are suitably attractive, and there's a great restaurant on site. **¥15,000**

ASAKUSA
SEE MAP PAGE 75

Asakusa Central 浅草セントラルホテル 1-5-3 Asakusa, Taitō-ku ☏ 03 3847 2222, ⊛ pelican.co.jp/asakusacentralhotel; Asakusa station. Modest business hotel which rises above local competition thanks to a winning combination of English-speaking staff, a convenient location on Asakusa's main street, and small but well-appointed rooms, all of which come with TV and telephone. **¥14,000**

BAYSIDE TOKYO
SEE MAP PAGE 88

Grand Nikkō ホテルグランドニッコー 2-6-1 Daiba, Minato-ku ☏ 03 5500 6711, ⊛ tokyo.grand-nikko.com; Daiba monorail. Rising up over the bay, the most luxurious of Odaiba's hotels has a light-filled lobby, walls peppered with contemporary art and, from all but the lower levels, great views of the Rainbow Bridge and the city across Tokyo Bay. Rooms are spacious (you'll pay a bit more for bridge views), and staff helpful to a tee. **¥51,000**

AKASAKA AND ROPPONGI
SEE MAP PAGE 98

ANA InterContinental Tokyo ANAインターコンチネンタルホテル 1-12-33 Akasaka, Minato-ku ☏ 03 3505 1111, ⊛ anaintercontinental-tokyo.jp; Tameike-sannō station. Offering great views across to Tokyo Midtown and the National Diet Building, this stylish hotel has contemporary decoration, attentive staff, a swimming pool, scores of restaurants (including the Tokyo home of

French super-chef Pierre Gagnaire) and attractive public areas. **¥42,000**

Andaz アンダズ 1-23-4 Toranomon, Minato-ku ☏ 03 6830 1234, ⊛ tokyo.andaz.hyatt.com; Toranomon station. Japan's first branch of Hyatt's luxury Andaz offshoot has touched down in Tokyo, taking up the upper section of the new Toranomon Hills complex. No attention to detail has been spared, from the perfumed lobby to the immaculate rooms, all decorated with Japanese-style flourishes from award-winning interior designers. **¥48,000**

The b Roppongi ザb六本木 3-9-8 Roppongi, Minato-ku ☏ 03 5412 0451, ⊛ roppongi.theb-hotels.com; Roppongi station. A boutique-style hotel that won't break the bank or offend the eyes, even if uninspiring plastic-unit bathrooms are the norm throughout. **¥19,500**

The Glanz ホテルザグランツ 2-21-3 Azabu-Jūban, Minato-ku ☏ 03 3455 7770, ⊛ theglanz.jp; Azabu-Jūban station. Highly appealing option with sleek, designer-style rooms including spa-style bathrooms and glimpses of Tokyo Tower. There are reduced rates on weekdays and if you check in after 10pm. Breakfast included. **¥15,000**

★ **Grand Hyatt Tokyo** グランドハイアットホテル 東京 6-10-3 Roppongi, Minato-ku ☏ 03 4333 1234, ⊛ tokyo.grand.hyatt.jp; Roppongi station. Glamour is the order of the day at this big-player hotel. The rooms' appealing design uses wood and earthy-toned fabrics, and restaurants and bars are all very chic, particularly The Oak Door and the slick sushi bar Roku Roku. **¥62,000**

Ōkura ホテルオークラ 2-10-4 Toranomon, Minato-ku ☏ 03 3582 0111, ⊛ www.hotelokura.co.jp/tokyo; Kamiyachō station. Although only one wing remains of the iconic Ōkura (augmented by one of more recent vintage), it remains a Tokyo classic with its 1970s time-warp lobby and beguiling garden view. The rooms are more contemporary, but really it's the retro ambience of the public areas that's the sell here. **¥49,000**

The Ritz-Carlton リッツカールトン東京 Tokyo Midtown, 9-7-1 Akasaka, Minato-ku ☏ 03 6434 8100, ⊛ ritzcarlton.com; Roppongi station. Occupying the top nine floors of the 53-floor Midtown Tower, this ultra-luxury hotel has a more contemporary look than usual for a Ritz-Carlton. The choice is between deluxe rooms or suites – both offering the height of comfort. **¥81,000**

EBISU, MEGURO AND THE SOUTH
SEE MAP PAGE 108

Claska クラスカホテル 1-3-18 Chūō-chō, Meguro-ku ☏ 03 3719 8121, ⊛ claska.com; Meguro station. This oversized Rubik's Cube is a real hipster's choice. A 10min bus or taxi ride from Meguro station, it makes up for a relatively remote location with an abundance of contemporary Tokyo style. Some rooms have been individually decorated by different local artists – worth considering, although they're not the largest or most practical in the hotel. There's also

13

a stylish lobby café/bar and very classy gift shop, Do (see page 207). Cheaper rates for weekly stays are available. **¥30,000**

Dormy Inn ドーミーイン目黒青葉台 3-21-8 Aobadai, Meguro-ku ☎03 3760 2211; Nakameguro station. Within walking distance of trendy Nakameguro and a stone's throw from the banks of the delightful Meguro-gawa (see page 110), this functional business hotel is a good deal. Each room has a hotplate and small fridge, so it's feasible to self-cater. There's also a large communal bathroom and sauna, plus free bike rental. **¥17,000**

The Strings ストリングスインターコンチネンタル Shinagawa East One Tower, 2-16-1 Konan, Minato-ku ☎03 4562 1111, ⓦintercontinental-strings.jp; Shinagawa station. Watch the Shinkansen come and go from this chic eyrie, part of the Intercontinental chain, located 26 floors up in one of the brace of towers next to Shinagawa station. The airy atrium lobby, with its combination of water, wood and stone, evokes traditional Japanese design in a contemporary way. **¥35,000**

Tōyoko Inn Takanawaguchi 東横　高輪口 4-23-2 Takanawa ☎03 3280 1045, ⓦtoyoko-inn.com; Shinagawa station. Close to the Shinkansen, this is a handy branch of the bargain business hotel chain that doesn't stint on facilities (including trouser press), although rooms are tiny. Rates include a continental breakfast. **¥9000**

HARAJUKU, AOYAMA AND SHIBUYA
SEE MAPS PAGE 116, PAGE 119 AND
PAGE 124

Caravan Tokyo キャラバントウキョウ 3-13 Minami-Aoyama, Minato-ku ☎080 4145 3422, ⓦcaravantokyo. com; Omotesandō station. Glamping in Tokyo? Yep, it's quite possible, at this custom-built caravan located in the

Commune 246 snack-courtyard complex (see page 168); mod-cons include a/c, heating, a shower and a real bed. Not quite the great outdoors, but pretty great nonetheless. Book on Airbnb. **¥15,000**

Cerulean Tower Tōkyū Hotel セルリアンタワー 東急ホテル 26-1 Sakuragaoka-chō, Shibuya-ku ☎03 3476 3000, ⓦceruleantower-hotel.com; Shibuya station. Shibuya's ritziest accommodation, with a range of intriguingly designed rooms, some featuring bathrooms with glittering views of the city. Also on site are a pool and gym (free to guests on the executive floor), several restaurants, a jazz club (see page 189) and even a nō theatre in the basement (see page 192). **¥52,000**

Granbell グランベルホテル 15-17 Sakuragaoka-chō, Shibuya-ku ☎03 5457 2681, ⓦgranbellhotel. jp; Shibuya station. This boutique hotel has a hip feel, courtesy of curtains with Lichtenstein-style prints, kettles and TVs from the trendy local electronics range Plus Minus Zero, and a neutral palette of greys, crisp whites and natural colours. **¥22,000**

★**Tōkyū Stay Aoyama** 東急ステイホテル青山 2-27-18 Minami-Aoyama, Shibuya-ku ☎03 3497 0109, ⓦtokyustay.co.jp; Gaienmae station. Designed for long-staying guests, but open to short-stay visitors too, this high-rise hotel and apartment complex scores for facilities, location and slick decor. There's a women-only floor and wonderful views, and rates include breakfast. There are thirteen other Tōkyū Stays around the city. **¥32,400**

Trunk トランク 5-31 Jingu-mae, Shibuya-ku ☎03 5766 3210, ⓦtrunk-hotel.com; Jingumae station. A new addition to the area's accommodation options, this boutique offering rises in stylish, sharp-edged layers from the side-road it calls home. Prices are a little ridiculous for the suites, but the standard rooms are certainly pretty

LOVE HOTELS

Generally clustered in entertainment districts such as Shibuya, Shinjuku, Ueno and Ikebukuro, **love hotels** are places where you can rent rooms by the hour. Often sporting ornate exteriors and a sign quoting prices for "rest" or "stay", they're not as sleazy as they might sound, and the main market is young people or married couples taking a break from crowded apartments. For the bold, they can be a cheaper and far more interesting place to stay than a bland business hotel.

All kinds of tastes are indulged at love hotels, with rotating beds in mirror-lined rooms being almost passé in comparison to some of the fantasy creations on offer. You usually choose your room from a backlit display indicating those available, and then pay a cashier lurking behind a tiny window (eye-to-eye contact is avoided to preserve privacy). "Rest" **rates** cost ¥3000–5800 for two hours in the evening or night-time, and are around the same for a "day-pack", which usually gives you from noon to about 6pm. The price of an **overnight stay** can cost the same as a basic business hotel (¥7800–9800, in general), though you usually can't check in until around 10pm. Double these rates for fancier love hotels, with rooms featuring four-poster beds, jacuzzi pools, swings and the like.

Several love hotels have been included in the listings here, including J-Mex in Shinjuku (see page 151), Two Way in Shibuya (see page 151), and Zebra in Ikebukuro (see page 151); all three are surrounded by umpteen other options.

enough, filled with art and local cosmetics. The lounge often hosts parties on weekends. **¥35,000**

Two Way ホテルツーウェイ 15-2 Maruyama-chō, Shibuya-ku ☎ 03 3476 2020, ⊛ hotel-twoway.jp; Shinsen station. Of Tokyo's hundreds upon hundreds of love hotels, this place in Shibuya is one of the best value. There's even a "group" room, the infamous #405: goodness only knows what might occasionally go on in here, but on more innocent evenings it's home to groups of university students enjoying a party, or even groups of locals watching a Premier League football game. "Rest" from **¥3600**, "stay" from **¥5700**

SHINJUKU AND THE WEST
SEE MAP PAGE 128

Century Southern Tower ホテルセンチュリーサザンタワー 2-2-1 Yoyogi, Shibuya-ku ☎ 03 5354 0111, ⊛ southerntower.co.jp; Shinjuku station. Smart, stylish place that's better value than similar options in Nishi-Shinjuku. Come evening time, the views overlooking the station lend the place a *Blade Runner*-ish feel. **¥29,000**

★ **J-Mex** 2-5-6 Kabukichō, Shinjuku-ku ☎ 03 3205 2223; Higashi-Shinjuku station. This love hotel stands out from the crowd in Kabukichō (where, as you may have noticed, there are quite a few). The racy rooms all have big TVs and karaoke machines, as well as – drum roll, please – built-in sauna units, and glowing spa tubs. It's not even that pricey, and bookable on some of the main international accommodation websites. "Rest" from **¥5800**, "stay" from **¥11,500**

★ **Gracery Shinjuku** ホテルグレイスリー新宿 1-19-1 Kabukichō, Shinjuku-ku ☎ 03 6833 2489, ⊛ shinjuku.gracery.com; Seibu-Shinjuku station. Yes, this is the "Godzilla hotel" that you may have spotted on your walk around Shinjuku. Despite the presence of the hulking beast by the upper-level lobby (he looks particularly fine when guarding you over breakfast), and the stylish rooms, it's not all that expensive a place to stay. **¥21,000**

Kadoya かどやホテル 1-23-1 Nishi-Shinjuku, Shinjuku-ku ☎ 03 3346 2561, ⊛ kadoya-hotel.co.jp; Shinjuku station. This efficient business hotel is a little charmer. Single rooms (from ¥9980) are a bargain for such a handy location, and the doubles won't break the bank either. A major plus is the lively *izakaya* in the basement. **¥16,000**

Keiō Plaza 京王プラザホテル 2-2-1 Nishi-Shinjuku, Shinjuku-ku ☎ 03 3344 0111, ⊛ keioplaza.co.jp; Tochōmae station. Though it's long since been knocked off its perch as the tallest, most glamorous hotel in Shinjuku, this enormous place nevertheless retains some of its original cachet. The premier rooms, in grey and brown tones, are very stylish, and those on the west side have sweeping views across to the Tokyo Metropolitan Government Building; there are also garish Hello Kitty rooms available. An outdoor pool opens up in summer. **¥29,500**

★ **Park Hyatt Tokyo** パークハイアット東京 3-7-1-2 Nishi-Shinjuku, Shinjuku-ku ☎ 03 5322 1234, ⊛ tokyo. park.hyatt.jp; Tochōmae station. Occupying the upper section of Tange Kenzō's Shinjuku Park Tower (see page 129), this is the epitome of sophistication, and holding up very well to newer rivals. All the huge rooms have breathtaking views, as do the restaurants and spa, pool and fitness centre at the pinnacle of the tower. **¥74,000**

Super Hotel Kabukichō スーパーホテル歌舞伎町 2-39-9 Kabukichō, Shinjuku-ku ☎ 03 6855 9000, ⊛ superhoteljapan.co.jp; Higashi-Shinjuku station. A budget treat, with small but comfortable en-suite rooms, rather beautiful communal bathing areas, well-trained staff, and a surprisingly generous free breakfast. Rates for a double room occasionally drop below ¥10,000. **¥12,000**

★ **Yuen Shinjuku** 由縁新宿 5-3-18 Shinjuku, Shinjuku-ku ☎ 03 5361 8355, ⊛ ryokan-yuen.jp; Shinjuku-gyoemmae station. This brand new "onsen ryokan" combines traditional styling with modern-day luxury – after entering what initially seems like a low-rise building, you may be surprised to find that it's actually 18 storeys high, and topped with onsen pools providing gorgeous views of Shinjuku. Rooms are a little small, but delightful in any case. **¥15,500**

IKEBUKURO AND THE NORTH
SEE MAPS PAGE 138 AND PAGE 140

Metropolitan ホテルメトロポリタン 1-6-1 Nishi-Ikebukuro, Toshima-ku ☎ 03 3980 1111, ⊛ www. metropolitan.jp; Ikebukuro station. Part of the *Crowne Plaza* group, Ikebukuro's plushest hotel offers all the facilities you'd expect, including several restaurants, a fitness club (¥2400) and limousine bus connections to Narita airport. The rooms are comfortable and well priced, and the hotel is located on the more interesting west side of Ikebukuro. **¥22,000**

★ **OMO5** 2-26-1 Kita-Ōtsuka, Toshima-ku ☎ 03 5961 4131, ⊛ omo-hotels.com; Ōtsuka station. A new breed emerging from the *Hoshinoya* stable, this hotel appeals to modern, youthful tastes, with a relaxed vibe, spacious rooms – all duplex in nature – and a snazzy common lounge that also plays host to the odd event. Their ranger tours are worth taking (especially since some are free to guests) if you'd like an in-depth look around the charming area. **¥13,000**

Zebra ホテルゼブラ 1-37-1 Higashi-Ikebukuro, Toshima-ku ☎ 03 3986 5015, ⊛ hotel-zebra.net; Ikebukuro station. Even amidst the "soaplands" of Ikebukuro, it's hard to miss this love hotel, which is adorned not only with the stripes hinted at in the name, but also all sorts of buttons, spikes and glowing panels. Considering the fact that there are costumes to borrow in the lobby, the rooms come across as surprisingly functional. "Rest" from **¥4800**, "stay" from **¥7800**

13

STAYING AT A RYOKAN

Staying at a traditional Japanese inn, known as a **ryokan** or **minshuku**, is one of the best experiences that a trip to Tokyo can throw at you. However, as exotic as these stays may be, many components can be utterly unfamiliar to Westerners – there are countless ways in which you may find yourself losing face, and as such it's essential to know what you're getting into before taking the plunge. However, most Japanese are pretty forgiving, and in many establishments you'll be handed an English-language printed list of dos and don'ts.

Upon entry, there'll be a row of **slippers** ready for you to change into – wear these at all times, since bare feet are a no-no in common areas. You'll be ushered to your bedroom, which will have **tatami** (rice-straw matting) on the floor, and little else beyond a low table, dresser and a few cushions. At almost all places, you'll be sleeping on futons on the floor – this may seem alien at first, but most people find them just as comfortable as a bed. The bedding is stored behind sliding doors during the day, and laid out in the evening. In most establishments, this is done for you, usually when you're having dinner.

All ryokan provide a **yukata**, a loose cotton robe tied with a belt, and a short jacket in cold weather. Always wrap the left side of the *yukata* over the right; the opposite way is used to dress bodies for a funeral. You may wear this to your evening **meal**; these tend to be served at 6pm or 7pm, and you may be asked to stipulate a set time on check-in. Smarter ryokan generally serve meals in your room, while communal dining is the norm in cheaper places. At night, some ryokan **lock their doors** pretty early, so check before going out – they may let you have a key.

Lastly, all ryokan and most minshuku feature a **traditional Japanese bath** (*furo*), a luxurious experience with its own set of rules (see page 29). Note that ryokan usually have separate bathrooms for men and women, while minshuku may only have one bathroom, in which case there'll either be designated times for males and females, or guests take it in turn. It's perfectly acceptable for couples and families to bathe together, though there's not usually a lot of space.

RYOKAN AND MINSHUKU

One of the highlights of a visit to Tokyo is staying in a **ryokan**, a traditional inn (see page 152). **Minshuku**, the Japanese equivalent of a bed-and-breakfast, are generally cheaper and more informal, but the same basic rules apply. The more expensive ryokan usually include two traditional meals – dinner and breakfast – as part of the price; it's usually possible to forgo them for a cheaper rate, but the meals are usually excellent and form part of the experience.

UENO AND AROUND
SEE MAP PAGE 66

Ryokan Katsutarō 旅館勝太郎 4-16-8 Ikenohata, Taitō-ku ☎03 3821 9808, ⓦkatsutaro.com; Nezu station. Handily located within walking distance of Ueno Park, this homely place has just seven slightly faded tatami rooms, plus coin laundry and complimentary coffee. They also run a newer annexe in Yanaka (see website for details). No meals. Singles **¥6680**, doubles **¥11,250**

★**Ryokan Sawanoya** 旅館澤の屋 2-3-11 Yanaka, Taitō-ku ☎03 3822 2251, ⓦsawanoya.com; Nezu station. This welcoming family-run inn is a real home from home in a very convivial neighbourhood within walking distance of Ueno Park. Though nothing fancy, it offers good-value tatami rooms, all with washbasin, TV, telephone and a/c. Few are en suite, but the two lovely Japanese-style

baths more than compensate. Facilities also include bike hire (¥300 per day), coin laundry and complimentary tea and coffee. No meals. Singles **¥5600**, doubles **¥10,600**

ASAKUSA AND AROUND
SEE MAP PAGE 75

★**Andon Ryokan** 行燈旅館 2-34-10 Nihonzutsumi, Taitō-ku ☎03 3873 8611, ⓦandon.co.jp; Minowa station. At this architectural gem, fusing traditional ryokan design with modern materials, the owner's fantastic antique collection is displayed alongside kitsch toys – and somehow it works. The dimly lit tatami rooms share bathrooms and are tiny, but sport DVD players and very comfortable futons. Other pluses include a top-floor jacuzzi spa you can book for private dips, regular events such as sake tastings and tea ceremonies, and super-friendly, English-speaking staff. Breakfast included. Singles **¥6500**, doubles **¥8100**

New Koyo ホテルニュー紅陽 2-26-13 Nihonzutsumi, Taitō-ku ☎03 3873 0343, ⓦnewkoyo.com; Minowa station. Tiny little place with tatami rooms that's about as cheap as you can get for a private room in Tokyo; there are also Western-style rooms available for the same price. It's a bit out of the way, but still within walking distance of Asakusa, and bike hire is available. No meals. Singles **¥2900**, doubles **¥5200**

Ryokan Kamogawa 旅館加茂川 1-30-10 Asakusa, Taitō-ku ☎03 3843 2681, ⓦf-kamogawa.jp; Asakusa station. Simple but well-maintained tatami rooms, with or without bath, in a welcoming minshuku one block west of Nakamise-dōri; still a popular choice, despite a recent spike in prices. Breakfast and dinner extra. Singles ¥11,600, doubles ¥23,400

Ryokan Shigetsu 旅館指月 1-31-11 Asakusa, Taitō-ku ☎03 3843 2345, ⓦshigetsu.com; Asakusa station. Just off bustling Nakamise-dōri, this smart little ryokan is a haven of kimono-clad receptionists and tinkling *shamisen* (Japanese lute) music, with a choice of small rooms, all en suite. There's a Japanese bath on the top floor, with views over temple roofs. Breakfast extra. Western singles ¥8000, tatami twins ¥17,000

★ **Sukeroku-no-yado Sadachiyo** 助六の宿 貞千代 2-20-1 Asakusa, Taitō-ku ☎03 3842 6431, ⓦsadachiyo.co.jp; Asakusa or Tawaramachi stations. Step back into Edo-era Asakusa in this delightful old inn marked by a willow tree and stone lanterns, northwest of Sensō-ji. The elegant tatami rooms are all en suite, though you can also use the traditional Japanese-style baths. Dinner and breakfast are included, and they can also arrange performances of traditional arts, including geisha dances. ¥21,600

★ **Tokyo Ryokan** 東京旅館 2-4-8 Nishi-Asakusa, Taitō-ku ☎090 8879 3599, ⓦwww.tokyoryokan.com; Tawaramachi station. Beautifully rendered traditional design elements and attention to detail make this modern establishment stand out from the crowd. With just three tatami rooms (including one triple; ¥10,500) above a communal lounge area and a shared bathroom, it feels like you're staying in someone's home. No meals. ¥7000

EBISU, MEGURO AND THE SOUTH
SEE MAP PAGE 108

Akimoto 旅荘秋元 3-2-8 Nakameguro, Meguro-ku ☎03 3711 4553; Nakameguro station. This minshuku is a super little find in fashionable Nakameguro, an area which is pricey at the best of times. There are a few floors of small tatami rooms (not en-suite), a general air of calm and an extremely relaxed manager. No wi-fi; no meals. Singles ¥2800, doubles ¥4000

Ryokan Sansuisō 旅館山水荘 2-9-5 Higashi-Gotanda, Shinagawa-ku ☎03 3441 7475, ⓦsansuiso.net; Gotanda station. This modest ryokan is beautifully maintained and run by friendly people. Only a few of the simple tatami rooms have en-suite bath. It's a 5min walk from the station, near the Meguro-gawa – quite convenient, despite the out-of-the-way location, thanks to its location on the Yamanote line. No meals. Singles ¥5500, doubles ¥9200

IKEBUKURO AND THE NORTH
SEE MAPS PAGE 138 AND PAGE 140

★ **Hōmeikan Daimachi Bekkan** 鳳明館台町別館 5-12-9 Hongō, Bunkyō-ku ☎03 3811 1187, ⓦhomeikan.com; Hongō San-chōme or Kasuga station. Of the three ryokan under the *Hōmeikan* name, this one is the real looker, with its ancient carpentry and traditional design. There are no en-suite bathrooms, but all rooms have tatami mats and look out on an exquisite little Japanese garden. Service is impeccable, too. The sister establishment across the road, the Meiji-era *Honkan*, is the only inn in the city that's a listed cultural property. No meals. ¥13,000

Kimi Ryokan 貴美旅館 2-36-8 Ikebukuro, Toshima-ku ☎03 3971 3766, ⓦkimi-ryokan.jp; Ikebukuro station. A great-value institution on Tokyo's budget scene, and a good place to meet fellow travellers – make sure you book well ahead. Rooms are compact but clean, access to a kitchen helps keep eating costs down and staff are friendly and speak English. There's a 1am curfew, and the place is a bit tricky to find, in the backstreets of west Ikebukuro. Singles ¥5400, doubles ¥8100

CAPSULE HOTELS

Capsule hotels used to be functional places for people who'd missed their trains. However, the last few years have witnessed a blooming in the industry, with flashy variants opening up all around the city.

CAPSULE HOTELS

Catering mainly to drunken salarymen who have missed their trains home, **capsule hotels** are made up of floors lined with two levels of tiny rooms, each containing a thin mattress, a comfy blanket, and (in most) a TV and radio built into the plastic surrounds. A metre wide, a metre high and two metres long, the rooms are just about big enough to stand in, but not much else.

However, the clichéd description of them as being "coffin-like" is rather wide of the mark: while claustrophobics and anyone over 2m tall should give them a miss, most actually find these minuscule rooms surprisingly comfortable. Capsule hotels are generally clustered around major train stations, and cost ¥3000–4000. Some are for men only, but these days most have female-only floors too.

13

GINZA AND AROUND
SEE MAP PAGE 53

Ginza Bay Hotel 銀座ベイホテル 7-13-15 Ginza, Chūō-ku ☎03 6226 1078, ⓦbay-hotel.jp; Higashi-Ginza station. Though no more expensive than most capsule hotels, this one has far more little flourishes such as gorgeous pine fittings in the bathing areas, and USB ports in the pods. It's also the cheapest place to stay in the Ginza area, and has a female-only floor. For ¥500 extra, you can choose a berth with a small TV inside. **¥3800**

AKIHABARA AND AROUND
SEE MAP PAGE 60

Glansit Akihabara グランジット秋葉原 4-4-6 Sotokanda, Chiyoda-ku ☎03 3526 3818, ⓦglansit.jp; Suehirocho or Akihabara stations. Now here's a fancy one. The lobby of this upscale capsule hotel would put many hotels to shame, with a snazzy design throughout. Rates vary widely depending upon which day you stay; book online. **¥5000**

HARAJUKU, AOYAMA AND SHIBUYA
SEE MAP PAGE 124

The Millennials Shibuya 1-20-13 Jinnan, Shibuya-ku ☎03 6824 9410, ⓦthemillennials.jp; Shibuya station.

One of the new breed of stylish capsule hotels now popping up around Tokyo, this has been a real hit with younger travellers, and not just due to the central-Shibuya location. Most of the pods here have been given artistic makeovers (some very jazzy), and the happy hours in the lobby lounge give guests a great chance to mingle. Prices are on the high side, though they do include breakfast, and are usually discounted on weekdays. **¥10,000**

IKEBUKURO AND AROUND
SEE MAP PAGE 138

Capsule Inn Komagome カプセルイン駒込 2-4-8 Nakazato, Kita-ku ☎03 3915 6670; Komagome station. A little way out in Komagome, this is one of the cheapest capsule hotels in Tokyo, and has a dedicated female-only floor. The communal hot tubs are a nice touch. No wi-fi. **¥3000**

NARITA

9 Hours ナインアワーズ Narita Airport, Terminal 2 ☎0476 335109, ⓦninehours.co.jp. If you have a late arrival or early departure flight to or from Narita, this slick airport capsule hotel can save you heaps on a taxi ride. Overnight **¥4900**, "nap" **¥1500** for first 2hr then **¥500** for each 1hr

HOSTELS

Until fairly recently, hostelling in Tokyo meant staying in one of the few municipal-run youth hostels. Now, however, you can forget about evening curfews and three-night maximum stays, since a glut of excellent privately run hostels have come on the scene, driving prices down and standards up. The majority are in, or near, the Asakusa area – another plus. Dormitories can be cramped but are kept clean; free wi-fi and 24hr hot water are a given; and most places have common areas which make good places to socialize.

GINZA AND AROUND
SEE MAP PAGE 53

Imano Tokyo Ginza いまの東京銀座 1-5-10 Shintomi, Chūō-ku ☎03 5117 2131, ⓦimano.jp; Shintomicho station. Backpackers rejoice – the Ginza area finally has a decent hostel! Somehow it even manages to look quite swanky, especially the almost naval blue-and-pine colour scheme of the lobby. The second-floor lounge makes for a great hangout spot, and the rooms are all spick and span too. Dorms **¥3400**, twins **¥10,000**

AKIHABARA AND AROUND
SEE MAP PAGE 60

★**Citan** シタン 15-2 Nihambashiodenma-chō, Chūō-ku ☎03 6661 7559, ⓦbackpackersjapan.co.jp;

Bakuroyokoyama station. The best hostel choice in the wider Akihabara area, even though it's basically a two-star hotel; you can have a great coffee at this little slice of hipster paradise, and they've a surprisingly good wine list at the bar. Dorms **¥3000**, twins **¥9000**

ASAKUSA AND AROUND
SEE MAP PAGE 75

1980 Hostel 1泊1980円ホテル 3-10-10 Shitaya, Taitō-ku ☎03 6240 6027, ⓦ1980stay.com; Inya station. The numbers in the name are the price, not the year – this is basically the cheapest hostel in Tokyo, and its capsule-like beds are just fine. Dorms **¥1980**

★**Bunka Hostel** ブンカホステル 1-13-5 Asakusa, Taitō-ku ☎03 5806 3444, ⓦbunkahostel.jp; Asakusa station. A remarkably stylish addition to the Asakusa hostel scene, with comfy, curtained-off berths adding some rare privacy to the dorm experience – a true bargain, as far as Tokyo accommodation goes. The lobby bar is a real winner, too (see page 180). Dorms **¥3550**

★**Khaosan Tokyo Origami** カオサン東京オリガミ 3-4-12 Asakusa, Taitō-ku ☎03 3871 6678, ⓦkhaosan-tokyo.com; Asakusa station. Part of the *Khaosan* chain, but a far more appealing option than the unfriendly original – rooms have been given Japanese stylings, and you'll see a fair few paper cranes around the place. There are grand views of Asakusa from the lounge, and the location can't be sniffed at; book online for discounted rates. Dorms ¥3800, doubles ¥10,000

★ **Retrometro Backpackers** レトロメトロバックパッカーズ 2-19-1 Nishi-Asakusa, Taitō-ku ☎ 03 6322 7447, ⓦ retrometrobackpackers.com; Asakusa or Tawaramachi stations. As far as backpackers go, it takes one to know one, and the owner of this tiny, two-dorm hostel (one dorm is female-only) certainly knows her stuff. Balinese and Thai stylings betray her favourite former travel destinations, and there's a sense of cosiness here absent from some of Tokyo's larger hostels. Dorms ¥2600

Sakura Hostel サクラホステル 2-24-2 Asakusa, Taitō-ku ☎ 03 3847 8111, ⓦ sakura-hostel.co.jp; Asakusa station. This friendly, well-run hostel occupies a cherry-pink building a couple of minutes' walk northwest of Sensō-ji. Each floor has its own shower and toilet area and there's a good kitchen and TV lounge; book online for discounted rates. Dorms ¥3300, twins ¥9300

RYŌGOKU AND KIYOSUMI
SEE MAP PAGE 83

Anne Hostel 庵ホステル 2-21-14 Yanagibashi, Taitō-ku ☎ 03 5829 9090, ⓦ j-hostel.com; Asakusabashi or Kuramae station. A lovely little place: part hostel, part traditional minshuku (see page 152), it's tremendously popular with international guests. Most rooms, even a couple of the dorms, boast tatami flooring, and prices include a decent little breakfast. Dorms ¥2600, twins ¥6800

★ **K's House Tokyo** ケイズハウス東京 3-20-10 Kuramae, Taitō-ku ☎ 03 5833 0555, ⓦ kshouse.jp/tokyo-e; Kuramae station. This spick-and-span hostel, just south of Asakusa, gets lots of accolades, and has spawned other branches across Japan. There's no shortage of showers and toilets, plus there's an attractive lounge area with a well-equipped kitchen and a roof terrace. Dorms ¥2900, twins ¥7200

Nui Hostel & Bar Lounge ヌイホステルバーラウンジ 2-14-13 Kuramae, Taitō-ku ☎ 03 6240 9854, ⓦ backpackersjapan.co.jp/nui; Kuramae station. Just 15min on foot from Asakusa, this hostel is an excellent choice. The funky common area features a bar that's hugely popular with locals, and a great mingling spot; the pine beds in the dorms aren't quite as fancy, but they do the job. Dorms ¥3000, doubles ¥7600

AKASAKA AND ROPPONGI
SEE MAP PAGE 98

★ **Kaisu** カイス 6-13-5 Akasaka, Minato-ku ☎ 03 5797 7711, ⓦ kaisu.jp; Akasaka station. Think you might prefer Akasaka to Asakusa? This is one of the only hostels in the club-heavy Roppongi area – it's not cheap, but being able to stagger home certainly saves money over a long cab ride. This is no party hostel, however, but a beautiful place set into an old geisha house; they do, however, also have an excellent on-site bar. Dorms ¥4300

HARAJUKU, AOYAMA AND SHIBUYA
SEE MAP PAGE 116

Turntable Hostel ターンテーブル ホステル 10-3 Shinsen-chō, Shibuya-ku ☎ 03 3461 7733, ⓦ turntable.tokyo; Shinsen station. The best hostel option in the Shibuya area – indeed, this whole chunk of Tokyo – is a chic, hipster-friendly place with a bar and restaurant abutting the lobby. The dorms are slightly capsule-like in nature, and there are socializing spots even within the corridors. Breakfast included. Dorms ¥4500

IKEBUKURO AND AROUND
SEE MAP PAGE 138

Unplan アンプラン 23-1 Tenjinchō, Shinjuku-ku ☎ 03 6457 5171, ⓦ unplan.jp; Kagurazaka station. One of the new wave of flashpacker hostels offering capsule-like dorm "rooms"; set in pine frames and concealed by curtains, they're quite cosy. Dorms ¥4500

TO BE, OR NOT TO AIRBNB?

The world's largest city it may be, but Tokyo suffers from something of a **dearth of accommodation** at more or less all budget levels – a problem sure to raise its head during the 2020 Olympic Games. A combination of high occupancy rates and high accommodation prices have led many travellers to give **Airbnb** (ⓦ airbnb.com) a go; the bulk of apartments go for ¥10,000–20,000 per night, and private rooms ¥3000–12,000. Tokyo duly became the site's fastest-growing market worldwide in early 2016, bringing the government under pressure from a hotel industry haemorrhaging revenue. Fears of a total crackdown were allayed in August of that year, when restrictions were lowered, rather than raised, though new registration rules introduced in 2018 removed thousands of Tokyo listings from the site. With the situation still somewhat up in the air, you're advised to check the site, and news organs like the *Japan Times* (ⓦ japantimes.co.jp), for updates far in advance of your visit.

13

LONG-TERM ACCOMMODATION

Gaijin houses Those on a budget usually start off in what's known as a *gaijin* house – a privately owned house or apartment consisting of shared or private rooms with communal kitchen and bathroom. They're usually rented by the month, though if there's space, weekly or even nightly rates may be available. Monthly rates start at ¥35,000–45,000 per person for a shared room and ¥40,000–70,000 for a single; a deposit may also be required. Try looking at *Metropolis* (see page 25) for listings.

Private apartments Private apartments are usually rented out by real-estate companies, although agencies recommended here (see below) have apartments on their books. Apart from the first month's rent, be prepared to pay a deposit of 1–2 months' rent in addition to key money (usually 1–2 months' non-refundable rent when you move in), and a month's rent in commission to the agent. You may also be asked to provide information about your financial situation and find someone – generally a Japanese national – to act as a guarantor. Rentals in Tokyo start at ¥60,000 per month for a one-room box, or ¥100,000 for somewhere with a separate kitchen and bathroom. For serviced apartments, figure on daily rates of ¥13,000 and up, and minimum terms of one month.

GAIJIN HOUSE AGENCIES

★ **Freshroom** ☎ 03 3851 6707, ⓦ freshroom.jp. Growing year by year, this excellent agency often houses *gaijin* in slightly larger buildings than others – great for students or businessfolk who'd like to make a few friends, especially since many guests are Japanese.

Kimi Information Center 8F Oscar Building, 2-42-3 Ikebukuro ☎ 03 3986 1604, ⓦ kimiwillbe.com. Runs a useful letting agency, with plenty of budget choices; they can also help with shorter-term arrangements.

Sakura House 2F K-1 Building, 7-2-6 Nishi-Shinjuku, Shinjuku-ku ☎ 03 5330 5250, ⓦ sakura-house.com. One of the biggest and best-known agencies for *gaijin* houses, with a tremendous range of places to stay across the city and helpful, well-informed staff.

APARTMENT RENTALS

Hikari Tokyo Apartment ⓦ tokyoapartment81.com. Agency used to dealing with foreign clients, with a wide range of affordable options.

Mori Living ⓦ www.moriliving.com. Excellent upper-end choice, mostly serviced apartments; a good option for those in Tokyo on business, or with a family.

Tōkyū Stay ⓦ tokyustay.co.jp. Good range of upmarket serviced apartments, many of which are in highly convenient locations.

Eating

Get ready for the gastronomic experience of a lifetime: when it comes to eating and drinking, few places in the world can compare to Tokyo. The number, range and quality of places is outstanding, with practically any world cuisine you can think of available alongside all the usual – and many unusual – Japanese dishes. The city's range of places to dine runs the gamut from simple noodle bars up to high temples of gastronomy where the eye-popping beauty of the food on the plate is matched by an equally creative approach to interior design. This being Japan, there are also scores of novelty theme restaurants, where the food plays second fiddle to the wacky atmosphere.

14

There's no need to panic about prices. Practically everywhere, including Michelin-starred restaurants, offers bargain **set-meal specials** for lunch, and there's a plethora of **fast-food** options, including stand-up noodle bars and conveyor-belt sushi restaurants, many clustered around and inside train stations. If you'd rather eat well and party at the same time, then **izakaya** (bars that serve food) are the way to go; a few with especially good food are reviewed here, others in the "Drinking and nightlife" chapter. There are also a great number of local **chain restaurants** (see page 162), where prices are at a minimum, and English-language menus are guaranteed; the quality of food at these places is often surprisingly good.

You can hardly walk a block of central Tokyo without passing a chain **café** – as often as not a *Starbucks*, although local operations such as *Doutor*, *Tully's* and *Caffe Veloce* are also common. Despite the convenience of these places, one of Tokyo's great joys is whiling away time in non-chain cafés (sometimes called *kissaten*), where the emphasis is on service and creating an interesting, relaxing, highly individual space. Recently, a glut of hipster-style coffee joints has sprung up around the country – to Western travellers, they'll feel a lot more familiar than the *kissaten*. Apart from drinks, many of the cafés listed in this chapter also serve wonderful pastries and a fine selection of more substantial foods which means they're good places for snacks and light meals. Some offer alcohol, too, making for a more relaxed alternative to bars. Do note, however, that many of Tokyo's cafés have no dedicated nonsmoking areas.

Traditional **teahouses** (*sabō*) are thinner on the ground than cafés; track one down and you can sample Japanese sweets made from compounded sugar or pounded rice cake (*mochi*) and red bean paste, the sweetness of which balances the bitterness of the tea. It's worth noting that while cafés often keep late hours, teahouses are generally a daytime affair.

ESSENTIALS

INFORMATION

Listings For up-to-date information on Tokyo's restaurant scene, check out *Metropolis* (ⓦ metropolis.co.jp), *Time Out* (ⓦ timeout.com/tokyo), and the rather more homespun Tokyo Belly (ⓦ tokyobelly.com) and Tokyo Cheapo (ⓦ tokyocheapo.com).

PRACTICALITIES

Breakfast The traditional Japanese breakfast features miso soup, fish, pickles and rice, washed down with green tea, though many Japanese now prefer a quick *kōhii* and *tōsuto* (coffee and toast), served at most cafés on the "morning service" menu (from ¥500 up). If you really want to jump into local culture, eat a tray of *nattō*: part-fermented soya beans served with soy sauce and mustard – it'll certainly wake you up. Many ryokan and top hotels offer a choice between a Western- or Japanese-style breakfast, which is sometimes included in the rates (see page 147).

Meal times Hardly any locals linger over lunch (usually taken from noon to 2pm) but that's no reason why you should follow suit. Dinner can be eaten as early as 6pm (with many places taking last orders around 9pm), although Tokyo is not short of options for late-night dining. Opening times are given throughout this chapter, though note that last orders tend to fall either 30min or an hour before the stipulated closing time; this goes for lunch too. These timings are just like the Shinkansen – arrive a minute late, and you've missed it.

Set meals Many restaurants offer set menus (*teishoku*), usually at around ¥1000 for a couple of courses plus a drink, and only rarely topping ¥3000 per person. At both lunch and dinner you may also come across what is described as a "course menu" (*kōsu menyū*), which is in fact a set menu of several courses and more expensive than the *teishoku*.

Reservations are advisable for many places, especially on Friday, Saturday and Sunday nights. At some popular venues you may have to queue at lunch- and dinnertime, even if a reservation system is in place.

ETIQUETTE

Reading the menu These days more places provide menus translated into English, and it's always worth asking for one (*Eigo no menyū ga arimasu ka?*) if it's not automatically presented. To assist with ordering, consult our Food and drink glossary (see page 278).

Table manners Before you start eating, you'll usually be handed an *oshibori*, a damp, folded hand towel, usually steamed hot, to clean your hands. When the food arrives, wish your companions bon appétit by saying *itadakimasu*. Don't stick chopsticks (*hashi*) upright in your rice – this is an allusion to death (relatives traditionally pass pieces of bone from the cremation pot to the funeral urn with long

TOKYO'S BEST RESTAURANTS

Best budget chain *Yoshinoya* (see page 162)
Best okonomiyaki *Sometarō* (see page 164) or *Sakuratei* (see page 169)
Best veggie ramen *T's Tantan* (see page 159)
Best views *Hibiki* (see page 161)
Best udon *Udon Shin* (see page 171)
Best sushi *Sushibun* (see page 164) or *Iroha Sushi* (see page 166)
Best tempura *Hachimaki* (see page 161) or *Suzuya* (see page 170)
Best tonkatsu *Tonki* (see page 168)
Best tofu *Sasa-no-yuki* (see page 163) or *Ume-no-hana* (see page 161)
Best yakitori *Omoide Yokochō* (see page 170)

14

chopsticks). Never cross your chopsticks when you put them on the table, and don't point at things with them. When eating soupy noodles it's considered good manners to slurp them noisily from the bowl.

Service, taxes, tipping and the bill When you want the bill, say *o-kanjō o kudasai* ("bill please"); the usual form is to pay at the till on the way out. Consumption tax (ten percent) will push up the total cost if not included in the prices; prices given in the reviews include tax. Some restaurants and bars serving food, especially those in hotels, add on a service charge (typically ten percent), which has also been included in prices given here. Tipping is not expected, but it's polite to say *gochisō-sama deshita* ("that was delicious") to the waiter or chef. Payment by credit card is becoming more common, but having enough cash to cover your tab is still a good idea.

RESTAURANTS

THE IMPERIAL PALACE AND AROUND
SEE MAP PAGE 42

Matsumotorō 松本楼 1-2 Hibiya-kōen, Chiyoda-ku ☎03 3503 1451, ⓦmatsumotoro.co.jp; Hibiya station. On a sunny day it's a pleasure to sit on the terrace of this venerable restaurant, which is as old as the park – Hibiya-kōen, Tokyo's first Western-style park – in which it's located. The food is pretty standard, along the lines of *omu-raisu* (rice-filled omelette; ¥1400), hamburgers and other Western "favourites". Daily 10am–9pm.

The Oyster Shack かき小屋 1-6-1 Uchisaiwai-chō, Chiyoda-ku ☎03 6205 4328, ⓦkakigoya.jimdo.com; Shimbashi station. One of the city's most atmospheric oyster bars, snuggled under the train track arches north of Shimbashi station. Oysters cost from ¥300, and there's a whole aquarium's worth of scallops, turban shells, garlic calamari and other stuff to slurp down. Mon–Fri 4–11.30pm, Sat & Sun noon–11pm.

Ren Ren Ren 人人人 1F Tokia Tokyo Building, 2-7-3 Marunouchi, Chiyoda-ku ☎03 5252 7361; Tokyo station. Cheap-but-attractive Chinese lunch option in the Tokyo station area. Sets of chilli shrimp, *mapo tofu* (chunks of tofu with minced meat in an oily, spicy sauce) or fried rice go for just ¥1100, and you can wash it down with some Shaoxing rice wine, which is something of an acquired taste. Mon–Fri 11am–4am, Sat & Sun 11am–10pm.

★ **Ryugin** Tokyo Midtown Hibiya, 1-1-2 Yurakuchō, Chiyoda-ku ☎03 6630 0007, ⓦnihonryori-ryugin.com; Hibiya station. Voted among the world's top 50 restaurants on several occasions, this is a prime place for a kaiseki meal, which is one of the best culinary experiences Japan can throw at you (see page 165), given a twist of molecular gastronomy. It's not cheap (around ¥40,000 or so), and getting a reservation is not always easy, but it's certainly worth it. Daily 5.30–11pm.

Sawamura 登運とん 7F Shin-Marunouchi Building, 1-5-1 Marunouchi, Chiyoda-ku ☎03 3240 0033, ⓦb-sawamura. com; Tokyo station. The best food on the restaurant level of the Shin-Marunouchi building, serving a mix of Japanese and Italian cuisine at fair prices; opt for pasta choices such as crab and avocado cream tagliatelle (¥1880), or meat and fish dishes involving beef cheek in wine, grilled mackerel and the like. Mon–Sat 11am–3am, Sun 11am–10pm.

Tonton 登運とん 2-1-10 Yurakuchō, Chiyoda-ku ☎03 3508 9454; Hibiya station. One of the most famous under-the-tracks restaurants in all Tokyo – not entirely on account of its food, most of which is served in grilled-skewer form (offal being the speciality), but more due to its superb location, and an atmospheric, ever-present cloud of smoke which can make the chefs hard to see. Daily 11.30am–10.30pm.

★ **T's Tantan** T'sたんたん Keiyo Street, 1-9-1 Marunouchi, Chiyoda-ku ☎03 3218 8040, ⓦts-restaurant.jp; Tokyo station. Veggies and vegans, if you want to have a crack at ramen or Japanese noodles, this is your place. Most go for the vegan ramen, but the spicy, drier *tantan-men* is even better (¥850), while they also have vegan *gyōza* and spicy tofu. It's actually located inside Tokyo station, so you'll need a train ticket – an ideal pit-stop on your way into or out of Tokyo. Daily 7am–10.30pm.

14

JAPANESE STAPLE DISHES

With Japanese food now popular across the globe, most visitors will, before even setting foot in the country, have sampled at least a couple of its main staple dishes. However, any national cuisine is best tasted in its homeland, and chances are that it'll be cheaper here, too. **Sushi** is perhaps the country's most famous food; go to a good restaurant and you'll never want to eat it outside Japan again.

SUSHI

Unless you're totally disgusted by the thought of raw fish, you absolutely have to give sushi a go during your time here. The name refers not to the fish, but to the vinegared rice it (or other ingredients) are laid upon; simple raw fish is actually known as **sashimi**. At a traditional *sushi-ya*, each plate is freshly made by a team of chefs working in full view of the customers. Choices include tuna (*maguro*), salmon (*sāmon*), shrimp (*ebi*), eel (*unagi*), scallop (*hotate*) and egg (*tamago*); order by pointing, or going for a set (*mori-awase*; usually served at lunch). **Kaiten-zushi** shops, where you pluck your selections from a conveyor belt, are an inexpensive, convenient way of sampling the cuisine; plates are colour-coded according to price, and the total number of plates is totted up at the end. You'll be served green tea with your meal, and expected to pour your own soy sauce, into which some stir *wasabi* (already included beneath the fish in some sushi); note that it's the fish, not the rice, which is supposed to be dipped into the soy, though this is only possible if you have good chopstick skills.

NOODLES AND RAMEN

There are three main types of noodle to try in Tokyo. The first two usually go side by side in simple noodle restaurants (see page 162): **soba**, a thin, grey noodle made from buckwheat powder; and **udon**, a fatter, white noodle made from wheat flour. These come with all sorts of toppings, and in either a hot or a cold broth (the latter usually a bit more expensive). King of the noodles, however, is **ramen**, a Chinese-style yellow noodle served in dedicated, often atmospherically steamy establishments; this can come in a soy or miso-based broth, and the additional ingredients vary. It's not unusual for long lines to form outside hit ramen stalls and there are scores of blogs devoted to the quest for the best bowl – English ones include Ⓦ www.ramenadventures.com and Ⓦ ramentokyo.com. Lastly, **tsukemen** is a sort of ramen in which the broth is served separately – often lukewarm, and with less liquid to slurp, many prefer it in the summertime, when it can be tough to pluck up the courage to fill oneself with boiling soup.

OKONOMIYAKI, MONJAYAKI AND ODEN

Savoury **okonomiyaki** are fast gaining currency outside Japan. Restaurants specializing in this pancake-like batter dish have tables featuring hot plates; usually the batter and ingredients are brought out for you to cook yourself. Fillings can vary, but seafood, noodles and veggies are popular choices. Tokyo has its own variant, known as **monjayaki**; with a far looser consistency than *okonomiyaki*, this is always a DIY job, though staff will do the necessaries for you if you ask.

A popular winter dish (though available all year round) is **oden**, large chunks of simmered tofu, *daikon* (radish), root-vegetable jelly, seaweed, hard-boiled eggs and fishcakes, traditionally eaten with a smear of mustard; *oden* is best eaten in *izakaya*, though convenience stores also sell it.

GRILLED MEATS, CUTLETS AND TEMPURA

Yakitori are delicious skewers of grilled chicken (or sometimes other meats, offal and vegetables). Traditionally seen as something of a non-gourmet, working-class meal, it has recently undergone a popularity explosion; inexpensive places to enjoy it include the atmospheric stalls under the tracks at Shimbashi and Yurakuchō. Similar to *yakitori* are **kushiage**: skewers of meat, seafood and vegetables, coated in breadcrumbs and deep-fried.

If your tastes turn to pork, then you'll not want to miss out on **tonkatsu**, larger cuts of meat also coated in breadcrumbs and usually served on shredded cabbage with a brown, semisweet sauce. This forms part of the king of comfort foods – **katsu-karē**, a breaded cutlet (usually pork) served with Japanese-style curry, sometimes served on a bed of rice.

Lastly, there's **tempura**, a series of battered, deep-fried comestibles including okra, shrimp (particularly tasty) and sweet potato; some restaurants serve a few varieties on a bed of rice (*tendon*).

GINZA AND AROUND
SEE MAP PAGE 53

Aoki 寿司屋青木 6-7-4 Ginza, Chūo-ku ☎03 6228 6436; Ginza station. This may look like a conventional sushi spot, but one look at the menu will prove otherwise: additions such as avocado, camembert and foie gras may offend the purists, but they taste rather good. You can have as much or as little as you like; a full meal will cost ¥2000–3000. Daily 11.30am–3pm & 5–11pm.

Dhaba India ダバインディア 2-7-9 Yaesu, Chūo-ku ☎03 3272 7160, ⓦdhabaindia.com; Kyōbashi station. Give your taste buds a workout at this bustling South Indian restaurant, one of the best of its kind in Tokyo. The blue decor avoids the usual clichés, and the specialities include a prawn and fish curry (¥1530), and a range of *dosa* (from ¥1200); lunch specials available for under ¥1000. Mon–Fri 11.15am–3pm & 5–10pm, Sat & Sun noon–3pm & 5–9pm.

★**Ginza Hirai** 銀座ひらい 5-9-5 Ginza, Chūo-ku ☎03 6280 6933; Higashi-Ginza station. About as old-school Ginza as you can get: mustard-yellow walls and dark-wood furnishings make this back-street venue an atmospheric place to tuck into conger eel on rice. ¥1800 will get you a bowl of the stuff, plus pickles and miso soup, which is very cheap for good eel. Daily 11.30am–2.30pm & 5.30–10pm.

Hibiki 響 46F Caretta Shiodome Building, 1-8-1 Higashi-Shinbashi, Minato-ku ☎03 6215 8051, ⓦdynac-japan.com/hibiki; Shiodome station. This modern *izakaya* boasts some of Tokyo's best views, high up on the 46th floor with large windows facing out over Tokyo Bay. The cuisine is contemporary Japanese, and lunch sets (¥1300 for the daily special, ¥1200 for a fried fish set) are particularly good value; count on more like ¥6000 a head in the evening. Mon–Fri 11am–3pm & 5–11.30pm, Sat & Sun 11am–4pm & 5–11pm.

Little Okinawa リトル沖縄 8-7-10 Ginza, Chūo-ku ☎03 3572 2930; Shimbashi station. The welcome at this cosy Okinawan restaurant is as warm as it would be in the southern islands. Try Ryūkyū dishes such as *goya champurū* (noodles with stir-fried bitter melon; ¥840), washed down with the strong rice liquor *awamori*. Mon–Fri 5pm–3am, Sat & Sun 4pm–midnight.

Old Thailand オールドタイランド 2-15-3 Shimbashi, Minato-ku ☎03 6206 1532; Shimbashi station. Lively Thai restaurant whose menu eschews the regular rundown, instead offering unusual creations such as specialities from the northeastern Isaan region, and delectable Chiang Mai curry noodles (¥1100). Mon–Sat 11.30am–3pm & 5pm–11pm.

Sakyō Higashiyama 左京ひがしやま B1F Oak Ginza, 3-7-2 Ginza Chūo-ku ☎03 3535 3577, ⓦsakyo higashiyama.com; Ginza station. Refined *kyō-ryōri* (Kyoto-style cuisine) is served at this rustic basement space, decorated with bamboo and with an open kitchen

that feels a million miles from Ginza's bustle. The lunch set (¥2200) includes six delicious, seasonal courses. Mon–Sat 11.30am–3pm & 5.30–11pm.

Taimeiken たいめいけん 1-12-10 Nihombashi, Chūo-ku ☎03 3271 2463, ⓦtaimeiken.co.jp; Nihombashi station. Tokyoites love the nostalgia of one of Tokyo's original Western-style restaurants, whose *omu-raisu* (fried rice wrapped in an omelette; ¥1700) featured in the cult movie *Tampopo*. Staff bustle about the cheap and cheerful downstairs section, serving large portions of curry rice, *tonkatsu* and noodles. Upstairs is a more formal restaurant serving the same menu at slightly higher prices. Mon–Sat 11am–9pm, Sun 11am–8.30pm.

★**Torigin Honten** 鳥ぎん本店 5-5-7 Ginza, Chūo-ku ☎03 3571 3333, ⓦtorigin-ginza.co.jp; Ginza station. Bright, popular restaurant hidden away on a side street – look for the red sign. They serve snacks like *yakitori* (from ¥170 per stick) and *kamameshi* (kettle-cooked rice with a choice of toppings; from ¥880). Their ¥750 weekday *toridon* (chicken on rice) lunch sets are a real bargain. Daily 11.30am–10pm.

Ume-no-hana 梅の花 5F 2-3-6 Ginza, Chūo-ku ☎03 3538 2226, ⓦumenohana.co.jp; Ginza-itchōme station. Trickling streams and bamboo screens set the mood in this elegant restaurant specializing in melt-in-the-mouth tofu creations. The tofu comes natural, deep-fried, boiled, grilled or sweetened for dessert; sets change by the season, but lunch courses generally go from ¥2100, while dinner sets start at ¥3560. Daily 11am–4pm & 5–10pm.

AKIHABARA AND AROUND
SEE MAP PAGE 60

Botan ぼたん 1-15 Kanda-Sudachō, Chiyoda-ku ☎03 3251 0577; Awajichō station. Chicken *sukiyaki* (a stew-like dish served in a hotpot) is the order of the day at this atmospheric old restaurant, tucked into the backstreets of Kanda. At around ¥7000 a head it's not cheap, but this is the genuine article, where the chicken, vegetables and tofu simmer gently over individual braziers in small rooms. Daily (except Sun) 11.30am–9pm.

Go Go Curry ゴーゴーカレー 1-16-1 Kanda-Sakumachō, Chiyoda-ku ☎03 5256 5525, ⓦgogocurry.com; Akihabara station. No doubt about it, the official meal of Akihabara regulars is *tonkatsu* curry (fried pork cutlet on rice, smothered in curry sauce), and one of the heartiest you'll find is at this chain, whose main branch – complete with gorilla logo – is in Akihabara. Plates start at ¥730, and in keeping with the rather odd opening hours ("go" is Japanese for the number five), you get ¥100 off before 5.55pm. Daily 9.55am–9.55pm.

★**Hachimaki** はちまき 1-19 Kanda-Jimbōchō, Chiyoda-ku ☎03 3291 6222; Jimbōchō station. Dating back to 1931, this tempura specialist is one of Tokyo's best time-warp restaurants: black-and-white photos abound,

14

14

DINING ON THE CHEAP

Tokyo isn't exactly paradise for budget travellers, but as far as food goes there are some very good ways to stretch your yen. Most head straight to the city's chain **convenience stores** such as 7-Eleven, AM/PM and Lawson (see page 206), which sell snacks and meals round the clock; these include sandwiches and pastries, plus more intrinsically Japanese sustenance such as *oden* (see page 160) and *onigiri* (rice wrapped in layered seaweed, with various fillings). Not quite as numerous, but still found in all parts of town, **supermarkets** sell sandwich fodder and other staples such as bentō sets (rice with all manner of other ingredients, in a plastic tray) and super-cheap fresh noodles; note that in the hours before closing (9–11pm) they tend to lop up to half of the price off sushi and other bentō.

If you want to eat out, try a **standing noodle bar**; these are usually referred to as a *soba-ya* or *udon-ya*, though in practice the vast majority sell both. A bowl of soba or udon will cost from ¥250, though it can be tricky to operate the Japanese-only ticket machines. However, the best value is to be had at Tokyo's **fast-food** chains, almost all of which supply English-language menus. All of the following can be found in every single part of town; just ask around.

FAST-FOOD CHAINS

Caffè Veloce カフェベローチェ. In a city where a simple mug of Joe can easily set you back ¥600, this budget café chain is a great fallback option: in cheap but pleasing Italianate environs, their coffee costs from just ¥200, and doesn't taste bad at all. Typically daily 8am–7pm.

CoCo Ichiban-ya ココ壱番屋 ⓦichibanya.co.jp. A quirky curry chain which allows you to piece together your meal. First, choose the type of stock you desire, then the amount of rice you want (up to a mighty 900g), then your desired level of spice (level one barely registers as a hit; level ten provides a veritable spice-gasm). Then comes the fun add-your-ingredients bit: choices include beef, okra, scrambled egg, cheese, *tonkatsu*, *nattō* and a whole lot more. It'll end up costing ¥600–1100. Daily 8am–midnight, often later.

Fuji Soba 富士そば. Sometimes you just want something quick, cheap and easy. This simple, round-the-clock chain (not as ubiquitous as others on this list, but there's at least one in most major areas) certainly scratches those particular itches, with soba from ¥300, *curry katsudon* for ¥570 and a range of similarly priced

local staples – all surprisingly tasty. Daily, usually 24hr.

Matsuya 松屋 ⓦmatsuyafoods.co.jp. Fronted by yellow, Japanese-only signs with red and blue blobs on them, this chain specializes in cheap curry (from ¥330) and *gyūdon* (beef on rice; ¥380). They chuck in a steaming-hot bowl of miso soup with whatever you order. Daily 24hr.

Saizeriya サイゼリ屋 ⓦwww.saizeriya.co.jp. Budget Italian food, often surprisingly good; their tasty *doria* (meaty rice gratin) will fill a hole for ¥300, pasta dishes and small pizzas can be had from ¥399, or have a fried burger-and-egg set for ¥400. The wine prices are also ridiculous – ¥100 per glass, or an astonishingly cheap ¥1100 for a 1.5-litre bottle (in other words, two normal bottles). Daily 8am–midnight, often later.

★ **Yoshinoya** 吉野屋 ⓦyoshinoya.com. You can't miss the bright orange signs marking branches of the nation's favourite fast-food chain, famed for its cheap, tasty bowls of *gyūdon* (beef on rice) from just ¥380. When they started reselling this dish after sales were choked off by a BSE scare, there was a 1.5km-long line outside their main Shinjuku branch – evidence of how important *Yoshinoya* is to Japan. Daily 24hr.

yellowing walls makes it feel like the whole place has been dunked in tea, and there's nary a sign that you're in the twenty-first century. Have a crack at their delectable *tendon*, which gets you four freshly made tempura on rice (¥800), or a full set (¥2000). Daily 11am–9pm.

Kagawa Ippuku 香川一福 1-18-11 Uchi-Kanda, Chiyoda-ku ☎03 5577 3644; Kanda station. A cheap and simple, yet highly respected, udon restaurant; bowls go from ¥450, and though there's an English menu, staff will be able to help you out with the Japanese-language-only ticket machines. Mon–Sat 11am–7pm.

Toritsune Shizendo 鳥つね自然洞 5-5-2 Soto-Handa, Chiyoda-ku ☎03 5818 3566; Suehirochō

station. Simple place serving some of the best oyakodon (basically chicken and egg on rice) around, for the very fair price of ¥1100. Daily (except Sun) 1.30am–1.30pm & 5.30–10pm.

UENO AND AROUND
SEE MAP PAGE 66

Hantei はん亭 2-12-15 Nezu, Bunkyō-ku ☎03 3828 1440, ⓦhantei.co.jp; Nezu station. Stylish dining in a beautiful, three-storey wooden house. There's only one dish, *kushiage* (deep-fried pieces of meat, fish and vegetables skewered on sticks), served in combination plates, six at a time: ¥3000 for the first plate (plus two appetisers); ¥1500 thereafter, until you say stop. Tues–Sat noon–2.30pm & 5–10pm, Sun 11.30am–2.30pm & 4–9.30pm.

Izuei 伊豆榮 2-12-22 Ueno, Taitō-ku ☎ 03 3831 0954; Ueno station. Fancy eel specialist on the southern fringe of Shinobazu Pond, selling delectable unadon (eel on rice) from ¥3240, or ¥2700 if you're one of the first twenty in for lunch. If your budget doesn't stretch that far, try a *tenju* (tempura on rice) for ¥1620. Daily 11am–9.30pm.

Musashino 武蔵野 2F 2-8-1 Ueno, Taitō-ku ☎ 03 3831 1672; Ueno-Hirokōji station. One of Ueno's few remaining old-style restaurants serving *tonkatsu*, for which the area was once famed; they have, however, recently moved up a floor to a less visually appealing space. The tonkatsu come in big, thick, melt-in-the-mouth slabs; choose between standard *rōsu* (fatty belly meat) and the leaner *hire* (loin fillet), both costing ¥1000 including soup, rice and pickles. Daily 11.30am–9pm.

★**Sasa-no-yuki** 笹乃雪 2-15-10 Negishi, Taitō-ku ☎ 03 3873 1145, ⓦ sasanoyuki.com; Uguisudani station. Three centuries ago, the chef here was said to make tofu like "snow lying on bamboo leaves", and both the name and the quality have survived, though the old wooden house is now marooned among flyovers. Calm prevails over the tatami mats as you feast on delicately flavoured silk-strained tofu. Prices are reasonable, with most tofu plates priced at around ¥750, and full courses starting at ¥5000 (or ¥2200 for lunch). Tues–Sun 11.30am–9pm.

Yukikage ゆきかげ 2-18-3 Nezu, Bunkyo-ku ☎ 03 5809 0612; Nezu station. Not your typical ramen spot – this one almost looks more like a bar, thanks to the range of sake and shōchū (they even have local IPA on tap). The noodles themselves are great too (from ¥750), and you'll probably have to eat standing up at the counter – which can be a real positive in this sociable, foreigner-friendly place. Tues–Sun 11am–10pm.

ASAKUSA
SEE MAP PAGE 75

320 Ramen 320ラーメン 2-15-1 Asakusa, Taitō-ku; Asakusa station. Don't expect any culinary fireworks at this spit-and-sawdust ramen bar, but the bowls – at just ¥320 – are excellent backpacker fare, and they don't taste too bad at all. Daily (except Sat) 10am–7.30pm.

Amisei あみ清 ☎ 3 3844 1869, ⓦ amisei.com. This boat sets off from the southwest side of Azumabashi bridge, Asakusa. Two-hour evening cruises cost ¥8640, including all the tempura you can eat. More lavish menus can be ordered and, naturally, prices skyrocket for cruises on the night when Asakusa holds its annual fireworks extravaganza in July.

★**Bon** 梵 1-2-11 Ryusen, Taitō-ku ☎ 03 3872 0375, ⓦ fuchabon.co.jp; Iriya station. A rare chance to sample *fucha ryōri*, a distinctive style of Zen Buddhist cuisine in which each of the ornately presented vegetable dishes is traditionally served from one large bowl, and the meal

begins and ends with tea. The setting, a charming old Japanese house, and the calm service, make it an experience not to be missed. Reservations essential, with courses starting at ¥5400. Mon & Tues, Thurs & Fri noon–1.30pm & 5–7pm, Sat noon–7pm, Sun noon–6pm.

Chin-ya ちんや 1-3-4 Asakusa, Taitō-ku ☎ 03 3841 0010, ⓦ www.chinya.co.jp; Asakusa station. Founded in 1880, this famous *shabu-shabu* and *sukiyaki* (styles of Japanese hotpots) restaurant offers sets from ¥5500. The place occupies seven floors, with more casual dining in the basement, where you can go for steak instead (from ¥2500). Mon & Wed–Fri noon–3.30pm & 4.30–9.30pm, Sat & Sun 11.30am–9pm.

Hatsuogawa 初小川 2-8-4 Kaminarimon, Taitō-ku ☎ 03 3844 2723; Asakusa station. Look for the profusion of potted plants outside this tiny, rustic eel restaurant. It's a lovely place to experience one of Japan's most delectable fish dishes (eel sets from ¥2900), but they often sell out or fill up long before closing time – arrive early. Mon–Sat noon–1.30pm & 5–7.30pm, Sun 5–7.30pm.

La Sora Seed ラソラシド 31F Solamachi, 1-1-2 Oshiage, Sumida-ku ☎ 03 5414 0581, ⓦ kurkku.jp; Oshiage station. Ecologically sound operation boasting one of the best possible views of the huge Skytree tower (see page 78). It leans on European flavours, including great meatballs made with organic pork. Lunch sets go from ¥3100, dinner for almost three times that. Daily 11am–4pm & 6–11pm.

Maguro Bito まぐろ人 1-21-8 Asakusa, Taitō-ku ☎ 03 3844 8736, ⓦ magurobito.com; Asakusa station. Fuji TV viewers once voted this the top *kaiten-zushiya* in Japan, and it's easy to see why: the quality of fish and other ingredients is excellent, the turnover fast and the decor on the ritzy side. Expect a queue (but it moves fast). Electronically price-coded plates range from ¥170 to ¥530. Mon–Fri 11.30am–9.30pm, Sat & Sun 11am–10pm.

Matsunami ステーキハウス松波 1-11-6 Asakusa, Taitō-ku ☎ 03 3844 3737, ⓦ matsunami.net; Asakusa or Tawaramachi stations. If you want to try some of Japan's melt-in-the-mouth beef, head to this traditional steakhouse, where the chef cooks the meat in front of you. Lunchtime plates start at ¥1800, including a coffee, so it won't break the bank. At night, prices begin at ¥4200 per portion, and quickly go up. Mon–Sat 11.30am–2pm & 5–11pm, Sun 11.30am–2pm & 5–10pm.

Nakae 中江 1-9-2 Nihonzutsumi, Taitō-ku ☎ 03 3872 5398, ⓦ sakuranabe.com; Minowa station. This venerable restaurant specializes in dishes made with horse meat, including *sukiyaki* (hotpot). The interior, decorated with beautiful ink paintings of horses, looks pretty much like it did a century ago when the whole area was a thriving red-light district. Their famous hotpots start at ¥3000, but consider splashing out ¥8000 on the full meal. Tues–Fri 5–10pm, Sat & Sun 11.30am–9pm.

14

14

DINING ON THE WATER

Lunch and dinner cruises on **yakatabune**, low-slung traditional boats lit up with paper lanterns, are a charming Tokyo eating institution, dating back to the Edo period. The boats accommodate anything from sixteen to a hundred people on trips along the Sumida-gawa and out on Tokyo Bay. Options listed in this chapter include *Amisei* (see page 163) and *Funasei* (see page 164); for a bar-like alternative, see *Jicoo* (see page 181).

Ōtafuku 大多福 1-2-6 Hanakawado, Taitō-ku ☎03 3871 2521, ⊛otafuku.ne.jp; Asakusa station. Recently relocated from its near century-old roost to the northwest, this restaurant has lost little of its charm, with customers clamouring to sample its delicious selection of *oden* boiled in a soy and *dashi* broth. Wash it all down with a glass of pine-scented *tarozake* (sake). There's a picture menu (individual pieces ¥130–600) or you can sit at the counter and point at what you want in the bubbling brass vats. Mon–Fri 5–10pm, Sat & Sun 11am–1pm & 4–8pm.

★ **Sometarō** 染太郎 2-2-2 Nishi-Asakusa, Taitō-ku ☎03 3844 9502; Tawaramachi station. This rambling, wooden restaurant specializing in *okonomiyaki*, but also offers some quirky house creations such as *osomeyaki* (a variation of *okonomiyaki*, made with Worcester sauce), all costing ¥550–1380. There are English instructions on the menu, and staff are pleased to help out with your on-the-table creations. Daily noon–10.30pm.

RYŌGOKU AND KIYOSUMI
SEE MAP PAGE 66

Ryōgoku Terrace 両国テラス 1-11-21 Yokoami, Sumida-ku ☎03 5608 7580, ⊛ryogokuterrace.jp; Ryōgoku station. A good option if you don't want the local speciality, *chanko-nabe* – simple Western meals, including pasta, salads and good pizza (all from ¥1000), served in a pretty settling, including an outdoor patio fringed with greenery. Mon–Fri 11.30am–3pm & 5.30–11pm, Sat & Sun 11am–11pm.

Tomoegata 巴潟 2-17-6 Ryōgoku, Sumida-ku ☎03 3632 5600, ⊛tomoegata.com; Ryōgoku station. In the heart of sumo territory, and a grand place to head if you're off to a tournament, this is a good place to sample *chanko-nabe*, the wrestlers' protein-packed meat, seafood and vegetable stew. Their sets (¥860–4860) come in sizes named after sumo rankings – the *yokozuna* course would fill a whale, but even the cheapest one (weekdays only) is pretty hearty. Daily 11.30am–2pm & 5–11pm.

Yoshiba 吉葉 2-14-5 Yokoami, Sumida-ku ☎03 3623 4480, ⊛kapou-yoshiba.jp; Ryōgoku station. Set in an old sumo *dōjō* (practice hall); book ahead for the prime tables around the ring), this is a richly atmospheric place to come for *chanko-nabe* (from ¥3000; minimum two persons); cheaper sets with sushi, *tendon* and the like are also available for lunch. On Mon, Wed and Fri there's live

singing of traditional songs. Mon–Sat 11.30am–1.30pm & 5–10pm.

BAYSIDE TOKYO
SEE MAP PAGE 88

The Canteen ザキャンティーン 1F The Soho, 2-7-4 Aomi, Koto-ku ☎03 5530 0261; Fune-no-Kagakukan monorail. Cosy up in the booths and flip through the glossy mags with creative types at this hip office complex near the Odaiba waterfront. Expect to pay around ¥1000 for Japanese home cooking such as fried chicken and rice, or just grab a coffee or fruit juice. Mon–Fri 9am–10pm, Sat 10am–6pm.

Funasei 船清 ☎03 5479 2731, ⊛funasei.com. Bay cruises, lasting two and a half hours, run out of Shinagawa and offer a choice of Japanese- and Western-style menus, with unlimited bar access, for around ¥10,800 per person.

Kondō 近どう 3-12-10 Tsukushima, Chūō-ku ☎03 3533 4555; Tsukishima station. This is the best *monjayaki* (see page 160) restaurant in a part of town that's absolutely full of them, striking just the right note – classic in style, but not falling to bits. They've a wide range (¥700–1600), of which 14 are explained on their English menu; options for the mix include mentaiko (spicy roe), tuna-corn-cheese, curry, or chicken and plum paste. Mon–Fri 5–10pm, Sat & Sun noon–10pm.

★ **Ramen Kokugikan** ラーメン国技館 5F Aqua City, 1-7-1 Daiba, Minato-ku ☎03 3599 4700; Odaiba Kaihin-kōen monorail. Six top ramen chefs from around Japan square off against each other in this section of Aqua City's restaurant floor. A bowl will cost you from ¥800; the Hakata variety, from Fukuoka, is well worth trying, as is the tsukemen wing. The outdoor balcony, when it's open, boasts fantastic views across the bay towards Tokyo's twinkling lights. Daily 11am–11pm.

★ **Sushibun** 鮨文 6-5 Toyosu, Koto-ku ☎03 3541 3860; Shijō-mae monorail station. One of the most *gaijin*-friendly options among the rows of sushi stalls within the new Toyosu fish market. Sets go from ¥3550, though you won't regret spending ¥1200 more for their top-quality ten-piece selection, including creamy *uni* (sea urchin). Daily (except Sun) 6.30am–2pm.

Sushi-zanmai Honten すしざんまい本店 4-11-9 Tsukiji Chūō-ku ☎03 3541 1117; Tsukiji station. Still going despite the relocation of the massive fish market it used to sit alongside, this pleasantly noisy place is the main, and best, branch of a popular chain of sushi restaurants run by Kimura Kiyoshi, the self-proclaimed "King of Tuna". Filling sushi sets go from ¥1620. Daily 24hr.

AKASAKA AND ROPPONGI
SEE MAP PAGE 98

Felafel Brothers 5-1-10 Roppongi, Minato-ku ☎03 6459 2844; Roppongi station. Vegan snack-shack, with sandwiches and salad bowls going from ¥1000; as you may have inferred from the name, felafel is a popular (and wise) choice, and there's Israeli beer and wine to wash it down with. There are only four seats inside, so most choose to take away; they've opened up a bigger, but less convenient, place near Ebisu. Mon–Sat 11am–10pm.

Gold Scorpion 金蠍 4-2-8 Shiba-kōen, Minato-ku ☎03 6380 0138; Kamiyachō station. The best place to eat in the Tokyo Tower complex (not much of a boast, admittedly), a simple place specialising in tantan-men (ramen noodles with minced pork and a spicy, oily sauce). Have it dry (¥780), in a soup (¥900), or with pork rib (¥1080), and choose your spice level from the ticket machine. Daily 11am–10pm.

Gonpachi 権八 1-13-11 Nishi-Azabu, Minato-ku ☎03 5771 0170, ⓦgonpachi.jp; Roppongi station. A faux-Edo-period storehouse is home to this atmospheric Japanese restaurant. Take your pick between reasonably priced soba (from ¥800) and grilled items (¥270–500) on the ground and second floors, or sushi on the third floor – a full meal will set you back around ¥3000. There's a wonderful samurai drama atmosphere, and it's easy to see how the place inspired the climactic scenes of Quentin Tarantino's *Kill Bill Vol. 1*. Daily 11.30am–3.30am.

★ **Kurosawa** 黒澤 2-7-9 Nagatachō, Chiyoda-ku ☎03 3580 9638, ⓦ9638.net/nagata; Tameike-sannō station. The design of this atmospheric restaurant was inspired by the sets from Akira Kurosawa's movies *Yojimbo* and *Red Beard*, and a meal here is a superb experience. Given the quality, the prices in the downstairs soba section (bowls from under ¥800) are a real steal; the refined upstairs rooms are for grander set meals only (from ¥5000). Mon–Fri 11.30am–3pm & 5–10pm, Sat noon–9pm.

L'Atelier de Joël Robuchon 2F Roppongi Hills Hillside, 6-10-1 Roppongi, Minato-ku ☎03 5772 7500, ⓦrobuchon.jp; Roppongi station. The French master chef has six Tokyo outposts; this one in Roppongi Hills is the best, offering tasting menus starting at ¥3520 for lunch, ¥5720 for dinner. There's a no-bookings policy, so you may have to wait to get a seat at the long counter, facing the open kitchen where black-garbed chefs create culinary mini-masterpieces before your very eyes. Daily 11.30am–2.30pm & 6–10pm.

Nobu Tokyo 東京 Toranomon Towers Office, 4-1-28 Toranomon, Minato-ku ☎03 5733 0070, ⓦnobu restaurants.com; Kamiyachō station. There's a dramatic Japanese-style design for Nobu Matsuhisa's Tokyo operation, where you can sample the famous black-cod dinner (Robert de Niro's favourite) for around ¥5550. For something a bit different, try *tiradito*, their South American twist on sashimi. Mon–Fri 11.30am–2pm & 6–10.30pm, Sat & Sun 6–10.30pm.

★ **Nodaiwa** 野田岩 1-5-4 Higashi-Azabu, Minato-ku ☎03 3583 7852, ⓦnodaiwa.co.jp; Kamiyachō station. Kimono-clad waitresses shuffle around this 160-year-old *kura* (storehouse), converted into one of Tokyo's best eel restaurants; a set meal will cost around ¥5000. The private rooms upstairs can only be booked by parties of four or more; if it's busy, they may guide you to the annexe around the corner, which has an almost identical interior. Mon–Sat 11am–1.30pm & 5–8pm.

Shunjū 春秋 27F Sannō Park Tower, 2-11-1 Nagatachō, Chiyoda-ku ☎03 3592 5288, ⓦshunju.com; Tameike-sannō station. Great modern Japanese dining experience, matching stylish interior design with food made from the freshest seasonal ingredients, including good seafood. The ¥1200 lunch deals are good (although the place gets busy with office workers); ¥400 extra gets you a go at the veggie buffet. In the evening it's overpriced, as you can easily spend ¥6000 on a set. Daily (except Sun) 11.30am–2.30pm & 5–11pm.

★ **Sukiyabashi Jiro** すきやばし次郎 3F Ark Mori Building, 6-12-2 Roppongi, Minato-ku ☎03 5413 6626, ⓦsushi-jiro.jp; Roppongi station. You may have heard of Jiro Dreams of Sushi, but people also dream about getting a seat at Jiro's restaurant; for the next best thing, head to this offshoot, stewarded by the famed chef's son. Although it's not cheap by any means (¥22,000 for lunch, ¥30,000 for

14

KAISEKI-RYŌRI: JAPAN'S BANQUET MEALS

Gourmands will not want to miss the opportunity to sample Japan's finest style of cooking, **kaiseki-ryōri**, while in Tokyo. A *kaiseki* meal consists of a series of small, carefully balanced and beautifully presented dishes, the ingredients reflecting the seasons, served by a waitress in kimono on exquisite china and lacquerware. It began as an accompaniment to the tea ceremony and still retains the meticulous design of that elegant ritual. While a *kaiseki* dinner can easily run to ¥10,000 or more, a *kaiseki* bentō (boxed lunch) is a more affordable option. Apart from recommended restaurants such as *Kakiden* (see page 170) and *Tōfuya-Ukai* (see above), top hotels are the best places for enjoying this style of cuisine.

14

dinner), those who can afford it will find the quality beyond reproach. Daily (except Wed) 11.30am–2pm & 5.30–9pm.

Suzunami 鈴波 B1F Galleria, Tokyo Midtown, 9-7-4 Akasaka, Minato-ku ☎03 5413 0335, ⓦsuzunami. co.jp; Roppongi station. Try the house speciality at this restaurant, hidden behind a shop in Tokyo Midtown's basement level – silver cod marinated in what's left of the rice mash after it's been used to make sake. Their filling set meals, rounded off with a glass of plum wine, are great value, starting at ¥1400. Daily 11am–10pm.

★ **Tōfuya-Ukai** とうふ屋うかい 4-4-13 Shiba-kōen, Minato-ku ☎03 3436 1028, ⓦukai.co.jp; Akabanebashi station. At the foot of Tokyo Tower, this stunning re-creation of an Edo-era mansion, incorporating huge beams from an old sake brewery, serves unforgettable tofu-based *kaiseki*-style cuisine. Book well ahead, especially for dinner (at least a month in advance). Set meals only, with lunch from ¥5940 on weekdays, and dinner from ¥10,800. Daily 11am–10pm.

EBISU, MEGURO AND THE SOUTH
SEE MAP PAGE 108

Chano-ma チャノマ 6F Nakameguro Kangyō Building, 1-22-4 Kami-Meguro, Meguro-ku ☎03 3792 9898; Nakameguro station. Dining while seated on the floor is not exactly uncommon in Tokyo, but at this casual eatery the dining space is actually a padded, bed-like platform – this is true lounging. (They do also have regular tables.) Overlooking the river in swanky Nakameguro, they serve some very tasty rustic-style Japanese fusion dishes (lunch sets from ¥1000), as well as a great selection of teas and flavoured lattes. Mon–Thurs & Sun noon–2am, Fri & Sat noon–4am.

Ebisu Yokochō 千恵比寿横丁 Ebisu, Minato-ku; Ebisu station. Not a restaurant, but a whole clutch of them, crammed into a hugely atmospheric covered arcade east of Ebisu station. Come in the evening and take your pick – there's a curry stand, several noodle joints, places specializing in seafood, and even a miniature karaoke bar. In addition, the venues and the tables in them are arranged in a way that lends itself to mingling. Daily 5pm–late.

Futatsume ふたつめ 3-9-5 Kami-Meguro, Meguro-ku ☎03 3712 2022; Nakameguro station. Grand little *kushiage* (deep-fried sticks) place, selling skewered snacks from just ¥100; choices include breaded camembert, shiitake and salmon, and they're all best washed down with a gigantic highball (¥980). Mon–Sat 6pm–3am.

Higashiyama 東山 1-21-25 Higashiyama, Meguro-ku ☎03 5720 1300, ⓦhigashiyama-tokyo.jp; Nakameguro station. An elegant restaurant and bar that's the epitome of Tokyo cool. The multilevel space has an open kitchen that allows you to watch the delicious range of dishes being prepared. The lunchtime "course menus" (see page

158) are just about affordable at ¥3500 (dinner's more like ¥6000), and they have a fine selection of sake and *shōchū* to match. Mon–Sat 11.30am–3pm & 6pm–midnight.

★ **Iroha Sushi** いろは寿司 1-5-13 Kami-Meguro, Meguro-ku ☎03 5722 3560, ⓦirohasushi.com; Nakameguro station. Relaxed sushi den that's the diametric opposite of most diners in this fancy part of town – you won't see any hipsters or bohos here, just salary-folk and older locals. Every single piece is freshly made, yet the place remains cheaper than any *kaiten-zushiya*, especially on weekday lunchtimes, when huge sets go from just ¥680; the largest is just ¥1050, and will fill almost any belly. Daily 11.30am–2.30pm & 5–10.30pm.

Ivy Place アイヴィプレイス 16-15 Sarugakuchō, Shibuya-ku ☎03 6415 3232, ⓦtysons.jp; Daikanyama station. This large, attractive venue is *so* Daikanyama – always full at brunchtime with shopping-bag-toting folk, tucking into buttermilk pancakes (¥1300), eggs with chorizo and potatoes (¥1400) and more. Good coffee, too. Daily 7am–11pm.

Jasmine 5-22-3 Hiro-o, Shibuya-ku ☎03 5421 8525, ⓦjasmine310.com; Hiro-o station. Michelin-recommended restaurants usually have mammoth queues at mealtimes, but you often don't have to wait at all at this pretty Chinese restaurant. It's cheap, too – just ¥1100 for their lunch special, a delicate cold chicken dish, served in sesame-topped soy, and highly photogenic; for an extra ¥250 you can have a mini spicy mapo tofu. You'll be spending a lot more at dinnertime; again, it's worth the price. Daily 11.30am–3pm & 6–11pm.

★ **Kosyu Ichiba** 広州市場 1-29-12 Aobadai, Meguro-ku ☎03 3760 7147; Nakameguro station. This chain sells fantastic *tantan-men* (ramen noodles with a spicy, oily sauce and minced pork; ¥920), and their delectable *gyōza* (¥330) aren't far off. The attractive Nakameguro branch basically does the simple things really, really well, and every customer walks out rubbing their belly. Daily 11am–2am.

Longrain 39F Ebisu Garden Place Tower, 4-20-3 Ebisu, Shibuya-ku ☎03 5424 1300; Ebisu station. The city's top Thai restaurant, in at least one sense, boasting phenomenal views over Tokyo from atop the mighty Ebisu Garden Place Tower. The food is cheap, considering, with lunch sets from ¥1300, including curry and pad Thai options. The atmosphere is loungey, though the music may be a little loud for some. Mon–Fri 11.30am–4pm & 5.30–11pm, Sat & Sun 11.30am–11pm.

Pizzeria da Isa ピッツェリアダイーサ 1-28-9 Aobadai, Minato-ku ☎03 5768 3739, ⓦda-isa.jp; Nakameguro station. The Japanese head chef at this authentically Italian-style pizzeria scooped a clutch of awards in Napoli – if he made his mark in the very home of pizza, you can be sure that this is the best you'll find in all Japan. Pizzas go from ¥1500, though note that every

14

TOKYO FOR VEGETARIANS

It may be the capital of a historically Buddhist nation, but Tokyo is a surprisingly bad place in which to be **vegetarian**. The problem stems from the fact that, although the average Japanese eats far less meat than the average Westerner, vegetarianism is extremely rare here: you might ask for a vegetarian (saishoku) dish in a restaurant, and still be served something with meat or fish in it. For example, the popular tofu dish hiya yakko (a small slab of chilled tofu topped with grated ginger, spring onions and soy sauce) is usually sprinkled with flakes of bonito (dried tuna). If you're a committed vegetarian, things to watch out for include dashi stock, which contains bonito; breads and cakes, as these can contain lard; and omelettes, which can contain chicken stock.

The good news is that places specializing in vegetarian and vegan food in Tokyo are on the rise. In this chapter, see the reviews for Bon (see page 163), Ain Soph Journey (see page 170), Land (see page 169), T's Tantan (notably offering veggie ramen; see page 159) and Felafel Brothers (see page 165); in addition, the Happy Cow phone app works well here, with over 450 options in Tokyo alone.

---

diner needs to order one dish and a drink; service is also notoriously uppity. Tues–Sun 11.30am–2pm & 5.30–11pm.

★**Tonki** とんき 1-1-2 Shimo-Meguro, Meguro-ku ☏03 3491 9928; Meguro station. This minimalist, sharp-looking, family-run restaurant – where a seemingly telepathic team create order out of chaos – is the most famous place in town for tonkatsu. Expect to have to queue up for a seat at mealtimes. Sets cost from ¥1900, cutlet alone ¥1300; you'll have to choose between hire (fillet) and rosu (sirloin). Daily (except Tues) 4–10.45pm.

HARAJUKU, AOYAMA AND SHIBUYA
SEE MAPS PAGE 116, PAGE 119 AND
PAGE 124

Bepokah ベポカ 2-17-6 Jingūmae, Shibuya-ku ☏03 6804 1377, ⓦbepocah.com; Meiji-jingūmae station. Given their mutual adoration of raw fish, you'd think that Peruvian cuisine would have a bigger impact in Japan. This is one of the only places in Tokyo in which you'll find quality ceviche (dishes from ¥1800), as well as Andean staples such as lomo saltado (stir-fried beef on rice; ¥2600) and ají de gallina (chicken in an almost curry-like yellow cream; ¥1800). Pricey, but just about worth it. Mon–Fri 6pm–1am, Sat 5pm–midnight.

Commune 2nd コミューン2nd 3-13 Minami-Aoyama, Minato-ku; ⓦcommune2nd.com; Omotesandō station. This open-air courtyard space is almost like a boho slice of London, San Francisco or Melbourne – a clutch of small snack shacks selling all sorts, from gourmet hot dogs and burgers to Thai food and ramen. It's also a good drinking spot (see page 184). Daily 11am–10pm; usually closed Dec–Feb.

★**Florilège** 2-5-4 Jingūmae, Shibuya-ku ☏03 6440 0878, ⓦaoyama-florilege.jp; Gaiemmae station. Not just any old French restaurant – chef Hiroyasu Kawate is something of a culinary superstar in Tokyo, and his fusion of Japanese and French tastes is something to behold, if you can afford it (¥6500 for a six-course lunch, ¥12,500 for an 11-course dinner). At these prices you'd expect a fancy setting too, and this restaurant certainly doesn't disappoint, with its rich carpets, dim lighting and flashes of greenery. Daily (except Wed) 12pm–1.30pm & 6.30–8pm.

Ganso Kujiraya 元祖くじら屋 2-9-22 Dōgenzaka, Shibuya-ku ☏03 3461 9145, ⓦwww.kujiraya.co.jp; Shibuya station. Like it or not, the Japanese have eaten whale meat for centuries, and this smart, surprisingly cheap venue is a good option if you'd like to see – and taste – what the fuss is about; if you're curious, it tastes a bit like liver. You may not be able to make head or tail of the menu (though it does feature pictures of the latter), so take a Japanese-speaker along if possible; most dishes are ¥780–980, but it's best visited at lunch when you'll get a hearty set from ¥1000. Mon–Fri 11am–2pm & 5–10.30pm, Sat & Sun 11.30am–11.30pm.

Gonpachi 権八 14F E-Space Tower, 3-6 Maruyama-chō, Shibuya-ku ☏03 5784 2011, ⓦgonpachi.jp; Shibuya station. A sister restaurant to the famous one in Roppongi (see page 165), this fourteenth-floor spot is great for a meal with a view – even Bill Clinton came along once. Under an elegant grid of dangling lamps, sushi sets go from ¥2000; the other wing has even cheaper lunchtime donburi and soba dishes (¥800–1200). Daily 11.30am–2am.

Hanamaru はなまる B1, 2-1 Udagawa-chō, Shibuya-ku ☏03 5428 0870, ⓦhanamaruudon.com; Shibuya station. Simple noodle restaurant that's a touch classier than the bigger chains, and certainly makes tastier food. Their cheapest udon is around ¥300, and though nothing's in English, picture menus help out somewhat. Daily 9am–10pm.

Harajuku Gyōzaro 原宿餃子楼 6-2-4 Jingūmae, Shibuya-ku ☏03 3406 4743; Meiji-jingūmae station. Though there are few Japanese customers (or, indeed, kitchen staff) at this atmospheric dumpling spot, the fare on offer is cheap and tasty. It's just over ¥300 for a round of succulent *gyōza*; your choices can be fried or boiled, and with or without garlic, and you can chase them down with draught beer. Mon–Sat 11.30am–4am, Sun 11.30am–11pm.

Land ランド 3-27-1 Shibuya, Shibuya-ku ☎03 3312 6791; Shibuya station. Decent western and Japanese food in a very pleasant environment. Pasta and rice dishes, as well as Okinawan "taco rice" (really quite tasty) go for ¥1000–1400, and seafood a little more; there are also some excellent vegan options. Daily (except Fri) 11.30am–3pm.

★ **Los Barbados** ロスバルバドス 41-26 Udagawachō, Shibuya-ku ☎03 3496 7157; Shibuya station. This little *izakaya* is, well, a little different from the norm. Under a large map of the Congo, the Africaphile owner whips up great food from across the African continent, including Senegambian rice-and-meat staples such as *maafe* and *yassa*; lunch meals cost under ¥1000, and there are always vegan options. Wash it all down with some Kenya Cane. Mon–Sat noon–3pm & 6–11pm.

Maisen まい泉 4-8-5 Jingūmae, Shibuya-ku ☎03 3470 0071, ⊚mai-sen.com; Omotesandō station. Located in an old bathhouse, this long-running *tonkatsu* restaurant serves up superb set meals from just ¥1580; prices dip under ¥1000 for lunch, though you'll probably have to queue for a while. Daily 11am–10pm.

Murugi ムルギ 2-29-1 Dōgenzaka, Shibuya-ku ☎03 3462 0241; Shibuya station. In the heart of Shibuya's sleazeland, this curry restaurant has been going for decades – since 1951, in fact – perhaps thanks to their distinctive Fuji-shaped rice mounds (actually more like the Matterhorn, but whatever). The curries will set you back ¥1000 (or ¥50 more with an egg), and taste just fine; the only problem is that the restaurant is only open for lunch. Daily (except Fri) 11.30am–3pm.

★ **Out** 2-7-14 Shibuya, Shibuya-ku, ⊚out.restaurant; Shibuya station. A small and uncommonly focused restaurant, where there's only one dish on the menu, only one wine served alongside, and only Led Zeppelin on the sound system. The dish in question is truffle pasta (¥4000 with wine, ¥2900 without), which is quite superb; the truffles and paired wines vary with the season. Tues–Sat 6pm–late; Sun 11am–2.30pm & 6pm–late.

Ramen Nagi ラーメン凪 1-3-1 Higashi, Shibuya-ku ☎03 3499 0390, ⊚n-nagi.com; Shibuya station. At this busy ramen joint, the waiter will give you a choice of how soft or hard you'd like your noodles cooked. There are a few interesting selections available on the fun cross-section menu, including the "Midorio", made with basil and cheese – weird, but it works. More regular varieties are served in a rich broth, topped with delicious pork slices and a heap of chopped spring onions – a bargain at ¥880 a bowl. Mon–Sat 11am–11pm, Sun 11am–10pm.

Royal Garden Café 2-1-19 Kita-Aoyama, Minato-ku ☎03 5414 6170, ⊚royal-gardencafe.com; Gaienmae station. With its spacious reclaimed-wood interior, on-site bakery and wraparound terrace sheltered by an umbrella of ginkgo trees (which look amazing in the autumn), this organic food café at the entrance to Meiji-jingū Outer Garden strikes all the right notes. Good set lunches, including pasta or salad as a main, are ¥1000 during the week; it's around ¥2000 for weekend brunch. Daily 11am–11pm.

★ **Sakuratei** さくら亭 3-20-1 Jingūmae, Shibuya-ku ☎03 3479 0039, ⊚sakuratei.co.jp/en; Meiji-jingūmae station. Funky, cook-your-own *okonomiyaki*, *monjayaki* and *yakisoba* joint behind the weird and wonderful Design Festa gallery (see page 120). Dishes start at ¥950, and feature some quirky options such as curry, Okinawan or pizza-style ingredients. A good drinks selection means it's a fun place at night. Daily 11am–11pm.

Two Rooms 5F AO Building, 3-11-7 Kita-Aoyama, Minato-ku ☎03 3498 0002, ⊚tworooms.jp; Omotesandō station. Sophisticated, high-end restaurant featuring a relaxed bar, and a spacious outdoor terrace that provides striking views. Perfectly cooked European food using top-quality Japanese ingredients is enhanced by wonderfully polite service. On Sunday they do a brunch

14

JAPANESE COOKERY COURSES

Learning to cook is currently very popular in Tokyo, with cooking schools setting up shop in big shopping malls. You'll usually need to book well in advance.

ABC Cooking Studio In the basement of Tokyo Midtown ☎03 5413 3476, ⊚www.abc-cooking. co.jp. Though this school focuses on Japanese students baking Western-style treats such as bread and cake, they have English-speaking instructors on hand to guide you through the basics of Japanese and other Asian cuisines.

Arigato Japan ☎090 6484 9577, ⊚arigatojapan. co.jp. Highly popular dining tours around Japanese markets, helping you to identify all those weird and wonderful Japanese products.

Buddha Bellies ☎03 5716 5751, ⊚buddhabellies tokyo.jimdo.com. Cultivate your own Buddha belly after lessons in making sushi, bentō, udon or even *washoku* (traditional meals) at this foreigner-friendly school.

Mayuko's Little Kitchen ☎080 3502 2005, ⊚mayukoslittlekitchen.com. Learn Japanese home-cooking skills at the home of the eponymous Mayuko, a highly personable local. Options include sushi, bentō and "everyday meals", and guests get a printed recipe sheet and apron to take home.

14

for ¥3600; otherwise lunch sets start at ¥2200, and dinner mains from ¥4400. Daily 11.30am–2.30pm & 6–10pm; bar open until 2am Mon–Sat.

Uobei 魚べい 2-29-1 Dōgenzaka, Shibuya-ku ☎ 03 3462 0241; Shibuya station. Searingly bright restaurant in which your sushi is ordered by touch screen, then delivered by rail on automated plates – the only humans you see are those who point you to your table and take your cash. Gimmicky, yes, but it's a lot of fun – not to mention cheap, since sushi plates go from ¥108. Daily 11am–midnight.

SHINJUKU AND THE WEST
SEE MAPS PAGE 128, PAGE 133 AND
PAGE 134

Acacia アカシア 3-22-10 Shinjuku, Shinjuku-ku ☎ 03 3354 7511; Shinjuku station. This old-school, shades-of-brown spot would suit Ginza more than Shinjuku, but local suits love the curry and (oddly) cabbage meat-rolls; you can have both on the same place, with some rice and pickles, for ¥850. A weird mix of India, Russia and retro Japan, with a painting of a cabbage on the wall – somehow, it works. Daily (except Tues) 11am–10pm.

Ain Soph Journey 3-8-9 Shinjuku, Shinjuku-ku ☎ 03 5925; Shinjuku-sanchōme station. Popular, presentable vegan restaurant doling out salads, veggie soups, green curry and the like, all costing ¥1200 or so for lunch, and a bit more at dinnertime. They also make delectable vegan pancakes (¥1620). Daily 11.30am–5pm & 6–10pm.

J.S. Burgers Café 3F 4-1-7 Shinjuku, Shinjuku-ku ☎ 03 5367 0185, ⓦ burgers.journal-standard.jp; Shinjuku station. A fab range of home-made chunky burgers, hot dogs and sandwiches are served at this retro-styled café – it's ¥1210 for a bacon-and-egg burger, and ¥1620 for the three-patty monster. Mon–Fri 11.30am–10pm, Sat 10.30am–10.30pm, Sun 10.30am–9pm.

Kakiden 柿傳 8F Yasuyo Building, 3-37-11 Shinjuku, Shinjuku-ku ☎ 03 3352 5121, ⓦ kakiden.com; Shinjuku station. One of the best places in Tokyo to sample *kaiseki-ryōri* (see page 165). There's a lunch set for ¥4320, but you won't regret investing in the eighteen-course dinner for ¥8640. They also conduct *kaiseki* appreciation classes. Daily 11am–9pm.

Konjiki Hototogisu 金色不如帰 2-4-1 Shinjuku, Shinjuku-ku ☎ 03 3373 4508; Shinjuku-gyoemmae station. There's always a long queue outside this esteemed noodle restaurant, but it says something that people are prepared to wait – sometimes for well over an hour – to nab one of the eleven seats. Two types of ramen soba are available, as well as a *tsukesoba* (dry noodles with dipping stock), and all cost under ¥1000, unless you go for some of the highly tempting add-ons. Mon–Fri 11am–3pm & 6.30–10pm.

Nakajima 中嶋 3-32-5 Shinjuku, Shinjuku-ku ☎ 03 3356 4534, ⓦ shinjyuku-nakajima.com; Shinjuku

station. At lunch all the delicious dishes served here are made with sardines – they're a bargain at around ¥1000 a plate, though you'll need a few to fill up. For dinner it's worth the expense (over ¥8000 per person) to sample the chef's Kansai *kapo* style of cooking, similar to *kaiseki-ryōri*; after all, it's earned him a Michelin star. Daily (except Sun) 11.30am–1.45pm & 5.30–8.30pm.

Nanban-tei なんばん亭 2F 2-12-3 Kitazawa, Setagaya-ku ☎ 03 3419 6938, ⓦ nanbantei.net; Shimokitazawa station. Highly atmospheric *okonomiyaki* restaurant (mains from ¥900) in Shimokitazawa, with lampshades that seem vaguely medieval, latticed windows looking down onto the street, and staff who amble around with cooking utensils in their holsters, like culinary cowboys. Daily 5pm–1am.

New York Grill 52F Park Hyatt Tower, 3-7-1-2 Nishi-Shinjuku, Shinjuku-ku ☎ 03 5323 3458, ⓦ tokyo.park. hyatt.jp; Tochōmae station. Sitting pretty on the 52nd floor of the *Park Hyatt*, this joint offers great views and Stateside-sized portions – after the buffet lunch (¥6800, including taxes and service charge) you won't n–eed to eat much else all day. Bookings essential. Daily 11.30am–2.30pm & 5.30–10.30pm.

★ **Omoide Yokochō** 思い出横丁 1-2-7 Nishi-Shinjuku, Shinjuku-ku; Shinjuku station. It's almost pointless recommending specific establishments on this hugely atmospheric *yokochō* alley (see page 171) – just stroll along a few times, until you've spied both the food you desire, and a free seat. Most places daily 4pm–midnight.

Suzuya すずや Kabukichō Ichibangai-iriguchi, Shinjuku-ku ☎ 03 3209 4408; Shinjuku station. Famous *tonkatsu* restaurant, which first opened just after World War II. Their twist on the breaded pork cutlet dish is to serve it *ochazuke* style (¥1530) – you pour green tea over the meat and rice to make a kind of savoury porridge. Daily 11am–10.30pm.

★ **Tensuke** 天すけ 3-22-7 Kōenji-kita, Suginami-ku ☎ 03 3223 8505, ⓦ nakadori.jp; Kōenji station. Perhaps the only restaurant in Tokyo famed for its eggs, mainly thanks to the often theatrical way they're prepared in this cute little space, which suits Kōenji down to the ground. A tamago-tempura set will cost ¥1100/1600 for lunch/dinner, with the egg served on top of rice, and followed by a selection of excellent tempura. Daily (except Mon) noon–2pm & 6–10pm.

★ **Tsunahachi** つな八 3-31-8 Shinjuku, Shinjuku-ku ☎ 03 3352 1012, ⓦ tunahachi.co.jp; Shinjuku station. This famous tempura restaurant almost always has a queue outside, though you're likely to get seated quickly if you settle for the upstairs rooms away from the frying action. Everything is freshly made, and the bowls, cups and plates are all little works of art. Even the smallest lunch set (just over ¥1500, including soup, rice and pickles) will fill you up, but somewhat unfairly, it's not listed on the

YOKOCHŌ

A trip to Tokyo is not complete without a night out at one of the city's many **yokochō**. These market-style areas often focus on food and drink, and many are packed with dozens upon dozens of minuscule eateries. With smoke and steam rising from the open-air "kitchens" (often nothing more than a small grill), they can be hugely photogenic. English-language menus and signage are rare at these places, but many places specialize in a particular type of food, making selection and ordering a simple exercise in walking around and pointing. Almost all stalls will sell beer, as well as sake.

The most famous *yokochō* in Tokyo is Shinjuku's *Omoide Yokochō* (see page 170), but *Ebisu Yokochō* (see page 166) down south is very good too (and covered, which is handy when it's cold or rainy), and there are several under the tracks south of Tokyo station. However, there are atmospheric *yokochō* all around the city – just ask around for the nearest one.

14

English menu; dinner sets will cost around double. Daily 11am–10pm.

Udon Shin うどん 慎 2-20-16 Yoyogi, Shibuya-ku ☎03 6276 7816; Shinjuku station. It's worth braving the Michelin-issue queues at this small, venerable udon joint – it'll give you plenty of time to peruse the various options on their menu (most bowls ¥900–1300), which include some featuring flying-fish tempura, others with yuzu sauce, and even a carbonara-like choice with parmesan cheese and bacon tempura. Sun–Thurs 11am–11pm, Fri & Sat 11am–midnight.

IKEBUKURO AND THE NORTH
SEE MAPS PAGE 138 AND PAGE 140

Akiyoshi 秋吉 3-30-4 Nishi-Ikebukuro, Toshima-ku ☎03 3982 0601, ⓦakiyoshi.co.jp; Ikebukuro station. Unusually large *yakitori* bar with a garrulous atmosphere and a helpful picture menu. Most deep-fried items are around ¥400 per plate, and there's plenty of booze on offer. Mon–Sat 5pm–midnight, Sun 5pm–11pm.

Bakudan ばくだん 1-21-1 Higashi-Ikebukuro, Toshima-ku; Ikebukuro station. Most *takoyaki* booths are much of a muchness, but the name of this place – "bomb" – hints at its super-sized servings. One of its *takoyaki* (octopus balls – ball-shaped snacks of batter filled with minced or diced octopus; from ¥370) is as large as a whole tray of normal-sized octopus balls. Long queues often form, giving you time to choose from toppings such as *yakitori* sauce, *kimchi* and lavered seaweed. Daily 10am–11pm.

Canal Café カナルカフェー 1-9 Kagurazaka, Shinjuku-ku ☎03 3260 8068, ⓦcanalcafe.jp; Iidabashi station. This is a surprisingly tranquil and appealing waterside spot, particularly romantic at night when the old clapperboard boathouses sparkle with fairy lights, or during the blossom-heavy *sakura* season. The café-restaurant has decent-value pasta and pizza meals (¥900–1400); for coffee alone, you can head to the outdoor section, though annoyingly they only serve in paper cups. Tues–Fri 11.30am–11pm, Sat & Sun 11.30am–9.30pm.

Hanagakura 花がくら 3-1 Kagurazaka, Shinjuku-ku ☎03 3260 0767; Iidabashi station. There are tables everywhere you look in this rambling, atmospheric Kagurazaka restaurant; perhaps most fun (unless you're quite tall) are the uppermost ones, from which you can even touch the ceiling from a seated position. The food is wholesome Japanese fare, with the lunch deals especially good value – meat and fish sets go for ¥900, and there's a "healthy" option for ¥1000. Mon–Fri 11.30am–2.30pm & 5pm–midnight, Sat 11.30am–11pm.

Hansarang ハンサラン 2F 1-16-15 Ōkubo, Shinjuku-ku ☎03 5292 1161; Shin-Ōkubo station. Designed like a Korean farmhouse with wooden beams and intimate booths, this restaurant is a good place to get acquainted with the diversity of Korean cuisine. Various set courses, served with multiple side-dishes (*banchan*) start at ¥1500, including cheesy "UFO" chicken, the latest fad to cross over the sea (though never called this in Korea itself). Daily 11am–midnight.

Isomaru Suisan 磯丸水産 3-25-10 Nishi-Ikebukuro, Toshima-ku ☎03 5953 2585; Ikebukuro station. This seafood *izakaya* is heaving all evening, every evening – in fact, it's so popular that it never shuts. There's no English menu, but there are plenty of pictures and live sea creatures to point at – try their colossal *sazae* (sea snails), or the splendid-value eel on rice (*unadon*; ¥980). Other branches around the city. Daily 24hr.

Le Bretagne 4-2 Kagurazaka, Shinjuku-ku ☎03 3235 3500; ⓦle-bretagne.com; Iidabashi station. Attractive French-run restaurant down a little side-street in Kagurazaka, offering authentic crepes (both sweet and savoury) from ¥780 and buckwheat *galettes* from ¥1180, as well as home-made Breton-style cider and good coffee. Tues–Sat 11.30am–10.30pm, Sun 11.30am–10pm.

Malaychan 3-22-6 Nishi-Ikebukuro, Toshima-ku ☎03 5391 7638, ⓦwww.malaychan-satu.jp; Ikebukuro station. Tiny, unpretentious Malay restaurant dishing up decent food, from grilled fish on a banana leaf and *mee goreng* (fried noodles) to winter steamboats (the Malay equivalent of *sukiyaki*). Weekday lunch menus start at

14

TOKYO'S TOP CAFÉS AND TEAHOUSES

Best for Japanese desserts *Umezono* (see page 176)
Best for tea *Cha Ginza* (see page 175)
Best for classical music *Lion* (see page 175)
Best for quirkiness *Maidreamin* (see pages 173 and 175) and *Swallowtail Café* (see page 175)
Best for Middle Eastern options *Mocha Coffee* (see page 174)
Best for aromas *Aoyama Flower Market* (see page 176)
Best animal café *Calico* (see page 175)
Best for a 1970s Tokyo vibe *Café de l'Ambre* (see page 172)
Best for views *L'Occitane* (see page 175)

¥850, and in general you'll eat well for under ¥2000. Mon 5–11pm, Tues–Sat 11am–2.30pm & 5–11pm, Sun 11am–11pm.

Mutekiya 無敵家 1-7-1 Minami-Ikebukuro, Toshima-ku ☎ 03 3982 7656, ⓦ mutekiya.com; Ikebukuro station. Popular with both tourists and locals, the queue at this ramen joint often stretches a full 40m from the door – don't worry, since it moves along fairly quickly. While you wait you can decide on the size, flavour and toppings or your ramen or *tsukemen*; bowls start at ¥800 or so. Daily 10.30am–4am.

★**Saemaeul Sikdang** セマウル食堂 1-1-4 Hyakuninchō, Shinjuku-ku ☎ 03 6205 6226; Shin-Ōkubo station. This outpost of an authentic Korean chain is by far the best *yakiniku* restaurant in Koreatown. Order some *yeoltan bulgogi* (like the meat from *shabu-shabu* without the soup, mixed with spicy paste; ¥950 per portion), and a

boiling *doenjang jjigae* (a spicier, chunkier miso soup served with rice; ¥840 per portion), and watch as the ethnic-Korean staff nonchalantly blanket the rest of your table with free side-dishes. To make things feel even more like Seoul, order a bottle of flavoured *soju* to wash everything down with. Daily 11.30am–2am.

Taishōken 大勝軒 2-42-8 Minami-Ikebukuro, Toshima-ku ☎ 03 3981 9360; Higashi-Ikebukuro station. Diners at this noodle restaurant are arranged almost as if they're praying to the chefs at work in the centre – and, in a sense, they are here to worship. This is the *honten* (head branch) of the eponymous noodle behemoth, and the very birthplace of *tsukemen* – try a bowl here (from ¥800) and you'll notice that the original taste is somewhat more subtle than the fattier broths in vogue these days. Daily (except Wed) 11am–10pm.

CAFÉS

GINZA AND AROUND
SEE MAP PAGE 53

Café de l'Ambre カフェドランブル 8-10-15 Ginza, Chūō-ku ☎ 03 3571 1551; Shimbashi station. One of Tokyo's best coffee venues – at least for those who don't mind the semi-permanent cloud of cigarette smoke. This old-school Ginza *kissaten* has been roasting up 300g batches of beans since the 1950s, achieving something approaching coffee perfection in the intervening years. Most cups (from ¥700) are made with a cotton-felt filter – the process is quite mesmerizing. Mon & Wed–Sat noon–9.30pm, Sun noon–6.30pm.

Henri Charpentier アンリシャルペンティエール 2-8-20 Ginza, Chūō-ku ☎ 03 3562 2721, ⓦ henri-charpentier.com; Ginza-itchōme station. This deep-pink boutique offers the ultimate in Tokyo patisseries on the ground floor, and a *salon de thé* below. Here you can enjoy crêpe suzette (¥2500, including a drink), flambéed at your table, as well as a range of gold-flecked chocolate morsels and seasonal specialities; unfortunately, their choice of coffees, teas and infusions can only be sampled if you're paying for a dessert. Don't leave before checking out the cleverly hidden toilets. Daily 11am–9pm.

Kiriko Lounge キリコラウンジ 6F Tokyo Tokyu Plaza 5-2-1 Ginza, Chūō-ku ☎ 03 6264 5590; Ginza station. Set in Tokyu Plaza, one of central Tokyo's newest large developments, this swanky place allows you to drain coffee (from ¥700) with a superlative view of Ginza's high-rises, through some truly gigantic windows. You can save a few hundred yen by taking it in a paper cup, and sitting in the common area. Mon–Sat 11am–11pm, Sun 11am–9pm.

AKIHABARA AND AROUND
SEE MAP PAGE 60

Gundam Café ガンダムカフェー 1-1 Kanda-Hanaokachō, Chiyoda-ku ☎ 03 3251 0078, ⓦ g-cafe.jp; Akihabara station. In the suitably sci-fi interior of this café you can experience what a pilot from the incredibly popular anime series *Mobile Suit Gundam* would eat – or at least our terrestrial equivalent. Café time and bar time (from 5pm) have different menus. Coffee from ¥400. Mon–Fri 10am–10pm, Sat 8.30am–11pm, Sun 8.30am–9.20pm.

★**Imasa** 井政 2-16-9 Sotokanda, Chiyoda-ku ☎ 03 3258 0059; Ochanomizu station. This café is something of a treat: essentially forming part of the Kanda Myōjin complex (see page 59), it's set in a wooden building dating from the

1920s, fringed with gardens and boasting a mix of traditional and modern fittings. The coffees and teas (from ¥600) are simple, and there's not usually any milk to go with it, but this place is still worth a visit. Mon–Fri 11am–4.30pm.

Maidreamin メイドリーミング 2F 1-8-10 Soto-Kanda, Chiyoda-ku ☎03 6252 3263, ⌨maidreamin.com; Akihabara station. The spangly, anime-like Akiba branch of the *Maidreamin* maid café chain (see page 173) draws a small stream of foreigners thanks to English-speaking staff – they'll let you know exactly which cute poses to make, which cute sounds to mimic and so on. It's all rather fun, and charged at ¥500 per person per hour, with an order from the menu mandatory: drinks cost ¥600–1000, with meals a little more expensive. Each of the seven levels of this building also host maid cafés, and there's another good branch in Shibuya (see page 175). Daily 10am–11pm.

Mai:lish マイリシ 2F FH Kowa Square, 3-6-2 Soto-Kanda, Chiyoda-ku ☎03 5289 7310, ⌨mailish.jp; Suehirochō station. Akiba's famed maid cafés (see page 173) come in all sorts of shapes, sizes and styles; this is one of the originals, a relaxed venue in which costumed girls pander to their customers' every whim. One order from the menu (from ¥600) will get you a 90min stay. Daily 11am–10pm.

Sabōru さぼーる 1-11 Kanda-Jimbōchō, Chiyoda-ku ☎03 3291 8404; Jimbōchō station. An appealingly rustic, treehouse-like *kissaten* tucked away on the alley running parallel to Yasukuni-dōri. Once a popular hideaway for school kids skipping lessons (the nearby bookshops presumably functioned as an excuse), it now attracts an older, more cosmopolitan clientele. Coffee from ¥450. Mon–Sat 9am–11pm.

UENO AND AROUND
SEE MAP PAGE 66

Hagiso はぎそ 3-10-25 Yanaka, Taitō-ku ☎03 5834 7301, ⌨hanare.hagiso.jp; Sendagi station. A black-painted building brooding on the corner of a Yanaka side-street, this is the best café in the area by far, with great coffee

14

MAIDS, BUTLERS AND CATS: TOKYO'S QUIRKY CAFÉS

Japan is famed for appropriating Western cultural standards, and Tokyo's various quirky takes on the humble café are all worth sampling – some would say that you haven't really visited Tokyo if you haven't tried at least one.

MAID AND BUTLER CAFÉS

The weird and wonderful **maid cafés** range in style from seedy to sci-fi via the unashamedly kitsch. Some visitors assume a link exists with the sex industry, but the majority of venues are actually rather tame, with nothing bar the weirdness to worry about. Most maid cafés are clustered among the electronics outlets to the west of Akihabara station; head there after sunset and you'll see lines of girls clamouring for custom. The deal is usually the same: costumed girls (and sometimes guys) serve up food and drink in an excruciatingly "cute" manner, their voices screeching a full two octaves above their natural pitch. There's usually an hourly fee, and you're also expected to order some food or drink from the menu. Keep an eye on the other customers, too: the mix of office groups, courting couples, old sleazebags and lonely young men can be a fascinating window onto contemporary Japanese culture, though remember that you're not usually allowed to take pictures. Recommended places to try include *Mai:lish* (see page 173), and the *Maidreamin* branches in Akihabara (see page 173) and Shibuya (see page 175).

The success of maid cafés spawned a male equivalent: the equally interesting **butler cafés**, where handsome, dressed-up young chaps (often Westerners) serve coffee, cake and wine to an exclusively female clientele. Though the format is essentially the same as that for the maid café, butler cafés tend to be fancier and are often rather more expensive. A good one to try is *Swallowtail Café* in Ikebukuro (see page 175).

ANIMAL CAFÉS

The current hit formula in Tokyo's polymorphous *kissaten* culture is the **animal café**. The craze started relatively tamely with cat cafés; offering quality time with pedigree cats, these cafés have long been popular, and the concept has since been extended to China, South Korea and even Europe. In recent years, cafés have popped up offering experiences with other animals – rabbits, hedgehogs, snakes, owls and even penguins. However, some establishments are clearly putting profit over animal welfare. Recommended establishments listed in this guide include the *Calico* (see page 175) and *Nekorobi* (see page 175) cat cafés, and *Tokyo Snake Center* (see page 175), all of which treat their animals well. If you are visiting an animal café, things to bear in mind are whether or not the animals are kept in cages, if they are allowed "off-time" away from visitors, and whether they have enough space to wander.

14

(from ¥500), a choice of desserts including cheesecake and parfaits, and an artistic atmosphere often enlivened by small exhibitions. It's also home to Hanare guesthouse (see page 149). Daily 8am–10.30am & noon–9pm.

ASAKUSA
SEE MAP PAGE 75

★ **Gallery éf** ガラリーエフ 2-19-18 Kaminarimon, Taitō-ku ☎03 3841 0442, ⓦgallery-ef.com; Asakusa station. The *kura* (traditional storehouse) at the back of this appealing café provides an intimate venue for an eclectic mix of concerts, performance art, and exhibitions that cover most of the space – the rest is taken up by the café's collection of retro goods. Drinks, meals (mostly Western-style, like chilli beans and spaghetti), and desserts are served using vintage tableware, and they carry a few import beers as well. Choose from four different types of blended coffee (¥590), or plum for a tasty fruit juice (¥660). Daily (except Tues): café and gallery 11am–7pm, bar 6pm–midnight.

RYŌGOKU AND KIYOSUMI
SEE MAP PAGE 83

Allpress 3-7-2 Hirano, Kōtō-ku ☎03 5875 9131, ⓦallpress.shop; Kiyosumi-shirakawa station. A couple of blocks away from the Museum of Contemporary Art (see page 84), this roastery café is also convenient for a bunch of other local sights. Most coffees cost ¥400–520, and you can buy beans to go too. Thurs–Mon 9am–6pm.

Cielo y Rio シエロイリオ 2-15-5 Kuramae, Taitō-ku ☎03 5820 8121, ⓦcieloyrio.com; Kuramae station. Precious few places make use of the Sumida-gawa's visual appeal, but this cool little café does just that. Espresso is cheap (¥300), there are plenty of types of tea available and they also serve good Western-style lunch specials. Daily 11am–11pm.

BAYSIDE TOKYO
SEE MAP PAGE 88

Starbucks スターバックス Venus Fort, Kōtō-ku ☎03 5500 5090; Aomi station. Recommending a *Starbucks* might be terribly uncool, but while the coffee here's the same old same old, this Venus Fort branch is nestled into a faux-Italian piazza, sitting under a permanently twilit "sky" like something out of *The Truman Show* – twee, but somehow rather satisfying, especially on a rainy day. Daily 9.30am–9pm.

AKASAKA AND ROPPONGI
SEE MAP PAGE 98

Bluebottle Coffee ブルーボトルコーヒー 7-7-7 Roppongi, Minato-ku ☎03 6804 6603; Roppongi station. Sleek, open, pine-lined space serving good coffee in the ¥500 region (or a little more for the day's single-origin

choice), from a whacking great espresso machine which looks like it may have been used on the Starship Enterprise. Daily 8am–8pm.

Gelateria Marghera ジェラテリア　マルゲラ 2-5-1 Azabu-Jūban, Minato-ku ☎03 5772 3283, ⓦgelateriamarghera.jp; Azabu-Jūban station. Though it's no looker, you won't find a better gelato – or sorbet, for that matter – in the area than at this offshoot of a Milanese gelateria. They go from ¥550 per scoop, and for an extra ¥150 you'll get a decent espresso to go with it. Daily 11.30am–10.30pm.

EBISU, MEGURO AND THE SOUTH
SEE MAP PAGE 108

★ **Mocha Coffee** モカコーヒー 25-1 Sargaku-chō, Shibuya-ku ☎03 6427 8285, ⓦmochacoffee.jp; Daikanyama station. The most distinctive of Daikanyama's many, many cafés, with a Middle Eastern twist to its offerings – coffees and teas go for ¥850–1000, including masala chai-like karak tea, and Turkish coffee served with sweets. Try not to look at the sticky date cake, or you'll want some. Tues–Sun noon–7pm.

HARAJUKU, AOYAMA AND SHIBUYA
SEE MAPS PAGE 119 AND PAGE 124

Crisscross クリスクロス 5-7-28 Minami-Aoyama, Minato-ku ☎03 6434 1266; Omotesandō station. One of Aoyama's "it" places, selling good coffee and dessert dishes such as buttermilk pancakes (both from ¥900). For cheaper eats, pick up something from the adjoining Breadworks bakery. Daily 8am–10pm.

FabCafe 1-22-7 Shibuya, Shibuya-ku ☎03 6416 9190; Shibuya station. This quirky café doubles as a centre for "fabbing" (digital fabrication). Coffee's cheap, starting at ¥300, and light meals are available. Sat–Wed 10am–8pm.

Koffee Mameya コーヒーまめや 4-15-3 Jingūmae, Shibuya-ku ☎03 5413 9422, ⓦkoffee-mameya.com; Omotesandō station. Something different in this café-infested area, and something like a laboratory for coffee. The staff here take their work very seriously, extolling the virtues of the many options – arrayed like lab specimens behind the counter – as they do their thing. Prices are ¥550 and up, and the end results are wonderful, though sadly there's nowhere to sit. Daily 10am–6am.

La Fée Délice ラフェデリース 5-11-13 Jingūmae, Shibuya-ku ☎03 5766 4084, ⓦlafeedelice.com; Meiji-jingūmae station. The best of Harajuku's many crêperies – some chefs here have actually trained in France, and the fact that people are here for the food and atmosphere, rather than simple photography potential, makes for shorter queues. Sweet and savoury crêpes go for ¥1080 and up. Mon–Sat 11.30am–11pm, Sun 11am–10pm.

★ **Lion** ライオン 2-19-13 Dōgenzaka, Shibuya-ku ☎03 3461 6858; Shibuya station. Not the place for animated conversations, this *Addams Family*-style institution, set amid the love hotels of Dōgenzaka, is where businessmen bunking off work come to appreciate classical music with their coffee (¥550 and up). Seats are arranged to face a pair of enormous speakers. Daily 11am–10.30pm.

L'Occitane 2F Likes Bldg, 2-3-1 Dōgenzaka, Shibuya-ku ☎03 5428 1564; Shibuya station. This café above the eponymous cosmetics store has one huge draw – it's a prime viewing spot for the Shibuya crossing. Thankfully, the coffee's fine; better, at least, than at the crammed Starbucks on the other side of the crossing. Daily 10am–9pm.

★ **Maidreamin** メイドリーミング B1 30-1 Udagawachō, Shibuya-ku ☎03 6427 8938, Ⓦmaidreamin.com; Shibuya station. This sci-fi-style maid café (see page 173) is an all-out cuteness assault, its glammed-up staff sporting inch-long fake eyelashes and umpteen petticoat layers. The food follows suit – think curry served in heart-shaped rice mounds and burgers cut up to look like teddy bears – and there's also a range of soft and alcoholic drinks. Entry ¥500 per hour, plus you have to make one order from the menu. Mon–Fri 1–11pm, Sat & Sun 10.30am–11pm.

Streamer Coffee Company 1-20-28 Jingūmae, Shibuya-ku ☎03 6427 3705; Meiji-jingūmae station. Set just a block or two from trendy Cat Street, this café is Harajuku through and through – award-winning barista, and a small line of clothing on sale in store. The coffee here is great but can (intentionally) taste a little burnt; you may want to sit nearer the window to avoid the espresso-making noises. Mon–Fri 8am–6pm, Sat & Sun 10am–6pm.

Tokyo Snake Center 東京スネークセンター 8F Sanpo-Sogo Building, 6-5-6 Jingūmae, Shibuya-ku ☎03 6427 9912, Ⓦsnakecenter.jp; Meiji-jingūmae station. One of the better "weird-animal" cafés in Tokyo, and decently priced at ¥1000 entry, including a drink; it's ¥540 more to pet a couple of small snakes. Daily (except Tues) 11am–8pm.

SHINJUKU AND THE WEST
SEE MAPS PAGE 128 AND PAGE 134

Ballon d'Essai バロンデッセ 2-30-11 Kitazawa, Setagaya-ku ☎03 6407 0511, Ⓦballondessai.com; Shimokitazawa station. Most caffeine-hunters in Shimokitazawa make a bee-line for *Bear Pond*, a café that can take up to an hour to enter. Those without the Japanese love of queuing should head instead to this little hipster hidey-hole, which makes equally good coffee, purportedly from a blend of five types of bean – at least take a photo of the artwork before downing your flat white (¥360). Mon–Fri 11.30am–9pm, Sat & Sun 10.30am–9pm.

Calico きゃりこ 6F, 1-16-2 Kabukichō, Shinjuku-ku, ☎03 6457 6387, Ⓦcatcafe.jp; Shinjuku station. A great place to experience the cat café phenomenon (see page 173); ¥600 gets you thirty minutes of quality time with some fifty gorgeous kitties. With instructions and menu in English, it's very foreigner friendly, and offers inexpensive drinks and food. No kids under 12 are allowed. Daily 11am–10pm.

Tajimaya 但馬屋 Omoide Yokochō, Shinjuku-ku ☎03 3342 0881; Shinjuku station. Surprisingly genteel for this ragged area of dining and drinking alleys (see *Omoide Yokochō*, page 170), this elegant café serves quality drinks and cakes on a pretty assortment of china. Most coffees ¥720. Daily 10am–10.30pm.

IKEBUKURO AND THE NORTH
SEE MAP PAGE 140

Fukuroshosabo 梟書茶房 1-12-1 Nishi-Ikebukuro, Toshima-ku ☎03 3971 1020; Ikebukuro station. Extremely popular book-café abutting Ikebukuro station. Unless your Japanese skills are decent there won't be much for you to read, but the atmosphere is lively and the coffee very decent (from ¥550). Daily 10.30am–10pm.

Nekorobi ねころび 3F Tact TO Bldg, 1-28-1 Higashi-Ikebukuro, Toshima-ku ☎03 6228 0646, Ⓦnekorobi.jp; Ikebukuro station. This cat café (see page 173) has a minimum ¥1100 cover charge for the first hour (¥1300 on weekends), which gets you unlimited drinks, though most go straight for the cat toys, and a play with the felines. Daily 11am–10pm.

Swallowtail Café スワロウテイル B1F 3-12-12 Higashi-Ikebukuro, Toshima-ku Ⓦbutlers-cafe.jp; Ikebukuro station. A butler café (see page 173) where young men dressed like Jeeves are the solicitous waiters in a room hung with chandeliers and antique-style furniture. Booking through the (mostly Japanese) website is essential. Expect to spend at least ¥2500 per head. Daily 10.30am–9pm.

TEAROOMS

GINZA AND AROUND
SEE MAP PAGE 53

Cha Ginza 茶銀座 5-5-6 Ginza, Chūō-ku ☎03 3571 1211; Ginza station. This teahouse, run by a tea wholesaler, offers a modern take on the business of sipping *sencha*. Iron walls add a contemporary touch, and the rooftop area, where they serve *matcha*, is the place to hang out with those Tokyo ladies who make shopping a career. ¥700 gets you three small (and different) cups of the refreshing green stuff, plus a traditional sweet. Daily (except Mon) 11am–6pm.

14

14

Higashiya Ginza 東家銀座 2F Pola Ginza, 1-7-7 Ginza, Chūō-ku ☎03 3538 3230; Ginza station. This utterly gorgeous tearoom and shop is known for its relaxing atmosphere and delicious assortments of seasonal Japanese sweets (from ¥1500); the tea itself goes from a pricey ¥1700 per head, though a pot will be enough for three cups. Daily 11am–9pm.

Sabō Nonohana 茶房 野の花 3-7-21 Ginza, Chūō-ku ☎03 5250 9025; Ginza station. Lovely tearoom on the second floor of Nonohana Tsukasa, a shop that specializes in traditional flower arrangements and crafts. The *teishoku* (set meal) lunches – starting at ¥1000 – are beautifully presented, and the green-tea ice cream (¥770) is hard to turn down. Mon–Sat 11am–7pm, Sun 11.30am–6pm.

ASAKUSA
SEE MAP PAGE 75

Suzukien 壽々喜園 3-4-3 Asakusa, Taitō-ku ☎03 3873 0311; Asakusa station. First things first – this isn't a tearoom, and in addition, it isn't a very attractive place. However, it has become hugely popular on account of its green-tea ice cream, which is sold in seven "grades" – the #7 is purportedly the strongest *matcha* substance in the world. A scoop will cost ¥370 (or ¥560 for the #7), and you'll get a tiny cup of tea to wash it down with. Daily 10am–5pm.

Umezono 梅園 1-31-12 Asakusa, Taitō-ku ☎03 3841 7580; Asakusa station. This traditional tearoom in the heart of Asakusa is famous for its *awa-zenzai*, millet flour cakes wrapped in sweet azuki bean paste, served with seeds of Japanese basil for contrast. Alternatively, choose a bowl

of *anmitsu* from the window display: a colourful concoction of agar jelly, azuki beans and sticky rice topped with a variety of fruits (and, if you're really hungry, whipped cream or ice cream; from ¥800). Daily (except Wed) 10am–8pm.

AKASAKA AND ROPPONGI
SEE MAP PAGE 98

Toraya とらや 4-9-22 Akasaka, Minato-ku ☎03 3408 4121; Akasaka-mitsuke station. This confectionery chain has branches all over town, but the third floor of their extremely beautiful main store (see page 207) is also a great place for tea; it costs from ¥750, and can usually be served with seasonal mochi (traditional rice cakes). Mon–Fri 8.30am–7pm, Sat & Sun 9.30am–6pm.

EBISU, MEGURO AND THE SOUTH
SEE MAP PAGE 108

Ganchabō 岩茶房 3-15-5 Kami-Meguro, Meguro-ku ☎03 3714 7425; Nakameguro station. Housed in a lovely residential-style building in the backstreets off Yamate-dōri, this place specializes in Chinese teas (¥800–1600), and has some good Chinese food too. Tues–Sun 11am–7pm.

HARAJUKU, AOYAMA AND SHIBUYA
SEE MAPS PAGE 119 AND PAGE 124

★**Aoyama Flower Market** 青山フラワーマーケット B1 5-1-2 Aoyama, Minato-ku ☎03 3400 0887, ⍟afm-teahouse.com; Omotesandō station. Yes, it's a flower shop – but one whose heady aromas also permeate a

---

THE WAY OF TEA

Tea was introduced to Japan from China in the ninth century and was popularized by Zen Buddhist monks, who appreciated its caffeine kick during their long meditation sessions. Gradually, tea drinking developed into a formal ritual known as *cha-no-yu*, the **tea ceremony**, whose purpose is to heighten the senses within a contemplative atmosphere.

In its simplest form the ceremony takes place in a tatami room, undecorated save for a hanging scroll or display of *ikebana* (traditional flower arrangement). Using beautifully crafted utensils of bamboo, iron and rustic pottery, your host will whisk **matcha** – the strong powdered form of green tea – into a thick, frothy brew and present it to each guest in turn. First, eat the accompanying sweet (*wagashi*), then take the bowl in both hands, turn it clockwise a couple of inches and drink it down in three slow sips.

The *Imperial* (see page 147) and *Ōkura* hotels (see page 149) all have traditional rooms in which tea ceremonies are regularly held; the cost will be around ¥1000. Some of the most appealing places to take tea are the city's **parks**, where small tearooms charge around ¥500 for a cup, often served with a small sweet treat. The best are located in Hama Rikyū Teien (see page 54), Shinjuku Gyoen (see page 133), Happōen (see page 111), Kyū Iwasaki-tei Gardens (see page 69) and Kyū Furukawa Gardens (see page 142).

Japan's tea culture embraces many **types of tea**. **Bancha**, the cheapest grade of tea is for everyday drinking and, in its roasted form, is used to make the smoky **hōjicha**, or mixed with popped brown rice for the nutty **genmaicha**. Medium-grade **sencha** is commonly served in upmarket restaurants, while top-ranking, slightly sweet **gyokuro** (dewdrop) is reserved for special occasions. Although usually reserved for tea ceremonies, thick and strong **matcha** is often available in regular teahouses, and is a great local alternative to an espresso.

KOREATOWN EATS

There's a point as you walk north from Kabukichō where you'll notice that the Japanese characters on shop signs are matched or replaced by *hangul* – Korean script. Welcome to Tokyo's **Koreatown**, where you can not only pick up K-pop boy-band music or posters, but also tuck into excellent Korean cuisine. Apart from *yakiniku* (beef or pork strips sizzled atop a grill at your table), *bibimbap* (rice topped with vegetables, egg and meat) and *kimchi* (the fiery fermented cabbage pickle) there's a vast range of other Korean dishes to sample, including *bindaeddeok* (pancakes made with yellow mung beans); *sundubu* (tofu stews); and *samgyetang* (chicken in a herb and ginseng soup).

For tasty Korean staples, try *Han Sarang* (see page 171); for barbecued meat, *Saemaeul Sikdang* (see page 172) is your best bet. Both are near Shin-Ōkubo station, within walking distance of Shinjuku.

14

fantastic tea-space, tucked away through a door at the back. They've a good range of herbal and green-tea concoctions on offer in the ¥750 range, though prepare for a queue on weekends. Daily 11am–8pm.

The Alley Lujiaoxiang THE ALLEY 表参道店 6-6-6 Jingūmae, Shibuya-ku ☎03 6712 5185, ⓦthe-alley.jp; Meiji-jingūmae station. Not so long ago it was buttermilk pancakes, but now if you see lengthy queues developing in Harajuku, it's most likely to be a bubble tea stand. For the actual tea, this one's best – just be prepared to wait a little while. Daily 10am–10pm.

IKEBUKURO AND THE NORTH SEE MAP PAGE 138

Saryō 茶寮 5-9 Kagurazaka, Shinjuku-ku ☎03 3266 0880, ⓦsaryo.jp; Iidabashi station. This is the head branch of an ever-growing tearoom chain, of which there are now more than a dozen nationwide; this one has a charming, backstreet setting in Kagurazaka, with outdoor seating on a wooden veranda. As well as good tea (from ¥650), they have yummy strawberry fondue (¥1000) and a variety of ice creams. Mon–Sat 11.30am–11pm, Sun 11.30am–10pm.

BEERS AND SNACKS AT AN *IZAKAYA*

Drinking and nightlife

If you thought that Tokyo had more than enough restaurants to last several lifetimes, then take a deep breath before diving into its equally vast and inventive bar scene. Take your pick from a myriad of cocktail bars, pubs and *izakaya* (traditional bars serving food), offering practically any brand of booze from around the world as well as local tipples such as sake and *shōchū* (two clear local spirits), as well as award-winning Japanese whisky. Tokyo is a key destination on the international clubbing scene, too, with big-name overseas DJs regularly jetting in to play alongside talented local mix masters. If you prefer live music, then you'll be happy to hear the city has an incredibly varied appetite for music from all corners of the globe.

Tokyo's drinking establishments range from shoebox-sized bars for regular patrons only to sophisticated cocktail lounges in hotels. The most common type are **izakaya**, which are generally cramped affairs, serving a good range of drinks and food and amid a lively atmosphere. **Chains** include *Kirin City*, Sapporo's *Lions Beer Hall*, identikit Irish bar *The Dubliners* and the faux-British pubs *The Hub* and the *Rose & Crown*.

Typically being smoky, cramped, exclusively male and expensive, the appeal of **nomiya** is not immediately apparent. However, the close quarters means you can't help but start chatting with fellow drinking companions and you're sure to be looked after by the bar keeper – often a genial woman called a *mama-san* (a male owner is called a master). *Nomiya* act like private clubs where regular customers keep a bottle of their favourite tipple behind the counter with their name on it. Many *nomiya* can be found under the tracks at Yūrakuchō (see page 48), along Shinjuku's *Omoide Yokochō* (see page 170) and Golden Gai (see page 133), and on Nonbei Yokochō, the alley running alongside the train tracks just north of Shibuya station; *gaijin*-friendly ones are listed in this chapter.

Tachinomiya (bars without seats) continue to be popular, with venues serving not just beer and nibbles but also specialist sake, *shōchū* and wines. Café-bars are covered in the "Eating" chapter.

There's a healthy **clubbing** scene in Tokyo, with high-profile international DJs regularly roped in for a spin (and an ever-increasing number of Japanese doing likewise abroad). While Tokyo still plays second fiddle to Ōsaka for **live music**, there's still a fair bit of variety here, while the city also boasts a lively **LGBTQ scene**.

15

BARS

Tokyo's bars can be a little confusing to the first-time visitor, but you should be able to work things out before too long. One common source of confusion is the **table charge** levied at some places, including almost all *izakaya*; it'll be anything from ¥200 to ¥1000. The small snack you may be served with your first drink is the official justification for the charge, though some places levy one without providing anything extra. If there's live music, you'll often pay for it through a cover charge or higher drink prices. **Opening hours** are long, generally from 5pm (often much earlier) until around midnight Sunday to Thursday, extended to 4am on Friday and Saturday. If you're socializing with Japanese it's polite to pour your companions' drinks, and let them pour yours. You can make a **toast** by lifting your glass and saying "*kampai*".

THE IMPERIAL PALACE AND AROUND
SEE MAP PAGE 42
Marunouchi House 丸の内ハウス 7F Shin-Marunouchi Bldg, 1-5-1 Marunouchi, Chiyoda-ku ☎03 5218 5100; Tokyo station. The best thing about the open-plan space here, with its seven different restaurants and bars, is that you can take your drinks out on to the broad wraparound terrace for great views of Tokyo station and towards the Imperial Palace. *Raimu Raitu* is probably the best of the three bars; this one's an enclosed space, with a distinct bubble-era feel, and cocktails for ¥800. Mon–Sat 11am–4am, Sun 11am–11pm.

★**Old Imperial Bar** Imperial Hotel, 1-1-1 Uchisaiwaichō, Chiyoda-ku ☎03 3539 8088, ⓦwww.imperialhotel.co.jp; Hibiya station. All that remains in

TOKYO'S TOP PLACES TO DRINK

Best for cheapskates *300 Bar* (see page 180), *Coins Bar* (see page 184) and *Gas Panic* (see page 188)
Best for Art Deco stylings *Old Imperial Bar* (see page 179)
Best for a sake education *Bunka Hostel* (see page 180) and *Buri* (see page 182)
Best for budding Bill Murrays *New York Bar* (see page 189)
Best for events *Pink Cow* (see page 182)
Best for microbrewed beer *Nakameguro Taproom* (see page 182) and *Hitachino Brewing Lab* (see page 180)
Best for Japanese whisky *Cask Strength* (see page 181)
Best for weirdness value *The Lockup* (see page 184)
Best club *Womb* (see page 188)
Best LGBTQ venue *Aiiro Café* (see page 190)

15

Tokyo of Frank Lloyd Wright's Art Deco *Imperial Hotel* (see page 147) is this re-created bar. Try its signature Mount Fuji cocktail (¥1800), a wickedly sweet blend of gin, cream, egg white and sugar syrup with a cherry on top, which was invented here in 1924. While you sip it, ask to see the photo albums of how the hotel once looked. Smart attire recommended. Daily 11.30am–midnight.

Shin Hi No Moto 新日の基 2-4-4 Yūrakuchō, Chiyoda-ku ☎ 03 3214 8021; Yūrakuchō or Hibiya stations. Known to all and sundry as "Andy's", this is a lively English-owned *izakaya* under the tracks just south of Yūrakuchō station. Prices are fair, but reservations are advisable. Daily (except Sun) 5pm–midnight.

GINZA AND AROUND
SEE MAP PAGE 53

300 Bar ３００円バー B1 Fazenda Building, 5-9-11 Ginza, Chūō-ku ☎ 03 3572 6300; Ginza station. The bargain-basement face of Ginza is this unusually large standing-only bar, where all food and drinks are ¥300 (plus a little more, for tax): cheap by the standards of rural Japan, let alone Ginza. Needless to say, it can get pretty full and fun. Mon–Fri 5pm–2am, Sat & Sun 2pm–2am.

Dry Dock ドライドック 3-25-10 Shimbashi, Minato-ku ☎ 03 5777 4755; Shimbashi station. Cosy craft-beer bar with a nautical theme nestling beneath the train tracks. Its no-smoking policy is a welcome change, and patrons often spill outside to enjoy the regularly changing menu of Japanese and overseas microbrews. No food served on Saturday. Mon–Fri 5pm–midnight, Sat 5pm–10pm.

Lion ライオン 7-9-20 Ginza, Chūō-ku ☎ 03 3571 2590; Ginza station. Opened in 1934, this flagship beer hall of the Sapporo chain is a rather baronial place, with dark tiles and mock wood panelling. As well as good draught beer (giant ones ¥1080), there are sausages, sauerkraut and other German snacks on offer alongside international pub grub. You'll find other branches scattered around Tokyo, all using the same formula. Mon–Sat 11.30am–11pm, Sun 11.30am–10.30pm.

Marugin マルギン 7-1 Ginza, Chūō-ku ☎ 03 3571 8989; Ginza station. Unlike many of the tourist-trap places abutting the tracks here, this *tachinomiya* (standing bar) is manifestly local, and often completely packed. Very little is in English, but all the more reason to chat to locals for their kushiyaki (fried sticks, from ¥130) or alcohol recommendations. Mon–Fri 5pm–midnight, Sat 5pm–10pm.

AKIHABARA AND AROUND
SEE MAP PAGE 60

Hitachino Brewing Lab 常陸野ブルーイングラボ mAAch-Ecute Building, 1-25-4 Kanda-Sudachō, Chiyoda-ku ☎ 03 3254 3434, ⓦ hitachino.cc; Akihabara station. Set under the train tracks, this is one of Tokyo's most attractive microbreweries, serving Hitachino's famous Nest

ale and another eight varieties on tap (¥680 for a small one), as displayed in a beer-rainbow array of test tubes. Try a taster set for ¥980. Mon–Sat 11am–11pm, Sun 11am–9pm.

UENO AND AROUND
SEE MAP PAGE 66

Echigoya Honten 越後屋本店 3-13-2 Yanaka, Taitō-ku ☎ 03 3821 0983; Sendagi station. Not a bar at all, really, but this liquor store has developed quite a following among locals, and often arouses the curiosity of foreigners wandering down Yanaka Ginza. The reason? Some of their offerings are sold outside by the glass (mostly ¥500), with old beer crates used for tables and chairs – an earthy kind of cool, and quite tempting on a nice evening. Daily 10am–9pm.

★ **Kadokura** カドクラ 6-13-1 Ueno, Taitō-ku ☎ 03 3832 5335; Ueno station. Bustling *tachinomiya* that usually gets boisterous even before office kicking-out time – a great place to make new friends over a freezing beer or highball (from ¥400). Daily 10am–11pm.

Sumire すみれ 2-24-8 Nezu, Bunkyō-ku ☎ 03 3821 8941; Nezu station. Located in ever-more-trendy Nezu, this izakaya is a good way to square the circle – cheap and extremely local in nature, yet with an English-speaking menu and mama-san for the benefit of the few tourists who pop in, it's a great introduction to *izakaya* culture. Thurs–Mon 6pm–1am.

Warrior Celt ウオリアーケルト 3F Ito Building, 6-9-22 Ueno ☎ 03 3836 8588, ⓦ warriorcelt.jp; Ueno station. Occasionally wild bar whose regulars are led on by a veritable United Nations of bar staff. Key ingredients include a fine range of beers, good food, a nightly happy hour (5–7pm), live bands and, last but not least, "Ladies Night" on Thursdays (cocktails ¥500 for female customers). Mon–Thurs 5pm–midnight, Fri & Sat 5pm–5am.

ASAKUSA
SEE MAP PAGE 75

★ **Bunka Hostel** ブンカホステル 1-13-5 Asakusa, Taitō-ku ☎ 03 5806 3444, ⓦ bunkahostel.jp; Asakusa station. The lobby of this excellent hostel (see page 154) doubles as a bar, as stylish as any in the area – the wall of Bunka-labelled sake jars behind the bar is extremely photogenic. They've more than thirty varieties of sake on offer, with the type (dry, sweet, strong, etc) explained on the English-language menu – a perfect place in which to get acquainted with Japan's most traditional drink. Daily (except Mon) 6pm–2am.

Campion Ale カンピオンエール 2-2-2 Nishi-Asakusa, Taitō-ku ☎ 03 6231 6554, ⓦ campionale.com; Tawaramachi station. Brew-pubs are ten-a-penny in Tokyo these days, but this one is ideally located for the Asakusa backpacker and tourist crowds. British-owned, it serves suitably authentic ales (usually 15 on tap; ¥1000/pint, or ¥2800 for 2hr all-you-can-drink) and hearty pub dishes. Mon–Fri 5–11.30pm, Sat & Sun noon–11.30pm.

Gin Maku Roku 銀幕ロック 2F 1-41-5 Asakusa ☏ 03 5828 6969; Asakusa or Tawaramachi stations. The Asakusa spirit is alive and kicking in this intimate, backstreet bar, festooned with homely bric-a-brac and full of colourful characters. A stage is squeezed in for the occasional gig (around ¥1000), which could feature anything from rockabilly to Balkan gypsy music. Daily 9pm–5am.

Ichimon 一文 3-12-6 Asakusa, Taitō-ku ☏ 03 3875 6800; Tawaramachi station. Traditional *izakaya* with a cosy atmosphere, specializing in various types of sake and dishes made with a range of unusual meats, including ostrich, turtle, crocodile and (ethics alert) whale. Payment is by wooden tokens, which you purchase on entering. Daily (except Mon) 3pm–2am.

Kamiya 神谷 1-1-1 Asakusa, Taitō-ku ☏ 03 3841 5400; Asakusa station. Established in 1880, this was Tokyo's first Western-style bar. It's famous for its Denki Bran ("electric brandy" – a mix of gin, wine, Curaçao and brandy), invented in 1883. It's a potent tipple (and just ¥270 a shot), though they also make a "weaker" version. It's a restaurant of sorts, so choose the lively ground floor if you're only after a drink; pay for your first round as you enter. Daily (except Tues) 11.30am–10pm.

BAYSIDE TOKYO
SEE MAP PAGE 88

Jicoo ジコー ☏ 0120 049490, ⓦ jicoofloatingbar.com; Hinode station. This night-time persona of the futuristic ferry *Himiko* shuttles between Hinode, under the Rainbow Bridge, and Odaiba. To board costs ¥2600 (it takes half an hour from point to point, but you can stay on as long as you like), drinks run from ¥700 and there's a DJ playing so you can take to the illuminated dancefloor and show off your best John Travolta moves. Daily 8am–11pm.

AKASAKA AND ROPPONGI
SEE MAP PAGE 98

BrewDog 5-3-2 Roppongi, Minato-ku ☏ 03 6447 4160, ⓦ brewdogbar.jp; Roppongi station. Craft beer has undergone a second wave in Japan, and this is your best bet in the Roppongi area, with their own five brews – including the excellent Punk IPA – forming part of a boozy constellation of 20 beers on tap, plus 60 bottled varieties (from ¥700). Mon–Fri 5pm–midnight, Sat & Sun 3pm–midnight.

Cask Strength B1 3-9-11 Roppongi, Minato-ku ☏ 03 6432 9772, ⓦ cask-s.com; Roppongi station. Attractive basement venue with one of Tokyo's best selections of whisky, including some rare Japanese choices – those with a nose for Karuizawa or Yamazaki Single Malt will be in paradise. Daily 6pm–late.

★ **Gen Yamamoto** 元山本 1-6-4 Azabu-jūban, Minato-ku ☏ 03 6434 0652, ⓦ genyamamoto.jp; Azabu-jūban station. This is one of those small, secretive Tokyo bars which makes you wonder what goes on inside. Nothing seedy at all here, merely the creation of some of the best cocktails in the city, often made with fresh fruits and veggies sourced from across the land (and all by "feel",

15

JAPANESE BEER

American brewer William Copeland set up Japan's first brewery in Yokohama in 1870 to serve fellow expats streaming into the country in the wake of the Meiji Restoration. Back then the Japanese had to be bribed to drink beer, but these days they need no such encouragement, knocking back a whopping **5.5 billion litres** of the stuff a year – almost 60 litres per adult.

Copeland's brewery eventually became **Kirin**, now one of Japan's big four brewers along with **Asahi**, **Sapporo** and **Suntory**. All turn out a range of lagers and dark beers, as well as low-malt beers called *happōshu*, and no-malt varieties called *dai-san-no-biiru*, which are popular because of their lower price (the higher the malt content, the higher the government tax), even if they generally taste insipid. Some of the standard cans and bottles are **design classics**, among them Kirin Ichiban, Asahi Super Dry and a couple of the Sapporo beers; beautiful seasonal additions to the cans and bottles feature the likes of snowflakes, red leaves or *sakura* flowers.

Standard-size **cans** of beer cost around ¥150 from convenience stores, while **bottles** (*bin-biiru*) usually start at ¥500 in restaurants and bars. **Draught beer** (*nama-biiru*) is sometimes available and, in beer halls, will be served in a *jokki*, a mug-like glass which comes in three sizes: *dai* (big), *chū* (medium) and *shō* (small).

An increasing number of Tokyo bars – try *Campion Ale* (see page 180), *Dry Dock* (see page 180), *Nakameguro Taproom* (see page 182) and the *Hitachino Brewing Lab* (see page 180) for starters – serve **microbrew craft beers** from around Japan (sometimes called *ji-biiru* – "regional beer"). Most of these ales have way more character than the products of the big four, though prices are not cheap – figure on ¥1000 for a half-litre at most establishments. For more information on the craft-beer scene there's the bilingual free magazine *The Japan Beer Times* (ⓦ japanbeertimes.com), which is also available in app form.

15

SUMMER BEER GARDENS

Helping to mitigate Tokyo's sticky summers are the **outdoor beer gardens** that sprout around the city from late May through to early September, typically on the roofs of department stores such as Tobu in Ikebukuro, or in street-level gardens and plazas. A couple of the best beer gardens can be found in Meiji-Jingū's Outer Garden close to Shinanomachi station; try the *Forest Beer Garden* (see page 184) or *Sekirei* (see page 184). **Rooftop bars** are also very pleasing places to drink in warm months; *Xex* (see page 182) is a good option.

rather than by measure). The results can be astonishingly good; if your wallet stretches far enough, consider going for the tasting sets of four to seven cocktails (¥4600–7900). Tues–Sat 3–11pm.

Hobgoblin ホッブゴッブリン Aoba Roppongi Building, 3-16-33 Roppongi, Minato-ku ☎03 3568 1280, ⊚hobgoblin.jp; Roppongi station. British microbrewery Wychwood serves up its fine ales at this spacious bar where you'll be part of a very boozy, noisy crowd of *gaijin* at weekends and on nights when sport events are shown on the big-screen TVs. A plus is the very comforting English pub-style food, including pie of the day (¥1700) and Sunday roast (¥1500). Mon–Fri 5pm–late, Sat & Sun noon–late.

Pink Cow ピンクカーウ 2-7-6 Akasaka, Minato-ku ☎03 6441 2998, ⊚thepinkcow.com; Tameike-sanno station. There's always something interesting going on – book readings, art classes, comedy improv nights – at this funky haven for local artists and writers. Has a good range of imported wines, and tasty Tex-Mex-style food. Daily 5pm–late.

Public Six 6-8-22 Roppongi, Minato-ku ☎03 5413 3182, ⊚bagus-99.com/public6; Roppongi station. A sports bar like no other – this gastropub boasts a truly zany design both inside and out, and has become a popular place to watch big games over some good food and drink. Food is generally Western in nature, though often with Japanese flourishes; drinks-wise, they have at least six craft beers on tap, as well as house cocktails, and plenty of varieties of sake. Mon–Sat 5pm–5am, Sun 5pm–3am.

Warayakiya わらやき屋 6-8-8 Roppongi, Minato-ku ☎03 5410 5560; Roppongi station. Appealingly gloomy *izakaya* that looks like it was pieced together from a fallen-down temple. As well as reasonable fish and meat dishes, it serves a full range of drinks, including some rare chestnut *shōchū*. Daily 5pm–5am (Sun until 11pm).

EBISU, MEGURO AND THE SOUTH
SEE MAP PAGE 108

★**Baja** バハ 1-16-12 Kami-Meguro, Meguro-ku, no phone; Nakameguro station. Seemingly decorated with everything the owner could find in his garage, this is one of the most entertaining bars in the Nakameguro area,

with a good mix of foreigners and oddball Japanese. Drinks (including cocktails) cost ¥500; no tax, no table charge, cool music, and they also whip up yummy tacos – a winner. Daily 5pm–5am.

★**Buri** ぶり 1-14-1 Ebisu-nishi, Shibuya-ku ☎03 3496 7744; Ebisu station. The fifty-strong range of chilled "one-cup sake" (a sealed glass, the size of a small can, ready filled with sake that you just pull the top off; ¥800) is the speciality at this trendy *tachinomiya* that's one of the best in town. Good *yakitori*, too, and just wait until you see the toilet door. Daily 3pm–midnight.

Footnik フットニック 1F Asahi Building, 1-11-2 Ebisu, Shibuya-ku ☎03 5795 0144, ⊚footnik.net; Ebisu station. A bar devoted to football, with a game or two on the big screen every night, pints of imported beer for ¥1000 or so, and reasonable food. For popular matches you'll have to pay an entry charge. Daily 3pm–1am, later at weekends.

★**Nakameguro Taproom** 中目黒タップルーム GT Plaza C-Block 2F, 2-1-3 Kami-Meguro, Meguro-ku ☎03 5768 3025, ⊚bairdbeer.com; Nakameguro station. This sleek real-ale nirvana serves beers (¥1000) from Baird Brewing Company, which started life out west in Numazu, on the Izu Peninsula. It also serves good food, and gets nice and busy on weekends. Mon–Fri 5pm–midnight, Sat & Sun noon–midnight.

Spring Valley Brewery スプリングバレーブルワリー 13-1 Daikanyama, Shibuya-ku ☎03 6416 4960; Daikanyama station. Owned by Kirin, one of the most famous beer names in Japan, this large brew-pub – part of the new Log Road development – produces ales far better than the cans of Kirin Ichiban you'll find at the 7-Eleven. You can try samples of six ales for ¥1000, then go for a large glass of your favourite. Mon–Sat 8am–midnight, Sun 8am–10pm.

Xex 3F La Fuente, 11-1 Sarugaku-chō, Shibuya-ku ☎03 3476 065, ⊚xexgroup.jp; Daikanyama station. This sleek rooftop bar is more like something you'd expect to find in Southeast Asia than Tokyo, with loungey seating dotted around a small pool. Pizza and sushi are on offer to augment the wine selection, and there's occasional live jazz. Mon–Fri 5.30pm–4am, Sat & Sun 5.30pm–midnight.

HARAJUKU, AOYAMA AND SHIBUYA
SEE MAPS PAGE 116, PAGE 119 AND PAGE 124

Coins Bar コインズバー B1 Noa Shibuya Building, 36-2 Udagawa-chō, Shibuya-ku ☏03 3463 3039; Shibuya station. This cool little basement bar offers most drinks for ¥320, making it a top choice if you're on a budget. Music is usually hip-hop and r'n'b; they also bring in DJs most weekends, when there's a ¥300 entry fee. Daily 4pm–12.30am, later at weekends.

★**Commune 2nd** コミューン2nd 3-13 Minami-Aoyama, Minato-ku; ⓦcommune2nd.com; Omotesandō station. Even better for drinking than it is for food (see page 168), this outdoor court is a real hub of the area; most of the eateries sell drinks, including bottled local craft beer, but special mention should be made of Beer Brain, which doesn't do food at all (¥600 for a small draught beer). Daily 11am–10pm; usually closed Dec–Feb.

★**Far Yeast** ファーイースト 2-6-8 Shibuya, Shibuya-ku ☏03 6874 0373, ⓦfaryeast.com; Shibuya station. Though it would be worth mentioning for the ace name alone, this is the best craft beer in the Shibuya area, despite substantial competition. There are usually up to a dozen beers on offer (¥1000 a glass), including their own blond, saison, pale and session ales. Mon–Fri 11.30am–3pm & 5–11pm, Sat & Sun 11.30am–10pm.

Fight Club 428 ファイトクラブ428 2-27-2 Dōgenzaka, Shibuya-ku ☏03 3464 1799; Shibuya station. Of Shibuya's array of weird bars, this is one of the oddest – part of a fitness centre, the bar itself is set right next to a functional kickboxing cage. You can spar there yourself for ¥1000, though staff will only allow you to do this before your drink (most priced at ¥500). Mon–Thurs 6pm–midnight, Fri & Sat 6pm–5am, Sun noon–6pm.

Forest Beer Garden 森のビアガーデン 14-13 Kasumigaoka-machi, Minato-ku ☏03 5411 3715; Shinanomachi station. This open-air beer garden, fronting the Meiji Kinenkan wedding hall, offers an eat-and-drink-all-you-can deal (*tabe-nomi-hōdai*) for men (¥4200) and women (¥3900). June–Sept only: Mon–Fri 5pm–10pm, Sat & Sun noon–10pm.

Goodbeer Faucets グッドビアフォーセツ 2F 1-29-1 Shoto, Shibuya-ku ☏03 3770 5544, ⓦgoodbeerfaucets.jp; Shibuya station. An excellent place for craft beer, selling over forty varieties on draught – some made by the Goodbeer brewery, others from across Japan and abroad. Large glasses of the good stuff cost ¥750–1300, with ¥200 off during happy hour (Mon–Thurs 5–8pm, Sun 1–7pm). Mon–Thurs 5pm–midnight, Fri 5pm–3am, Sat & Sun 1pm–midnight.

Legato レガート 15F E-Space Tower, 3-6 Maruyama-chō, Shibuya-ku ☏03 5784 2121, ⓦlegato-tokyo.jp; Shibuya station. This fancy Italian restaurant's bar offers a memorable floor-to-ceiling view over Shibuya from fifteen floors up. It feels higher than that, for some reason, even without the booze – plenty of wines from under ¥1000 a glass, plus house cocktails and Japanese craft gin. Sun–Thurs 11.30am–2pm & 5.30pm–midnight, Fri & Sat 11.30am–2pm & 5.30pm–4am.

Montoak モントオーク 6-1-9 Jingūmae, Shibuya-ku ☏03 5468 5928; Meiji-jingūmae station. Stylish but rather snooty café-bar which faces Harajuku's famous shopping street, with no sign whatsoever – look for the large glass facade. DJs create a suitable loungey vibe, and there's live music sometimes at weekends. Daily 11am–3am.

Sekirei 鶺鴒 2-2-23 Moto-Akasaka, Minato-ku ☏03 3403 1171, ⓦmeijikinenkan.gr.jp; Shinanomachi station. Inside the Meiji Kinenkan wedding hall complex, this swanky bar overlooks a floodlit garden where classical Japanese dance (Nihon Buyō) is performed nightly at around 8pm. June–Sept only: Mon–Sat 4.30–10.30pm, Sun 5.30–10.30pm.

Shisha Salon シーシャサロン 31-4 Udagawa-chō, Shibuya-ku ☏03 6427 0826, ⓦshisha-chillin.com; Shinanomachi station. Festooned with cushions and dangling lampshades of a Middle Eastern ilk, this is a great pick for those in the mood for a shisha; figure on ¥1500 per pipe. Daily 2pm–4am.

SHINJUKU AND THE WEST
SEE MAPS PAGE 128 AND PAGE 134

★**Champion** チャンピオン Golden Gai, off Shiki-no-michi; Shinjuku-sanchōme station. At the western entrance to the Golden Gai stretch (see page 133), this is the largest bar in the area. There's no cover charge and most drinks are a bargain ¥500 – some even less. The catch? You have to endure tone-deaf patrons crooning karaoke for ¥100 a song, though after a few drinks, you'll probably want to join in, or make your own request. Mon–Sat 6pm–6am.

Hair of the Dogs ヘアオヴザドッグ 1st Street, Golden Gai; Shinjuku-sanchōme station. Punk rockers will get a kick from this tiny bar, whose location in Golden Gai (see page 133) is indicated by a Sex Pistols poster on the door and a thudding soundtrack of rebellious music inside. Cover charge ¥800. Mon–Sat 6pm–4am.

Kushikatsu Dengana 串かつでんがな 1-11-1 Kabukichō, Shinjuku-ku ☏03 3209 011; Seibu-Shinjuku station. A good, unpretentious place for cheap fried *kushiage* sticks, a beer or three, and a chat with whoever's sat next to you. Daily 6pm–3am.

★**The Lockup** ザロックアップ 6/7F 1-16-3 Kabukichō, Shinjuku-ku ☏050 5305 7370; Shinjuku station. It's quite a trip merely walking into this house-of-horrors/prison themed bar. You'll be handcuffed then led to a cell-like room where you can take your pick of weird cocktails: some arrive in test tubes; others have fake eyeballs inside. Periodically, the lights dim and staff try their best to

KARAOKE BARS AND BOXES

Legend has it that **karaoke**, literally translated as "empty orchestra", was invented by an Ōsaka record-store manager in the early 1970s. Today the mainstay of this ¥1 trillion-a-year business are **karaoke boxes** – buildings packed with comfy booths kitted out with a karaoke system. Rental of these boxes is by the hour and they have proved particularly popular with youngsters, women and families, who prefer them to the smoky bars frequented by salarymen that were the original preserve of karaoke.

You'll find branches of the biggest chains – *Karaoke-kan*, *Shidax* and *Big Echo* – all over the city; the charge is typically ¥800–1000 per person per hour, but some independent bars are cheaper. There are always plenty of English-language songs to butcher, although it certainly helps to have a Japanese-speaker on hand to operate the karaoke system. Almost all venues serve alcohol, and many have drink-all-you-can (*nomi-hōdai*) specials; two hours of booze costs ¥3000 or so, plus the actual singing fee, and as a rule of thumb these deals usually work out cheaper if you're planning to have four or more drinks. If you're a first-timer, alcohol certainly helps to ease things along – those who are too shy to sing at the beginning of a session often end up hogging the microphone all night long.

Big Echo ビッグエコ 4-2-14 Ginza, Chūō-ku ☎ 03 3563 5100; Ginza station. The most appealing branch of this major chain, with a few interesting themed rooms, including a Hello Kitty one. From ¥850 per person, with a minimum order of one drink. Daily 24hr.

Fiesta フィエスタ B1 6-2-35 Roppongi, Minato-ku ☎ 03 5410 3008; ⓦ fiesta-roppongi.com; Roppongi station. A particularly good karaoke bar for newbie *gaijin*, offering thousands of songs in English, as well

as several other languages – 26,000 hits, in all. ¥3500 including three drinks. Mon 7pm–midnight, Tues–Sat until 5am.

Karaoke-kan カラオケ館 30-8 Udagawachō, Shibuya-ku ☎ 03 3462 0785; Shibuya station. Japan's premier karaoke-box operator has branches liberally peppered across the capital. Rooms 601 and 602 in their Udagawachō branch were featured in the movie *Lost in Translation*. An hour of karaoke here costs from ¥900 per person, with a minimum order of one drink. Daily 24hr.

terrify customers – brilliant fun, believe it or not. Mon–Fri 5pm–midnight, Sat & Sun noon–midnight.

Moto スタンド戻 5-17-11 Shinjuku; Shinjuku-sanchōme station. One for the sake aficionados – there are usually 50–60 varieties for the tasting in this standing-only basement lair, and they're all excellent. Most cost just ¥380 per glass, making a tasting session almost inevitable. Mon–Fri 3–11pm, Sat noon–11pm.

Ren 蓮 1-7-1 Kabukichō, Shinjuku-ku ☎ 03 6273 9736; Shinjuku-sanchōme station. Shows at the *Robot Restaurant* (see page 194) are fantastic fun but rather overpriced. However, you can sample the surreal, wacky-and-tacky atmosphere at its sister bar, which opens up to non-customers after showtime. Drinks are surprisingly reasonable, going from ¥500. Daily 10pm–5am.

★**Shisha** シーシャ 3-30-3 Kitazawa, Setagaya-ku ☎ 03 3468 0601; Shimokitazawa station. This tiny, loungey Shimokitazawa bar has perhaps the city's cheapest shisha (from ¥800 per person), with a wide range of flavours to choose from. Drop by before 5pm and you can have a drink for an extra ¥100 – they're usually affordable at ¥400, in any case. Daily 2pm–3am or so.

Square スクエーア 2F 3rd Street, Golden Gai; Shinjuku-sanchōme station. Cute, squashed little upper-floor bar in Golden Gai (see page 133) with cheery staff, cheery customers, decent drinks, and some dangerous-

looking bras on the wall. Look out for the blue sign, which is, ironically, a circle. Cover charge ¥500. Mon–Sat 6pm–4am.

Vagabond ヴァガボンド 1-4-20 Nishi-Shinjuku, Shinjuku-ku ☎ 03 3348 9109; Shinjuku station. A local institution, with jazz pianists who tinkle the ivories every night and colourful art plastered on the walls, and a ¥500 cover charge. Also has a downstairs bar, without live music. Daily 5–11.30pm.

Zoetrope ゾートロープ 7-10-14 Nishi-Shinjuku, Shinjuku-ku ☎ 03 3363 0162; Seibu-Shinjuku station. The most vaunted whisky bar in the Shinjuku area, with umpteen varieties of foreign and Japanese scotch and single malts (if rather unfriendly management). Look for the small red sign with a eye and "shot bar" next to the katakana. Mon–Sat Sun 7pm–4am.

IKEBUKURO AND THE NORTH
SEE MAP PAGE 140

Hub 1-33-4 Nishi-Ikebukuro, Toshima-ku ☎ 03 3989 8682, ⓦ pub-hub.com; Ikebukuro station. There are a few branches of this chain in Ikebukuro (and, indeed, all over central Tokyo), but this particular one provides a particularly good balance – it doesn't get too busy (as many do), but it's always full enough to be fun, and there's space to mingle. Drinks are cheap, with cocktails going down to ¥190 during the 5–7pm happy hour; Western bar snacks are available too, including cheap fish and chips. Mon–Thurs 5pm–1am, Fri 5pm–3am, Sat 4pm–3am, Sun 4pm–1am.

Tachinomiya Kippei 立ち飲み屋喜平 2-29-16 Minami-Ikebukuro, Toshima-ku ☏03 3987 0081; Higashi-Ikebukuro station. Plastered with yellowing posters and (oddly) marathon number tags, this *tachinomiya* (standing bar) perfectly suits the working-class vibe of Ikebukuro. Drinks go from just ¥290; most fun are the sake and shōchū, which you select from the shelves and bring over to the master for a pour. Daily (except Sun) 4–9.30pm.

Torikizoku 鳥貴族 1-26-2 Minami-Ikebukuro, Toshima-ku ☏03 5944 9844; Ikebukuro station. This chain has branches all over the city, but somehow the raucous vibe suits Ikebukuro best. Absolutely everything on the menu, whether food or drink, costs ¥298 (plus tax); in 2018, this was raised for the first time in 28 years, causing consternation among the largely student clientele, but in reality it's still one of the cheapest watering holes around, especially if you take advantage of their eat- and/or drink-all-you-can deals. Daily 4pm–3.30am.

CLUBS

The Tokyo **clubbing** scene took a turn for the better in 2016, when a *Footloose*-like law forbidding dancing was finally repealed; the law, on the books since 1948, banned dancing in licensed premises after midnight (and in unlicensed premises at all), though in practice it was ignored for much of the twentieth century and only enforced occasionally since 2001, so not all that much has changed, especially in the main clubbing regions, **Roppongi** and **Shibuya**. Local **DJs** to look out for are Satoshi Tomiie, a house legend since the early '90s; Ken Ishii, well known for his techno sets; EDM attitude-monger Mitomi Tokoto; and quirky dubstep star Ajapai.

ESSENTIALS

Prices and times Cover charges are typically ¥2500–3500, usually including your first drink; the majority of venues don't really get going until after 11pm, especially at weekends, with most staying open until around 4am.

ID At many clubs you'll have to show some ID to get in – national ID cards or a driving licence should be fine (though some clubs also insist on proof of your profession!), otherwise you may need to risk losing your precious passport.

Information Check listings magazines and online resources to see what's on before heading out; most major

---

SAKE AND SHŌCHŪ

It's said that Japan's ancient deities brewed **sake** from the first rice of the new year. Over ten thousand different brands of the clean-tasting rice wine (also known as *nihonshu*) are now produced across Japan by some two thousand breweries. Pronounced more like "sah-kay" than the "sah-kee" Westerners usually go for, sake primarily comes in sweet (*amakuchi*) and dry (*karakuchi*) varieties. Some types are cloudier and less refined than others, while a few are aged. If you're after the best quality, take a look at bottles labelled *ginjō-zukuri* (or *ginjō-zō*), the most expensive and rare of the *junmai-shu* pure rice sake.

In restaurants and *izakaya* you'll have the choice of drinking sake warm (*atsukan*), with water (*mizu*), iced (*rokku*) or cold (*reishu*). Drinking it cold will enable you to properly taste the wine's complex flavours; you should never drink premium sake warm. Warm sake is always served in a small flask (*tokkuri*), but cold sake is sometimes poured directly from a large bottle into a small wooden box (*masu*), with a smidgen of salt on the rim to counter the slightly sweet taste. Glasses are traditionally filled right to the brim and often placed on a saucer to catch any overflow; they're generally small because, with an alcohol content of fifteen percent or more, sake is a strong drink – note that it goes to your head even more quickly if drunk warm. For more on sake, check out the books and informative website (ⓦ sake-world.com) of long-time resident expert John Gautner.

Shōchū is another clear spirit that is generally stronger and more flavoursome than sake – with an alcohol content of anything from twenty to fifty percent, it's no surprise that some call it "white lightning". Served in the same variety of ways as sake, it can be made from many different ingredients, all with their own particular taste: ask your bartender for sweet potato (*imo*), brown sugar (*kurozatō*), rice (*kome*), barley (*mugi*) or the nettle-like perilla leaf (*shiso*). The best is said to come from Kagoshima and Miyazaki prefectures, both in the far south of Japan on the island of Kyūshū; non-purists mix it with lemon sour, or even oolong tea.

Glasses of sake and *shōchū* tend to **cost** from ¥350 at cheaper **bars and restaurants**, though they can easily start at double that at regular bars; at places selling premium varieties, the prices rise higher still. If you want to drink on the cheap, try a **convenience store**, which all sell large (and usually extremely beautiful) bottles of both sake and *shōchū* from around ¥900; sake also comes in jar-like "cups" from ¥200, and even in carton form from ¥100.

PECHAKUCHA NIGHT

It started in 2003 as an idea to bring people to a new "creative art" basement venue called *SuperDeluxe* in the then pre-Roppongi Art Triangle days, but in a few short years **PechaKucha Night** (@pechakucha.org) became a worldwide **phenomenon** – it has now spread to over 700 cities and counting. Co-created by Tokyo-based architects Astrid Klein and Mark Dytham (KDa), the presentation format – 20 images shown for 20 seconds each, with the exhibitor talking along in time – keeps participants on their toes, often forcing funny ad-lib moments due to the high pace. More importantly it acts as a platform for these creators to share their ideas. PechaKucha ("chit-chat") has ended up being the perfect platform for Tokyo's **young, up-and-coming creators** who would never previously have had a place to share their works in front of a large audience.

PechaKucha usually takes place once a month, with regular venues including the CORE Kitchen/Space in Shintoranomon, and Shibuya's Hikarie Building (see page 123).

clubs post their schedules online. The @iflyer.jp website provides a good overview of the clubbing scene, and offers discounts from the cover charge at some venues.

BAYSIDE TOKYO
SEE MAP PAGE 88

Ageha アゲハ Studio Coast, 2-2-10 Shin-Kiba, Kōtō-ku ☎03 5534 2525, @ageha.com; Shin-Kiba station. Ultra-cool club with an outdoor pool, body-trembling sound system and roster of high-profile events. It's out by Tokyo Bay, but there's a free shuttle bus here from Shibuya – check the website for details. Entry usually ¥3000. Usually Fri & Sat only.

AKASAKA AND ROPPONGI
SEE MAP PAGE 98

Alife 1-7-2 Nishi-Azabu, Minato-ku ☎03 5785 2531, @e-alife.net; Roppongi station. Closed for a while, this famed venue reopened in 2016, and is setting about reclaiming its mantle as one of Roppongi's top spots. As with the earlier incarnations, the second-floor lounge area is a good place to chill out after you've worked up a sweat to the house and techno being spun on the large dancefloor below. The cost of entry varies, but expect to pay more on weekends, even more after 11pm, and yet more again if you're a guy. Events most nights except Sun.

Esprit エスプリー 2/3F B&V Bldg, 5-1-6 Roppongi, Minato-ku ☎03 3470 1371, @esprit-tokyo.net; Roppongi station. Mega-club with state-of-the-art sound and lighting systems, and a roster of high-end local and international DJs. Entry around ¥3500 for guys, ¥2000 for girls. Events most nights.

Jumanji 55 ジュマンジ Marina Building 3-10-5 Roppongi, Minato-ku ☎03 5410 5455, @jumanji55. com; Roppongi station. Aptly, considering its name, *Jumanji* can be a bit of a zoo: with the ¥1000 early-entry fee often including a couple of drinks (and sometimes, particularly for women, unlimited trips to the bar within a certain time window), there's essentially no entry charge,

meaning that on weekends there's barely any wiggle-room. Great fun, though, and a hugely popular pick-up spot. Open most nights.

Muse ミューズ B1 4-1-1 Nishi-Azabu, Minato-ku ☎03 5467 1188, @muse-web.com; Roppongi station. A pick-up joint, but an imaginatively designed one, with lots of interesting little rooms to explore or canoodle in. The dancefloor at the back gets packed at weekends (there's room for 1200 people, in theory), when they mostly play r'n'b. Free entry weekdays, weekends ¥3000; women usually free. Closed Mon.

EBISU, MEGURO AND THE SOUTH
SEE MAP PAGE 108

★**Unit** ユーニット Za-House Bldg, 1-34-17 Ebisu-Nishi, Shibuya-ku ☎03 5459 8630, @unit-tokyo.com; Ebisu or Daikanyama stations. DJ events and gigs from an interesting mix of artists and bands at this cool three-floor club, café and lounge bar. Events most nights.

HARAJUKU, AOYAMA AND SHIBUYA
SEE MAPS PAGE 116 AND PAGE 124

★**Bonobo** ボノボ 2-23-4 Jingūmae, Shibuya-ku ☎03 6804 554, @bonobo.jp; Meiji-jingūmae or Sendagaya stations. Walk past this place in the daytime, and you'll usually think it's nothing more than a wooden house. Come evening, however, it transforms into a highly intimate club, with a surprisingly good sound system; entry is usually just ¥1000–1500 plus a drink, and the DJs are often young up-and-comers. Events most nights.

Club Asia クラブアシア 1-8 Maruyamachō, Shibuya-ku ☎03 5458 2551, @clubasia.co.jp; Shibuya station. A mainstay of the clubbing scene, with the emphasis on techno and trance nights, though they occasionally wander into other territories such as reggae and new wave. It's in the heart of the Dōgenzaka love hotel district, and a popular place for one-off gigs by visiting DJs. Entry usually ¥3000 plus a drink. Open Fri & Sat, and sometimes Sun & Thurs.

15

15

Gas Panic ガスパニック B1 21-7 Udagawachō, Shibuya-ku ☎03 3462 9099, ⓦgaspanic.co.jp; Shibuya station. For many a year, the various *Gas Panic* clubs have, between them, constituted Tokyo's main meat markets, with this one the biggie. Free entry, cheap drinks, and lots of youngsters (both Japanese and foreign) doing things their parents wouldn't be proud of. Daily 6pm–late.

★**Harlem** ハーレム 2-4 Maruyama-chō, Shibuya-ku ☎03 3461 8806, ⓦwww.harlem.co.jp; Shibuya station. The city's prime hip-hop venue for two full decades, keeping abreast of the genre's undulations with a roster of young, energetic DJs. The crowd are almost all dressed to the nines – do likewise or you might as well not be here. Usually ¥3000 with a drink. Events most nights; sometimes closed Sun or Mon.

The Ruby Room ルビールーム 2-25-17 Dōgenzaka, Shibuya-ku ☎03 3780 3022, ⓦrubyroomtokyo.com; Shibuya station. Cosy, unpretentious cocktail bar-club with frequent live music. Their open-mic night on Tuesdays (from 7pm) is a long-running affair that attracts a diverse crowd and throws up some talented performers. Events most nights.

Sound Museum Vision サウンドミュージアムヴィジョン B1F 2-10-7 Dōgenzaka, Shibuya-ku ☎03 5728 2824, ⓦvision-tokyo.com; Shibuya station. 1500-capacity club with four giant rooms, a bunch of regular club nights, and some seriously heavy sound systems. Their EDM events are best of all. Usually ¥2500 with a drink. Events Fri & Sat.

★**Womb** ウーム 2-16 Maruyama-chō, Shibuya-ku ☎03 5459 0039, ⓦwomb.co.jp; Shibuya station. Mega-club with a spacious dancefloor and pleasant chill-out space. Top DJs often work the decks, but be warned that at big events it can get ridiculously crowded. Usually ¥3000 with a drink; discount before midnight. Events most nights.

SHINJUKU AND THE WEST
SEE MAP PAGE 128

Garam ガラム 7F Dai-Roku Polestar Bldg, 1-16-6 Kabukichō, Shinjuku-ku ☎03 3205 8668; Shinjuku station. This tiny, Jamaican-style dancehall is very friendly, and the place to head if you're into reggae. The cover charge is unusually reasonable and includes one drink. Entry ¥1000–1500. Daily 9pm–6am.

LIVE MUSIC VENUES

Pop and **rock** acts usually play in "**live houses**", many of which are little more than a pub with a small stage, although some clubs such as *SuperDeluxe* (see page 187) and *Unit* (see page 187) also have live music events. **Jazz** and **blues** are also incredibly popular in Tokyo, with scores of clubs across the city. There are several **larger venues** where top local and international acts do their thing, most notably the cavernous Tokyo Dome (see page 143), and the Nippon Budōkan (see page 45). **Tickets** for concerts can be bought through ticket agencies (see page 192).

ROCK AND POP

Billboard Live Tokyo ビルボードライブ東京 4F Tokyo Midtown 9-7-4 Akasaka, Minato-ku ☎03 3405 1133, ⓦbillboard-live.com; Roppongi station. A relatively intimate space at which everyone on the three levels gets a great view of the stage. Acts tend to appeal to an older crowd, with everything from jazz to bossa nova (Sergio Mendes has performed here a few times), and R&B to funk. Tickets usually from ¥5800, but can be much higher for the big names. Events most nights.

BYG 2-19-14 Dōgenzaka, Shibuya-ku, ⓦwww.byg.co.jp; Shibuya station. Tiny rock venue which has been around since the late 1960s – the acts often play music of a similar vintage. Tickets ¥1500–5000. Usually a few events each week, 5.30pm–2am.

Club Citta クラブチッタ 5-7-26 Ogawachō, Kawasaki ☎044 246 8888, ⓦclubcitta.co.jp; Kawasaki station. A major live-music venue in Kawasaki, around 20min from central Tokyo, hosting a variety of local and international rock bands. It's part of an entertainment and shopping complex called La Cittadella. Tickets ¥2000–3000. Events most nights.

Club Quattro クラブクアットロ 5F Quattro Building, 32-13 Udagawa-chō, Shibuya-ku ☎03 3477 8750, ⓦclub-quattro.com; Shibuya station. Intimate rock music venue which tends to showcase up-and-coming bands and artists, though it also plays host to well-known local and international acts. Tickets ¥2000–4500. Events most nights.

Crocodile クロコダイル 6-18-8 Jingūmae, Shibuya-ku ☎03 3499 5205, ⓦcrocodile-live.jp; Meiji-jingūmae or Shibuya stations. You'll find everything from samba to blues and reggae at this long-running basement space on Meiji-dōri, between Harajuku and Shibuya. Tickets ¥3000–4000. Events most nights.

Liquid Room リキッドルーム 3-16-6 Higashi, Shibuya-ku ☎03 5464 0800, ⓦliquidroom.net; Ebisu station. Live-music venue hosting some pretty prominent bands; they also throw DJ events from time to time in their *Liquid Loft* space. Tickets ¥2800–5800. Events most nights.

Red Shoes レッドシューズ B1F Chigau Aoyama Building, 6-7-14 Minami-Aoyama, Minato-ku ☎03 3486 1169, ⓦredshoes.jp; Omotesandō station. Fledgling bands try out their stuff at this place south of Omotesandō station – worth a look. Tickets range from free to ¥3000. Events most weekends.

Shelter シェルター 2-6-10 Kitazawa, Setagaya-ku ☎03 3466 7430, ⓦloft-prj.co.jp; Shimokitazawa station. This is the most reliable of the many live-music venues in Shimokitazawa, and one of the oldest, too. Acts

MUSIC FESTIVALS

Music fans visiting in the summer can get their teeth into a few excellent **music festivals**. Fuji Rock is still the biggest such event in Asia, and Summer Sonic quite possibly the second-largest.

Fuji Rock Three days at the end of July; Naeba Ski Resort, Niigata prefecture Ⓦen.fujirockfestival. com. The most established event, as far as foreign bands go, hosting a wide range of top-name acts covering musical genres from dance and electronica to jazz and blues on multiple stages. It takes place at Naeba Ski Resort in Niigata prefecture, easily accessible from Tokyo by train (around 1hr 25min from Tokyo station to Echigoyuzawa by Shinkansen, then a short shuttle-bus ride). It's possible to visit for the day, camp, or stay in the hotels that, in winter, cater to the ski crowd.

Summer Sonic Two days in early August; Chiba, Chiba prefecture Ⓦsummersonic.com. A two-day event split between Ōsaka and Chiba, the latter a 30min train ride east of central Tokyo. An audience of well over 100,000 line up to see a terrific mix of both local and overseas bands over nine stages – Muse, Jay-Z, Metallica and local rock legend Eikichi Yazawa are among the many star acts to have performed here.

Rock in Japan Two weekends in August; Hitachi Seaside Park, Ibaraki-ken Ⓦrijfes.jp. Held north of Tokyo, and accessible from Ueno station, this smaller event focuses on home-grown bands.

15

are usually young four-piece guitar bands with stars in their eyes. Tickets ¥2000–3000. Shows most days from 7pm, and sometimes also at noon.

Tsutaya O-East 2-14-8 Dōgenzaka, Shibuya-ku ☎03 5458 4681, Ⓦshibuya-o.com; Shibuya station. This complex has several venues, all hosting live-music events, ranging from J-pop to hard rock. International bands also play here. Tickets from ¥2500. Events most nights.

★**WWW** B1F Rise Building, 13-17 Udagawachō, Shibuya-ku ☎03 5458 7685, Ⓦwww-shibuya.jp; Shibuya station. Once an arthouse cinema, with its extant tiered hall now functioning as a place to stand and tap your feet. Acts are a mixed bag of genres, from shoegaze to electronica, but they're all pretty high quality; all-night events sometimes take place in the upper level, and they sell out fast. Tickets from ¥2500. Events most nights.

JAZZ AND BLUES

Blue Note ブルーノート 6-3-16 Minami-Aoyama, Minato-ku ☎03 5485 0088, Ⓦbluenote.co.jp; Omotesandō station. Tokyo's premier jazz venue, part of the international chain, attracts world-class performers. Entry for shows is ¥6000–10,000 (including one drink) depending on the acts, though prices hit the stratosphere for the global stars. Events most evenings.

Blues Alley Japan ブルーズアリー B1F Hotel Leon, 1-3-14 Meguro, Meguro-ku ☎03 5740 6041, Ⓦbluesalley.co.jp; Meguro station. This offshoot of the Washington DC blues and jazz club occupies a small basement space near the station. Apart from blues, you can expect to hear jazz, soul and various Latin sounds. Ticket prices average ¥4500. Performances usually daily 6pm & 7.30pm.

Cotton Club コットンクラブ 2F Tokia Building, 2-7-3 Marunouchi ☎03 3215 1555, Ⓦcottonclubjapan.co.jp; Tokyo station. Ritzy jazz club with top-class performers,

from the same stable as the *Blue Note* (see above). It's run as a supper club with two shows a night; ticket prices vary (¥5000–12,000) depending on where you sit and who's on. Two shows per evening.

JZ Brat 2F Cerulean Tower Tōkyū Hotel, 26-1 Sakuragaoka-chō, Shibuya-ku ☎03 5728 0168, Ⓦjzbrat.com; Shibuya station. Swanky jazz club and restaurant in a top Shibuya hotel, with a spacious contemporary design and a respectable line-up of artists. Cover charge from ¥3000. Daily 3–9pm.

New York Bar Park Hyatt Hotel, 3-7-1-2 Nishi-Shinjuku, Shinjuku-ku ☎03 5322 1234, Ⓦtokyo.park.hyatt.jp; Tochōmae station. Top-class live jazz, plus the glittering Shinjuku night views seen in Lost in Translation, are the attractions of this sophisticated bar atop the *Park Hyatt* (see page 151); the cover charge (¥2700) is waived if you eat there. Smart attire recommended. Evening shows start 8pm (7pm Sun).

Shinjuku Pit Inn 新宿ピットイン B1F Accord Shinjuku Building, 2-12-4 Shinjuku, Shinjuku-ku ☎03 3354 2024, Ⓦpit-inn.com; Shinjuku station. Serious, long-standing jazz club which has been the launch platform for many top Japanese performers. Tickets cost ¥3000 in the evening, and less for daytime shows. Shows 2.30pm & 7.30pm most days.

TRADITIONAL JAPANESE MUSIC

Waentei-Kikkō 和えん亭吉幸 2-2-13 Asakusa, Taitō-ku ☎03 5828 8833, Ⓦwaentei-kikko.com; Asakusa station. A rare chance to see an excellent live performance of the *shamisen* (Japanese lute) in a delightful wooden house transported to Asakusa from Takayama. The lunch bentō is beautifully presented *kaiseki*-style food (see page 165) and costs ¥2500; dinner starts at ¥6800. There are five performances daily; see the website for the schedule. Daily (except Wed) 11.30am–1.30pm & 5–9.30pm.

LGBTQ FESTIVALS

Out-and-proud LGBTQ life in Tokyo is still somewhat coming out of its shell, and until recently there were no concrete annual events. However, there are now at least a couple of established fixtures on the calendar.

Rainbow Reel Late July ⓦrainbowreeltokyo.com. This annual film festival is a permanent fixture of Tokyo's LGBTQ calendar, showing films from around the world with English subtitles. A dance party typically rounds things off.

Tokyo Pride Parade Two days in May ⓦtokyorainbowpride.com. The city's Pride Parade acts as the hub of a full-on Rainbow Week. However, the dates have been in flux – check the website for details.

LGBTQ BARS

With over 150 bars and clubs, **Shinjuku-Nichōme** is the most densely packed area of LGBTQ venues in Japan, but clubbing events are held around the city. Check websites for regular monthly standbys such as Shangri-la at *Ageha* (see page 187), Goldfinger (ⓦgoldfingerparty.com) and Diamond Cutter (ⓦdiamondcutter.jp), all of which will have a cover charge of around ¥3000. Check our Basics section for more general advice on Tokyo's LGBTQ scene (see page 190).

SHINJUKU AND THE WEST
SEE MAP PAGE 128

★**Aiiro Café** アイイロカフェ Tenka Building 7, 2-18-1 Shinjuku, Shinjuku-ku ☎03 3358 3988, ⓦaliving.net; Shinjuku-sanchōme station. Many a night in Nichōme starts with a drink at this place, and quite a few finish here too. The bar itself is tiny, which is why scores of patrons hang out on the street corner outside, creating a block party atmosphere on weekends. Daily 6pm–4am (Sun until 1am).

Arty Farty アーティファーティ 2F Dai 33 Kyutei Building, 2-11-7 Shinjuku, Shinjuku-ku ☎03 5362 9720, ⓦarty-farty.net; Shinjuku-sanchōme station. As the night draws on, this pumping bar with a small dancefloor gets packed with an up-for-fun crowd. Their annexe bar, within staggering distance, hits its stride later in the evening and draws a younger clientele. Daily 6pm–1am.

A-Un 阿吽 3F 2-14-16 Shinjuku, Shinjuku-ku ☎070 6612 9014; Shinjuku-sanchōme station. A quirky bar in many ways: it's lesbian-friendly but doesn't mind fellas coming in; the sound system is unusually good; and you can bring your own booze for ¥500. Entry is usually ¥1000 including a free drink. The bar's name represents the first

and last letters of the Sanskrit alphabet. Daily 6pm–2am, Fri & Sat until 4am.

Campy! カンピー 2-13-10 Shinjuku, Shinjuku-ku ☎03 6273 2154; Shinjuku-sanchōme station. This highly colourful venue is perhaps the tiniest of the area's many minuscule LGBTQ bars, but what it lacks in size it makes up for in pizzazz – the drag queen staff sure help. One of the better local venues for straight folk. Daily 6pm–2am (Fri & Sat until 4am).

Dragon Men ドラゴンメン 2-11-4 Shinjuku, Shinjuku-ku ☎03 3341 0606; Shinjuku-sanchōme station. The average Nichōme bar is pretty tiny, but this is a relative whopper – big enough for a proper dancefloor. Good music, a street-side terrace, daily happy-hour specials and strong drinks served by tattooed *gaijin* waiters clad only in underpants also account for its popularity. Daily 6pm–3am (Fri & Sat until 5am).

Goldfinger ゴールドフィンガー 2-12-11 Shinjuku, Shinjuku-ku ☎03 6383 4649; Shinjuku-sanchōme station. This fun, female-only bar is famed for the regular wild parties it runs (ⓦgoldfingerparty.com), and though these are actually held elsewhere, the bar itself is a fun drinking hole, styled something like an old motel and presided over by glamourpuss DJs. Daily 6pm–2am (Fri & Sat until 4am).

Kinsmen キンズメン 2F 2-18-5 Shinjuku, Shinjuku-ku ☎03 3354 4949; Shinjuku-sanchōme station. Long-running and unpretentious bar – you're as likely to be carousing with a mixed group of office workers here as with a drag queen. Check out their famous *ikebana* – traditional flower displays. Tues–Sun 8pm–1am (Fri & Sat until 3am).

ROBOT RESTAURANT

Entertainment and the arts

When it comes to exploring Tokyo's diverse theatre scene, it's easy to enjoy colourful extravaganzas like Takarazuka or the more traditional kabuki even if you don't understand the language. The notoriously difficult nō and butō are also worth trying at least once. Tokyo can be a good place for English-language drama too, with international theatre groups often passing through on foreign tours, while opera is slowly gaining currency. Moving from the highbrow to slightly lower ground, there are numerous multiplex and independent cinemas, as well as a handful of fun, glitzy shows featuring drag queens, robots and more. Tokyo does a fine line in fun theme parks, too, which are great if you are travelling with children.

16

TICKET AGENCIES

To buy tickets for theatre performances, concerts and sporting events, it's simplest to head to the venue in advance. However, using one of the ticket agencies listed below may save a lot of time. In addition, major events sell out quickly; don't expect to be able to buy tickets at the venue door unless you get them some time beforehand. All of the online ticketing agencies below have Japanese-only websites, and English is rarely spoken at their ticket booths – the best plan is to get a Japanese-speaker to assist you.

CN Playguide ⓦ www.cnplayguide.com. Japanese-only website covering almost all major events.
HMV ⓦ l-tike.com. Connected to Lawson, a convenience-store chain with thousands of branches across the country, and hundreds in Tokyo alone. Tickets can be purchased online, or from in-branch machines.
Ticket Pia ⓦ t.pia.co.jp. As well as offering tickets online, branches can be found in shopping malls and department stores in main city areas.

TRADITIONAL THEATRE

The easiest of Japan's traditional performance arts for foreigners to enjoy are **kabuki** and the puppet theatre of **bunraku**. If you don't want to sit through a full performance, which can last up to four hours, single-act tickets are often available. **Nō** (sometimes Romanized as "Noh"), the country's oldest form of theatre, isn't as appealing, though some find the rarefied style incredibly powerful; **kyōgen**, short satirical plays with simple plots, liven up the intervals. Take advantage of hiring recorded commentaries in English at the theatre to gain a better understanding of what's happening on stage. Subtitles displayed on a screen beside the performers (or, at some venues, on the back of each seat) are also sometimes used. Apart from the lines being spoken, information on the background of the story and the characters is also provided. For more on traditional theatre, se.

Cerulean Tower Nō Theatre セルリアンタワー能楽堂 26-1 Sakuragaoka-chō, Shibuya-ku ☎ 03 3477 6412, ⓦ www.ceruleantower-noh.com; Shibuya station. In the basement of the luxury *Cerulean Tower* hotel (see page 150), this theatre provides an elegant setting for both professional and amateur nō and *kyōgen* performances (tickets typically ¥3500 and up).

★ **Kabukiza** 歌舞伎座 6-18-2 Ginza, Chūō-ku ☎ 03 3541 2600, ⓦ kabukiweb.net; Higashi-Ginza station. Tokyo's oldest and largest kabuki theatre, this is the best place to head if you're at all interested in catching a performance. Getting a ticket (¥4000–22,000) can be tricky; they usually become easier to buy after the fifteenth

of each month. Single-act tickets (¥800–2000) are available on the door for those who don't want to commit to a whole performance.

Kanze-Nō-Gakudō 観世能楽堂 1-16-4 Shōtō, Shibuya-ku ☎ 03 3469 5241, ⓦ kanze.net; Shibuya station. The home theatre of Kanze, the best-known of Tokyo's several nō troupes, and one of the city's most traditional nō theatres. Tickets from ¥3000.

National Nō Theatre 国立能楽堂 4-18-1 Sendagaya, Shibuya-ku ☎ 03 3230 3000, ⓦ ntj.jac.go.jp; Sendagaya station. Hosts nō performances several times a month, with tickets starting at around ¥2700. Printed English explanations of the plot help make some sense of what's going on.

National Theatre 国立劇場 4-1 Hayabusachō, Chiyoda-ku ☎ 03 3230 3000, ⓦ www.ntj.jac.go.jp; Hanzōmon station. In its two auditoria, Tokyo's National Theatre puts on a varied programme of traditional theatre and music, including kabuki, *bunraku*, court music and dance. English-language earphones and programmes are available. Tickets start at around ¥1500 for kabuki and ¥4500 for *bunraku*.

Shimbashi Embujō 新橋演舞場 6-18-2 Ginza, Chūō-ku ☎ 03 3541 2600, ⓦ shinbashi-enbujo.co.jp; Higashi-Ginza station. This large theatre stages a range of traditional dance, music and theatre, including the "Super-kabuki" (kabuki with all the bells and whistles of modern musical theatre). Single-act tickets for regular kabuki performances range from ¥800 to ¥1500 depending on the length of the act.

CONTEMPORARY AND INTERNATIONAL THEATRE

Camp as a row of tents, the most unique theatrical experience you can have in Tokyo is **Takarazuka** (see page 193), the all-singing, all-dancing, all-female revue which appears occasionally at the Takarazuka Theatre (see page 193). If your Japanese is up to it, you'll find plenty of modern **Japanese dramas** to enjoy: look out for productions by Chelfitsch (see below), or anything by the

director Ninagawa Yukio, famous for his reinterpretations of Shakespeare. **Overseas theatre companies** often appear at the Tokyo Globe or Shinjuku's New National Theatre, though seats sell out months in advance for the bigger names.

Black Stripe Theater B1 Sangubashi Guesthouse, 4-50-8 Yoyogi, Shibuya-ku ☎ 080 4184 0848, blackstripetheater.com; Sangubashi station. A relatively recent addition to the expat theatre scene, this company has staged plays by Harold Pinter and David Mamet. Tickets ¥4000.

Chelfitsch ⓦ chelfitsch.net. Founded by award-winning writer Okada Toshiki, this internationally acclaimed group put on excellent shows in Tokyo when they're not busy touring the globe (which is most of the time). They can usually be relied on for one new performance each year, although the venues and prices vary.

★**The Globe Tokyo** 東京グローブ座 3-1-2 Hyakunin-chō, Shinjuku-ku ☎03 3366 4020, ⓦ www.tglobe.net; Shin-Ōkubo station. A variety of works, including Shakespearean plays and Western-style operas, are performed in this modern-day replica of the famous Elizabethan stage in London. Tickets from ¥4500.

New National Theatre 新国立劇場 1-20 Honmachi, Shinjuku-ku ☎03 5352 9999, ⓦ nntt.jac.go.jp; Hatsudai station. Just behind Tokyo Opera City, the New National Theatre comprises three stages specially designed for Western performing arts, including opera, ballet, dance and drama. Discount tickets (under ¥2000) for restricted-view seats are sold from 10am on the day; you'll otherwise pay at least double that.

★**PUK** 2-12-3 Yoyogi, Shibuya-ku ☎03 3370 5128, ⓦ puppettheatrepuk.wordpress.com; Shinjuku station. This charming puppet theatre was founded in 1929 as La Pupa Klubo, and survived a government witch-hunt during the war. It's home to a resident group of puppeteers, as well as visiting troupes, and puts on shows that both young and old can enjoy.

Setagaya Public Theatre 世田谷パブリックシアター 4-1-1 Taishido, Setagaya-ku ☎03 5432 1526, ⓦ setagaya-pt.jp; Sangenjaya station. One of Tokyo's most watchable contemporary theatre companies, spread across two auditoria and specializing in contemporary drama and dance.

★**Takarazuka Theatre** 宝塚劇場 1-1-3 Yūrakuchō, Chūō-ku ☎03 5251 2001, ⓦ kageki.hankyu.co.jp; Hibiya station. Mostly stages musicals, punched out by a huge cast in fabulous costumes. The theatre, immediately north of the *Imperial Hotel* (see page 147), also stages regular Takarazuka performances (see page 193). Tickets start at ¥3500; performances run most days except Wed at either 11am or 1pm, and at 3pm.

Theatre Cocoon シアターコクーン 2-24-1 Dōgenzaka, Shibuya-ku ☎03 3477 9999, ⓦ www.bunkamura.co.jp; Shibuya station. Part of Shibuya's Bunkamura arts centre, this modern theatre hosts some of Tokyo's more accessible fringe productions.

Tokyo International Players ⓦ tokyoplayers.org. Tokyo International Players has been going since 1896 (in other words, exactly as long as the modern Olympics), feeding off the ever-changing cast of foreign acting talent that passes through the city. Their website lists their productions, mounted four or five times a year at venues across the city (though their Facebook site is kept more up-to-date); details can also be found in the English-language press.

Za Kōenji 座高円寺 2-1-2 Kōenji-Kita, Suginami-ku ☎03 3223 7300, ⓦ za-koenji.jp; Kōenji station. Managed by the nonprofit Creative Theater Network, and set in a suitably dramatic building designed by leading architect Itō Toyō, this venue presents a high-quality programme of drama, dance and music performances.

16

DANCE

The highly expressive avant-garde dance form of **butō** (also Romanized as "butoh"), which originates from Japan, shouldn't be missed if you're interested in modern dance. It can be minimalist, introspective, and often violent or

---

TAKARAZUKA

There's a long tradition of men performing female roles in Japanese theatre, acting out a male fantasy of how women are supposed to behave. It's not so strange, then, that actresses playing idealized men have struck such a chord with contemporary female audiences. Along with glitzy productions, this has been the successful formula of the all-female **Takarazuka Revue** (ⓦ kageki.hankyu.co.jp), founded in 1914 in Takarazuka, a town 20km northwest of Ōsaka.

The company's founder, Kobayashi Ichizō, was mightily impressed by performances of Western operas he'd seen in Tokyo. He sensed that Japanese audiences were ripe for lively Western musical dramas, but he wanted to preserve something of Japan's traditional theatre, too. So, as well as performing dance reviews and musicals, Takarazuka act out classical Japanese plays and have developed shows from Western novels, including *Gone With the Wind* and *War and Peace*.

Thousands of young girls apply annually to join the troupe at the age of 16, and devote themselves to a punishing routine of classes that will enable them to embody the "modesty, fairness and grace" (the company's motto) expected of a Takarazuka member. They must also forsake boyfriends, but in return are guaranteed the slavish adoration of an almost exclusively female audience, who go particularly crazy for the male impersonators or *otoko-yaku*.

16

TOKYO'S RARE GEISHA

Less than a century ago, **geisha** – female performers of traditional music and dance – were a common sight around certain areas of Tokyo. The capital had certain geisha quarters – the so-called *roku kagai* (meaning "six flower districts") – where geisha lived and entertained clients in teahouses and *ryōtei* (banqueting houses): Akasaka, Asakusa, Kagurazaka, Mukōjima and Yoshi-chō were the most prominent. Today, however, even in **Mukōjima**, once the largest of these districts, the number of *ryōtei* is down from 400 to fewer than 20 and it's thought that there are only around 600 geisha practising their arts nationwide.

As a result of this rarity, an audience with a geisha is far from being a cheap affair, costing in the region of ¥50,000–100,000. There are, however, occasional chances to see geisha in their finery for much less, and even for free. The main opportunity is when geisha **parade** during the Sanja Matsuri (see page 27); if you're not in town then, the tourist centre in Asakusa (see page 74) sometimes hosts weekend performances. Special **performances** by geisha of Japanese dancing at theatres such as the Shimbashi Embujō (see page 192) or at top hotels, often during the cherry blossom season, are also affordable, often ¥10,000 or under.

sexually explicit. *Butō* aside, there's a vast range of other types of dance shows staged in Tokyo, including **ballet**, **tap** and **tango**. It's also possible to sometimes see **geisha** perform their beautiful dances (see page 194).

Dairakudakan Kochūten 大駱駝艦壺中天 B1 2-1-18 Kichijōji-Kitamachi, Musashinoshi, ☎ 0422 214982, ⓦ dairakudakan.com; Kichijōji station. The studio of legendary *butō* troupe Dairakudakan; sometimes there are joint productions here with visiting foreign dancers.

Plan B B1F Monark Nakano Building, 4-26-20 Yayoi-chō, Nakano-ku ☎ 03 3384 2051, ⓦ i10x.com/planb; Nakano-Fujimichō station. Apart from dance or musical performances, you might also catch documentary film screenings or experimental music nights here.

COMEDY

Punchline Comedy Club 3F Pizza Express, 4-30-3 Jingūmae, Shibuya-ku ☎ 03 5775 3894, ⓦ punchline comedy.com. This international organization occasionally brings top foreign talent to the city, with an event every month or so; see website for details. Tickets ¥6500, or ¥8500 with dinner buffet and two drinks.

Tokyo Comedy Store ⓦ tokyocomedy.com. For comedy in English, this team hosts well-attended shows at several venues across the city; there are usually two or three performances per week, and sometimes they also venture into musical or sketch shows. See website for details. Tickets ¥500–1500.

CABARET BARS

A couple of **cabaret bars** host glitzy shows with drag queen performers in fabulous costumes. They usually open up around an hour before the performance – plenty of time to get in the mood with a drink or three.

Black Swan Lake 黒鳥の湖 2-25-2 Kabukichō, Shinjuku-ku ☎ 03 3205 0128, ⓦ kokucho.com; Shinjuku station. It shouldn't come as much of a surprise to learn that there's something like this in Kabukichō – drag shows have been performed here since the early 1980s, and today the cast usually features men, women and transsexuals

DINING WITH ROBOTS

Opened in 2012, the **Robot Restaurant** (ロボットレストラン; 1-7-1 Kabukichō, Shinjuku-ku ☎ 03 3200 5500, ⓦ shinjuku-robot.com; Shinjuku station) is perhaps Tokyo's zaniest attraction, and provides a little trip back to the wild days before Japan's financial bubble burst. It all starts at the entrance foyer, where there's nary an inch of regular, boring space – everything glistens, shines, flashes or reflects. There's far more of the same heading down the stairs to the trippy, video-screen-lined hall where you'll be sat with other excited tourists and locals. Though the website, and plenty of YouTube clips, will give you a great idea of what to expect, the performances are far more fun if you have no idea what's coming – for now, it should suffice to say that dozens of robots, scantily dressed girls, more LEDs than anyone could ever count, and a wall of roaring music are on the cards. Most visitors enjoy it, but a fair few leave grumbling about the price – ¥8000 per head, plus ¥1000 (optional) for a light bentō meal. Performances run daily at noon, 2pm, 4pm, 6.30pm & 8.30pm.

(sometimes referred to in Japan as "newhalfs"). Nightly shows at 7.30pm & 10pm. Tickets ¥2500. Closed Sun.

Kaguwa 香和 3-8-15 Roppongi, Minato-ku ☏03 5414 8818, ⓦkaguwa-roppongi.com; Roppongi station. Hidden away in the Roppongi back alleys, and concealed with an unassuming facade of lanterns and lacquer, this is Tokyo's prime cabaret venue, putting on a couple of performances most nights, plus afternoon shows on weekends. Tickets ¥4200.

CLASSICAL MUSIC AND OPERA

The city is well stocked with Western **classical music** venues, and there are usually one or two concerts every week, either by one of Tokyo's several resident symphony orchestras or by a visiting group, as well as occasional performances of **opera**. Concerts of **traditional Japanese music**, played on instruments such as the *shakuhachi* (flute), the *shamisen* (a kind of lute that is laid on the ground), and the *taiko* (drum), are much rarer, though you may get lucky in Asakusa at *Waentei-Kikkō* restaurant.

NHK Hall NHKホール 2-2-1 Jinnan, Shibuya-ku ☏03 3465 1751, ⓦwww.nhk-sc.or.jp/nhk_hall; Harajuku or Shibuya stations. One of Tokyo's older auditoria for classical concerts, but still well thought of and home to the highly rated NHK Symphony Orchestra. It's next to the NHK Broadcasting Centre, south of Yoyogi-kōen. Tickets cost from ¥2000 to ¥10,000, depending upon the performance.

Orchard Hall オーチャードホール 2-24-1 Dōgenzaka, Shibuya-ku ☏03 3477 9111, ⓦwww.bunkamura. co.jp; Shibuya station. Part of the Bunkamura arts centre, this large concert hall hosts a wide range of classical music performances throughout the year, and has very good acoustics.

★ **Suntory Hall** Ark Hills サントリーホール 1-13-1 Akasaka, Minato-ku ☏03 3505 1001, ⓦsuntory.co.jp/ suntoryhall; Roppongi-itchōme station. Reputed to have the best acoustics in the city, this elegant concert hall has one of the world's largest pipe organs, which is sometimes

CINEMA

There are numerous multiscreen **cinemas** that show Hollywood blockbusters – usually with Japanese subtitles – while a decent number of smaller venues specialize in independent and art-house releases. On "First Day" (in other words the first day of the month, though some chains have their own monthly "Cinema Day" on different dates), **tickets** cost ¥1100, as opposed to the regular price of around ¥1800, or ¥2500 for a reserved seat (*shitei-seki*). Women can also get discounted tickets (¥1000) on Ladies Day, usually Wednesday. Otherwise, you can buy slightly reduced tickets in advance from a ticket agency (see page 192). Note that the last screening of the day can be as early as 7 or 8pm. **Listings** are published on Friday in *The Japan Times*, and can also be found on online sources

AMUSEMENT AND THEME PARKS

Amusement and **theme parks** are huge business in Japan, and they can certainly come in handy if you're dragging around kids – or if you simply want to bring out the kid in yourself.

Aqua Park (see page 112)
Asakusa Hanayashiki (see page 77)
Joypolis (see page 94)
KidZania Tokyo (see page 90)
Namco Namja Town (see page 141)
Tokyo Disney Resort (see page 95)
Tokyo Dome City (see page 143)

used for free lunchtime recitals; check the website for details of this and other events. Prices vary by performance.

Tokyo Bunka Kaikan 東京文化会館 5-45 Ueno, Taitō-ku ☏03 3828 2111, ⓦt-bunka.jp; Ueno station. Tokyo's largest classical music venue, with an extravagantly designed main hall seating over 2300. It has a busy and varied schedule of performances and a marvellous interior dating back to the 1960s, while ticket prices tend to be cheap.

Tokyo International Forum 東京国際フォーラム 3-5-1 Marunouchi, Chiyoda-ku ☏03 5221 9000, ⓦwww.t-i-forum.co.jp; Yūrakuchō station. The Forum's four multipurpose halls (including one of the world's largest auditoria, with over five thousand seats) host an eclectic mix of performing arts, including classical music and opera.

Tokyo Opera City 東京オペラシティ 3-20-2 Nishi-Shinjuku, Shinjuku-ku ☏03 5353 9999, ⓦoperacity.jp; Hatsudai station. This stunningly designed concert hall, with a giant pipe organ, seats over 1600 and has excellent acoustics – though despite its name it hosts only music concerts, not full-blown opera. There's a more intimate recital hall too.

16

such as *Metropolis* (ⓦmetropolisjapan.com) and *Time Out* (ⓦtimeout.com/tokyo). Apart from cinemas listed here, which tend to specialize in independent films, there are many more **multiplexes** in Ginza, Ikebukuro, Shibuya and Shinjuku, mostly showing the latest Hollywood releases.

★ **Cinema Vera** シネマヴェーラ 4F Kinohaus, 1-5 Maruyama-chō, Shibuya-ku ☏03 3461 7703, ⓦcinemavera.com; Shibuya station. The vast majority of films here are Japanese-language only; however, they're mainly black-and-white or Technicolor classics dating from the 1950s to the 1970s, and the location in the heart of Shibuya's raucous love-motel district makes this a good date spot.

Iwanami Hall 岩波ホール 10F, 2-1 Kanda-Jimbōchō, Chiyoda-ku ☏03 3262 5252, ⓦiwanami-hall.com;

TOKYO FILM AND THEATRE FESTIVALS

The biggest of the city's several **film festivals** is the **Tokyo International Film Festival** (🌐 tiff-jp.net), held each autumn at Roppongi Hills (see page 27) and other venues around Tokyo. It's one of the few opportunities to catch Japanese and world cinema with English subtitles, not to mention seeing some films that would never get a general release, although it's increasingly becoming a vehicle for promoting major releases from the US. Also worth catching is the annual LGBTQ **Rainbow Reel Festival** (see page 27).

The city's major **theatre** event is **Festival/Tokyo** (🌐 www.festival-tokyo.jp), held annually in October and November. It showcases a diverse range of productions, with performances both from Japanese and visiting international troupes.

Jimbōchō station. Long-established venue showing non-commercial European films from places as diverse as Greece and Poland, as well as quirky Japanese movies, often from female directors.

★**Meguro Cinema** 目黒シネマ B1F Meguro Nishiguchi Buidling, 2-24-15 Kamiosaki, Shinagawa-ku ☎ 03 3491 2557, 🌐 okura-movie.co.jp; Meguro station. With just one screen and a ten-by-ten seat formation, seeing a film here is a bit like taking a trip back through time to the dawn of cinema. Staff sometimes wear dickie-bows, or costumes related to the films on show – a mix of genres, and very cheap too, with double-bill tickets just ¥1500.

National Film Archive 東京国立近代美術館フィルムアーカイブ 3-7-6 Kyōbashi, Chūō-ku ☎ 03 3272 8600, 🌐 nfaj.go.jp; Kyōbashi station. A treasure-trove for cinephiles, with a small gallery on the seventh floor for film-related exhibitions and two small cinemas screening retrospectives from their vast movie archive. Most are Japanese classics, though they occasionally dust off their collection of foreign films.

Shin-Bungei-za 新文芸坐 3F Maruhan-Ikebukuro Building, 1-43-5 Higashi-Ikebukuro, Toshima-ku ☎ 03 3971 9422, 🌐 shin-bungeiza.com; Ikebukuro station. Amid the game parlours and sex venues ("soaplands") of Ikebukuro is this theatre specializing in classic reruns and art-house movies. All-night screenings on Sat.

Toho Cinemas Roppongi Hills TOHOシネマズ六本木ヒルズ Roppongi Hills, Roppongi, Minato-ku ☎ 03 5775 6090; Roppongi station. Ultra-modern multiplex cinema with bookable seats, late-night screenings and popular Japanese films with English subtitles.

Uplink アップリンク 37-18 Udagawa-chō, Shibuya-ku ☎ 03 6825 5502, 🌐 uplink.co.jp; Shibuya station. World cinema is a staple at this arts centre, which combines a couple of cinemas with a gallery, live music, bar and various workshops.

Waseda Shōchiku 早稲田松竹 1-5-16 Takadanobaba, Shinjuku-ku ☎ 03 3200 8968, 🌐 waseda shochiku.co.jp; Takadanobaba station. Popular with students from the nearby university, this cinema is cheaper (¥1300 for a double bill) and less fancy than others in town, but still shows a decent selection of mainstream and non-commercial releases.

Yebisu Garden Cinema 恵比寿ガーデンシネマ Yebisu Garden Place, 4-20 Ebisu, Shibuya-ku ☎ 03 5420 6161; Ebisu station. There are two screens at this modern cinema, with numbered seating, showing an interesting range of non-mainstream US and British releases.

16

AKIHABARA, OR "ELECTRIC TOWN"

Shopping

Cruising the boutiques while toting a couple of designer-label carrier bags is such a part of Tokyo life that it's hard not to get caught up in the general enthusiasm. There are shops to suit every taste and budget, including some great crafts shops and wonderfully quirky souvenir and novelty stores. Antique and bargain hunters shouldn't miss out on a visit to one of the city's flea markets, which if nothing else can turn up some unusual curios. Always at the cutting edge of consumerism, the city is also a prime hunting ground for the latest electronic gadgets, as well as fashions in both what to wear and how to style your home.

17

DUTY-FREE SHOPPING

Tourists to Japan can make purchases **duty-free** – that is, without the ten percent consumption tax – in a whole bunch of shops around the country. Participating outlets usually have a Duty Free or Tax Free sticker in the window by the entrance.

To take advantage of the scheme, you'll need a **minimum total spend** of ¥5000 at a single store; there's an upper limit of ¥500,000 on **perishable goods** such as food, drinks, tobacco, cosmetics and film, which have to be taken out of the country within 30 days, and cannot be used while still inside the country. Your passport will be required on purchase, and it must have an **entry stamp** from customs; if you manage to enter Japan without one (such as by using the automatic gates at the airport), ask for a stamp from an immigration officer. The shop will attach a copy of the **customs document** (*wariin*) to your passport, which will be removed by customs officers when you leave Japan.

Ginza, stacked with department stores and brand shops, is still regarded as Tokyo's traditional shopping centre, although **Shinjuku** has long put up a strong challenge. Young and funky, **Shibuya** and **Harajuku** are probably the most enjoyable places to shop: even if you don't want to buy, the passing fashion parade doesn't get much better. **Asakusa** is home to a plethora of small, traditional crafts shops, particularly on and around Nakamise-dōri. **Akihabara** has long been known as "electric town" thanks to its myriad high-tech emporia, but is also now the go-to location for manga and anime goods. **Ueno** is famous for the lively Ameyokochō market (see page 69), while **Ikebukuro** is home to two mammoth department stores and many discount outlets. Also worth a look are the shopping malls out at **Odaiba**, such as Venus Fort (see page 92).

Chic **Daikanyama** has an appealing village atmosphere and is a good place to check out up-and-coming Japanese designers; nearby **Nakameguro** is better for "multi-shops" (which contain several brands in one space) than individual labels, with a host of small, funky stores lining the streets beside the Meguro-gawa. **Shimokitazawa** has a studenty, bohemian air with shops selling secondhand clothes, where you can scoop big-name labels at bargain prices – and keep an eye open too for fashion and art creations by local students.

ANIME AND MANGA

Manga (see page 269) are available just about everywhere, from train station kiosks to bookshops – at the latter and in CD shops (see page 200) you'll also find **anime** DVDs. **Akihabara** is the key shopping area for anime, manga and associated character goods, though with some time on your hands you could also give Ikebukuro or Nakano a try. Apart from the places listed below, devoted fans should schedule time at the shops in the **Ghibli Museum** (see page 135).

Radio Kaikan ラジオ会館 1-15-16 Soto-Kanda, Taitō-ku; Akihabara station. This complex is a real nirvana for *otaku* (obsessive fans). Originally an electronics specialist, this huge store now caters to a rich and varied set of anime and manga tastes – everything from lifelike dolls, figurines and model kits to fantasy and sexually charged items. Mon–Sat 10.30am–8pm, Sun 10.30am–7.30pm.

AKIHABARA AND AROUND
SEE MAP PAGE 60

Comic Tora-no-ana コミックとらのあな 4-3-1 Soto-Kanda, Chiyoda-ku ☎ 03 3526 5330; Akihabara station. Seven floors of manga- and anime-related products, including self-published works and secondhand comics on the top floor. There are several other branches across the city. Daily 10am–10pm.

HARAJUKU, AOYAMA AND SHIBUYA
SEE MAP PAGE 124

Mandarake まんだらけ 31-2 Udagawachō, Shibuya-ku ☎ 03 3477 0777, ⊕ mandarake.co.jp; Shibuya station. If you're into character dolls and plastic figures based on anime and manga, this subterranean operation is the place to head. They also have a wide range of second-hand manga as well as posters, cards and even costumes. There's another branch in Akihabara. Daily noon–8pm.

ARTS AND CRAFTS

Tokyo has a wealth of specialist arts and crafts shops, with the largest concentration in and around **Asakusa**. All the following outlets are good places to hunt for souvenirs, including **paper** products, satin-smooth **lacquerware** and sumptuous **textiles**. Also check out the splendid gift shop at the Japan Folk Crafts Musem (see page 125) for folk craft items, and the ones in the basement of the National Art Center (see page 102) for great contemporary gifts.

GINZA AND AROUND
SEE MAP PAGE 53

★ **Ginza Natsuno** 銀座夏野 6-7-4 Ginza, Chūo-ku ☎03 3569 0952, ⓦwww.e-ohashi.com; Ginza station. Stuffed to the rafters with an incredible collection of over 1000 types of chopstick, plus chopstick rests and rice bowls. Prices go very high, but you'll find good ones for under ¥1000. Several other branches around the city. Mon–Sat 10am–8pm, Sun 10am–7pm.

Haibara はいばら 2-7-1 Nihombashi, Chūo-ku ☎03 3272 3801, ⓦhaibara.co.jp; Nihombashi station. This shop has been selling traditional *washi* paper – and everything made from it – since 1806. They've moved a couple of times since, and are now located in more modern-looking environs, but their products are just as great. Mon–Fri 10am–6.30pm, Sat & Sun 10am–5.30pm.

★ **Itō-ya** 伊東屋 2-7-15 Ginza, Chūo-ku ☎03 3561 8311, ⓦito-ya.co.jp; Shibuya station. This fabulous stationery store comprising 11 floors and two annexes (Itō-ya 2 & 3), is a treasure-trove full of packable souvenirs such as traditional *washi* paper, calligraphy brushes, inks and so on. There are several other branches around the city, including one in Ginza station. Mon–Sat 10.30am–8pm, Sun 10.30am–7pm.

★ **Kyūkyodō** 鳩居堂 5-7-4 Ginza, Chūo-ku ☎03 3571 4429; Ginza station. Filled with the dusty smell of *sumi-e* ink, this venerable shop has been selling traditional paper, calligraphy brushes and inkstones since 1800. During Edo times, they provided incense to the emperor but the shop's history actually goes back even further – it was first founded in Kyoto in 1663 and, amazingly, the same family still runs it. Daily 10am–7pm.

S Watanabe 渡邊木版美術画舗 8-6-19 Ginza, Chūo-ku ☎03 3571 4684; Shimbashi station. Small shop specializing in woodblock prints at a range of prices, with designs both modern and traditional in nature. You'll spy original *ukiyo-e* as well as reproductions of works by famous artists. Mon–Sat 9.30am–8pm.

AKIHABARA AND AROUND
SEE MAP PAGE 60

★ **Origami Kaikan** おりがみ会館 1-7-14 Yushima, Bunkyō-ku ☎03 3811 4025, ⓦorigamikaikan.co.jp; Ochanomizu station. This outpost for the production and dyeing of *washi* (Japanese paper) was founded in 1858, and to this day they continue to sell it on the premises – there's also an exhibition hall on the second floor. It's possible to take lessons (some free) in the art of paper folding here. Mon–Sat 9.30am–6pm.

UENO AND AROUND
SEE MAP PAGE 66

★ **Jūsan-ya** 十三や 2-12-21 Ueno, Taitō-ku ☎03 3831 3238; Ueno-Hirokōji station. Tiny shop across the road from Shinobazu Pond, where a craftsman sits making beautiful boxwood combs – just as successive generations have done since 1736. A truly beautiful place to visit, even if you're not buying. Mon–Sat 10am–6.30pm.

Yanaka Matsunoya 谷中松野屋 3-14-14 Yanaka, Taitō-ku ☎03 3823 7441; Nippori station. Appealing hand-crafted everyday items such as shopping bags, baskets, brooms and stools are the stock-in-trade of this artfully rustic shop, at the top of the steps linking Nippori station with Yanaka Ginza. Daily (except Tues) 11am–7pm.

ASAKUSA AND AROUND
SEE MAP PAGE 75

Bengara べんがら 1-35-6 Asakusa, Taitō-ku ☎03 3841 6613; Asakusa station. This tiny store is crammed with a wide variety of *noren*, the split curtain seen hanging outside every traditional shop or restaurant. Even if you don't own a shop or restaurant, there'll be somewhere suitable in your own home for one of these. Daily 10am–6pm; closed third Sun of month.

Bunsendō 文扇堂 1-20-2 Asakusa, Taitō-ku ☎03 3841 0088; Asakusa station. Shops selling paper fans are ten-a-penny in Asakusa, but this is one of the higher-grade offerings, and one of the most notable stalls on Nakamise-dōri. Daily 10.30am–6pm.

Fujiya ふじ屋 2-2-15 Asakusa, Taitō-ku ☎03 3841 2283; Asakusa station. Hand-printed cotton towels (*tenugui*) designed by the Kawakami family; some end up becoming collectors' items, so choose carefully. Daily (except Thurs) 10am–6pm.

Kanesō かね惣 1-18-12 Asakusa, Taitō-ku ☎03 3844 1379; Asakusa station. A mind-boggling array of knives, scissors, shears and files, crafted by the Hirano family over five generations. Daily 11am–7pm.

Kurodaya 黒田屋 1-2-5 Asakusa, Taitō-ku ☎03 3844 7511; Asakusa station. Kurodaya has been selling woodblock prints and items made of traditional *washi* paper since 1856. Tues–Sun 11am–7pm.

Takahisa 高久 1-21-7 Asakusa, Taitō-ku ☎03 3844 1257; Asakusa station. Shop selling row upon row of richly decorated *hagoita*: battledores which are traditionally used by young girls playing shuttlecock at New Year. You wouldn't want to be playing sport with these fancy, lacquered versions, but they make great souvenirs. Daily 10am–8pm.

Yonoya Kushiho よのや櫛舗 1-37-10 Asakusa, Taitō-ku ☎03 3844 1755; Asakusa station. Tokyo's finest hand-crafted boxwood combs and hair decorations; much of the wood used here is sourced from forest land south of Kagoshima, and it's reputed to be particularly suitable for hair. Daily (except Wed) 10.30am–6pm.

17

AKASAKA AND ROPPONGI
SEE MAP PAGE 98

Art & Design Store 3F Roppongi Hills West Walk, 6-10-1 Roppongi, Minato-ku ☎03 6406 6654; Roppongi station. A wonderful store near the entrance to Roppongi Hills' City View. The selection is ever-changing, but often features products from some of Japan's most famous contemporary designers; look out for the polka-dot-splashed produce of Yayoi Kusama. There's also a small gallery space here. Daily 11am–9pm.

Asa-no-ha 麻の葉 1-5-24 Azabu-Jūban, Minato-ku ☎03 3405 0161, ⓦwww.artsou.co.jp; Azabu-Jūban station. Small shop selling some wonderful handkerchiefs, fans and other implements. All designs feature, or at least reference, traditional Japanese styles and patterns. Daily 10.30am–7pm.

★ **Blue & White** ブルー＆ワイと 2-9-2 Azabu-Jūban, Minato-ku ☎03 3451 0537; Azabu-Jūban station. Small store that sells exclusively blue-and-white-coloured products made in Japan including *yukata*, *furoshiki* (textile wrapping cloths), quilts, pottery and traditional decorations. Mon–Sat 10am–6pm, Sun 11am–6pm.

Japan Traditional Craft Centre 伝統工芸青山スクエア 1F Akasaka Ouji Building, 8-1-22 Akasaka, Minato-ku ☎03 5785 1001, ⓦkougeihin.jp; Aoyama-itchōme station. This centre showcases the works of craft associations across the nation – everything from finely crafted chopsticks to elegant lacquerware and metalwork. Great stuff, but not cheap by any means. Daily 10am–7pm.

EBISU, MEGURO AND THE SOUTH
SEE MAP PAGE 108

Kamawanu かまわぬ 1-19-23 Sarugaku-chō, Shibuya-ku ☎03 3797 4788; Daikanyama station. Small shop selling excellent *tenugui* cloths in a variety of styles which, although modern, also make use of Japanese motifs. They also have a very nice looking range of traditional fans. Daily 11am–7pm.

Yamada Heiandō 山田平安堂 2F Hillside Terrace, 18-12 Sarugaku-chō, Shibuya-ku ☎03 3464 5541, ⓦheiando.com; Daikanyama station. Hunt down this store for lacquerware – both traditional and contemporary – found on tables no less distinguished than those of the imperial household and Japan's embassies. Mon–Sat 10.30am–7pm, Sun 10.30am–6.30pm.

HARAJUKU, AOYAMA AND SHIBUYA
SEE MAPS PAGE 116 AND PAGE 119

Beniya べにや民芸店 1-33-8 Komaba, Meguro-ku ☎03 5875 3261, ⓦbeniyamingeiten.com; Aoyama-itchōme station. It's a bit out of the way, but this place stocks one of Tokyo's best ranges of folk crafts (*mingei*). They also stage craft exhibitions at which you may get to meet the artist. Daily (except Wed) 10am–7pm.

Musubi むす美 2-31-8 Jingūmae, Shibuya-ku ☎03 5414 5678; Meiji-jingūmae station. Pick up beautifully printed fabric *furoshiki* here to use instead of wrapping paper – they're also great gifts in themselves. Their origami design prints are particularly unusual. Note that there's no obvious sign on the store – look for the handbags on the ground level of a silver building. Daily (except Wed) 11am–7pm.

Oriental Bazaar オリエンタルバザー 5-9-13 Jingūmae, Shibuya-ku ☎03 3400 3933, ⓦorientalbazaar.co.jp; Meiji-jingūmae station. Although it may seem like a tourist trap, this very popular, one-stop souvenir emporium, selling everything from secondhand kimono to origami paper and top-class antiques, offers great deals and an almost unbeatable selection. Daily (except Thurs) 10am–7pm.

BOOKS AND MUSIC

Despite high prices, it can be enjoyable to browse the city's many **bookshops**, and bookworms should also rummage around the secondhand outlets of Jimbōchō (see page 62). Most big hotels have a shop stocking English-language books on Japan, as well as imported newspapers and magazines. In an age of digital downloads, Tokyo bucks the trend by sustaining many **CD and record shops**. The range of music on offer is impressively eclectic, with a huge range of foreign imports boosting an already mammoth local output of cheesy J-pop. Shibuya has the city's highest concentration of recorded music shops: head to the Udagawachō district near Tōkyū Hands to find scores of outlets specializing in hip-hop, house and techno. The music stores of Shimokitazawa are another good place to root around.

AKIHABARA AND AROUND
SEE MAP PAGE 60

★ **Kitazawa Book Store** 北沢書店 2F 2-5 Jimbōchō, Chiyoda-ku ☎03 3263 0011; Jimbōchō station. The stately granite- and brick-fronted building houses one of the best selections of English-language titles among the dozens of secondhand stores in Jimbōchō – head up to the second level, which is absolutely gorgeous, almost like something from a film. Mon–Fri 11am–6.30pm, Sat noon–5.30pm.

EBISU, MEGURO AND THE SOUTH
SEE MAP PAGE 108

Bonjour Records 24-1 Sarugaku-chō, Shibuya-ku ☎03 5458 6020, ⓦwww.bonjour.co.jp; Daikanyama station. It may not be the biggest CD store in Tokyo, but it's certainly one of the trendiest; they sell their own designer T-shirts, and have an uber-cool curated music selection. Daily 11am–7pm.

★ **Tsutaya** 蔦屋 17-5 Sarugaku-chō, Shibuya-ku ☎03 3770 2525, ⓦtsite.jp; Daikanyama station. The design of this bookshop, whose exterior weaves together a lattice of

ANTIQUE AND FLEA MARKETS

There's at least one **flea market** in Tokyo every weekend, though you'll need to arrive early for any bargains; see below for a roundup of the main venues and ask at a tourist information office (see page 38) for the current schedule. Note that **outdoor markets** are cancelled if the weather is bad. Alternatively, head for the permanent **antique halls**, which gather various dealers under one roof.

Hanazono-jinja 花園神社 5-17-3 Shinjuku, Shinjuku-ku; Shinjuku-sanchōme station. You're more likely to find junk than real antiques at this market, but its setting in the grounds of a shrine, on the east side of Shinjuku (see page 132), is highly attractive. Most Sundays 6am–3pm.

Heiwajima Zenkoku Komingu Kottō Matsuri 平和島全国古民具骨董祭り Ryūtsū Center, 6-1-1 Heiwajima, Ōta-ku ☎ 03 3980 8228, ⓦ kottouichi. com; Ryūtsū Center monorail. One of the biggest antique fairs, this three-day event takes place about five times a year at the Ryūtsū Center, one stop on the monorail from Hamamatsuchō to Haneda. Usually Feb/March, May, June, Sept & Dec.

Ōedo Antique Market 大江戸骨董市 Tokyo International Forum, 3-5-1 Marunouchi, Chiyoda-ku ⓦ antique-market.jp; Yūrakuchō station. One of the largest regular flea markets in Tokyo, with some 250 vendors offering real antiques and interesting curios. Don't expect any bargains, though. Usually first and third Sun of month 9am–4pm.

Yasukuni-jinja 靖国神社 3-1-1 Kudankita, Chiyoda-ku; Kudanshita or Ichigaya stations. One of the few temple flea markets which actually takes place every week, the goods on offer here aren't always particularly impressive, but the dramatic setting (see page 45) makes it a great visit anyway. Sun dawn–dusk.

white letter Ts, has scooped architects Klein Dytham a bunch of awards. Filled all day, every day with a preening young crowd, it's now the fulcrum of the whole Daikanyama area. They've a tremendous selection of English-language books, as well as a *Starbucks* (good luck finding a seat) and lounge bar. Daily 7am–2am.

HARAJUKU, AOYAMA AND SHIBUYA
SEE MAP PAGE 124

Technique テクニーク 33-14 Udagawa-chō, Shibuya-ku ☎ 03 5458 4143; Shibuya station. Second-floor store with plenty of techno, electro, deep house and the like on vinyl. The wall opposite the entrance is a good listings spot for those into such music. Daily 2–10pm.

Tower Records タワーレコード 1-22-14 Jinnan, Shibuya-ku ☎ 03 3496 3661; Shibuya station. An entertainment superstore, with six floors of CDs, DVDs, books, magazines, videos and games. Other branches across

the city. Daily 10am–10pm.

SHINJUKU AND THE WEST
SEE MAPS PAGE 128 AND PAGE 134

Disk Union ディスクユニオン 1-40-6 Kitazawa, Setagaya-ku ☎ 03 3467 3231; Shimokitazawa station. Of the twenty-odd Disk Union branches scattered around Tokyo (there are several in Shinjuku), the Shimokitazawa one is by far the most notable – a huge venue with pretty much every major genre and subgenre covered, and one of Tokyo's best vinyl collections. Daily 11.30am–9pm.

★ **Kinokuniya** 紀伊國屋 Takashimaya Times Square, Annex Building, 5-24-2 Sendagaya, Shinjuku-ku ☎ 03 5361 3301; Shinjuku station. The sixth floor of Kinokuniya's seven-storey Shinjuku outlet offers Tokyo's widest selection of foreign-language books and magazines, including loads of Rough Guides. Daily 10am–8pm; closed one Wed each month.

CAMERAS AND ELECTRONIC GOODS

Akihabara boasts Tokyo's biggest concentration of stores selling **electronic goods**. **Shinjuku** is Tokyo's prime area for **cameras** and photographic equipment, though Ikebukuro also has a solid reputation for new and secondhand deals at reasonable prices. There are also plenty of **discount outlets** in Shinjuku and Shibuya. Compare prices – many shops are open to bargaining – and make sure there's the appropriate voltage switch (the Japanese power supply is 100V). It's also important to check that whatever you buy will be compatible with equipment you have at home. For English-language

instructions, after-sales service and guarantees, stick to export models, which you'll find mostly in the stores' duty-free sections. Some of the larger Akihabara stores offering export models are listed below and at ⓦ e-akihabara.jp.

IMPERIAL PALACE AND AROUND
SEE MAP PAGE 42

BIC Camera ビックカメラ 1-11-1 Yūrakuchō, Chiyoda-ku ☎ 03 5221 1111; Yūrakuchō station. The main branch of BIC offers hard-to-beat prices for cameras and audio and electronic goods – practically any gizmo you want can be found here. You'll find other branches scattered around Tokyo's main shopping centres, including several in Ikebukuro, Shinjuku and Shibuya. Daily 10am–10pm.

GINZA AND AROUND
SEE MAP PAGE 53
Shimizu Camera 清水カメラ 4-3-2 Ginza, Chūō-ku ☎03 3564 1008; Ginza station. Reputable used-camera specialist in the backstreets of Ginza, still going strong despite the decline of the industry. Mon–Sat 10.30am–8pm, Sun 11am–7pm.

AKIHABARA AND AROUND
SEE MAP PAGE 60
Laox ラオクス 1-2-9 Soto-Kanda, Chiyoda-ku ☎03 3255 9041; Akihabara station. One of the most prominent names in Akiba and probably the best place to start browsing: they have a well-established duty-free section with English-speaking staff, and nine stores

where you can buy everything from pocket calculators to plasma screen TVs. Mon–Fri 10am–8pm, Fri & Sat 10am–9pm.

Tsukumo Robot Kingdom ツクモロボット王国 1-9-9 Soto-Kanda, Chiyoda-ku ☎03 3253 5599; Akihabara station. Tsukumo is a general electrical store with three outlets – look for the one with the sign "Robot". Upstairs you'll find a floor aimed at model enthusiasts building their very own androids, but there are also a few demonstration models of working robots. The videos are fun to watch, too. Daily 10am–10pm.

Yodobashi Camera ヨドバシカメラ 1-1 Kanda-Hanaokachō, Chiyoda-ku; Akihabara station; 1-11-1 Nishi-Shinjuku, Shinjuku-ku ☎03 3346 1010; Shinjuku station. Vast electronics store selling everything from PCs to exercise bikes, by way of cameras. There are other branches throughout the city; the Shinjuku outlet claims to be the world's largest camera shop, and offers decent reductions. Daily 9.30am–10pm.

DEPARTMENT STORES

Although they're not as popular as they once were, Tokyo's massive **department stores** are likely to have almost anything you're looking for. They're also more likely to have English-speaking staff and a duty-free service than smaller shops, though prices tend to be slightly above average. Seasonal sales can offer great bargains.

GINZA AND AROUND
SEE MAP PAGE 53
Mitsukoshi 三越 1-4-1 Nihombashi-Muromachi, Chūō-ku ☎03 3241 3311; Mitsukoshimae station. Tokyo's most prestigious and oldest department store – dating back to 1673 – is elegant, spacious and renowned for its high-quality merchandise. Designer boutiques and more contemporary fashions are concentrated in the southerly *shin-kan* ("new building"). Daily 10.30am–7.30pm.
Takashimaya 高島屋 2-4-1 Nihombashi, Chūō-ku ☎03 3211 4111; Nihombashi station. Like Mitsukoshi, Takashimaya has a long and illustrious past, a great food hall and a very broad range of goods, though it appeals to decidedly conservative tastes. There's a huge branch in Shinjuku at Takashimaya Times Square. Daily 10am–8pm.

UENO AND AROUND
SEE MAP PAGE 66
Matsuzakaya 松坂屋 3-29-5 Ueno, Taitō-ku ☎03 3832 1111, ⓦwww.matsuzakaya.co.jp/ueno; Ueno-Hirokōji station. This 300-year-old store is based in Ueno, where its main outlet barely shows its age thanks to an updated look. Daily 10am–8pm.

HARAJUKU, AOYAMA AND SHIBUYA
SEE MAP PAGE 124
Tōkyū 東急 2-24-1 Dōgenzaka, Shibuya-ku ☎03 3477 3111; Shibuya station. Top dog in the Shibuya department store stakes, with branches all over the area, particularly around the train station. This main store specializes in designer fashions and interior goods. Daily 11am–7pm.

SHINJUKU AND THE WEST
SEE MAP PAGE 128
★ Isetan 伊勢丹 3-14-1 Shinjuku, Shinjuku-ku ☎03 3352 1111, ⓦisetan.co.jp; Shinjuku-sanchōme station. One of the city's best department stores, with an emphasis on well-designed local goods and a reputation for promoting up-and-coming fashion designers. Their annexe, housing men's clothing and accessories, is particularly chic. The daily opening ceremony, with all staff bowing as you walk through the store, is worth attending. Daily 10am–8pm.

IKEBUKURO AND THE NORTH
SEE MAP PAGE 140
Seibu 西武 1-28-1 Minami-Ikebukuro, Toshima-ku ☎03 3981 0111; Ikebukuro station. Sprawling department store with a reputation for innovation, especially in its homeware store *Loft*, and its clothing and lifestyle offshoot *Parco*. There's a great chill-out area on the rooftop. Mon–Sat 10am–9pm, Sun 10am–8pm.

17

FASHION AND COSMETICS

The city's epicentre of clothing chic is **Omotesandō**, where dazzlingly designed **boutiques** for famed brands such as Chanel, Ralph Lauren and Louis Vuitton vie to outdo each other in extravagance. Alongside you'll also find top **Japanese labels** such as Issey Miyake and Comme des Garçons, while the area's backstreets are prime hunting grounds for fashionistas searching for up-and-coming designers. **Daikanyama**, **Nakameguro** and **Shimokitazawa** are also worth browsing around – shops in the last two areas tend to be slightly cheaper. Finding clothes that fit is still a challenge (especially, it has to be said, for many foreign females), but is becoming easier as young Japanese are, on average, substantially bigger than their parents; **shoes** remain more of a problem, with the range of larger sizes still pretty limited. Along with department stores (see page 202), the ubiquitous ABC-Mart and Ginza's Washington shoe shop are usually your best bet. Good places to hunt for bargain footwear are Shinjuku, especially around Studio Alta, and Ueno's Ameyokochō market.

GINZA AND AROUND
SEE MAP PAGE 53

★ **Dover Street Market** 6-9-6 Ginza, Chūō-ku ☎ 03 6228 5080, ⓦ ginza.doverstreetmarket.com; Ginza station. This large new complex has started to draw fashionistas back to Ginza from the west, and with good reason – the several floors here feature clothing from almost every major Japanese designer, plus a few of the Antwerp Six, without the department-store atmosphere that usually goes with such choice. Mon–Sat 11am–8pm.

Mikimoto 三木本 4-5-5 Ginza, Chūō-ku ☎ 03 3535 4611, ⓦ www.mikimoto.com; Ginza station. The famous purveyor of cultured pearls has branched out into diamonds and other jewellery lines, all shown off to perfection in its dramatic main store in the heart of Ginza. An annexe aound the corner focuses on high-fashion clothes, accessories and beauty products – look for the pale, pearly pink building with holes punched in it, the work of architect Itō Toyō. Daily 11am–7pm.

Shiseidō 資生堂 8-8-3 Ginza, Chūō-ku ☎ 03 3572 3913, ⓦ shiseido.co.jp; Ginza or Shimbashi stations. One of the oldest cosmetics companies in the world, and the fourth largest globally, Shiseidō was established in Tokyo in 1872. Their main branch occupies a distinctive red building that also features a gallery (see page 56) and several places to eat and drink. Mon–Sat 11.30am–7.30pm, Sun 11.30am–7pm.

Uniqlo ユニクロ 5-7-7 Ginza, Chūō-ku ☎ 03 3569 6781 ⓦ www.uniqlo.co.jp; Ginza station. Inexpensive but still cool, this local brand has found mammoth success overseas. This is their flagship Tokyo store, designed by Klein Dytham,

also responsible for the Tsutaya bookshop in Daikanyama (see page 200). Other branches all over the city. Daily 11am–9pm.

EBISU, MEGURO AND THE SOUTH
SEE MAP PAGE 108

Evisu エヴィス 1-1-5 Kami-Meguro, Meguro-ku ☎ 03 3710 1999, ⓦ evisu.com; Nakameguro station. Main branch of the ultra-trendy – and ultra-pricey – Japanese jeans designer. Stock up here on shirts, T-shirts, sweatshirts and a full range of accessories. Daily noon–8pm.

Jun Ashida ジュン アシダ 17-16 Sarugakuchō, Shibuya-ku ☎ 03 3462 5811, ⓦ jun-ashida.co.jp; Daikanyama station. The headquarters of Jun Ashida, one of Japan's top designers of womenswear, as well as his daughter Tae, who recently achieved fame by becoming the first ever designer of luxury spacewear. Daily 11am–7pm.

★ **Okura** オクラ 20-11 Sarugaku-chō, Shibuya-ku ☎ 03 3461 8511; Daikanyama station. Youthful boutique specializing in indigo-dyed traditional and contemporary Japanese fashions, from jeans and T-shirts to kimono and *tabi* socks. No English sign – look for a low, wooden-style building, usually with some form of indigo fabric hanging outside. Daily 11am–8pm.

HARAJUKU, AOYAMA AND SHIBUYA
SEE MAPS PAGE 116, PAGE 119 AND
PAGE 124

6% Dokidoki ロクパーセントドキドキ 2F 4-28-16 Jingūmae, Shibuya-ku ☎ 03 3479 6116, ⓦ dokidoki6.com; Meiji-jingūmae station. Focusing on the "Kawaii" clothing genre (see page 115), this second-floor store is as loud as it gets: loud clothing, loud decor, loud music. Daily noon–8pm.

Arts & Science 6-6-20 Minami-Aoyama, Minato-ku ☎ 03 3498 1091, ⓦ arts-science.com; Omotesandō station. Sonya Park, the Korean-born, Hawaii-raised owner of this boutique, has a great eye for what works in fashion. Her collection includes original pieces alongside such things as sheepskin Scandinavian army coats and French perfumes. Daily noon–8pm.

★ **Bapexclusive** 5-5-8 Minami-Aoyama, Minato-ku ☎ 03 3407 2145, ⓦ bape.com; Omotesandō station. A Bathing Ape, the streetwear brand of designer Nigo, has a string of boutiques all over Aoyama and Harajuku, of which this is the main showroom. One of their T-shirts will set you back at least ¥6000. Daily 11am–8pm.

Billionaire Boys Club ビリオネールボイズクラブ 4-5-21 Jingūmae, Shibuya-ku ☎ 03 5775 2633, ⓦ bbcicecream.com; Meiji-jingūmae station. Boutique selling the hip-hop-inspired clothes of Pharrell Williams and the tutti-frutti-coloured sneaker line Ice Cream (his collaboration with Japanese designer Nigo, of A Bathing Ape fame). Daily 11am–7pm.

CA4LA 1-18-2 Kaminami, Shibuya-ku ☎ 03 3770 5051, ⓦ ca4la.com; Shibuya station. Hat shop to the eternally trendy, with everything from foppish fedoras and broad-brimmed sun hats to hip-hop beanies and designer baseball caps. The name is pronounced "Ka-shi-ra", by the way. Daily 11am–8pm.

Comme des Garçons 5-2-1 Minami-Aoyama, Minato-ku ☎ 03 3406 3951, ⓦ comme-des-garcons.com; Omotesandō station. More like an art gallery than a clothes shop, this beautiful store is a suitable setting for the high-fashion menswear and womenswear by renowned designer Kawakubo Rei. Daily 11am–8pm.

★ **Hysterics** 5-5-3 Minami-Aoyama, Minato-ku ☎ 03 6419 3899, ⓦ hystericglamour.jp; Omotesandō station. The premier outlet for Hysteric Glamour, a fun, retro-kitsch Americana label which is one of Japan's leading youth brands. Daily noon–8pm.

Isehan Honten 伊勢半本店 6-6-20 Minami-Aoyama, Minato-ku ☎ 03 5467 3735, ⓦ isehanhonten.co.jp; Omotesandō station. Traditional cosmetics are the speciality of Isehan Honten. Their key product is *beni*, a safflower-based lip colour with a lustrous green glow in its concentrated form, though it paints on red; only one percent of the yellow flower's pigment is red, making it expensive. It's sold in lovely china pots, and you can learn about its history in the attached small museum. Tues–Sun 11am–7pm.

★ **Issey Miyake** 三宅一生 3-18-11 Minami-Aoyama, Minato-ku ☎ 03 3423 1407, ⓦ isseymiyake.co.jp; Omotesandō station. One of the top names in world fashion, famous for his elegant, eminently wearable designs. This flagship store, a pink building with Art Deco touches, is suitably fancy. Daily 11am–8pm.

★ **Kura Chika Yoshida** クラチカヨシダ 5-6-8 Jingūmae, Shibuya-ku ☎ 03 5464 1766, ⓦ www.yoshidakaban.com; Omotesandō station. Access the full range of bags, wallets and luggage at this shrine to the hip Japanese brand Porter. It's just off Omotesandō, behind Tokyo Union Church. Daily (except Wed) noon–8pm.

Laforet ラフォレー 1-11-6 Jingūmae, Shibuya-ku ☎ 03 3475 0411, ⓦ laforet.ne.jp; Meiji-jingūmae station. This pioneering "fashion building" is packed with boutiques catering to the fickle tastes of Harajuku's teenage shopping mavens. Wander through and catch the zeitgeist. Daily 11am–8pm.

Omotesando Hills 表参道ヒルズ 4-12-10 Jingūmae, Shibuya-ku ☎ 03 3497 0310, ⓦ omotesandohills.com; Omotesandō station. Like a mini-mall for upscale local designers, this stylish, Andō Tadao-designed building is a must-visit for those with an interest in fashion. Daily 11am–8pm.

Onitsuka Tiger おにつかタイガー 4-24-14 Jingūmae, Shibuya-ku ☎ 03 3405 6671, ⓦ onitsukatiger.com; Meiji-jingūmae station. Selling trainers as seen on the most fashionable feet, this Japanese brand started business back in 1949. Other branches across the city. Daily 11am–8pm.

Prada プラダ 5-2-6 Minami-Aoyama, Shibuya-ku ☎ 03 6418 0400, ⓦ prada.com; Omotesandō station. Without doubt the most attractive shop in Aoyama – which is saying something. Walk in like you own the place, head up to the top floor, and walk down the spiral stairs feeling like a superstar. Mon–Thurs 11am–8pm, Fri–Sun 11am–9pm.

★ **Ragtag** ラグタグ 6-14-2 Jingūmae, Shibuya-ku ☎ 03 6419 3770, ⓦ ragtag.jp; Meiji-jingūmae station. A great place selling secondhand goods from selected designers, including local über-brands Comme des Garçons, Yohji Yamamoto and United Arrows. Daily 11am–8pm.

Solakzade ソラクザデ 4-29-4 Jingūmae, Shibuya-ku ☎ 03 3478 3345, ⓦ solakzade.com; Meiji-jingūmae station. Set discreetly below street level, this is the place for vintage shades – most are from the 1980s, and you'll sense it wouldn't be beyond the realms of possibility to find something much older... Daily (except Wed) 2–7pm.

★ **Sou Sou** そうそう 5-4-24 Minami-Aoyama, Minato-ku ☎ 03 3407 7877, ⓦ sousou.co.jp; Omotesandō station. After the Japanese saying "sō sō", meaning "I agree with you", this range of modern design shoes and clothes based on traditional forms, such as split-toe *tabi* (socks), is eminently agreeable. Their plimsolls are an ideal match for jeans. There's also an outlet in Venus Fort (see page 92). Daily 11am–8pm.

★ **Tsumori Chisato** 津森千里 4-21-25 Minami-Aoyama, Minato-ku ☎ 03 3423 5170; Omotesandō station. Girlish streetwear that captures the Harajuku look, but with better tailoring, materials and attention to detail. Daily 11am–8pm.

UnderCover アンダーカバー 5-3 Minami-Aoyama, Minato-ku ☎ 03 3407 1232; Omotesandō station. Jun Takahashi's UnderCover brand of clothing isn't that underground at all, but remains youthful and eclectic. Daily 10am–8.30pm.

United Arrows ユナイテッドアローズ 3-28-1 Jingūmae, Shibuya-ku ☎ 03 3479 8180, ⓦ united-arrows.co.jp; Meiji-jingūmae station. Main store of the upmarket fashion chain, famous for its clean-cut men's shirts and suits. Head to the top floor to have your measurements taken for a custom-made kimono or cotton shirt. Mon–Fri noon–8pm, Sat & Sun 11am–8pm.

Yohji Yamamoto 山本耀司 5-3-6 Minami-Aoyama, Shibuya-ku ☎ 03 3409 6006, ⓦ yohjiyamamoto.co.jp; Omotesandō station. Flagship store of Japanese fashion icon Yohji Yamamoto, famed for his edgy, single-colour designs. Daily 11am–8pm.

CONVENIENCE STORES

It's fair to say that Tokyo has a fair few convenience stores: some estimates clock a figure approaching ten thousand. Wherever you are in the city, there are always a Dozen or so within easy walking distance, selling food, soft drinks and alcohol (and often spare underwear) at every hour of the day, every day of the year. Locals also use them for tasks such as bill paying and booking concert tickets. The largest chains of **kombini**, as locals usually call them, are **7-Eleven**, **Lawson**, **Family Mart** and **Mini Stop**. Most offer fried snacks from ¥85, cup noodles from ¥120, cartons of sake from ¥100, and cans of beer for ¥150 and up. Indeed, with liberal public drinking laws, and the price of a beer running to over ¥500 in most Tokyo bars (plus sit-down charge), it's no surprise that students, backpackers and others on tight budgets often end up racing to their nearest store for a "*kombini* martini".

SHINJUKU AND THE WEST
SEE MAPS PAGE 128 AND PAGE 134

The Four-Eyed 2-8-2 Kabukichō, Shinjuku-ku, no phone, ⓦthefoureyed.shop; Higashi-Shinjuku station. This shop has an impeccably selected range of pricey menswear, but that's only half the story – it's set in a former love motel, off a hidden courtyard that can only be accessed by bypassing the lobby of another love motel (the Avyss)... Kabukichō in a nutshell. Daily 1–9pm.

New York Joe ニューヨークジョー 3-26-4 Kitazawa, Setagaya-ku ☎03 5738 2077; Shimokitazawa station. Set in what was once a bathhouse, this is the best of the area's many vintage clothing stores, selling a wide range of first-rate secondhand goods. All items are under ¥10,000, and you can get a big discount if taking suitable goods to swap. Daily noon–8pm.

IKEBUKURO AND THE NORTH
SEE MAP PAGE 140

Assist Wig アシストウイッグ 3-4-1 Higashi-Ikebukuro, Toshima-ku ☎079 228 9625, ⓦassistcosplay.com; Ikebukuro station. Ape the wild Harajuku hairstyles with a cartoonish wig from this store, which claims to have more colours on offer than any other wig-shop in the world; at 500 and counting, perhaps they're right. Daily 11.30am–9pm.

FOOD AND DRINK

The best one-stop places to find unusual and souvenir food and drink items – such as beautifully boxed biscuits, cakes and traditional sweets (*wagashi*), and sake from across the country – are the department store **food halls** (see page 202). There are also some highly regarded food and drink shops in Tokyo, some of which have been around for centuries. Premium **teas** are sold at Cha Ginza and Higashiya Ginza teahouses (see pages 175 and 176). General foodstuffs and snacks are easily bought from 24-hour **convenience stores** (see page 206).

IMPERIAL PALACE AND AROUND
SEE MAP PAGE 42

Amano Freeze-Dry Station アマノフリーズドライステーション B1F Kitte Building, 2-7-2 Marunouchi, Chiyoda-ku ☎03 6256 0911; Tokyo station. A fun little shop where everything for sale is freeze-dried – take some soups, curries or risotto home, boil some water, and dine like a Japanese astronaut. Daily 10am–8pm.

Sake Plaza 酒プラザー 1-1-21 Nishi-Shinbashi, Minato-ku ☎03 3519 2091, ⓦwww.japansake.or.jp/sake/know/data; Toranomon or Uchisai-wachō stations. Run by the Japan Sake Brewers Association, this shop and tasting room has an excellent range of sake from all over the country, and they often offer cheap sample tastings. It promotes a different region each season, and the sakes on offer change daily. Mon–Fri 10am–6pm.

BAYSIDE TOKYO
SEE MAP PAGE 88

Tenyasu Honten 天安本店 1-3-14 Tsukuda, Chūō-ku ☎03 3532 3457; Tsukishima station. This ancient shop specializes in *tsukudani*, delicious morsels of seaweed and fish preserved in a mixture of soy sauce, salt and sugar – a speciality of the local area. A wooden box of six different types from their selection of eighteen costs ¥2050; the preserves last for three weeks. Daily 9am–6pm.

AKASAKA AND ROPPONGI
SEE MAP PAGE 98

Fukumitsuya 福光屋 B1 Tokyo Midtown Galleria, 9-7-4 Akasaka, Minato-ku ☎03 6804 5341, ⓦfukumitsuya.co.jp; Roppongi station. Tucked away in the basement level of Tokyo Midtown, this boutique sake shop represents the oldest brewery in Kanazawa (founded 1625), in north central Japan. There are fifty different sakes on offer, from which you can taste a selection of three for ¥1100. Otherwise, prices start at ¥400 a shot. Daily 11am–9pm.

★**Toraya** とらや 4-9-22 Akasaka, Minato-ku ☎03 3408 4121, ⓦtoraya-group.co.jp; Akasaka-Mitsuke station. Makers of *wagashi* (traditional confectionery, often used in tea ceremonies) for the imperial family. Everything is beautifully packaged, and products vary with the season; sample them, along with green tea, in the upstairs café of this lovingly redesigned building, a symphony in pine. Other branches around Tokyo. Mon–Fri 11am–7pm, Sat & Sun 11am–5.30pm.

HOMEWARE AND INTERIOR DESIGN

Japan is justly famous for the delicate beauty and practicality of its **interior design**, particularly the ingenious way it makes the most of limited space, and for its *wabi-sabi* sensibility, which finds beauty in imperfection. In Tokyo's top interior design shops you can find products by legendary designers such as Isamu Noguchi and Yanagi Sori, as well as up-and-coming and overseas talents.

IMPERIAL PALACE AND AROUND
SEE MAP PAGE 42

Pass the Baton Brick Square, 2-6-1 Marunouchi, Chiyoda-ku ☎03 6269 9555; Tokyo station. Styling itself a "personal culture marketplace", this curate's egg of a shop is like a boutique recycling store, with carefully chosen new and old decorative objects as well as a few fashion items – from time to time, the previous owners were local household names. Mon–Sat 11am–9pm, Sun until 8pm.

GINZA AND AROUND
SEE MAP PAGE 53

★**Muji** 無印良品 3-3-5 Ginza, Chūō-ku ☎03 5367 2710; Shinjuku station. One of the newest and biggest branches of this homeware, lifestyle and fashion chain, a "no-brand" concept whose logo is now, ironically, seen across the world. Carries the widest range of their goods, and there's a good gallery section on the top floor, which is also the lobby of the Muji Hotel (see page 148). Other branches around the city. Daily 10am–9pm.

EBISU, MEGURO AND THE SOUTH
SEE MAP PAGE 108

National Azabu ナショナル麻布 4-5-2 Minami-Azabu, Minato-ku ☎03 3442 3181, ⓦnational-azabu. com; Hiro-o station. Supermarket firmly geared towards the tastes of the expat community, with a great selection of international foods as well as fresh veggies, fruits, meat and fish. Daily 9.30am–8pm.

AKASAKA AND ROPPONGI
SEE MAP PAGE 98

★**The Cover Nippon** 3F Galleria, Tokyo Midtown, 9-7-3 Akasaka, Minato-ku ☎03 5413 0658, ⓦthecover nippon.jp; Roppongi station. The most interesting shop on Tokyo Midtown's interior design floor, with a fantastic selection of Japanese designer goods made by small, quality manufacturers – everything from cotton fabric and furniture to lacquerware. Daily 11am–9pm.

Nuno ぬの B1 Axis, 5-17-1 Roppongi ☎03 3582 7997, ⓦnuno.com; Roppongi station. In the basement of the Axis Building (which has several other good interior design shops), Nuno stocks its own range of exquisite original fabrics made in Japan, either sold on their own by the metre or made into clothes, cushions and other items. Mon–Sat 11am–7pm.

EBISU, MEGURO AND THE SOUTH
SEE MAP PAGE 108

Do Claska, 1-3-18 Chūō-chō, Meguro-ku ☎03 3719 8124, ⓦclaskashop.com; Meguro station, then bus or taxi. The shop and gallery of the fab *Claska* hotel (see page 149) is packed with beautiful pieces of Japanese contemporary design – everything from straw hats and fish-shaped soaps to woven lacquerware boxes and sleek wooden chopsticks. There's also an online store. Daily 11am–7pm.

NEO-KIMONO

Demand for new kimono has dipped in recent years, a trend that has gone hand in hand with Japan's declining birth rate and the antipathy of the younger generation to this style of clothing. A bright spot for the industry is the trend to adapt old kimono to **new uses**: young women sometimes wear kimono like a coat over Western clothes, or coordinate it with coloured rather than white *tabi* (traditional split-toed socks). At the same time, **fashion designers** are turning to kimono fabrics and styles for contemporary creations. **Do Justice** (ⓦwww.dojustice.jp) uses antique kimono and *obi* fabric to decorate jeans and create ties, shirts and other fashion items (available online); it's not cheap but each one-off item is utterly original.

17

HARAJUKU, AOYAMA AND SHIBUYA
SEE MAPS PAGE 116, PAGE 119 AND PAGE 124

Cibone 2F Aoyama Bell Commons, 2-27-25 Minami-Aoyama, Minato-ku ☎03 3475 8017, ⓦcibone.com; Gaienmae station. All kinds of furniture and interior design goods can be purchased at this stylish store, which has a strong representation of local designers, as well as good books and CD sections. Daily 11am–9pm.

Francfranc フランフラン 3-1-3 Minami-Aoyama, Minato-ku ☎03 5413 2511, ⓦfrancfranc.com; Omotesandō station. You can get an idea of how free-spending young and on-trend Japanese like to decorate their homes at this fun interior design store, which offers an appealing range of colourful, affordable items that wouldn't look out of place at Ikea. Daily 11am–10pm.

KIMONO AND YUKATA

Japan's national costume, the kimono, is still worn by both sexes for special occasions, such as weddings and festival visits to a shrine. Ready-made kimono can easily cost ¥100,000, while ¥1 million is not uncommon for the best made-to-measure garments. Secondhand or **antique kimono**, with prices as low as ¥1000, can be found at tourist shops, flea markets or in the kimono sales held by department stores, usually in spring and autumn; *Oriental Bazaar* (see page 200) also offers a good selection of pre-loved kimono. You'll pay more for the highly decorated **wedding kimono** (they make striking wall hangings), as well as for the most beautifully patterned *obi*, the broad, silk sash worn with a kimono. Light cotton **yukata** are popular with both sexes as dressing gowns; you'll find them in all department stores and many speciality stores, along with *happi* coats – the loose jackets that just cover the upper body. To complete the outfit, pick up a pair of traditional wooden sandals (*geta*).

ASAKUSA AND AROUND
SEE MAP PAGE 75

Sakura 桜 2-41-8 Asakusa, Taitō-ku ☎03 5826 5622; Asakusa station. Not your regular kimono shop – this tiny store sells Gothic-style clothing made with patches of old kimono fabric (see page 207). Their pantaloons, which

TOYS, GAMES AND NOVELTIES

The land that gave the world Super Mario Brothers, Hello Kitty and Pokemon is forever throwing up new **must-have toys**, games and novelties – Tokyo's top stores are prime hunting grounds for the next big craze before it hits the world market. For more traditional playthings, poke around the **craft stalls** of Asakusa's Nakamise-dōri. Also keep an eye out for "**¥100 Shops**" (everything's actually ¥108, including tax), which can yield a crop of bargain souvenirs.

Hakusan 白山 Floor G, From First Bldg, 5-3-10 Minami-Aoyama, Minato-ku ☎03 5774 8850; Omotesandō station. Sophisticated, award-winning porcelain produced at the Kyūshū town of Hasami, near Nagasaki. Daily 11am–8pm.

★**Tōkyū Hands** 東急ハンズ 12-10 Udagawachō, Shibuya-ku ☎03 5489 5111; Shibuya station. This offshoot of the Tōkyū department store is the place to head if you're planning home improvements or have practically any hobby – they stock everything you could possibly need, from paper, paints and pencils to backpacks and kayaks. It's also a great place to look for quirky souvenirs. Other branches across the city. Daily 10am–8pm, except second and third Wed of the month.

morph from skirts to trousers by way of hidden buttons, are fantastic. Daily 12.30–9.30pm.

RYŌGOKU AND KIYOSUMI
SEE MAP PAGE 83

Merikoti メリコティ 1-12-10 Kamezawa, Sumida-ku ☎070 6986 0708, ⓦmeri-koti.tokyo; Ryogoku station. No kimono or *yukata* here, or even geta, but zori – traditional sandals for indoor use, in a range of beautiful designs. Daily 10am–6pm.

HARAJUKU, AOYAMA AND SHIBUYA
SEE MAP PAGE 119

Chicago シカゴ 4-26-26 Jingūmae, Shibuya-ku ☎03 5414 5107, ⓦwww.chicago.co.jp; Meiji-jingūmae station. There's a fine selection of kimono, *obi* and so on at this Harajuku thrift store, as well as rack upon rack of good used clothes – plus more at another branch, just along the road. Daily 11am–8pm.

Gallery Kawano ギャラリー　川野 102 Flats-Omotesandō, 4-4-9 Jingūmae, Shibuya-ku ☎03 3470 3305; Omotesandō station. Excellent selection of vintage kimono, *yukata* and *obi*, with swatches of gorgeous kimono fabric available too. Daily 11am–6pm.

GINZA AND AROUND
SEE MAP PAGE 53

Hakuhinkan Toy Park 博品館 8-8-11 Ginza, Chūo-ku ☎03 3571 8008, ⓦhakuhinkan.co.jp; Shimbashi station. This huge toy shop also houses a theatre, staging Japanese-language shows which might entertain little ones – or at least distract them from spending up a storm on your behalf. Daily 11am–8pm.

Tamiya Plamodel Factory タミヤプラモデルファク トリー 6 Toyokaiji Building, 4-7-2 Shimbashi, Minato-ku ☎03 3719 8124, ⓦtamiya-plamodelfactory.co.jp; Shimbashi station. Model-kit enthusiasts rejoice – the Japanese manufacturer's entire range is available in this three-level emporium, showcasing thousands of scale and radio-controlled models of automobiles, planes, boats and military hardware. Mon–Fri noon–10pm, Sat & Sun noon–6pm.

ASAKUSA
SEE MAP PAGE 75

Ganso Sample-ya 元祖サンプル屋 3-7-6 Nishi-Asakusa, Taitō-ku ☎0120 171839, ⓦganso-sample.com; Tawaramachi station. The most traveller-friendly shop in "Kitchenware Town" (see page 78), selling fun items such as sushi key-fobs and fake bowls of miso soup – great souvenir fodder. Daily 10am–5.30pm.

AKASAKA AND ROPPONGI
SEE MAP PAGE 98

Don Quijote ドンキホーテ 3-14-10 Roppongi, Minato-ku ☎03 578 6811, ⓦdonki.com; Roppongi station. Fancy some sushi-print socks? A mind-boggling array of stuff is piled high and sold cheap here – everything from liquor to sex toys, as well as gadgets galore. A national institution, it's worth visiting just for the gawp factor. Several branches around the city. Daily 24hr.

HARAJUKU, AOYAMA AND SHIBUYA
SEE MAPS PAGE 119 AND PAGE 124

Kiddyland キッディランド 6-1-9 Jingūmae, Shibuya-ku ☎03 3409 3431, ⓦkiddyland.co.jp; Meiji-jingūmae station. Flagship store boasting six full floors of toys, stationery, sweets and other souvenirs. Daily 10am–8pm, closed every third Tues.

Village Vanguard ヴィレジヴァンガード 23-3 Udagawa-chō, Shibuya-ku ☎03 5281 5535; Shibuya station. This self-described "exciting bookstore" (and really, it is) stocks an amazing hotchpotch of toys and novelties, from inflatable bananas to Batman accessories – and a few fun books and CDs. You'll find quite a few branches around the city. Daily 10am–11pm.

KENDO PRACTICE

Sport and health

In 1964, Tokyo became the first Asian city to host the Olympic Games; in 2020, it then became the first to do so twice. Together with the World Cup that Japan hosted in 2019, these events hint at a surprisingly sporty scene in a country that most outsiders might associate more closely with academic performance than with athletic endeavour. It's not uncommon for parts of Tokyo to come to a complete standstill during crucial baseball games as fans gather around television screens in homes, offices, bars and even on the street. Baseball is the city's premier sporting obsession, but hot on its heels is football (soccer), with the Japanese national team improving every decade.

Although its popularity has oscillated in recent decades, **sumo wrestling** also has a high profile, with big tournaments (*basho*) televised nationwide and wrestlers enjoying celebrity status. Tokyo also has numerous *dōjō* (practice halls) where it's possible to watch **martial arts** such as aikido, judo and karate, and learn about these ancient fighting methods.

Check local media for details of events. For tickets, approach one of the major **ticket agencies** (see page 192).

18

BASEBALL

The baseball season (ⓦnpb.jp) runs from April–Oct, and watching a **professional match** is great fun; even if you're not a fan, the audience enthusiasm can be infectious. Tickets start at under ¥2000, and go on sale on the Friday two weeks prior to a game. It's rare to find anyone who doesn't support one of Tokyo's two main baseball (*yakyū*) teams, the **Yomiuri Giants** and the **Yakult Swallows**; Yokohama has the Yokohama Baystars. As well as the two professional leagues (Central and Pacific), there's the equally popular All-Japan High School Baseball Championship, and you might be able to catch one of the local play-offs before the main tournament held each summer in Ōsaka; check with the tourist office for details.

Meiji Jingū Baseball Stadium 神宮球場 13 Kasumigaoka, Shinjuku-ku ☎03 3404 8999, ⓦwww.jingu-stadium.com; Gaienmae station. One of the stadia grouped in Meiji-jingū's Outer Gardens, this is the base of the Yakult Swallows, and hosts the college baseball Tokyo Big Six league.

Tokyo Dome 東京ドーム 1-3 Koraku, Bunkyō-ku ☎03 5800 9999, ⓦtokyo-dome.co.jp; Suidōbashi station. This huge covered arena, affectionately nicknamed the "Big Egg", is home to the Yomiuri Giants, and is a great place to take in a night game.

FOOTBALL

The national "sakaa" team didn't qualify for the FIFA World Cup until 1998, but have made every finals since – they even co-hosted the 2002 edition with South Korea. This has helped make the game a huge crowd-puller here; professional **J-League** (ⓦjleague.jp) games are held from March to October, with a break in August. Eighteen clubs play in the top J1 division, and together with teams from lower leagues, they also participate in the **Emperor's Cup**; primarily a winter event, its final takes place on New Year's Day (oddly meaning that the cup of any given year is actually won the day after that year ends). At an **amateur level**, there's the Tokyo Metropolis League (ⓦfootyjapancompetitions.com); check the website for

games, or if you're interested in taking part. Other than the clubs mentioned below, look out for Kawasaki Frontale (ⓦfrontale.co.jp) and Yokohama F Marinos (ⓦwww.f-marinos.com), both based in the wider Tokyo area.

STADIA

Ajinomoto Stadium 味の素スタジアム 376-3 Nishi-machi, Chōfu ☎0424 400555; Tobitakyū station. Head west on the Keiō line to reach this stadium, home to FC Tokyo (ⓦfctokyo.co.jp) and Tokyo Verdy (ⓦwww.verdy.co.jp).

National Stadium 国立競技場 10 Kasumigaoka-chō, Shinjuku-ku ☎03 3403 1151; Sendagaya station. Big

---

BATTING STATIONS

If you fancy practising to be the next baseball superstar, or just want to let off some steam, then a trip to one of Tokyo's **batting stations** is what's called for. You'll pay around ¥400 for 20 balls; machines fire these your way one by one, and you're sometimes able to adjust the speed of their flight.

Asakusa Batting Stadium 浅草バッティングスタジアム 1-27 Asakusa, Taitō-ku; Asakusa station. Just what you need in the centre of Tokyo's most traditional area – a complex featuring several batting cages, as well as a whole clutch of zany arcade games. Daily 10am–2am.

★**Meiji-jingū Gaien** 明治神宮外苑 2-2-1 Kasumigaoka-machi, Shinjuku-ku; Gaienmae station. Set of practice cages abutting the Yakult Swallows stadium in the Outer Gardens area of Meiji-

jingū. This place is special, since the balls come from the hands of actual pitchers – okay, clever projections of actual pitchers, but the effect is surprisingly realistic. Daily 9am–8.30pm; Nov–Feb until 7.30pm.

Shinjuku Batting Center 新宿バッティングセンター 2-21-14 Kabukichō, Shinjuku-ku; Shinjuku-nishiguchi station. In the heart of Kabukichō, the Shinjuku Batting Center allows you to choose between balls pitched at a leisurely 70kph or super-fast 130kph. Daily 10am–4am.

18

A TRIP TO THE HOT SPRINGS

Until a few decades ago life in Tokyo's residential neighbourhoods focused round the **sentō**, the public bath. A surprising number of *sentō* survive; those with at least one bath fed by natural spring water are usually referred to as onsen (the term that is more familiar to the Western world), though there are few such places in Tokyo. Then there are the larger **hot-spring resorts** – good fun, though in terms of traditional atmosphere they're not a patch on the smaller *sentō* facilities found elsewhere in the city. Wherever you head, note that it's hugely important to observe local bathing etiquette (see page 29).

Establishments listed in the Guide include the large **Ōedo Onsen Monogatari** (see page 92) and **Spa LaQua** (see page 143) complexes, as well as the smaller **Komparu-yu** (see page 52) in Ginza, **Take-no-yu** (see page 105) near Roppongi and **Somei Onsen Sakura** (see page 142) near Ikebukuro.

Japanese and international games have long been held here, at a stadium that was reconstructed for the 2020 Olympics. **Saitama Stadium** 埼玉スタジアム 2002 500 Nakanoda, Saitama ☎048 812 2002; Urawa Misono station. The home of the Urawa Red Diamonds (Ⓦwww.urawa-reds.co.jp), this is Japan's largest soccer-only stadium, seating 63,700.

MARTIAL ARTS

Japan has a pleasing selection of indigenous **martial arts**, and it's fairly easy to see events at any time of year. Studying is a different matter, however; martial arts require time and patience, meaning that it's only really going to be worth your while taking **classes** if you're in Tokyo for an extended period. Even then, the best first step is usually the relevant federation in your home country.

AIKIDO

Blending elements of judo, karate and kendo is aikido, which translates as "the way of harmonious spirit". Created in Japan in the 1940s, it is a form of self-defence performed without weapons. For a painfully enlightening and humorous take on the rigours of aikido training, read Robert Twigger's *Angry White Pyjamas* (see page 264).
International Aikido Federation 全日本合気道連盟 17-18 Wakamatsu-chō, Shinjuku-ku ☎03 3203 9236, Ⓦaikikai.or.jp; Wakamatsu-Kawada station. You can learn more about the sport by heading here – if you like what you see and are in Tokyo for a while, it's quite possible to participate in their classes.

JUDO

Probably the martial art most closely associated with Japan, judo is a self-defence technique that developed out of the Edo-era style of fighting called *jujutsu*.
All-Japan Judo Federation 全日本柔道連盟 ☎03 3818 4199, Ⓦjudo.or.jp. Federation controlling judo activities throughout Japan.
Kōdōkan 講道館 1-16-30 Kasuga, Bunkyō-ku ☎03 3818 4172, Ⓦkodokanjudoinstitute.org; Kasuga or Kōrakuen stations. This *dōjō* has an upper-floor spectators' gallery open to visitors free of charge, with classes held most evenings. There's also a hostel here where you can stay

if you have an introduction from an authorized judo body or an approved Japanese sponsor. Classes Mon–Fri 5–8pm, Sat 5–7.30pm.
Nippon Budōkan 日本武道館 2-3 Kitanomaru-kōen, Chiyoda-ku ☎03 3216 5143, Ⓦnipponbudokan.or.jp; Kudanshita station. Around fifty free martial-arts exhibition matches are held annually at this large, octagonal arena, an important centre for all martial arts, as well as judo.

K-1

K-1 isn't exactly an ancient fighting form, and as far as mixed modern martial arts go its global standing has taken a bit of a kicking with the rise of the rival UFC (Ultimate Fighting Championship). However, the upside of its declining global popularity is that Tokyo now gets to host the vast majority of K-1 events (see Ⓦk-1.co.jp), since the form remains popular in Japan; these usually take place at Shinjuku FACE (1-20-1 Kabukichō, Shinjuku-ku) every couple of months.

KARATE

Karate has its roots in Okinawa and China, and only hit mainland Japan in 1922. Since then the sport has developed into many different styles, with several major governing bodies and federations based in Tokyo.
Japan Karate Association 日本空手協会 2-23-15 Kōraku, Bunkyō-ku ☎03 5800 3091, Ⓦjka.or.jp; Iidabashi or Kōrakuen stations. Home of the world's largest karate association teaching the Shokotan tradition. You can apply to train here, but it's best to call or email first.
Japan Karatedō Federation 全日本空手道連盟 6F, 2 Nippon Zaidan Building, 1-11-2 Toranomon, Minato-ku ☎03 3503 6640, Ⓦkaratedo.co.jp; Toranomon station. This umbrella organization can fill you

in on the main styles of karate, and advise on the best places to see practice sessions or take lessons.

KENDO

Kendo ("the way of the sword") is Japanese fencing using a long bamboo weapon (the *shinai*) or the metal *katana* blade. This is the oldest fighting skill in Japan, dating from the Muromachi period (1392–1573). It was developed as a sport in the Edo period and is now watched over by the All-Japan Kendo Federation.

All-Japan Kendo Federation 全日本剣道連盟 Nippon Budōkan, 2-3 Kitanomaru-kōen, Chiyoda-ku 📞 03 3211 5804; Kudanshita station. The Budōkan is the venue for the All-Japan Championships each autumn, and the children's kendo competition in the summer.

RUGBY

Rugby has been something of a niche sport in Japan. The national team was famously obliterated 145–17 by New Zealand in the 1995 World Cup (a record defeat), but the game in Japan has since come on leaps and bounds: Japan even provided the shock of the 2015 tournament – some would say the entire history of rugby – with a last-second win over South Africa. Partly as a result of said improvement, Japan was given hosting rights for the **2019 World Cup** tournament. On the **domestic** front, several teams from around Tokyo compete in the national Top League, which runs from August to January (check ⓦ en.rugby-japan.jp for schedule and venue information).

SUMO

Japan's national sport, **sumo**, declined substantially in popularity after the turn of the millennium, with successive **scandals** and a wave of **non-Japanese wrestlers** (see page 82) damaging the sport's reputation. However, it's currently undergoing something of a renaissance, and if you're in Tokyo at **tournament** (*basho*) time, it's certainly worth popping along – relatively devoid of the commercialism entwined with Western sports, and dripping with mesmerizing ritual, this is Japanese sporting culture at its finest.

TOURNAMENTS

National Sumo Stadium 国技館 1-3-28 Yokoami, Kōtō-ku 📞 03 3622 1100, ⓦ sumo.or.jp; Ryōgoku station. The National Sumo Stadium in Ryōgoku is the venue for Tokyo's three *basho* during the middle fortnights of January, May and September, with tickets going on sale a month before each tournament. They're available from ticket agencies (see page 192), but the cheapest ones (up in the gods) are only sold on the day (¥2200); these days you'll have to come early to get a ticket, especially on the first and last days of the 15-day tournament. For further information, consult the website.

PRACTICE SESSIONS

It's possible to watch practice sessions (*keiko*) at the stables (*heya*) where the wrestlers live and train. These take place in the early morning (usually from 5 or 6am to 10.30am) except during and immediately after a *basho* or when the wrestlers are out of town. A few stables accept visitors without an appointment, but double-check first at a tourist information office (see page 38) to make sure

---

STAYING FIT IN TOKYO

The success of the Tokyo Marathon, held in spring, has prompted a **running boom** in the city. Many people make circuits of Yoyogi-kōen, or jog around the 5km course encircling the Imperial Palace (don't dare to go clockwise, lest you flaunt one of Japan's litany of silent, unwritten laws). There are also running clubs such as Namban Rengo and several Hash House Harrier groups.

Gyms are liberally sprinkled around the city, with private chains including Tipness (ⓦ tipness.co.jp) and Gold's Gym (ⓦ goldsgym.jp) – if you're a member overseas you can use their facilities here, though if you're under 20 you might need a note from a parent or guardian (really). At some gyms you can take **yoga** classes, too.

Hash House Harriers ⓦ tokyohash.org. Tokyo's own branch of the international "drinkers with a running problem" society.

Namban Rengo ⓦ namban.org. Long-established running club that's highly popular with local expats.

Tokyo Marathon ⓦ marathon.tokyo. One of Asia's biggest marathons, with more than thirty thousand runners padding the Tokyo streets in late Feb or early March.

Tokyo Metropolitan Gymnasium 1-17-1 Senda-gaya, Shibuya-ku; Sendagaya station. Includes 25m and 50m pools, as well as a gym.

Yogajaya 1-25-11 Ebisu-nishi, Shibuya-ku 📞 03 5784 3622, ⓦ yogajaya.com; Daikanyama station. Yoga classes in Daikanyama.

they're actually training that day. Visitors are expected to watch in silence, and women must wear trousers. Some recommended stables include Dewanoumi-beya at 2-3-15 Ryōgoku, Sumida-ku (出羽海部屋; ☎03 3632 4920; Ryōgoku station); Kasugano-beya at 1-7-11 Ryōgoku, Sumida-ku (春日野部屋; ☎03 3631 1871; Ryōgoku station); and Tokitsukaze-beya at 3-15-4 Ryōgoku, Sumida-ku (時津風部屋; ☎03 5600 2561; Ryōgoku station).

VOLLEYBALL

Tokyo hosts the FIVB World Cup, volleyball's **top international tournament**, every single time it's held. It's on a four-year loop, with the next tournament set to take place in 2023 at the Tokyo Metropolitan Gymnasium (see page 213). It's usually held in late August and early September, though dates can vary. Tickets are pretty easy to buy on the door, and the arena hosts many other smaller events in addition to the World Cup.

18

Around Tokyo

Tokyo functions as a giant magnet to visitors from abroad – there's simply so much to see, eat and do in the capital that many never make it beyond the city centre, let alone the city limits. However, there's plenty to see within day-trip range, and many places fully deserve a night or two of their own. If you make one trip from Tokyo, it should be to the pilgrim town of Nikkō, famed for its World Heritage-listed, mountain-based shrine complex. Out west there is the scenic Fuji Five Lakes area, from which you'll be able to attack Japan's highest and most majestic peak; and Hakone, a mix of sulphur-seeping moonscapes, thrilling cable-car rides and hot springs. Closer to Tokyo are Yokohama, a huge city with plenty to see, and Kamakura, home to a famed giant Buddha statue.

Nikkō and around

日光

"NIKKŌ is Nippon", goes the town's slogan. It's only half-correct, though: visitors to Japan come prepared to take the ancient with the modern, but this town, 128km north of the capital, is up there with the most traditional in the country. It certainly lives up to its billing better than Kyoto, the vaunted dynastic capital way out west.

Most visit Nikkō to see the World Heritage-listed shrine complex of **Tōshō-gū**, which sits at the base of mountains crisscrossed by the outstanding hiking trails of **Nikkō National Park**. It's also worth investigating the far less crowded **Tōshō-gū Museum of Art**, and the **Tamozawa Imperial Villa Memorial Park**, before crossing the Daiya-gawa to explore the dramatically named **Ganman-ga-fuchi abyss**, which is in fact a modest gorge flanked by a tranquil walking path. The most beautiful parts of the aforementioned national park are around **Chūzenji-ko** lake, some 17km west of Nikkō, and the quieter resort of **Yumoto**, higher up in the mountains.

Despite its popularity as a tourist destination today, barely a century ago, in the wake of the Meiji Restoration, Nikkō was running to seed. It was foreign diplomats and businesspeople who began to favour it as a highland retreat from the heat of summer in Tokyo; grand villas such as the Meiji-no-Yakata (see page 221) were built and the *Kanaya Inn* – now the *Nikkō Kanaya Hotel* – was founded by Kanaya Zen'ichirō in 1873.

Outside the peak summer and autumn reasons, and with a very early start, it's possible to see both Tōshō-gū and Chūzenji-ko in a long day-trip from Tokyo, but to get the most out of the journey it's best to stay **overnight**. In contrast to most Japanese urban areas, the town is refreshingly quiet after dark: very little is open after 8pm, bar a couple of renegade bars and two convenience stores, allowing you to wander the town's lanes unmolested by traffic or flashing lights, drinking in the fresh air which remains clement all through the summer.

Shin-kyō

神橋 • Off Nihon Romantic Highway • Daily: April–Sept 8am–5pm; Oct to mid-Nov 8am–4pm; mid-Nov to March 9am–4pm • ¥300

At the top of Nikkō's main street is the red-lacquered **Shin-kyō**, a bridge that is one of the town's most famous landmarks. Legend has it that when the Buddhist priest Shōdō Shōnin visited Nikkō in the eighth century, he was helped across the Daiya-gawa at this very spot by the timely appearance of two snakes, which formed a bridge and then vanished. The original arched wooden structure first went up in 1636, but has been reconstructed many times since, most recently in 2005. There's no need to pay the entrance fee, since the structure is clearly visible (and more photogenic) from the road.

Rinnō-ji

輪王寺 • Daily: April–Oct 8am–5pm; Nov–March 8am–4pm • ¥400, or ¥900 including Taiyūin Reibyō (see page 220); Treasure House ¥300

North of Shin-kyō, an uphill pedestrian path works through gorgeous woodland; follow it up and you'll soon emerge in front of the main compound of **Rinnō-ji**, a

---

NIKKŌ IN WINTER

The one time of year when the crowds taper off at Nikkō is winter. Be sure to pack warm clothes, as there are **cross-country ski trails** and downhill slopes to be discovered; for those who haven't packed snowshoes, skis or a snowboard, the tourist offices (see page 222) will be able to advise on equipment hire. Winter is also the perfect time to enjoy Nikkō's **onsen** (see page 221); most ryokan have bathing facilities on site, though there are a few other pools around town. Another temptation to get you up here in winter is discounted rates at practically all accommodation.

AROUND TOKYO

Tendai Buddhist temple founded in 766 by Shōdō Shōnin, whose statue stands on a rock at the entrance. The large, red-painted hall, **Sanbutsu-dō**, finally reopened in 2019 after a decade of renovation work; it houses three giant gilded statues (the thousand-handed Kannon, the Amida Buddha and the fearsome horse-headed Kannon), and it's worth the entry fee to view these awe-inspiring figures from directly beneath their lotus-flower perches. Rinnō-ji's **Treasure House** (宝物殿, Hōmotsuden), opposite the Sanbutsu-dō, has some interesting items on display, but its nicest feature is the attached Shōyō-en, an elegant garden with a strolling route around a small pond.

Tōshō-gū

東照宮 • Daily: April–Oct 8am–5pm; Nov–March 8am–4pm • ¥1300

Although Nikkō has been a holy place in the Buddhist and Shinto religions for over a thousand years (a hermitage was built here in the eighth century), its fortunes only took off with the death of **Tokugawa Ieyasu** in 1616. In his will, the shogun requested that a shrine be built here in his honour. However, the complex, completed in 1617, was deemed not nearly impressive enough by Ieyasu's grandson, **Tokugawa Iemitsu**, who ordered work to begin on the elaborate mausoleum seen today. Iemitsu's dazzling vision was driven by practical as well as aesthetic considerations: he wanted to stop rival lords amassing money of their own, so he ordered the *daimyō* to supply the materials for the shrine, and to pay the thousands of craftsmen.

NIKKŌ FESTIVALS

Every year, on May 18, the **Grand Festival** restages the spectacular burial of Ieyasu at Tōshō-gū, with a cast of over one thousand costumed priests and warriors taking part in a colourful procession through the shrine grounds, topped off with horseback archery. It's well worth attending, as is the smaller-scale festival on October 17, which doesn't have the archery and only lasts half a day. This is followed by **"Light Up Nikkō"** (end of Oct/beginning of Nov), during which the major temple buildings are illuminated at night to great effect.

The mausoleum was completed in 1634, and ever since the jury has been out on its over-the-top design, the antithesis of the usually austere Shinto shrines, and often considered overbearingly gaudy. Whatever you make of it, **Tōshō-gū** (the name means "sunlight") certainly conveys the immense power and wealth of the Tokugawa dynasty.

The shrine complex

A broad, tree-lined lane leads up to the main **entrance** to Tōshō-gū, just to the northwest of Rinnō-ji. You'll pass under a giant stone *torii* (one of the few remaining features of the original 1617 shrine), while on the left is an impressive red and green five-storey pagoda, an 1819 reconstruction of a 1650 original, which burned down. Ahead is the Omote-mon gate, the entrance to the main shrine precincts. Once

DRINKING AND NIGHTLIFE
Bar Dacite	3
Family Mart	2
Murmur Beer Stand	1

ACCOMMODATION
Nikkō Kanaya	4
Nikkō Park Lodge	1/7
Nikkō Senhime-Monogatari	5
Nikkorisō Backpackers	2
Stay Nikkō	3
Turtle Inn Nikkō	6/8

EATING
Akinoya	5
Gyōshintei	1
Meiji-no-Yakata	2
Natural Saryo	3
Yuba Zen	4

Daiya-gawa

NIHON ROMANTIC HIGHWAY

Tōbu Nikkō Station

JR Nikkō Station

Nikkō Edo Village

Tokyo

Utsunomiya

NIHON ROMANTIC HWY

NIKKŌ UTSUNOMIYA DŌRI

N

0   200
metres

inside, turn left to reach the **Three Sacred Storehouses** (Sanjinko) on the right and the **Sacred Stables** (Shinkyūsha) on the left, where you'll spot some of Tōshō-gū's many famous painted woodcarvings – the "hear no evil, see no evil, speak no evil" **monkeys**, which represent the three major principles of Tendai Buddhism. The route leads to the steps up to the dazzling **Yōmei-mon** (Sun Blaze Gate), with its wildly ornate carvings, gilt and intricate decoration. A belfry and drum tower stand alone in front of the gate. Behind the drum tower is the **Honji-dō**; this small hall is part of Rinnō-ji and contains a ceiling painting of a "roaring dragon"; a priest will demonstrate how to make the dragon roar by standing beneath its head and clapping to create an echo.

Beyond the Yōmei-mon, just above the Sakashita-mon gate to the right of the inner precinct, the temple's famed **sleeping cat** (*nemuri neko*) is usually accompanied by gawping crowds – you'd otherwise easily miss this minute, underwhelming carving. Two hundred stone steps lead uphill from the gate to the surprisingly unostentatious **tomb of Ieyasu**, amid a glade of pines, and about the only corner of the shrine where tourists are generally absent.

Directly in front of the Yōmei-mon is the serene white and gold gate of **Kara-mon**, beyond which is the **Haiden**, or hall of worship. The side entrance to the hall is to the right of the gate; you'll need to remove your shoes and stop taking photographs. Inside, you can walk down into the Honden, the shrine's central hall, still decorated with its beautiful original paintwork.

Futarasan-jinja

二荒山神社 • Daily: April–Oct 8am–4.30pm; Nov–March 9am–3.30pm • Free; garden ¥200

A short tramp west of Tōshō-gū is the fantastic **Futarasan-jinja**, whose simple red colour scheme comes as a relief to the senses after the gaudiness of Tōshō-gū. This shrine, originally established by the priest Shōdō Shōnin in 782, is the main one dedicated to the deity of Mount Nantai, the volcano whose eruption created nearby Chūzenji-ko. There are some good paintings of animals and birds on votive plaques in the shrine's main hall, while the attached garden offers a quiet retreat, with a small teahouse serving *matcha* green tea and sweets. You can also inspect the *bakemono tōrō*, a "phantom lantern" made of bronze in 1292 and said to be possessed by demons.

Taiyūin Reibyō

大猷院霊廟 • Daily: April–Oct 8am–5pm; Nov–March 8am–4pm • ¥550, or ¥900 including Rinnō-ji (see page 216)

The charming **Taiyūin Reibyō** contains the mausoleum of the third shogun, Tokugawa Iemitsu, who died in 1651. This complex, hidden away on a hillside and surrounded by lofty pines, was deliberately designed to be less ostentatious than Tōshō-gū. Look out for the green god of wind and the red god of thunder in the alcoves behind the Futatsuten-no-mon gate, and the beautiful Kara-mon (Chinese-style gate) and fence surrounding the gold-and-black-lacquer inner precincts – extremely photogenic, especially when dusk begins to encroach.

Tōshō-gū Museum of Art

東照宮美術館, Tōshō-gū Bijutsukan • Daily: April–Oct 8am–5pm; Nov–March 8am–4pm • ¥800

Tucked away behind Tōshō-gū, the **Tōshō-gū Museum of Art** – the former head office of the shrine – is set in a huge, traditional, wooden mansion dating from 1928. Inside, the collection features little bar an array of sliding doors and screens decorated by the top Japanese painters of the early twentieth century; together, they constitute one of Japan's most beautiful collections of such art.

Meiji-no-Yakata

明治の館 • Daily 24hr • Free

The pretty gardens of **Meiji-no-Yakata** were formerly the grounds of American trade representative F.W. Horne's early twentieth-century holiday home. The various houses amid the trees are now fancy restaurants (see page 223), but even if you don't eat here, it's worth wandering around to take in the sylvan setting.

Tamozawa Imperial Villa

日光田母沢御用邸記念公園, Tamozawa Goyōtei Kinen Kōen • Off Nihon Romantic Highway • Daily (except Tues) 9am–4.30pm • ¥500

In stark contrast to Nikkō's temples and shrines is the Zen-like simplicity of the beautifully restored **Tamozawa Imperial Villa**, a ten-minute walk west of the Shin-kyō bridge along the main road. This 106-room residence, surrounded by manicured gardens (including a 400-year-old weeping cherry tree), combines buildings of widely different heritage, some parts dating back to 1632. Three emperors have lived in it, including Akihito, who was evacuated here during World War II. As you stroll the corridors, take time to appreciate the intricate details and the gorgeous screen paintings.

19

Ganman-ga-fuchi abyss

含満ヶ淵 • Daily 24hr • Free

The wonderfully named **Ganman-ga-fuchi abyss** is a rocky little gorge cut through by a river that, while crystal-clear, can be a roaring beast after the rains. Accessed via a small path from the road, a delightful, easy-to-walk **trail** hugs the south side of the rocky river valley. Part of the walk is lined by the **Narabi-jizō**, a few dozen decaying stone statues of Jizō, the Buddhist saint of travellers and children. Sporting scarlet bibs and woven caps, and backed by forest, they make for an absolutely enchanting sight; all in all, it's a place bound to remind you of just how special Japan is.

Yashio Onsen

やしおの湯, Yashio-no-Yu • 1726-4 Kiyotakiwanoshiro-machi • Daily (except Thurs) 10am–9pm • ¥510 • ☎ 0288 53 6611

Nikkō's municipal onsen, **Yashio**, is set a little way west of the town, and offers large communal baths and *rotemburo* (outdoor baths). It's quite possible to walk here from central Nikkō if you have an hour or so to spare; the most pleasant route is via the Ganman-ga-fuchi abyss (see above), after which you turn right onto the main road, then look for the signs.

ARRIVAL AND DEPARTURE   NIKKŌ

Nikkō is accessible on two lines from Tokyo, which serve stations sitting almost side-by-side in the east of the town. The JR station is a real beauty, a historic wooden building designed by Frank Lloyd Wright; however, unless you've got a JR Pass, the Tōbu line will generally be more convenient. **Tōbu train** The Tōbu-Nikkō line (w www.tobu.co.jp) runs from Tōbu-Asakusa Station, connected by tunnel to Asakusa subway station; an alternative access point for this line is

---

NIKKŌ TRAVEL PASSES

Tōbu offers **travel passes** to foreigners, covering the return trip from Tokyo and transport around the Nikkō area. These tickets, which can only be bought at Tōbu stations, include the fare from Asakusa to Nikkō, unlimited use of local buses, and discounts on entrance charges at many of the area's attractions. Cheapest are the **two-day passes** (¥2000 on local trains, ¥4320 on the express services); if you're planning a trip out to Chūzenji-ko (see page 223), it's better to get a **four-day pass** (¥4520 April–Nov, ¥4150 Dec–March on local trains; ¥6840 April–Nov, ¥6470 Dec–March on express services).

Kita-Senju Station, at the end of the Hibiya line. There are two types of train to choose from: the regular local ones (2hr 30min–3hr 30min; ¥1360), or the fancier limited express "Spacia" or "Revalty" services (1hr 50min; ¥2700); on local trains you'll need to change at Shimo-Imaichi (and probably a couple of other places, unless you're travelling on the commuter-time expresses).

JR train You can also reach Nikkō on JR trains but the fares are far higher (¥5370 each way if travelling with Shinkansen), so travelling this way only makes sense if you have a JR pass (see page 23). The fastest route (around 2hr total) is by Shinkansen from either Tokyo or Ueno to Utsunomiya (宇都宮), where you change to the JR Nikkō line for a local train to the JR Nikkō terminus, just east of the Tōbu station.

INFORMATION

Tourist information The main tourist office, the Nikkō Kyōdo Centre, is on the main road from the station to the Tōshō-gū complex (daily 9am–5pm; ☎0288 542496, ⓦnikko-jp.org). If you're planning on walking in the area, you can pick up the free *Tourist Guide of Nikkō*, which shows you all the hiking trails found within Nikkō National Park. There's also an excellent information desk at the Tōbu-Nikkō

station (daily 8.30am–5pm; ☎0288 53 4511).

ATMs The main post office (Mon–Thurs 8.45am–6pm, Fri 8.45am–7pm, Sat & Sun 9am–5pm) on the approach road to Tōshō-gū has an ATM which accepts foreign-issued cards, as do the town's two Family Marts, but otherwise it's hard to use cards in Nikkō.

ACCOMMODATION
SEE MAP PAGE 218

Nikkō has plenty of accommodation, and is the best base for the area. If you're looking for a quieter environment, consider staying up at Chūzenji-ko or Yumoto (see page 225). Rates at virtually all places are slightly higher in the **peak seasons**: August, from October to early November, and during major holidays. During these periods reservations are essential.

Nikkō Kanaya 日光金谷ホテル 1300 Kami-hatsuishi-machi ☎0288 54 0001, ⓦkanayahotel.co.jp. This charming heritage property, practically a museum piece, remains Nikkō's top Western-style hotel, harking back to the glamorous days of early twentieth-century travel. There are some cheaper rooms with en-suite shower or just a toilet (the hotel has a communal bath) but for the full effect, splash out on the deluxe grade. Note that there's another *Kanaya* up in Chuzenji-kō (see page 225). **¥17,800**

Nikkō Park Lodge 日光パークロッジ 11-6 Matsubara-chō & 2828-5 Tokorono ☎0288 53 1201, ⓦnikkoparklodge.com. This hostel has two locations in town: one right by the Tōbu station, and the other in a lovely spot high up on the north bank of the river – not terribly convenient, but it makes for a memorable stay. Vegan dinners are available. Dorms **¥2800**, doubles **¥9000**

Nikkō Senhime-Monogatari 日光千姫物語 6-48 Yasukawa-chō ☎0288 54 1010, ⓦsenhime.co.jp. Large, highly comfortable option in the calm western side of town, boasting a mix of tatami and Western-style rooms, and charming bathing facilities. Their meals are also quite

superb. **¥17,300**

★ **Nikkorisō Backpackers** にっこり荘バックパカーズ 1107 Naka-hatsuishi-machi ☎0288 54 0535, ⓦnikkorisou.com. Housed in a building which looks like a giant school carpentry experiment, this amiable hostel has a delightful location near the river, and small but cosy rooms. Discounts kick in if you're staying more than one night. Dorms **¥3000**, twins **¥7000**

★ **Stay Nikkō** ステーイ日光ゲストハウス 2-360-13 Inari-machi ☎0288 25 5303, ⓦstaynikko.com. Presided over by a super-friendly (and English-speaking) Japanese-Thai couple, this place is a real winner. The main building only has four tatami rooms, all with shared facilities, making for an atmosphere halfway between a guesthouse and a homestay; they also have two new villas, suitable for families or small groups. The breakfasts (¥800) go down very well, and the peaceful riverside location is another bonus. Rooms **¥8800**, villas **¥23,000**

Turtle Inn Nikkō タートルイン日光 2-16 Takumi-chō ☎0288 53 3168, ⓦturtle-nikko.com. Popular pension run by an English-speaking family, in a quiet location next to the river. There are small, plain tatami rooms with common bathrooms, and en-suite Western-style rooms, plus a cosy lounge. Add ¥1080 for breakfast, and ¥2160 for the evening meal. They also run a fancier, slightly more expensive annexe, the *Hotori-an*, down the road beside the path to the Ganman-ga-fuchi abyss; it boasts a pottery shop on site, as well as a bath with forest views, and meals are taken at the *Turtle Inn*. **¥9600**

EATING
SEE MAP PAGE 218

The Nikkō area's culinary speciality is **yuba-ryōri** – milky, thin strips of tofu, usually rolled into tubes and cooked in various stews; this can be enjoyed at many local restaurants, but you may well be served it as part of meals at your accommodation. Note that most **restaurants** in town

shut at around 8pm – the opening times listed here are the official ones, but don't take them as gospel.

★ **Akinoya** 晃のや 588 Gokō-machi ☎0288 25 7979. The best of the main road's several noodle restaurants, serving various strains of yakisoba (fried soba) for ¥580–

1080, including an unusual – and very spicy – tantan variety. The only drawback is that they close up rather early. Daily 11am–6pm.

Gyōshintei 堯心亭 2339-1 Sannai ☎ 0288 53 3751. Sample exquisitely prepared *shōjin-ryōri* (Buddhist vegetarian cuisine) in a traditional tatami room, served by kimono-clad waitresses: lunches cost from ¥3000, dinners more like ¥5500, and some sets include fish. It's part of the charming Meiji-no-Yakata complex (see page 221), so you can gaze out on a lovely garden as you eat, then walk off the calories in and around the surrounding sights. Daily (except Thurs) 11.30am–7pm.

★**Meiji-no-Yakata** 明治の館 2339-1 Sannai ☎ 0288 53 3751. If you get to this charmingly nostalgic stone villa (once a Meiji-era holiday home) at around 10am, you can make a table reservation, then go sightseeing; come back when it opens at 11am, and treat yourself to the best coffee this side of Tokyo, plus some cheesecake (¥1080 will get you both), possibly after some clam chowder (¥700). With everything served by starched-shirted sorts,

with fancy bowls and utensils, it's a small price to pay for some luxury. Otherwise, go the whole hog with their mix of Japanese and Western staples – mains such as bouillabaisse or beef tongue stew start at ¥1500. Daily 11am–7.30pm.

Natural Saryo 自然茶寮廻 909-1 Nakahatsuishi-machi ☎ 0288 25 3122. Run by a husband-and-wife team, this true vegan café – also known as Megumi – has a great laidback atmosphere. Meals (¥1200–1800) use vegetables grown in their own garden, as well as local organic produce. You'll also find some yummy dessert choices, mostly Western style (such as cakes), and plenty of fresh fruits. It's a little hard to spot; look for the sign saying "Oriental Fine Art & Curios". Daily 11.30am–6pm.

Yuba Zen 湯波巻 1007 Kamihatsuishi-machi ☎ 0288 53 3470. The best place to sample that local speciality, *yuba-ryōri*; sets including it as a main cost from ¥2000, or you can sample to the tofu (which is particularly fresh here) for just ¥600. They also have excellent tea on offer. Daily (except Tues) 11am–7pm.

19

DRINKING
SEE MAP PAGE 218

Bar Dacite バー「デイサイト」 1300 Kami-hatsuishi-machi ☎ 0288 54 0001, ⓦ kanayahotel.co.jp. The dark and cosy hotel bar at the swanky *Nikkō Kanaya* (see page 222) is the town's best spot for a nightcap – not that there's much competition. Cocktails suit the elegant atmosphere best, and the menu features some house specials. Daily 6–10.30pm.

Family Mart ファミリーマート 1-16 Yasukawa-chō. This convenience store may be a left-field drinking recommendation, but there are a few sound reasons behind it: first, its location – from the outdoor tables you'll be able to hear the rushing river, and see the dark mountains

behind; second, it has a splendid selection of boutique cup sake, including (if you're in luck) an exceedingly tasty local brown-glass number, long served by appointment to Tōshō-gū; and finally, after a certain hour, it's the only place in Nikkō you can go for a drink. Daily 24hr.

Murmur Beer Stand マービールスタンド 1013 Kamihatsuishi-machi, ⓦ facebook.com/murmurbiiru. A great recent addition to Nikkō, this small bar sells craft beer – usually a dozen varieties thereof – brewed on the premises (¥500). Often good fun, but also often closed at short notice; if so, try the Bar de Nikkō immediately opposite, which is also pretty decent. Fri–Tues noon–10pm.

Chūzenji-ko

中禅寺湖

Some 10km west of Nikkō lies the tranquil lake of **Chūzenji-ko**, most famed for the dramatic **Kegon Falls** that flow from it. Buses from Nikkō run east along Route 120 and up the twisting, one-way road to reach **CHŪZENJI**, the lakeside resort. Both the lake and waterfalls were created thousands of years ago, when nearby **Mount Nantai** (男体山, Nantai-san; 2486m) erupted, its lava plugging the valley.

Many buses from Nikkō continue northwest of Chūzenji to terminate 45 minutes later at the onsen village of **YUMOTO**, which nestles cosily at the base of the mountains on the northern shore of lake **Yuno-ko**.

Kegon Falls

華厳の滝, Kegon-no-taki • Daily: Jan, Feb & Dec 9am–4.30pm; March, April & Nov 8am–5pm; May–Sept 7.30am–6pm; Oct 7.30am–5pm • Lift ¥550 • ⓦ kegon.jp

The best view of the **Kegon Falls** can be had from the viewing platform at their base. The lift to this vantage point lies east across the car park behind the Chūzenji bus station; don't be put off by the queues of tour groups – a shorter line is reserved for independent travellers. The lift drops 100m through the rock to the base of the falls, from where you can see over a tonne of water per second cascading from the Ojiri River, which flows from the Chūzenji-ko lake.

Futarasan-jinja

二荒山神社 • Off Nihon Romantic Highway • 24hr • Free; Mount Nantai ¥500

This colourful shrine, around 1km west of the Kegon Falls along the shore of Chūzenji-ko, is the second **Futarasan-jinja** of the Nikkō area (the first is in Nikkō itself). The shrine, which once bore the name Chūzenji, has a pretty view of the lake, but is nothing extraordinary. There's also a third Futarasan-jinja, on the actual summit of Mount Nantai; to reach it you'll have to pay to climb the volcanic peak, which is owned by the shrine. The hike up is beautiful but takes around four hours, and should only be attempted in good weather; the tourist offices in Nikkō (see page 222) can provide you with maps.

Ryūzu Falls

竜頭の滝, Ryūzu no Taki • Daily 24hr • Free • ☎ 0288 55 0388

Heading 6km west around Chūzenji-ko from Futarasan-jinja, on a gorgeous lakeside path, you'll eventually spot the spectacular, 60m-high **Ryūzu Falls**, which boast clear views of the lake. At the base of the falls are several gift shops and noodle bars, one of which has a superb location overlooking the water as it gushes into the lake. Note that there's also a great hiking route from here to Yumoto (see below).

Yumoto

湯元

The village of **YUMOTO** nestles cosily at the base of the mountains on the northern shore of lake **Yuno-ko**, 15km northwest of Chūzenji-ko. A lovely way to take in the scenery is to rent a rowing boat at the lakeside *Yumoto Rest House* (¥1000 for 50min; May–Oct only). Alternatively, you could walk around the lake in about an hour.

Onsen-ji

温泉寺 • At the back of the village, 5min walk from the bus terminal • April–Nov daily 10am–2pm • ¥500

The small temple of **Onsen-ji** is notable for its onsen bath, which you can use. Nearby is **Yu-no-daira**, a field where bubbling water breaks through the ground – this is the source of the sulphur smell that hangs so pungently in the air. There's a free footbath, great for soaking weary feet, near the *Yumoto Hillside Inn*.

Senjōgahara marshland plateau

戦場ヶ原

If you're feeling energetic, it's worth embarking on the easy and enjoyable 10km **hike** from Yumoto across the **Senjōgahara marshland plateau**, past two spectacular waterfalls and back to Chūzenji-ko. First, follow the west bank of Yuno-ko around to the steps down to the picturesque Yudaki Falls (湯滝), where you can stop off at the lodge serving delicious grilled fish and rice cakes (*mochi*) dipped in sweet miso paste. The trail continues along the Yu-gawa through shady woods before emerging beside the Izumiyado, a large pond and the start of a two-hour tramp across the raised walkways above the Senjōgahara marshland, which blooms with many wild flowers during the summer. Roughly one hour further on, at the Akanuma junction, you can branch off back to the main road, or continue along the riverside path for thirty minutes to the main road and bridge overlooking the **Ryūzu Falls** (see page 224).

ARRIVAL AND DEPARTURE   **CHŪZENJI-KO AND YUMOTO**

By bus Buses up to Chūzenji-ko (¥1150 one-way) and on to Yumoto (¥1700) run at fairly frequent intervals from

outside both of Nikkō's train stations between 6am and 6pm, and usually take 45min, though travelling times can

MINAKAMI AND ADVENTURE SPORTS

The sprawling township of **Minakami** (水上), buried deep in the mountains of Gunma-ken, about 65km west of Nikkō, has become one of the hottest spots in Japan for adventure sports. No fewer than ten whitewater rafting companies, including **Canyons** (☎0278 72 2811, ⓦcanyons.jp), offer trips down the Tone-gawa. Other activities include paragliding, canyoning, abseiling, rock-climbing and a wide variety of treks, including the ascent to the summit of **Tanigawa-dake** (谷川岳; 1977m). To relax after all this, you can head to **Takaragawa onsen** (宝川温泉; daily 9am–5pm; ¥1500 before 4pm, ¥1000 after 4pm; ⓦtakaragawa.com), famous for its mixed-sex bathing (though it also has separated baths) and its four huge rotemburo.

To reach Minakami from Tokyo, take the Shinkansen (1hr; ¥5910) to **Jōmō-Kōgen** (上毛高原), from where the town is a 20min bus ride. The **tourist office** (daily 9am–5.15pm; ☎0278 72 2611, ⓦenjoy-minakami.com) is opposite the station. **Places to stay** include the Canyons-run *Alpine Lodge* (¥5000 per person, or less if also booking activities), which offers private rooms plus a lively bar; and the aforementioned **Takaragawa onsen** (from ¥21,600 per person).

19

easily double – or even triple – during *kōyō* in mid-October, the prime time for viewing the changing autumn leaves, when traffic is bumper to bumper. If you haven't bought a Tōbu pass (see page 221), it's still possible to save money on transport by buying a two-day bus pass at either train station; for unlimited return trips to Chūzenji-ko the cost is ¥2000, while to Yumoto it's ¥3000.

ACCOMMODATION

Unfortunately, there's little in the way of cheap accommodation in Yumoto, though searching online for specific dates often brings up one or two options in the ¥12,000 region – if you don't have any luck with the international engines, try asking at a local tourist office.
Chūzenji Kanaya Hotel 中禅寺金谷ホテル 2482

Chugushi ☎0288 51 0001, ⓦkanayahotel.co.jp. The most luxurious place to stay on the lake, and affiliated to the eponymous hotel in Nikkō (see page 222). It's a couple of kilometres away from the tourist village, en route to the Ryūzu Falls, and has been especially designed to blend in with the woodland surroundings. ¥24,000

Fuji Five Lakes

The best reason for heading 100km west from Tokyo towards the area known as **FUJI FIVE LAKES** is to climb **Mount Fuji** (富士山), Japan's most sacred volcano and, at 3776m, its highest mountain. Fuji-san, as it's respectfully known by the Japanese, has long been worshipped for its latent power (it last erupted in 1707) and near-perfect symmetry; it is most beautiful from October to May, when the summit is crowned with snow. The climbing season is basically July and August; even if you don't fancy the rather daunting ascent, just getting up close to Japan's most famous national symbol is a memorable experience. Apart from Mount Fuji, don't miss the wonderfully atmospheric shrine **Fuji Sengen-jinja**, in the area's transport hub of **Fuji-Yoshida**.

During the summer, the **five lakes** in the area are packed with urbanites fleeing the city. **Kawaguchi-ko** is not only a popular starting point for climbing Mount Fuji, but also features a kimono museum and the easily climbable Mount Tenjō, which has outstanding views of Mount Fuji and the surrounding lakes. The smallest of the other four lakes, horseshoe-shaped **Shōji-ko** (精進湖), 2km west of Kawaguchi-ko, is by far the prettiest. The largest lake, **Yamanaka-ko** (山中湖), southeast of Fuji-Yoshida, is just as developed as Kawaguchi-ko and has fewer attractions, while **Motosu-ko** (本栖湖) and **Sai-ko** (西湖) – both good for swimming and camping – are fine, but not so extraordinary that they're worth the trouble of visiting if you're on a short trip.

Fuji-Yoshida

富士吉田

FUJI-YOSHIDA, some 100km west of Tokyo, lies so close to Mount Fuji that when the dormant volcano eventually blows her top the local residents will be toast. For the time being, however, this small, friendly town acts as an efficient transport hub for the area, as well as the traditional departure point for journeys up the volcano, with frequent buses leaving for Mount Fuji's fifth station (see page 228) from outside the train station. If you're in town in late August, you'll find the main thoroughfare illuminated spectacularly, when seventy bonfires are lit along its length at night-time during the **Yoshida Fire Festival** (August 26 & 27).

Fuji Sengen-jinja

富士浅間神社 • Off Fuji Panorama Line road • 24hr • Free • Head uphill from the train station along the main street towards Mount Fuji; turn left where the road hits a junction and walk 200m

The volcano aside, Fuji-Yoshida's main attraction is its large, colourful Shinto shrine, **Fuji Sengen-jinja**, set in a small patch of forest. Sengen shrines, dedicated to the worship of volcanoes, encircle Fuji, and this is the most important, dating right back to 788. The beautiful main shrine was built in 1615. Look around the back for the jolly, brightly painted wooden carvings of the deities Ebisu the fisherman and Daikoku, the god of wealth, good humour and happiness, who appears content to let a rat nibble at the bales of rice he squats upon.

19

Togawa-ke Jutaku

戸川家受託 • Off Fuji-michi • Daily 9.30am–5pm • ¥100

Between the Fuji Sengen-jinja and the train station you'll likely spot a few old **pilgrims' inns** (*oshi-no-ie*) set back from the road, their entrances marked by narrow stone pillars. Some of these old lodging houses, where pilgrims used to stay before climbing Mount Fuji, still operate as minshuku today, and one, **Togawa-ke Jutaku**, has been opened up as a tourist attraction; its various tatami halls are worth pottering around, though the staff will want to explain every single thing to you in Japanese.

Fujikyū Highland

富士急ハイランド • Mon–Fri 9am–5pm, Sat & Sun 9am–6pm; closed second Tues of month • Most individual rides ¥800–1500; one-day pass ¥5700 • ⓦ www.fujiq.jp • One train stop west of Mount Fuji station

An appealingly ramshackle amusement park, **Fujikyū Highland** features a handful of hair-raising roller coasters, including the Takabisha, which claims to have the world's steepest drop – 121 degrees of terror. Avoid coming at weekends or holidays unless you enjoy standing in long queues.

Kawaguchi-ko

河口湖

The small lakeside resort of **KAWAGUCHI-KO** lies a couple of kilometres west of Fuji-Yoshida, and makes a more appealing place to stay. With its cruise boats and crass souvenir shops, it's the tourist hub of the area, and is often choked with traffic during the holiday season. However, the lake is placid and strikingly beautiful, especially at night, when the various visitors are clip-clopping around its southern fringes in their wooden *geta* sandals (said footwear being de rigueur for those staying at ryokan).

Tenjō-zan

天上山 • Off Misaka-michi • Cable car daily 9am–5pm • ¥500 one-way, ¥900 return

The fabulous view of Mount Fuji from the top of **Tenjō-zan** is probably the highlight of a trip to Kawaguchi-ko; of course, you'll also get a great view of the lake from here, since it's right next door. You can either take a three-minute cable-car ride up to the lookout, or get some exercise by hiking up, which takes around 45 minutes.

Itchiku Kubota Art Museum

久保田一竹美術館 Kubota Itchiku Bijutsukan • 2255 Guchiko, 4km northwest of Kawaguchi-ko • April–Nov daily 9.30am–5.30pm; Dec–March daily except Wed 10am–4.30pm • ¥1300 • ☎ 0555 76 8811, ⓦ itchiku-museum.com • Bus from Kawaguchi-ko station (25min)

One of the highlights of Kawaguchi-ko is the **Itchiku Kubota Art Museum**, on the northern shore of the lake. This small museum, housed in a Gaudí-esque building, showcases the work of Itchiku Kubota, who refined the traditional *tsujigahana* textile-patterning technique and applied it to kimono. Inside the pyramid-shaped building are pieces from the artist's *Symphony of Light* series, a continuous mountain landscape through the seasons, formed when the kimono are placed side by side.

Mount Fuji

19

富士山

"A wise man climbs Fuji once. A fool climbs it twice", says the Japanese proverb. Don't let the sight of children and grannies trudging up lull you into a false sense of security: at 3776m in height – more than enough for altitude sickness to take hold – this is a tough climb. There are several **routes** up the volcano, with the ascent on each divided into sections known as **stations**; the summit is the tenth station. Most people take a bus to the fifth station (*go-gōme*) on the **Kawaguchi-ko route**, about halfway up the volcano, where a Swiss-chalet-style gift shop marks the end of the road; for most people, it's four or five hours from here to the summit. The traditional hike, though, begins down at Fuji-Yoshida and ascends via the **Yoshida route**; it takes around five hours to walk up to this route's fifth station, and another six hours to reach the summit. The shortest route (around four hours from the fifth station) is the **Fujinomiya-guchi** to the south, accessible by bus from Shin-Fuji station, on the Shinkansen route; these buses also pass Fujinomiya JR station en route. Many climbers choose to ascend the mountain at **night** in order to reach the summit by dawn; during the season, the lights of climbers' torches resemble a line of fireflies trailing up the volcanic scree.

Essential items to carry include at least one litre of water and some food, a torch and batteries, a raincoat and extra clothes. However hot it might be at the start of the climb, the closer you get to the summit the colder it becomes, with temperatures dropping to well below freezing. Sudden rain and lightning strikes are not uncommon.

Mount Fuji's official **climbing season**, when all the facilities on the mountain are open, including lodging huts (see page 229) and phones at the summit, runs from July 1 to the middle of September. You can climb outside these dates, but don't expect all, or indeed any, of the facilities to be in operation, and be prepared for snow and extreme cold towards the summit. Once you're at the summit, it will take around an hour to make a circuit of the crater.

ARRIVAL AND DEPARTURE

FUJI FIVE LAKES

By bus The easiest way to reach the Fuji Five Lakes area is to take the bus (¥1950; 1hr 45min in good traffic) from the Shinjuku bus terminal in Tokyo, on the west side of the train station; there are also services from Tokyo station and Shibuya. During the climbing season there are frequent services, including at least three a day that run directly to the fifth station on the Kawaguchi-ko route, halfway up Mount Fuji (¥1540 one-way, ¥2100 return; 1hr 15min). If you're planning on visiting the Hakone area, the regular bus to Gotemba costs ¥1510 (hourly; 2hr); alternatively, the Fuji Hakone Pass allows you to combine the Fuji Five Lakes area with a trip around Hakone (see page 230).

By train Good news; there are now direct services from Shinjuku to Mount Fuji station (the old name, Fuji-Yoshida, is still commonly used) and Kawaguchiko, though only twice daily (7.35am & 9.30am; ¥3940–4060). Otherwise, the journey from Shinjuku involves transferring from the JR Chūō line to the Fuji Kyūkō line at Ōtsuki, then local trains (not covered by the JR Pass, though some have Thomas the Tank Engine decoration, which might make up for it; 2hr or so in total; ¥3340 using the limited express trains).

ACCOMMODATION ON MOUNT FUJI

There are seventeen **huts** on Fuji, most of which provide dorm accommodation from around ¥5500 per night (add ¥1000–2000 on weekends) for just a bed (no need for a sleeping bag), with an option to add meals for ¥1000 each. It's essential to book in advance during the official climbing season (July & Aug). The huts also sell snacks and stamina-building dishes, such as curry rice. To make reservations at the huts, you're best off contacting a tourist information office, either in the Fuji Five Lakes area, or in Tokyo.

GETTING AROUND

By bus A comprehensive system of buses will help you get around once you've arrived at either Fuji-Yoshida or Kawaguchi-ko. Two-day passes (¥1500) allow travel around the Fuji Five Lakes area.

On foot It's easy enough to walk from Kawaguchi-ko station down to the lake in 15min or so, and those without too much luggage can access most of its surrounding hotels on foot.

By bicycle You'll see plenty of tourists pedalling around the Kawaguchi-ko area. Most rent bikes from their accommodation, though there are plenty of other rental outlets around, including one just opposite the train station, on the left (¥500/hr, ¥1500/day).

19

INFORMATION

Fuji-Yoshida tourist office On the left as you exit Mount Fuji station (daily 9am–5pm; ☎ 0555 22 7000), with tons of information in English. If you're here to climb Fuji, pick up a free copy of the various maps on offer (also available at the Kawaguchi-ko tourist office).

Kawaguchi-ko tourist office Outside Kawaguchi-ko station, this branch (daily 8.30am–5.30pm; ☎ 0555 72 6700) is just as useful as its counterpart in Fuji-Yoshida.

ACCOMMODATION   SEE MAP PAGE 226

Fuji-Yoshida and Kawaguchi-ko have plenty of good places to stay, including youth hostels and hotels. Fuji **climbers** could consider overnighting in one of the mountain huts (see page 229), but the claustrophobic might prefer to stick to the roomier accommodation at the base of the mountain. There are also several **campsites** around the lakes.

FUJI-YOSHIDA

Daikoku-ya 大国屋 Honchō-dōri, Fuji-Yoshida ☎ 0555 22 3778. This original pilgrims' inn on the main road still takes guests in its very traditional and beautifully decorated tatami rooms (though the owner prefers guests who can speak some Japanese). Rate includes two meals. Closed Oct–April. **¥14,000**

Michael's マイケルズ 3-21-37 Shimo-yoshida ☎ 0555 72 9139, ⓦ mtfujihostel.com. American-run hostel with spick-and-span rooms, a quiet backstreet location – though one very close to the train station – and a lively bar (see page 230). Private rooms are a particularly good deal for single travellers. Dorms **¥3000**, private rooms (per person) **¥3600**

KAWAGUCHI-KO

★**Fuji Lake** 富士レークホテル 1 Funatsu, Kawaguchi-ko-machi ☎ 0555 72 2209, ⓦ fujilake.co.jp. Large lakeside hotel that dates back to the 1930s, making it one of Japan's oldest such facilities. Its rooms are all large and very stylish, and feature charming washrooms into which onsen water is piped. There's another fantastic onsen downstairs. **¥15,000**

★**K's House Mount Fuji** ケイズハウス富士山 6713-108 Funatsu, Kawaguchi-ko-machi ☎ 0555 83 5556, ⓦ kshouse.jp. Super-friendly hostel with a choice of either bunk-bed dorms or private tatami-style rooms, some en suite. Also on offer are a well-equipped kitchen, comfy lounge, internet access, laundry and bike rental, as well as a small bar. They'll even pick up from the station for free (8am–7.30pm). Their newer hostel, *Fuji View*, further up the slopes, is a similar operation. Dorms **¥2500**, doubles **¥7200**

Sunnide Village サンニデヴィレッジ Kawaguchi-ko ☎ 0555 76 6004, ⓦ www.sunnide.com. This attractive complex of hotel and holiday cottages offers spectacular views across the lake towards Mount Fuji, and has lovely public baths, too. It's on the north side of the lake, towards the Itchiku Kubota Art Museum. Doubles **¥12,600**, cottages **¥16,000**

EATING   SEE MAP PAGE 226

FUJI-YOSHIDA

★**Menkyo Kaiden** 麺許皆伝 849-1 Kami-Yoshida ☎ 0555 23 8806. This is the undisputed udon favourite with lunching locals; you may have to wait for a seat. The menu can be a little confusing, but staff recommend the *yokubari*, which comes in a miso-base soup (¥550). Mon–Sat 11am–2pm.

FUJI-NOODLES

Both Fuji-Yoshida and Kawaguchi-ko are renowned for their thick *teuchi* (handmade) **udon noodles**. Fuji-Yoshida udon comes topped with shredded cabbage and carrot, and is usually prepared and served in people's homes at lunchtime only; the tourist offices can provide a Japanese list and map of the best places serving it. Most of these will serve just three types of dish: *yumori*, noodles in a soup; *zaru*, cold noodles; and *sara*, warm noodles dipped in hot soup. In Kawaguchi-ko, be sure to try **hōtō**, a hearty broth served piping hot; ingredients vary, and some places serve it with exotic meats such as venison and bear, but sweet pumpkin is the local favourite.

19

KAWAGUCHI-KO

★ **Hōtō Fudo** ほうとう不動 Train station plaza ☎ 0120 41 0457. Right in front of the train station in a building with a wood-panelled exterior, this small restaurant serves decent *hōtō* (see page 230) for ¥1050, as well as *basashi* (raw horse meat; ¥1080) and a range of other tasty Japanese food. Daily 11am–9pm.

Tetsuyaki 鉄焼き 3486-5 Kawaguchiko-chō, no phone. This teppanyaki spot is frequently the only place in town open after 8pm. Mains go from ¥800, and include steak, *okonomiyaki* (pancake-like batter dish with various fillings) and rice dishes; mercifully, since few bars around the lake stay open too long after sundown, they also sell alcoholic drinks. Daily noon–10pm.

DRINKING

SEE MAP PAGE 226

Michael's マイケルズ 3-21-37 Shimo-yoshida ☎ 0555 72 9139, ⓦ mtfujihostel.com. Even if you're not staying overnight at this Fuji-Yoshida hostel (see page 229), it's worth swinging by the bar if you're in the area – the atmosphere can be surprisingly raucous for provincial Japan. Simple pub snacks are on offer alongside a modest range of drinks. Daily (except Thurs) 7pm–2am; lunch served daily (except Sat) 11.30am–4pm.

Hakone

箱根

South of Mount Fuji and 90km west of Tokyo is the lakeland, mountain and onsen area known as **HAKONE**, always busy at weekends and holidays. Most visitors follow the well-established day-trip route, which is good fun and combines rides on several trains or buses, a funicular, a cable car and a sightseeing ship, styled as a seventeenth-century galleon, across Ashino lake. However, the scenery is so pretty, and there's so much else to do – such as seeing great **art** at the Hakone Open-Air Museum and the Pola Museum of Art, not to mention soaking in numerous **onsen** – that an overnight stay is encouraged. Weather permitting, you'll also get great views of nearby Mount Fuji.

The traditional day-trip itinerary, described below, runs anticlockwise from **Hakone-Yumoto**, gateway to the **Fuji-Hakone-Izu National Park**, then over the peaks of **Sōun-zan**, across the length of **Ashino-ko** to **Moto-Hakone**, and back to the start. Approaching Hakone from the west, you can follow a similar route clockwise from Hakone-machi, on the southern shore of Ashino-ko, to Hakone-Yumoto.

Hakone-Yumoto

箱根湯元

HAKONE-YUMOTO, the small town nestling in the valley at the gateway to the national park, is marred by scores of concrete-block hotels and *bessō*, vacation villas for company workers – not to mention the usual cacophony of souvenir shops. It does, however, have some good **onsen** (see page 233) which are ideal for unwinding after a day's sightseeing around the park.

Miyanoshita

宮ノ下

HAKONE

N

0   1
kilometre

■ ACCOMMODATION
Fuji-Hakone Guesthouse   1
Fujiya   6
Gōra Kadan   4
Hakone Ginyu   5
Hakone Tent   2
Hyatt Regency Hakone   3
Moto-Hakone Guesthouse   8
Prince Hakone   7

● EATING
Amazake-chaya   6
Hatsuhana Soba   5
Hoshino-an   1
Karaage Karatto   7
Naokichi   4
Naraya Café   3
Orchid Lounge   2

Tokyo

Ashigara
Iskda

ODAKYŪ LINE
Midorichō
Odawara
JR TŌKAIDŌ LINE

Tokyo

Hayakawa
Hakone-itabashi

TŌKAIDŌ SHINKANSEN

Sagami-wan

Nebukawa

Nagoya & Ōsaka

Kazamatsuri

Iriuda

Hakone-Yumoto

Hakone Yuryō

Tonosawa

Tenzan Notemburo

HAKONE SHINDŌ TOLL ROAD

Ōhiradai

OLD TŌKAIDŌ HIGHWAY

Miyanoshita

Hatajjuku

Amazake-jaya teahouse

HAKONE TURNPIKE DRIVEWAY

Atami

Hakone Open-Air Museum
Tenoyu

Gōra
Kōen-shimo
Nakagora
Naka-gōra
Kami-gōra
Sōunzan

Chōkoku no-Mori
Hakone Museum of Art

Kowakudani

Okada Museum of Art

Mount Sengen (804m)

Pola Museum of Art

Mount Sōun (1153m)

Ōwakudani

Ōwakudani

Mount Kamiyama (1357m)

Mount Komaga-take (1357m)

Moto-Hakone

Hakone Gongen

AVENUE OF CRYPTOMERIA

Hakone Barrier

Onshi-Hakone Kōen

Hakone-machi

Sengokuhara

Lalique Museum Hakone

Gotemba & Mount Fuji

FUJI-HAKONE-IZU NATIONAL PARK

HAKONE-EN

Ashino-ko

Sightseeing Boats

Ubako

Tōgendai

Hamamatsu & Nagoya

ASHI-NO-KO SKYLINE DRIVEWAY

Rising up into the mountains, the Hakone-Tozan **switchback railway** zigzags for nearly 9km alongside a ravine from Hakone-Yumoto to the village of Gōra. There are small traditional inns and temples at several of the stations along the way, but the single best place to alight is the village onsen resort of **MIYANOSHITA**. Interesting antique and craft shops are dotted along its main road, and there are several hiking routes up **Mount Sengen** (804m) on the eastern flank of the railway – one path begins just beside the station. At the top (an hour's walk or so) you'll get a great view of the gorge below. After the walk you can relax in the appealing day-onsen **Tenoyu** (see page 233). Miyanoshita's real draw, however, is its handful of splendid **hotels**, the most historic of which is the *Fujiya* (see page 237), which opened for business in 1878; it's well worth a look even if you're not staying, and its *Orchid Lounge* is great for afternoon tea.

Hakone Open-Air Museum

彫刻の森美術館, Chōkoku-no-Mori Bijutsukan • 1121 Ninotaira • Daily 9am–5pm • ¥1600; small discounts if booked online • Ⓦ hakone-oam.or.jp

19

Travelling two stops uphill from Miyanoshita on the Hakone-Tozan railway brings you to Chōkoku no Mori (彫刻の森), where you should alight if you want to visit the nearby **Hakone Open-Air Museum**. This worthwhile museum is packed with sculptures, ranging from works by Rodin and Giacometti to Michelangelo reproductions and bizarre modern formations scattered across the landscaped grounds, which have lovely views across the mountains to the sea. There's an enclave of 26 pieces by Henry Moore; a "Picasso Pavilion", which houses over three hundred paintings, lithographs, ceramics and sculptures by the Spanish artist; and four galleries featuring works by Chagall, Miró and Renoir, plus work by modern Japanese artists such as Umehara Ryūzaburō and Hayashi Takeshi. You can rest between the various galleries at several restaurants or cafés, and there's also a traditional Japanese teahouse here.

Gōra to Ashino-ko

Funicular tram Every 10–15min • ¥420 one-way • **Cable car** Every 1–2min • ¥1450 one-way to Ashino-ko

The Hakone-Tozan railway terminates at **GŌRA** (強羅), where you can stop for lunch, or overnight. Continuing west on the day-trip route, you'll transfer to a **funicular tram**, which takes ten minutes to cover the short but steep distance to **Sōunzan**, the start of the cable-car ride. From here, the **cable car** floats like a balloon on its thirty-minute journey high above the mountain to the Tōgendai terminal beside Ashino-ko, stopping at a couple of points along the way.

Hakone Museum of Art

箱根美術館, Hakone Bijutsukan • 1300 Gōra • Daily (except Thurs) 9am–4pm • ¥1400 • Ⓦ moaart.or.jp/hakone

En route to Sōunzan, you might want to stop at Kōen-kami (公園上), a couple of stops on the funicular tram from Gōra, for the **Hakone Museum of Art**. Its collection of ancient ceramics – some of which date back as far as the Jōmon period – is likely to appeal to experts only, but the delicate moss gardens and the view from the traditional teahouse across the verdant hills are captivating.

Ōwakudani

大涌谷

If the weather is playing ball, you should get a good glimpse of Mount Fuji in the distance as you pop over the hill at the first cable-car stop, **ŌWAKUDANI**. This is the site of a constantly bubbling and steaming valley formed by a volcanic eruption three thousand years ago. A series of tectonic belches in recent years saw the cable-car station and surrounding area fully closed down, with visitors unable to get off and explore; the station and some surrounding paths were reopened in 2016. Should the remainder of Ōwakudani be opened up, you'll be able to hike through the lava formations to

TAKING AN ONSEN DIP IN HAKONE

The sulphuric steam rising from the mountain of Sōun-zan makes it clear that something is going on beneath the surface of Hakone. As with any such place in Japan, this volcanic activity also makes it a prime spot for a soak in mineral-heavy **onsen** water.

Hakone Yuryō 箱根湯寮 ⓦ hakoneyuryo.jp. Set back in the forest near Hakone-Yumoto, this onsen is a good option; bathing out by the trees is quite delightful, even if the weather's chilly. Free shuttle buses from Hakone-Yumoto Station. Daily 10am–8pm; ¥1500.

Tenoyu てのゆ ⓦ tenoyu.jp. Attractive onsen with rotemburo (outdoor hot springs), a short walk out of Miyanoshita along the main road to Gōra. Mon–Fri 11am–7pm, Sat & Sun 11am–8pm; ¥1600 Mon–Fri, ¥2100 Sat & Sun.

Tenzan Notemburo 天山野天風呂 ⓦ tenzan.jp. The most stylish bathhouse in the area is this luxurious riverside complex close to Hakone-Yumoto Station, and connected to it by free shuttle buses. There are outdoor baths for men and women, including waterfalls and jacuzzis in a series of rocky pools, plus a clay-hut sauna for men. For an extra charge both men and women can use the wooden baths in the building across the car park. Rarely for Japan, visible tattoos are allowed. Mon–Fri 11am–8pm, Sat & Sun 11am–9pm; ¥1100.

19

bubbling pools where eggs are traditionally boiled until they are black, then scoffed religiously by every tourist.

North from Gōra

North of Gōra are a couple of excellent museums, both worthy of a detour: the splendid **Pola Museum of Art** and the quirky **Lalique Museum Hakone**. The latter is in the pleasant village of **SENGOKUHARA** (仙石原), a good place to stay the night.

Pola Museum of Art

ポーラ美術館, Pōra Bijutsukan • 1285 Sengokuhara • Daily 9am–5pm • ¥1800 • ⓦ polamuseum.or.jp • Bus from Gōra station (15min; ¥300)

The superb **Pola Museum of Art** boasts a diverse and eclectic collection of Western art, predominantly from French Impressionists and École de Paris artists. When you've had your fill of checking out pieces by the likes of Renoir, Monet, Picasso, Van Gogh, Cezanne and Gallé, hunt down the glasswork section, and the Japanese paintings and ceramics. The artworks are all displayed in modern galleries in a stunning building that blends beautifully with the surrounding forest, and there's a café and restaurant on site too.

Lalique Museum Hakone

箱根ラリック美術館, Hakone Rarikku Bijutsukan • 186-1 Sengokuhara • Daily 9am–5pm • ¥1500, or ¥2100 including train carriage with drinks and dessert (reservation necessary) • ☎ 0406 84 2225, ⓦ lalique-museum.com • Bus from Gōra station (25min; ¥420)

Perhaps the most interesting – and certainly the most beautifully situated – of Sengokuhara's museums is the **Lalique Museum Hakone**, dedicated to the delicate glass pieces of the French artist René Lalique. At the entrance is a parked *Orient Express* Pullman train carriage, kitted out with Lalique glass panels, which is a great place for tea.

Ashino-ko and around

Sightseeing boats Tōgendai to Moto-Hakone or Hakone-machi ¥1000 one-way, ¥1840 return • Daily 9.30am–5pm, every 30–40min • ⓦ hakone-kankosen.co.jp • **Komaga-take cable-car** ¥1000 one way, ¥1800 return

From **Tōgendai** (桃原台) – the westernmost point of the cable-car route from Gōra – a shoreline trail winds along the western side of **Ashino-ko** (芦ノ湖) to the small resort of **HAKONE-MACHI** (箱根町) some 8km south, taking around three hours to cover. This western lakeshore is not covered by the Hakone Free Pass (see page 236) and is thus somewhat marginalized – and all the more peaceful for it. Most visitors, however,

19

> ### THE HAKONE BARRIER
>
> In 1618 the second shogun, Tokugawa Hidetada, put up the **Hakone Barrier** (Sekisho) – actually more of a large compound than a single gate – which stood at Hakone-machi until 1869. The shogun decreed that all his lords' wives and their families live in Edo (now Tokyo) and that the lords themselves make expensive formal visits to the capital every other year, a strategy designed to ensure no one attempted a rebellion. The Tōkaidō, on which the barrier stands, was one of the major routes in and out of the capital, and it was here that travellers were carefully checked to see how many guns they were taking into the Edo area; the barrier also ensured that the lords' families were prevented from escaping. Any man caught trying to dodge the barrier was crucified and then beheaded, while accompanying women had their heads shaved and were, according to contemporary statute, "given to anyone who wants them".

hop straight from the cable-car on to one of the colourful **sightseeing ships**, modelled after the seventeenth-century man o' war *The Sovereign of the Seas*, that regularly sail the length of the lake in around thirty minutes; you can see Fuji's peak reflected in the waters from the northern end of Ashino-ko. A cluster of upmarket hotels and ryokan can be found at Hakone-machi, where the sightseeing boats dock before or after hitting Moto-Hakone.

Boats also run from Tōgendai to the *Prince* hotel resort at **Hakone-en** (箱根園), midway down the east side of the lake. A cable-car here glides up the 1357m **Komagatake** (駒ヶ岳), from where there's a fabulous view; you can't use Hakone passes for this one, so it's usually pretty empty.

Hakone Barrier

箱根関所, Hakone Sekisho · Daily: March–Nov 9am–5pm; Dec–Feb 9am–4.30pm · ¥500

The southern end of the lake is the location of the **Hakone Barrier**, a gateway through which all traffic on the **Tōkaidō**, the ancient road linking Kyoto and Edo, once had to pass (see page 234). What stands here today is a reproduction, enlivened by waxwork displays which provide the historical background, and there's nothing much to keep you.

Onshi-Hakone Kōen

恩賜箱根公園 · Daily 9am–4.30pm · Free

North of the Hakone Barrier, the wooded promontory between Hakone and Moto-Hakone, **Onshi-Hakone Kōen**, is an easily accessible Fuji-viewing spot. After panting your way up 200-odd steps, you'll come to a garden area and an observation point; despite the hordes of tourists pouring off the ferries to the south, and padding their way through Moto-Hakone to the north, this place is usually pretty quiet.

Moto-Hakone

元箱根

Part of the Tōkaidō ancient road – shaded by 420 lofty cryptomeria trees planted in 1618 and now designated "Natural Treasures" – runs for around 1km beside the road leading from the Hakone Barrier to the lakeside **MOTO-HAKONE** tourist village. The prettiest spot around here is the vermilion *torii*, standing in the water just north of Moto-Hakone – a scene celebrated in many an *ukiyo-e* print and modern postcard. The gate belongs to the **Hakone Gongen** (箱根権現) and is the highlight of this small Shinto shrine, where samurai once came to pray.

Ashino-ko to Hakone-Yumoto

From either Hakone-machi or Moto-Hakone you can take a **bus** back to **Hakone-Yumoto** or Odawara. Far more rewarding, however, is the 11km **hike** along part of the

HAKONE TRAVEL PASSES

Touring the Hakone area is great fun, but the various train, funicular, cable-car and boat tickets can add up quickly. One way to prevent this, and save a bundle of cash, is to invest in one of the many **travel passes** covering the area. As well as covering almost all transport, they can be used to lop a little off entry prices to some sights. You can buy passes at the **Odakyū Sightseeing Service Centre** at the west exit of Shinjuku Station (daily 8am–6pm; ☏ 03 5321 7887, ⓦ odakyu. jp); the English-speaking staff here can also make reservations for tours and hotels.

Hakone Freepass If you plan to follow the traditional Hakone route, invest in this pass, which comes in either two- or three-day versions; from Shinjuku, it costs ¥5700/¥6100 (2/3 days); from Odawara or Gotemba it costs ¥4600/¥5000 (2/3 days). The pass covers a return journey on the Odakyū line from Shinjuku to Odawara, and unlimited use of the Hakone-Tozan line, Hakone-Tozan funicular railway, cable-car, boats across the lake and most local buses.

Hakone One-day Pass If you're already in Odawara or Gotemba you can buy a special one-day pass for ¥1540.

It doesn't cover the journeys to or from Tokyo, nor the boat, but unlimited use of the railways and cable-car.

Fuji Hakone Pass If you're going directly from Hakone to the neighbouring Fuji Five Lakes area (or vice versa) then the three-day Fuji Hakone Pass (¥9090 from Shinjuku, ¥6740 from Odawara) is the way to go. This offers the same deal as a Hakone Freepass, but also covers a one-way express bus trip between the Hakone area and Kawaguchi-ko; you can hit Fuji and Hakone in either order, returning from whichever one you like.

19

Tōkaidō ancient road, which begins five minutes up the hill from the Hakone-Tozan bus station in Moto-Hakone; to find the start of the route, keep an eye out for a spot where large paving stones are laid through the shady forests. After the first 2km the route is all downhill and takes around four hours.

When the path comes out of the trees and hits the main road, you'll see the Amazake-jaya teahouse. From here, the path shadows the main road to the small village of **HATAJUKU** (畑宿), where since the ninth century craftsmen have perfected the art of *yosegi-zaiku*, or marquetry. The wooden boxes, toys and other objects inlaid with elaborate mosaic patterns make great souvenirs; there are workshops throughout the village, including one right where the path emerges onto the main road. Hatajuku is a good place to pick up the bus the rest of the way to Hakone-Yumoto if you don't fancy hiking any further.

ARRIVAL AND INFORMATION
HAKONE

By train Most people visit Hakone aboard the Odakyū-line train from Shinjuku, using one of the company's excellent-value travel passes (see page 236). To get to Hakone-Yumoto – at the end of the line – on the basic trains (2hr; ¥1190), you may have to change in Odawara (小田原); for an extra fee you can take the more comfortable "Romance Car" (hourly; 1hr 30min; ¥2280) all the way. If you're using a JR Pass (see page 23), the fastest route is to take a Shinkansen to Odawara, from where you can transfer to an Odakyū train (16min; ¥310) or bus into the national park area.

By bus The Odakyū express bus (hourly; from ¥1680) from Shinjuku bus terminal will get you to Hakone in a couple of hours; buses stop first at Hakone-Yumoto, followed by

Moto-Hakone, the *Prince* hotel at Hakone-en (see 237) and finally Tōgendai. The company also run buses from Tokyo station (6 daily; ¥1650) and the Tokyo airports. It's also possible to visit by bus from the Fuji Five Lakes area, in which case you'll enter Hakone through Sengokuhara to the north, passing through the major town of Gotemba; passes will save you money (see page 236), as well as hassle on the local buses, which don't give any change.

Tourist information You can pick up a map of the area and plenty of other information at the very friendly Hakone tourist office (daily 9am–5.45pm; ☏ 0460 85 5700, ⓦ hakone.or.jp), situated in the buildings at the bus terminal, across the street from Hakone-Yumoto Station.

ACCOMMODATION
SEE MAP PAGE 231

Excellent transportation links mean you can stay pretty much anywhere in the national park and get everywhere else easily. There's a good range of budget options and some top-grade ryokan; a profusion of offerings on Airbnb has seen prices decrease slightly at the lower end of the spectrum.

ASHINO-KO

Moto-Hakone Guesthouse 元箱根ゲストハウス 103 Moto-Hakone ☏ 0460 83 7880, ⓦ motohakone. com. Simple guesthouse a short bus ride (get off at Ōshiba) or stiff 10min walk uphill from Moto-Hakone village. The reward for the journey is spotless Japanese-style rooms and extremely friendly service – a cup of coffee will be plonked in front of you in no time at all. Surcharge of ¥1000 at weekends. **¥5000** per person

Prince Hakone プリンス箱根 144 Moto-hakone ☎ 0460 83 1111, ⓦ princehotels.com. This hotel boasts a prime location on the eastern shore of Ashino-ko and a multitude of facilities, including access to an outdoor hot bath with a view of the lake. **¥24,000**

GORA

Gōra Kadan 強羅花壇 1300 Gōra ☎ 0460 82 3331, ⓦ gorakadan.com. One of Hakone's most exclusive ryokans is the stuff of legend, which means you might have to wait an eternity to secure a reservation. Expect beautiful tatami rooms, antiques, exquisite meals and a serene atmosphere. Rates include two meals. **¥100,000**

★ **Hakone Tent** 箱根テント 1320-257 Gōra ☎ 0460 83 8021, ⓦ hakonetent.com. Created from an old ryokan, this striking, modern guesthouse is a fantastic choice for those on a budget. The on-site onsen is a delight, and at the welcoming bar before collapsing onto their futons. The single room is great value at ¥4000, and if the place is full they have a similar new branch, the Irori, within walking distance. Dorms **¥3500**, doubles **¥9000**

Hyatt Regency Hakone ハイアット リージェンシー箱根 1320 Gōra ☎ 0460 82 2000, ⓦ hakone.regency. hyatt.com. This slickly designed hotel is a treat, offering some of the largest rooms in Hakone and elegant facilities, including a lounge, two restaurants and the Izumi onsen

spa. For those who can't bear to be parted from their pooch, there are even dog-friendly stone-floored rooms. **¥35,000**

MIYANOSHITA

Fujiya 富士屋ホテル 359 Miyanoshita ☎ 0460 82 2211, ⓦ fujiyahotel.jp. The first Western-style hotel in Japan, this place is a living monument to a more glamorous era of travel, and boasts lots of Japanese touches, including traditional gardens and decorative gables like those found in temples. The plush 1950s-style decor is retro-chic, the rooms are good value, and there are a couple of great on-site places to eat and drink; at the time of writing it was closed for restoration, but it should have reopened by April 2020. Check the website for details. **¥14,000**

Hakone Ginyu 箱根吟遊 100-1 Miyanoshita ☎ 0460 82 3355, ⓦ hakoneginyu.co.jp. Outstanding luxury ryokan, where guests are assured maximum comfort. The views across the valley are stunning and the interiors are a tasteful blend of old and new. Huge *hinoki* wood tubs on private verandas are a major plus. Rates include two meals. **¥66,000**

SENGOKUHARA

Fuji-Hakone Guesthouse 富士箱根ゲストハウス 912 Sengokuhara ☎ 0460 84 6577, ⓦ fujihakone. com. Tucked into a pleasingly secluded spot, this convivial guesthouse – run by the friendly, English-speaking Takahashi-san and his family – has comfortable tatami rooms, though the defining feature is the onsen water piped into no fewer than four separate baths. Breakfast available. **¥10,800**

EATING

SEE MAP PAGE 231

ASHINO-KO

Karaage Karatto 唐揚げKARATTO 10 Moto-Hakone ☎ 0460 83 5008. This is the best of the rather motley bunch of tourist restaurants in Moto-Hakone, specialising in karaage (deep-fried chicken; ¥800), with curry-rice pretty much your only other choice. Many end up here by default, since the area's other restaurants all shut even earlier – plus,

as the signboard outside states, they sell pints (full British ones!) of draught Guinness (¥850). Daily 11am–7pm.

HAKONE-YUMOTO

Hatsuhana Soba はつ花そば 635 Hakone-Yumoto ☎ 0460 85 8287. The Hakone area is famed for its soba, on account of the purity of the local water, and this restaurant

---

MOUNT TAKAO

An hour west of Shinjuku, **Mount Takao** (高尾山; 600m; ⓦ takaotozan.co.jp), also referred to as Takao-san, is a particularly pleasant place for a quick escape from Tokyo, and is a starting point for longer trails into the mountains in the **Chichibu-Tama National Park** (秩父多摩国立公園). The Keiō line from Shinjuku provides the simplest and cheapest way of reaching the terminus of Takao-san-guchi (1hr; ¥390). After a hike up or a ride on the cable car or chairlifts (both ¥470 one-way, ¥900 return), you'll get to **Yakuo-in** (薬王院; ⓦ takaosan.or.jp), a temple founded in the eighth century and notable for the ornate polychromatic carvings that decorate its main hall. It hosts the spectacular **Hiwatarisai** fire ritual on the second Sunday in March back in Takao-san-guchi, where you can watch priests and pilgrims march across hot coals – and even follow them yourself. From the temple, it's a relatively short walk to Takao's summit.

KAMAKURA THROUGH THE YEAR

The town's biggest **festivals** take place in early April (second Sun to third or fourth Sun) and mid-September, including displays of horseback archery and costume parades, though the summer fireworks display (second Tues in Aug) over Sugami Bay is the most spectacular event.

Kamakura is also well known for its **spring blossoms** and **autumn colours**, while many temple gardens are famous for a particular flower – for example, Japanese apricot at Zuisen-ji and Tōkei-ji (Feb) and hydrangea at Meigetsu-in (mid-June).

---

is the best place to try it. Several options are available, including the *teijo* and curry bowls, but you can't go wrong with the *teijo soba*, served with grated yam and raw egg (¥1050). To get here from the station, follow the riverbank into town, then turn left at the first bridge – it's right on the other side, overlooking the river. Daily 10am–7pm.

★ **Naokichi** 直吉 696 Hakone-Yumoto ☎ 0460 85 5148. Excellent, elegant restaurant serving the scrumptious local speciality, *yubadon* – soy milk skin in fish broth served on rice (¥980). Not sold yet? There's also a free onsen footbath just outside. To find it, head up the river path from the station; you'll soon spot the place on your right. Daily (except Tues) 11am–6pm.

HATAJUKU

Amazake-chaya 甘酒茶屋 Hatajuku. Rest at this charming teahouse, just as travellers did hundreds of years ago, and sip a restorative cup of the milky, sweet rice drink *amazake* (¥400), with some mochi (rice-cake; ¥250 each). Daily 7am–5.30pm.

MIYANOSHITA

★ **Naraya Café** ならやカフェー 404-13 Miyanoshita.

There's one major draw at this lovely café, just down the road from Miyanoshita Station – a footbath that runs under the table in the outdoor section, making it possible to bathe your toes while sipping a latte (¥450), or perhaps even a cocktail. Hot dogs and other snacks are available, and there's a gallery on the top level. Daily (except Weds) 10.30am–6pm.

Orchid Lounge 359 Miyanoshita ☎ 0460 82 2211, ⓦ fujiyahotel.co.jp. The tea lounge at the wonderful *Fujiya* hotel (see opposite) is a grand spot for coffee (¥1500 with cake) or afternoon tea (¥1000); it's a pleasure to sit down and relax with a view over the garden and carp-filled pond. Daily 9am–9pm.

SENGOKUHARA

Hoshino-an 穂し乃庵 817-88 Sengokuhara ☎ 0460 84 0055. If you're staying in the Sengokuhara area, this simple restaurant is a good bet for dinner and a drink, and with a little advance warning they'll collect you from nearby accommodation. They've a decent range of soba (from ¥750), plus heartier sets featuring deep-fried comestibles (from ¥1150), and a range of local drinks. Daily (except Weds) 11am–3pm & 5–8pm.

Kamakura and around

鎌倉

The small, relaxed town of **KAMAKURA** lies an hour's train ride south of Tokyo, trapped between the sea and a circle of wooded hills. The town is steeped in history, and many of its 65 temples and 19 shrines date back some eight centuries, when, for a brief and tumultuous period, it was Japan's political and military centre. Its most famous sight is the **Daibutsu**, a glorious bronze Buddha surrounded by trees, but its ancient **Zen temples** are equally compelling. Kamakura's prime sights can be covered on a day-trip from Tokyo, but the town more than justifies a two-day visit, allowing you time to explore the enchanting temples of **east Kamakura** and follow one of the gentle "hiking courses" up into the hills, or head out west to **Enoshima** and its own clutch of appealing sights.

Brief history

In 1185 the warlord **Minamoto Yoritomo** became the first permanent shogun and the effective ruler of Japan. Seven years later he established his military government – known as the Bakufu, or "tent government" – in Kamakura. Over the next century, dozens of grand monuments were built here, notably the great Zen temples founded by monks fleeing Song-dynasty China. Zen Buddhism flourished under the patronage of a warrior class who shared similar ideals of single-minded devotion to duty and rigorous self-discipline. The Minamoto rule was brief and violent. Almost immediately, Yoritomo turned against his valiant younger brother, Yoshitsune, who had led the clan's armies, and hounded him until Yoshitsune committed ritual suicide (*seppuku*) – a favourite tale of kabuki theatre. Both the second and third Minamoto shoguns were murdered, and in 1219 power passed to the Hōjō clan, who ruled as fairly able regents behind puppet shoguns. Their downfall followed the Mongol invasions in the late thirteenth century, and in 1333 Emperor Go-Daigo wrested power back to Kyoto; as the imperial armies approached Kamakura, the last Hōjō regent and an estimated eight hundred retainers committed *seppuku*. Kamakura remained an important military centre before fading into obscurity in the late fifteenth century. Its temples, however, continued to attract religious pilgrims until Kamakura was "rediscovered" in the last century as a tourist destination and a desirable residential area within commuting distance of Tokyo.

Kita-Kamakura

As the Tokyo train nears the station at **Kita-Kamakura**, the town's northern suburb, urban sprawl gradually gives way to gentle, forested hills which provide the backdrop for some of Kamakura's greatest Zen temples. Chief among these are **Kenchō-ji** and

ZAZEN

Zazen, or sitting meditation, is a crucial aspect of Zen Buddhist training, particularly among followers of the Rinzai sect. Several temples in Kamakura hold public *zazen* sessions at various levels, of which the most accessible are those at Engaku-ji (April–Oct daily 5.30am; Nov–March daily 6am; plus second and fourth Sun of month at 10am; ☏ 0467 22 0478) and Kenchō-ji (Fri & Sat 5pm in the Hōjō; ☏ 0467 22 0981). These hour-long sessions are free and no reservations are required, though it's best to check the current schedule with the temple or Kamakura tourist office (see page 246) before setting out, and you should get there at least fifteen minutes early. Though non-Japanese-speakers are welcome, you'll get much more out of it if you have someone with you who can translate.

19

the wonderfully atmospheric **Engaku-ji**. It takes over an hour to cover the prime sights, walking south along the main road, the Kamakura-kaidō, to the edge of central Kamakura. If you have more time, follow the Daibutsu Hiking Course (see page 241) up into the western hills.

Engaku-ji

円覚寺 • 409 Yama-no-uchi • Daily: April–Oct 8am–5pm; Nov–March 8am–4pm • ¥300; Butsunichi-an ¥100, or ¥650 including tea

The second most important – but most satisfying – of Kamakura's major Zen temples, **Engaku-ji** lies buried among ancient cedars just two minutes' walk east of Kita-Kamakura station. It was founded in 1282 to honour victims (on both sides) of the ultimately unsuccessful Mongolian invasions in 1274 and 1281. The layout follows a traditional Chinese Zen formula – a pond and bridge (now cut off by the train tracks), followed by a succession of somewhat austere buildings – but the encroaching trees and secretive gardens add a gentler touch.

The first building inside the compound is Engaku-ji's two-storey main gate, **San-mon**, a magnificent structure rebuilt in 1783; beneath it the well-worn flagstones bear witness to generations of pilgrims. Beyond, the modern **Butsu-den** (Buddha Hall) houses the temple's primary Buddha image, haloed in soft light, while behind it lies the charming **Shari-den**, tucked off to the left past an oblong pond. This small reliquary hall, usually closed to visitors, is said to contain a tooth of the Buddha brought here from China in the early thirteenth century. It's also considered Japan's finest example of Song-dynasty Zen architecture, albeit a sixteenth-century replica. The main path continues gently uphill to another pretty thatched building, **Butsunichi-an**, where regent Hōjō Tokimune was buried in 1284; in fine weather green tea is served in its attractive garden. Finally, you'll come to tiny **Ōbai-in**, which enshrines a pale-yellow Kannon statue, although its best attribute is a nicely informal garden with a grove of Japanese apricot.

On the way out, follow signs up a steep flight of steps to the left of San-mon to find Kamakura's biggest bell, **Ōgane**, forged in 1301 and an impressive 2.5m tall; the adjacent teahouse, *Bentendō* (see page 247), is a great place to relax.

Tōkei-ji

東慶寺 • 1367 Yama-no-uchi • Daily: March–Oct 8.30am–5pm; Nov–Feb 8.30am–4pm • ¥200 • **Treasure House** Tues–Sun 9.30am–3.30pm • ¥300 • ⦿ tokeiji.com

A short walk along the main road from Engaku-ji, **Tōkei-ji** was founded as a nunnery in 1285 by the young widow of Hōjō Tokimune. It's an intimate temple, with a pleasing cluster of buildings and a profusion of flowers at almost any time of year: Japanese apricot in February, magnolia and peach in late March, followed by peonies and then irises in early June; September is the season for cascades of bush clover. At the back of the temple, take a walk round the peaceful, mossy cemetery hidden among stately cryptomeria trees, where many famous and forgotten nuns lie buried.

Tōkei-ji is more popularly known as the **"Divorce Temple"**. Up until the mid-nineteenth century, when women were given the legal right to seek divorce, this was one of the few places where wives could escape domestic ill-treatment. If they reached the sanctuary, which many didn't, they automatically received a divorce after three years according to traditional temple law. Husbands could be summoned to resolve the dispute or, ultimately, sign the divorce papers. Some of these documents are preserved, along with other temple treasures, in the **Treasure House**, including two books detailing the women's reasons for seeking sanctuary – unfortunately, not translated.

Jōchi-ji

浄智寺 • 1402 Yama-no-uchi • Daily 9am–4.30pm • ¥200

Almost immediately to the south of Tōkei-ji, a sign to the right indicates **Jōchi-ji**, the fourth most important of Kamakura's great Zen temples, and the start of the wonderful Daibutsu Hiking Course (see page 241). Founded by the nephew of Hōjō Tokimune in 1283, Jōchi-ji was almost completely levelled by the 1923 earthquake. Nevertheless,

19

KAMAKURA HIKING COURSES

There are two extremely pleasant **hiking courses** to tackle in central Kamakura, both giving you the chance to enjoy some lovely wooded scenery. The hikes, while a decent workout, are both pretty straightforward and quite possible to do in flip-flops (though trickier if it has been raining).

DAIBUTSU HIKING COURSE

Beside the temple of Jōchi-ji (see page 241) you'll find the steps that mark the start of the **Daibutsu Hiking Course** (大仏ハイキングコース), a meandering 2.2km-long ridgetop path which makes an enjoyable approach to the **Daibutsu**, Hase's Great Buddha (see p.240). Even if you're not walking the whole route it's well worth going as far as the captivating cave-shrine dedicated to the goddess **Zeniarai Benten** (銭洗弁天), the "Money-Washing Benten", an incarnation of the goddess of good fortune, music and water. To find it, follow the somewhat erratic signs from **Genjiyama-kōen** (源氏山公園), a pleasant park, which lead you along a trail heading vaguely south through the park to a road junction where the main trail turns right; here, you'll pick up signs pointing steeply downhill to where a *torii* and banners mark the Zeniarai Benten shrine entrance. Duck under the tunnel to emerge in a natural amphitheatre filled with a forest of *torii* wreathed in incense and candle smoke. According to tradition, money washed in the spring, which gushes out of a cave on the opposite side from the entrance, is guaranteed to double at the very least, though not immediately.

If you're following the Daibutsu Hiking Course all the way to Hase, then rather than retracing your steps, take the path heading south under a tunnel of tightly packed *torii*, zigzagging down to the valley bottom. Turn right at a T-junction to find another avenue of vermilion *torii* leading uphill deep into the cryptomeria forest. At the end lies a simple shrine, **Sasuke Inari-jinja** (佐助稲荷神社), which dates from before the twelfth century and is dedicated to the god of harvests, whose messenger is the fox; as you head up the steep path behind, to the left of the shrine buildings, climbing over tangled roots, you'll find fox statues of all shapes and sizes peering out of the surrounding gloom. At the top, turn right and then left at a white signboard to pick up the hiking course for the final 1.5km to the Daibutsu (see page 244).

TEN'EN HIKING COURSE

The **Ten'en Hiking Course** (天園ハイキングコース) begins just behind the Hōjō in Kenchō-ji (see above). It takes roughly one and a half hours to complete the 5km trail, which loops round the town's northeast outskirts to Zuisen-ji (see page 244); for a shorter walk (2.5km), you can cut down earlier to Kamakura-gū (see page 243). This trail is less trafficked than the Daibutsu course, and even on a sunny weekend, it's quite possible to find yourself alone in the forest for decent periods of time; you'll likely find a few trekkers having a snack or vending-machine coffee at a curious pit-stop, hidden in the bamboo thickets just after the golf course as you approach from Kenchō-ji.

it's worth walking up the lane to see its beautifully proportioned Chinese-style gate which doubles as a bell tower. The small worship hall contains a trinity of Buddhas while, at the back, there's a graveyard, sheltered by a bamboo grove.

Kenchō-ji

建長寺 • 8 Yama-no-uchi • Daily 8.30am–4.30pm • ¥300 • ⊕ kenchoji.com

The greatest of Kamakura's Zen temples is **Kenchō-ji**, headquarters of the Rinzai sect and Japan's oldest Zen training monastery. More formal than Engaku-ji and a lot less peaceful, largely because of the neighbouring high school, Kenchō-ji contains several important buildings, most of which have been relocated here from Tokyo and Kyoto to replace those lost since the temple's foundation in 1253. Again, the design of the layout shows a strong Chinese influence; the founding abbot was another Song Chinese émigré, in this case working under the patronage of Hōjō Tokiyori, the devout fifth regent and father of Engaku-ji's Tokumine.

The main complex begins with the towering, copper-roofed **San-mon**, an eighteenth-century reconstruction, to the right of which hangs the original temple **bell**, cast in 1255 and considered one of Japan's most beautiful. Beyond San-mon, a grove of gnarled and twisted juniper trees hides the dainty, nicely dilapidated **Butsu-den**. The main image is, unusually, of Jizō (the guardian deity of children) seated on a lotus throne, his bright, half-closed eyes piercing the gloom. Behind is the **Hattō**, or lecture hall, one of Japan's largest wooden Buddhist buildings. The curvaceous Chinese-style gate, **Kara-mon**, and the **Hōjō** hall beyond are much more attractive structures. Walk round the latter's balcony to find a **pond-garden** generally attributed to a thirteenth-century monk, making it Japan's oldest-surviving Zen garden, though it's been spruced up considerably. Behind the Hōjō entrance, a path heads up the steep steps past **Hansōbō**, a shrine guarded by statues of long-nosed, mythical *tengu*; this is the start of the **Ten'en Hiking Course**.

Central Kamakura

Modern Kamakura revolves around the central **Kamakura station** and a couple of touristy streets leading to the town's most important shrine, **Tsurugaoka Hachiman-gū**. The traditional approach to this grand edifice lies along **Wakamiya-ōji**, which runs straight from the sea to the shrine entrance. Shops along here peddle a motley collection of souvenirs and crafts, the most famous of which is *kamakura-bori*, an 800-year-old method of laying lacquer over carved wood. More popular, however, is *hato*, a pigeon-shaped French-style biscuit first made by Toshimaya bakers a century ago. Shadowing Wakamiya-ōji to the west is **Komachi-dōri**, a narrow, pedestrian-only shopping street, packed with more souvenir shops, restaurants and, increasingly, trendy boutiques.

Tsurugaoka Hachiman-gū

鶴岡八幡宮 • 2-1-31 Yuki-no-shita • Daily 6am–8.30pm • Free

A majestic, vermilion-lacquered *torii* marks the south-facing front entrance to **Tsurugaoka Hachiman-gū**, the Minamoto clan's guardian shrine since 1063. Hachiman-gū, as it's popularly known, was moved to its present site in 1191, since when it has witnessed some of the more unsavoury episodes of Kamakura history. Most of the present buildings date from the early nineteenth century, and their striking red paintwork, combined with the parade of souvenir stalls and the constant bustle of people, create a festive atmosphere in sharp contrast to that of Kamakura's more secluded Zen temples.

Three humpback bridges lead into the shrine compound between two connected ponds known as **Genpei-ike**. These were designed by Minamoto Yoritomo's wife, Hōjō Masako, and are full of heavy, complicated symbolism, anticipating the longed-for victory of her husband's clan over their bitter enemies, the Taira; strangely, the bloodthirsty Masako was of Taira stock. The **Mai-den**, an open-sided stage at the end of a broad avenue, was the scene of another unhappy event in 1186, when Yoritomo forced his brother's mistress, Shizuka, to dance for the assembled samurai. Yoritomo wanted his popular brother, Yoshitsune, killed and was holding Shizuka prisoner in the hope of discovering his whereabouts; instead, she made a defiant declaration of love and only narrowly escaped death herself, though her newborn son was murdered soon after. Her bravery is commemorated with classical dances and nō plays during the shrine **festival** (Sept 14–16), which also features demonstrations of horseback archery on the final day.

Beyond the Mai-den, a long flight of steps leads up beside a knobbly, ancient ginkgo tree – reputedly a thousand years old and scene of the third shogun's murder by his vengeful nephew – to the **main shrine**. This is an attractive collection of buildings set among trees, though, as with all Shinto shrines, you can only peer in. Appropriately, the principal deity, Hachiman, is the God of War.

Near the front of the Tsurugaoka Hachiman-gū complex, you'll find the beautifully restrained, black-lacquered **Shirahata-jinja**, dedicated to the first and third Kamakura shoguns.

19

East Kamakura

The eastern side of Kamakura contains a scattering of less-visited shrines and temples, including two of the town's most enchanting corners. It's possible to cover the area on foot in a half-day, or less if you hop on a bus for the return journey.

Hōkoku-ji
報国寺 • 2-7-4 Jomyoji • Daily 9am–4pm • Bamboo gardens ¥200

The well-tended gardens and simple wooden buildings of **Hōkoku-ji**, or Take-dera, the "Bamboo Temple", are accessed via a small bridge off Kanazawa-kaidō. The temple is best known for a grove of evergreen bamboo protected by the encircling cliffs. This dappled forest of thick, gently curved stems, where tinkling water spouts and the soft creaking of the wind-rocked canes muffle the outside world, would seem the perfect place for the monks' meditation. Too soon, though, the path emerges beside the manicured rear garden, which was created by the temple's founding priest in the thirteenth century.

Sugimoto-dera
杉本寺 • 903 Nikaido • Daily 8am–4.30pm • ¥200

One of Kamakura's oldest temples, **Sugimoto-dera** is set at the top of a steep, foot-worn staircase lined with fluttering white flags, overlooking the main road. Standing in a woodland clearing, the small, thatched temple, founded in 734, exudes a real sense of history. Inside its smoke-blackened hall, spattered with pilgrims' prayer stickers, you can slip off your shoes and take a look behind the altar at the three wooden statues of Jūichimen Kannon, the eleven-faced Goddess of Mercy. The images were carved at different times by famous monks, but all three are at least a thousand years old. According to legend, they survived a devastating fire in 1189 by taking shelter – all by themselves – behind a giant tree; since then the temple has been known as Sugimoto ("Under the Cedar").

Kamakura-gū
鎌倉宮 • 154 Nikaido • Daily 9am–4pm • ¥300

Mainly of interest for its history and torchlight nō dramas in early October, **Kamakura-gū** was founded by Emperor Meiji in 1869 to encourage support for his new imperial regime. The shrine is dedicated to Prince Morinaga, a forgotten fourteenth-century hero who helped restore his father, Emperor Go-Daigo, briefly to the throne. The prince was soon denounced, however, by power-hungry rivals and held for nine months in a Kamakura cave before being executed. The small cave and a desultory treasure house lie to the rear of the classically styled shrine, but don't really justify the entry fee.

A road heading north from Kamakura-gū marks the beginning – or end – of the shortcut to the Ten'en Hiking Course (see page 241).

Zuisen-ji

瑞泉寺 • 710 Nikaido • Daily 9am–4.30pm • ¥200

Starting point of the main trail of the Ten'en Hiking Course (see page 241), **Zuisen-ji's** quiet, wooded location and luxuriant gardens make it an attractive spot, though the temple's fourteenth-century Zen garden, to the rear of the main building, is rather dilapidated.

Hase

長谷

The west side of Kamakura, an area known as **Hase**, is home to the town's most famous sight, the **Daibutsu** (Great Buddha), cast in bronze nearly 750 years ago. On the way, it's worth visiting **Hase-dera** to see an image of Kannon, the Goddess of Mercy, which is said to be Japan's largest wooden statue. These sights are within walking distance of Hase station, three stops from Kamakura station on the private Enoden line.

Hase-dera

長谷寺 • Daily: March–Sept 8am–5pm; Oct–Feb 8am–4.30pm • ¥400 • ⓦ www.hasedera.jp • Hase station

Hase-dera stands high on the hillside a few minutes' walk north of Hase station, with good views of Kamakura and across Yuigahama beach to the Miura peninsula beyond. Though the temple's present layout dates from the mid-thirteenth century, according to legend it was founded in 736, when a wooden eleven-faced Kannon was washed ashore nearby. The statue is supposedly one of a pair carved from a single camphor tree in 721 by a monk in the original Hase, near Nara; he placed one Kannon in a local temple and pushed the other out to sea.

Nowadays the **Kamakura Kannon** – just over 9m tall and gleaming with gold leaf (a fourteenth-century embellishment) – resides in an attractive, chocolate-brown and cream building at the top of the temple steps. This central hall is flanked by two smaller buildings: the right hall houses a large Amidha Buddha carved in 1189 for Minamoto Yoritomo's 42nd birthday to ward off the bad luck traditionally associated with that age; the hall on the left shelters a copy of an early fifteenth-century statue of Daikoku-ten, the cheerful God of Wealth. The real statue is in the small **treasure hall** immediately behind, alongside the original temple bell, cast in 1264. The next building along is the **Sutra Repository**, where a revolving drum contains a complete set of Buddhist scriptures – one turn of the wheel is equivalent to reading the whole lot. In the far northern corner of the complex, a **cave** contains statues of the goddess Benten and her sixteen children, or disciples, though it can't compete with the atmospheric setting of the Zeniarai Benten cave-shrine (see page 241).

Ranks of **jizō statues** are a common sight in Hase-dera, some clutching sweets or "windmills" and wrapped in tiny woollen mufflers; these sad little figures commemorate stillborn or aborted children.

The Daibutsu

大仏 • 4-2-28 Hase • Daily: April–Sept 7am–6pm; Oct–March 7am–5.30pm • ¥200 • **Entering statue** Daily 8am–4.30pm • ¥20

After all the hype, the **Daibutsu**, in the grounds of Kōtoku-in temple, can seem a little disappointing at first sight. But as you approach, and the Great Buddha's serene, rather aloof face comes more clearly into view, the magic begins to take hold. He sits on a stone pedestal, a broad-shouldered figure lost in deep meditation, with his head slightly bowed, his face and robes streaked grey-green by centuries of sun, wind and rain. The

13m-tall image represents Amida Nyorai, the future Buddha who receives souls into the Western Paradise, and was built under the orders of Minamoto Yoritomo to rival the larger Nara Buddha, near Kyoto. Completed in 1252, the statue is constructed of bronze plates bolted together around a hollow frame – you can climb inside for a fee – and evidence suggests that, at some time, it was covered in gold leaf. Amazingly, it has withstood fires, typhoons, the tsunami of 1495 which washed away its surrounding hall, and even the Great Earthquake of 1923.

Enoshima

江の島 • Elevators ¥350 for all three

Tied to the mainland by a 600m-long bridge, and easily reached from Kamakura, the tiny, sacred island of **Enoshima** has a few sights – some shrines, a botanical garden and a couple of caves – but its prime attraction is as a pleasant place to walk, away from motor traffic. Enoshima's eastern side shelters a yacht harbour and car parks, but otherwise the knuckle of rock – less than 1km from end to end – is largely covered with woods and a network of well-marked paths.

19

The private Enoden-line train rattles from Kamakura to Enoshima station, from where it's roughly a fifteen-minute walk southwest to the island, via a bridge constructed over the original sand spit. Once over the bridge, walk straight ahead under the bronze *torii* and uphill past restaurants and souvenir shops to where the steps to the main shrine begin; though the climb's easy enough, there are three **escalators** tunnelled through the hillside.

Enoshima-jinja

江の島神社 • Daily 9am–4.30pm • ¥200

The island features a wide-ranging shrine area. Most make a beeline for Hatsu-no-miya, inside which sits Enoshima's most famous relic – a naked **statue of Benten**, housed in an octagonal hall halfway up the hill. The statue has been here since the days of Minamoto Yoritomo (1147–99) of the Kamakura Shogunate, who prayed to it for victory over the contemporary Fujiwara clan. Although ranked among Japan's top three Benten images, it's a little hard to see what all the fuss is about.

Samuel Cocking Park

サムエル・コッキング苑, Samyueru Cokkingu-en • April–June, Sept & Oct Mon–Fri 9am–6pm, Sat & Sun 9am–8pm; July & Aug daily 9am–8pm; Nov–March Mon–Fri 9am–5pm, Sat & Sun 9am–8pm • Park ¥200, lighthouse ¥300

This nicely laid-out botanical garden is known as the **Samuel Cocking Park** after the English merchant and horticulturalist who built Japan's first greenhouse here in 1880. If it's a clear day, you'll get good views south to Ōshima's (occasionally smoking) volcano, and west to Fuji from the lighthouse inside the garden.

Iwaya

岩屋 • Daily: March–Oct 9am–5pm; Nov–Feb 9am–4pm • ¥500

From the botanical garden, the path drops down steeply past restaurant-bars perched over the cliff – great for a sunset beer in fine weather – to the island's rocky west shore and two caves known as **Iwaya**. The caves themselves aren't all that special; more enjoyable is the walk along the wave-side boardwalk that runs between them.

ARRIVAL AND DEPARTURE   **KAMAKURA AND AROUND**

KAMAKURA

By train You can take either the JR Yokosuka line from Tokyo Station, or the JR Shōnan-Shinjuku line from Shinjuku via Shibuya (every 5–10min; each around 1hr; ¥920); both go via Yokohama (25–30min; ¥340), and all trains stop at Kita-Kamakura Station before pulling into the main Kamakura Station a few minutes later. Tokyo travel cards can be used for all of these journeys.

19

ENOSHIMA

By train If you're visiting Enoshima after Kamakura, you can hop onto the Enoden line (ⓦenoden.co.jp) at Kamakura Station (every 12min; 25min; ¥260); trains pull in to Enoshima Station, from where it's roughly a 15min walk southwest to the island, over the bridge. Alternatively, if you're heading straight to Enoshima from Tokyo, the most straightforward route is the Odakyū-Enoshima line direct from Shinjuku to Katase-Enoshima Station (片瀬江ノ島駅), which lies just north of the bridge, on the western side

of the river; a helpful travel pass (see below) is available for this route.

Travel pass If you're planning to visit Enoshima, it's worth considering the Odakyū Enoshima-Kamakura Freepass, a one-day discount ticket (¥1470) covering a return trip to Katase-Enoshima Station on the Odakyū line from Shinjuku, and unlimited travel on the Enoden line; it means that you'll have to hit Enoshima first and last, while visiting Kamakura on a loop trip, but it's feasible.

GETTING AROUND

By train Given the narrow roads and amount of traffic, it's usually quickest to use the trains as far as possible and then walk. On the west side of Kamakura Station are ticket machines and platforms for the private Enoden line (ⓦenoden.co.jp) to Hase and Enoshima (every 12min; daily 6am–11pm); Kamakura to Hase costs ¥190, to Enoshima ¥260. If you plan to hop on and off the Enoden line a lot and haven't got any other form of discount ticket, it's worth investing in the Kamakura-Enoshima day-pass (¥700), which entitles you to unlimited travel on this line, plus JR services.

By bus The only time a bus might come in handy is for the more far-flung restaurants or the eastern shrines and temples. Local buses depart from the main station concourse; for the eastern shrines you want stand 4 for Kamakura-gū and stand 5 for Sugimoto-dera (¥200 minimum fare). To make three or more journeys by bus, you'll save money by buying a Kamakura Free Kippu day pass (¥550), which is available from the JR ticket office. The pass also covers JR trains from Kamakura to Kita-Kamakura and Enoden line services as far as Hase.

INFORMATION

Kamakura tourist office Outside the main, eastern exit of Kamakura Station, immediately to the right, there's a small tourist information window (daily: April–Sept 9am–5.30pm; Oct–March 9am–5pm; ☏0467 23 3050), with English-speaking staff.

Enoshima tourist office You can pick up an English-

language map of the island at the small tourist office, which is on your left as you come off the bridge (daily 10am–5pm; ☏0466 26 9544, ⓦfujisawa-kanko.jp).

Services There's an international ATM (Mon–Fri 8am–9pm, Sat & Sun 8am–7pm) at the post office on Wakamiya-ōji, and 24hr facilities in most major convenience stores.

ACCOMMODATION

SEE MAP PAGE 239

Most people visit Kamakura on a day-trip from Tokyo, but if you do want to stay over note that many places charge more at weekends and during peak holiday periods, when it can be tough to get a room. Central Kamakura offers little budget accommodation, but has a fair choice of mid-range hotels.

Kaihinsō かいひん荘 4-8-14 Yuigahama ☏0467 22 0960, ⓦkaihinso.jp. Nestled by the beach, this hotel is one for the romantics, with elegant rooms and a peaceful setting. The building went up in 1924; though added to since, the Western-style section is now protected property. You can stay in one of the two rooms here, or in tatami rooms in the newer Japanese section; some of the latter have views onto the garden. **¥27,000**

Kamakura Prince ホテル鎌倉プリンス 1-2-18 Shichirigahama-higashi ☏0467 32 1111, ⓦprincehotels.com/kamakura. Located by the beach, just a couple of stops west of Hase Station on the Enoden line, this hotel is a real winner. Guest rooms surround a delightful pool, while floor-to-ceiling windows offer generous ocean views (from some rooms you can see Mt Fuji, too); a golf range and excellent *teppanyaki* restaurant

round things off, but there's often a two-night minimum stay. **¥17,000**

New Kamakura ホテルニューカマクラ 13-2 Onari-machi ☏0467 22 2230, ⓦnewkamakura.com. One of the best-value places to stay in Kamakura is this early twentieth-century, Western-style building by Kamakura Station. It's a little bit worn, but most rooms are light and airy, with a choice of Western or Japanese style. **¥7000**

Villa Sacra ヴィラサクラ 13-29 Onari-machi ☏0467 22 5311, ⓦvillasacra.com. For something a bit different, give this modern ryokan a whirl. It's situated in an old Japanese house, renovated with funky artistic flourishes. Staff are switched on, and the common room is a nice place to hang out with other guests. No meals; breakfast available for an extra fee. **¥8500**

★ **WeBase Hostel** ウィーベースホステル 4-10-7 Yuigahama ☏0467 22 1221, ⓦwe-base.jp. Superbly convenient hostel, just over 15min on foot from Kamakura Station, and 2min from the beach. It's a large place which feels rather more modern than you'd expect in Kamakura – features include a couple of outdoor showers, a large veranda for coffee and chit-chat, and even a yoga studio. Dorms **¥3800**, doubles **¥9600**

EATING

SEE MAP PAGE 239

Kamakura is famous for its beautifully presented **Buddhist vegetarian cuisine**, known as *shōjin ryōri*, though there's plenty more casual dining on offer at local restaurants.

KAMAKURA

Bentendō 弁天堂 1-7-6 Ko-machi ☎ 0467 25 3500. At this wonderful teahouse in the grounds of Engaku-ji temple (see page 240), you can enjoy a cup of *matcha* (¥650) while admiring the view across the valley to Tōkei-ji (see page 240). Daily 11am–4pm.

Cafe Terrace Itsuki Garden カフェテラス樹ガーデン On Daibutsu Hiking Course. A fantastic place to get your breath back if you're panting your way along the Daibutsu Hiking Course (see page 241). There are seats inside, but in warmer months everyone's out on the steeply arrayed outdoor terraces. Coffees and teas cost around ¥600, alcoholic drinks a little more. Daily 10am–7pm.

Gokuraku Curry ごくらくカレー 3-9-47 Yuigahama ☎ 0467 61 1807. Vegan-friendly, gluten-free curry house serving just one type of curry per day (set meal ¥1500). They only make enough for 30 servings, meaning that it's best to visit for an early lunch, since they may be shut by dinner time. Mon–Fri 11.30am–2.30pm & 5.30–8pm, Sat & Sun 11.30am–2.30pm.

Hachi-no-ki 鉢の木 7 Yamanouchi ☎ 0467 22 8719; Kita-Kamakura branch ☎ 046 723 3722. Reservations are recommended for this famous *shōjin ryōri* restaurant beside the entrance to Kenchō-ji, though it's easier to get a table at the newer branch, just over the lane to the south. Whichever you opt for, prices start at around ¥2400, though the new branch also offers cheap soba (¥920). Mon, Tues, Thurs & Fri 11.30am–2.30pm, Sat & Sun 11am–3pm; new branch 11am–2.30pm & 5–7pm, closed Wed.

Paradise Alley Bakery 1-13-10 Ko-machi ☎ 0467 84 7203. Tucked into a cute little alley, this hipster bakery (all of the staff, and most of the customers) is a good place in which to load up on snacks before wandering around Kamakura. Most of them are sweet in nature, including a fair few curiously grey (but highly tasty) chocolate breads. Mon–Fri 8am–6pm, Sat & Sun 7am–6pm.

ENOSHIMA

Enoshima-tei 江之島亭 Enoshima ☎ 0466 22 9111. Pretty seafood restaurant on the island itself; no English, but the picture menu should help out. Most affordable are their donburi (rice bowls, ¥1100 and up); some have non-fishy toppings, but for a local treat go for the ones topped with perilla leaf and a miniature shoal of tiny sardines. Daily 10.30am–6pm.

Kinokuniya 紀伊国屋 1-3-16 Tasegaikan ☎ 0466 22 4247; Enoshima Station. Heading towards Enoshima from the station, you'll pass this simple ryokan-restaurant on your right. It's highly popular with locals on account of the cheap sets (most ¥1000–1500), most of which include tea or coffee; if it's on offer, the *kin-me-dai* (a delicious local red fish, served in soy) is best. Daily 11am–9pm.

DRINKING

SEE MAP PAGE 239

In summer, wooden **bars** line the beaches from Kamakura to Enoshima. The nightlife in Kamakura town itself won't exactly remind you of Shibuya, but for a small place there's still a fair bit of activity until the last trains zoom off.

Milk Hall ミルクホール 2-3-8 Ko-machi ☎ 0467 22 1179, �🌐 milkhall.co.jp. Dimly lit, jazz-playing coffee house-cum-antique shop buried in the backstreets west of Komachi-dōri. Best for an evening beer, wine or cocktail (all from ¥700), rather than as a place to eat. Occasional live music. Daily 11am–10.30pm.

★ **Tenshō** 天昇 1-3-4 Ko-machi ☎ 0467 22 6099. Get away from the tourists and down with the locals at this *tachinomiya*, whose raucous nature is the very antithesis of the regular genteel Kamakura atmosphere. *Yakitori* sticks go from ¥130, and sets of Hoppy (a type of fake beer to which alcohol is added) from ¥400. Daily (except Mon) 3–10pm.

Yokohama

横浜

On its southern borders Tokyo merges with **YOKOHAMA**, Japan's second most populous city (home to 3.6 million people) and a major international port. Though essentially part of the same mega-conurbation, central Yokohama feels far more spacious and airy than central Tokyo, thanks to its open harbour frontage and generally low-rise skyline, and though it can't claim any outstanding sights, the place has enough of interest to justify a day's outing from Tokyo.

Locals are proud of their city's international heritage, and there's definitely a cosmopolitan flavour to the place, with its scattering of Western-style buildings, Chinese temples and world cuisines, and its sizeable foreign community. The upmarket suburb of **Yamate** (also known as "the Bluff") is one of the city's highlights and boasts a

splendid museum; the area forms a pleasant contrast with the vibrant alleys, colourful trinket shops and bustling restaurants of nearby **Chinatown**. Near the seafront, the **harbour area** boasts a few grand old Western edifices, in complete contrast to the **Minato Mirai 21** development's high-tech skyscrapers in the distance.

Brief history

When Commodore Perry sailed his "Black Ships" into Tokyo Bay in 1853, Yokohama was a mere fishing village of some eighty houses on the distant shore. But it was this harbour, well out of harm's way as far as the Japanese were concerned, that the shogun designated one of the five **treaty ports** open to foreign trade in 1858.

From the early 1860s until the first decades of the twentieth century, Yokohama flourished on the back of raw silk exports, a trade dominated by British merchants. During this period the city provided the main conduit for new ideas and inventions into Japan: the first bakery, photographers', ice-cream shop, brewery and – perhaps most importantly – the first railway line, which linked today's Sakuragichō with Shimbashi in central Tokyo in 1872. The **Great Earthquake** levelled the city in 1923, and it was devastated again in air raids at the end of World War II; the rebuilt city is, however, among the world's largest ports.

19

Motomachi and Yamate

The narrow, semi-pedestrianized shopping street of **Motomachi** (元町) exudes a faint retro flavour with its European facades. You'll get more of the old Motomachi feel in the two streets to either side, particularly Naka-dōri to the south, with its funky cafés and galleries.

At the northeast end of Motomachi, a wooded promontory marks the beginning of the **Yamate** (山手) district. The panoramic view from **Harbour View Park** is particularly beautiful at night; if you look really hard, just left of the double chimney stacks, you'll see the Tokyo Skytree blinking away.

Yokohama Foreign General Cemetery

外国人墓地, Gaikokujin Bochi • 96 Yamate-chō • March–Dec Sat & Sun noon–4pm • ¥200 donation • ☎ 045 622 1311, ⓦ yfgc-japan.com

Just a few minutes' walk south of the Harbour View Park, you'll likely happen upon the **Yokohama Foreign General Cemetery**, which sits on a west-facing hillside. Over 4500 people from more than forty countries are buried here, the vast majority either British or American.

Yamate Museum

山手博物館, Yamate Hakubutsukan • 254 Yamate-chō • Daily 11am–4pm • ¥210 • ☎ 045 622 1188

The tiny **Yamate Museum** is housed in the city's oldest wooden building, a stunning, fairytale-like structure erected in 1909. Exhibits focus on life in the area during the foreign-settlement period, and include a collection of cartoons from *Japan Punch*, a satirical magazine published in Yokohama for a while in the late nineteenth century. However, it's the building itself that's the main draw.

Chinatown

中華街, Chūka-gai

Founded in 1863, Yokohama's **Chinatown** is the largest in Japan: its streets contain roughly two hundred restaurants and over three hundred shops, while some eighteen million tourists pass through its narrow byways every year; few leave without tasting what's on offer, from steaming savoury dumplings to a full-blown meal in one of the famous speciality restaurants.

Kantei-byō

関帝廟 • 140 Yamashita-chō • Daily 9am–7pm • Free; ¥500 to see main altar

The focus of community life is **Kantei-byō**, a shrine dedicated to Guan Yu, a former general and guardian deity of Chinatown. The building is a bit cramped, but impressive nonetheless, with a colourful ornamental gateway and writhing dragons wherever you look. You can pay to enter the main building to see the red-faced, long-haired Guan Yu, but it's not really worth it.

The harbour

From the eastern edge of Chinatown it's a short hop down to the harbour, which is fronted by **Yamashita-kōen**, a pleasant park – more grass than trees – created as a memorial to victims of the Great Earthquake. Here you can pick up a *Sea Bass* ferry (see page 252) or take a harbour cruise (see page 251) from the pier beside the **Hikawa-maru** (see below). The 106m-high **Marine Tower**, built in 1961, is still the focal point of the area after all these years, but it's better to save your money for the Landmark Tower's much higher observation deck (see page 250). Cruise ships pull up at **Ōsanbashi** pier to berth at Yokohama's International Passenger Terminal; a beautifully fluid, low-slung design inspired by ocean waves, it's a skateboarder's dream come true.

19

Hikawa-maru Museum

日本郵船氷川丸, Nikon Yūsen Hikowe-maru • Off Yamashita-kōen • Tues–Sun 10am–5pm • ¥300 • ☎ 045 641 4362, ⓦ nyk.com/rekishi

The *Hikawa-maru*, a retired passenger liner also known as the *Queen of the Pacific*, was built in 1930 for the NYK line Yokohama–Seattle service, though it was later commandeered as a hospital ship during World War II. It now serves as the **Hikawa-maru Museum**, with the ship done up to look as it did in its prime.

Minato Mirai 21

みなとみらい21 • ⓦ minatomirai21.com

Occupying over two square kilometres of reclaimed land and disused dockyards, **Minato Mirai 21**, or **MM21**, is an ever-expanding mini-city of apartment blocks, offices, recreational and cultural facilities.

Yokohama Port Museum

横浜みなと博物館, Yokohama Minato Hakubutsukan • 2-1-1 Minatomirai • Tues–Sun 10am–5pm • ¥400 for museum or ship, ¥600 for both• ⓦ nippon-maru.or.jp

Built in 1930, the **Nippon-maru** training sail ship saw service up until 1984 (during which time she sailed the equivalent of 45 times round the world) and now forms part of the enjoyable **Yokohama Port Museum**. You can explore the entire vessel, which has plenty of English labelling throughout, and alternating Japanese and English commentary over the loudspeakers.

Landmark Tower

横浜ランドマークタワー • 2-2-1 Minatomirai • **Observation deck** Daily 10am–9pm (Sat until 10pm) • ¥1000 • ⓦ yokohama-landmark.jp

You can't miss the awesome, 296m-tall **Landmark Tower** – Yokohama's tallest building by far, and still ranked second countrywide (Tokyo Tower and the Skytree are mere towers). The **Sky Garden observation deck** is on its 69th floor, and on clear days, when Fuji is flaunting her beauty, the superb views more than justify the entry fee. You can also enjoy a coffee for about the same price in the opulent *Sirius Sky Lounge*, another floor up in the *Royal Park Hotel*, or splash out on an early evening cocktail as the city lights spread their magic.

Yokohama Museum of Art

横浜美術館, Yokohama Bijutsukan • 3-4-1 Minatomirai • Daily (except Thurs) 10am–6pm • ¥1100; varying prices for special exhibitions • ☎ 045 221 0300, ⓦ yokohama.art.museum

YOKOHAMA SIGHTSEEING CRUISES

From Yamashita-kōen you can join the *Marine Shuttle* or *Marine Rouge* for a variety of **sightseeing cruises** round the harbour (from ¥1000 for 40min; ⓦ yokohama-cruising.jp); the *Marine Rouge* also offers lunch and dinner cruises (¥2520 plus ¥5500–11,000 for food). In addition, the bigger and more luxurious *Royal Wing* cruise ship (❶ 045 662 6125, ⓦ royalwing. co.jp) runs lunch, tea and dinner cruises from Ōsanbashi pier (¥1500–2500 plus ¥1500–5400 for food).

The centrepoint of the MM21 area is the splendid **Yokohama Museum of Art**, which is filled with mostly twentieth-century works of Japanese and Western art. Such refinement is set off to fine effect by designer Tange Kenzō's cool, grey space, which grabs your attention as much as the exhibits.

Shinkō island

Between MM21 and Ōsanbashi is **Shinkō island**, which was reclaimed about a hundred years ago as part of Yokohama's then state-of-the-art port facilities. Sights here include a huge Ferris wheel, and an even huger spa complex; on the eastern side of the island, two handsome red-brick warehouses dating from 1911 now form the attractive **Akarenga** shopping, dining and entertainment complex.

19

Cosmo Clock 21

コスモクロック21・2-8-1 Shinkō・Mon–Fri 11am–9pm, Sat & Sun 11am–10pm; occasionally closed Thurs・¥700

The slowly revolving **Cosmo Clock 21** is one of the world's largest Ferris wheels, with a diameter of 112m; one circuit takes around fifteen minutes, allowing plenty of time to take in the view, which is particularly spectacular at night. The clock's changing colours provide a night-time spectacle in their own right.

Manyō Club

万葉倶楽部, Manyō Kaiabu・2-7-1 Shinkō・Daily 10am–9pm・¥2700・❶ 045 663 4126

Spread over five floors, the **Manyō Club** spa complex offers a variety of hot-spring baths – the water is trucked in from Atami onsen down the coast – in addition to massages and treatments, restaurants and relaxation rooms. The rooftop is one of the best places from which to admire the night-time colour display of the Cosmo Clock.

Cup Noodle Museum

カップヌードルミュージアム・2-3-4 Shinkō・Daily (except Tues) 10am–6pm・¥500・❶ 045 345 0825, ⓦ cupnoodles-museum.jp

Instant noodles are one of Asia's most important snacks, and the contribution made since 1971 by the pioneering Japanese Cup Noodle brand is traced in the fun, beautifully designed **Cup Noodle Museum**. There are all sorts of interactive displays, though for many the main sources of enjoyment are sampling some of the many Cup Noodle varieties, and purchasing quirky branded souvenirs.

ARRIVAL AND DEPARTURE	**YOKOHAMA**

On the northwest side of town, Yokohama station functions as the city's main transport hub, offering train, subway and bus connections, as well as featuring several gargantuan department stores.

BY TRAIN

From Shibuya The fast Tōkyū-Tōyoko line runs via Nakameguro, calling at Yokohama Station (every 5–10min; 30min; ¥270) before heading off underground to Minato Mirai and terminating at Motomachi-Chūkagai Station. Some services actually start life way back in Saitama prefecture as Fukutoshin metro trains, stopping at Ikebukuro and Shinjuku-sanchōme stations before switching identity in Shibuya, then again in Yokohama. JR's Shōnan-Shinjuku line runs into Yokohama Station from Shibuya (every 20–30min; 25min; ¥390) and Shinjuku.

From Tokyo Station You can choose from the Tōkaidō or Yokosuka lines (both every 5–10min; 30min; ¥470), or the Keihin-Tōhoku line (every 5–10min; 40min; ¥470). All three are JR lines; the first two terminate at Yokohama Station, while the latter continues to Sakuragichō, Kannai and Ishikawachō.

GETTING AROUND

By train Getting around central Yokohama is easy on either the Tōkyū-Tōyoko line or the JR Negishi line (the local name for Keihin-Tōhoku trains). Trains on both lines run every 5min.

By subway A subway line connects Kannai and stations north to Shin-Yokohama, on the Shinkansen line; it's bisected by another line which few travellers will end up using. Services on both run every 5–15min.

By Akai Kutsu sightseeing bus A retro-style sightseeing bus runs from outside Sakuragichō Station's east exit via Minato Mirai, the Akarenga complex, Chinatown and Yamashita-kōen to Harbour View Park, then loops back via Ōsanbashi pier. Services run every 10–15min (¥220 per hop, or ¥500 for a day-pass).

By ferry Perhaps the most enjoyable way of getting about the city is on the *Sea Bass* ferries (ⓦ yokohama-cruising.jp) that shuttle between Yokohama Station (from a pier in the Bay Quarter shopping complex) and southerly Yamashita-kōen, with some services stopping at Minato Mirai and Akarenga en route. There are departures every 15min (daily 10am–7.30pm; ¥350–700).

INFORMATION

Tourist information The most useful centre (daily: April–Nov 9am–6pm; Dec–March 9am–7pm; ☎ 045 211 0111, ⓦ yokohamajapan.com) is immediately outside Sakuragichō station's east entrance, but there's also a booth in the underground concourse at Yokohama station (daily 9am–7pm; ☎ 045 441 7300).

ACCOMMODATION SEE MAP PAGE 248

★ **Edit** ホテルエジット 6-78-1 Sumiyoshi-chō, Naka-ku ☎ 045 680 0238, ⓦ hotel-edit.com. With its pleasing modern flourishes and winning location, this business hotel is excellent value, with rooms cheaper – and often more stylish – than anything else in this category. **¥7800**

Navios Yokohama ナヴィオス横浜 Shinkō-chō, Naka-ku ☎ 045 633 6000, ⓦ navios-yokohama.com. One of the best-value options in Yokohama, with rooms frequently discounted from the rack rates; ask for one facing the Landmark Tower for terrific night-time views. Western-style doubles **¥15,000**, Japanese-style doubles **¥19,000**

Royal Park Hotel ローヤルパークホテル 2-2-1-3 Minato Mirai, Nishi-ku ☎ 045 221 1111, ⓦ yrph.com. This hotel occupies the 52nd to 67th floors of the Landmark Tower, so spectacular views are guaranteed. Rooms are fairly spacious and come with good-sized bathrooms. As well as a fitness club and swimming pool (extra charges apply), facilities include a tea ceremony room and the *Sirius Sky Lounge*. **¥30,000**

Yokohama Central Hostel 横浜セントラルホステル 222 Yamashita-chō, Naka-ku ☎ 045 663 1890, ⓦ ychostel.com. Just a few minutes on foot from Chinatown, this is the best of Yokohama's several hostel options. The tatami common area is appealingly rustic, though the dorms themselves feel modern and spacious. Dorms **¥2000**

EATING SEE MAP PAGE 248

One of Yokohama's highlights is sampling the enormous variety of restaurants and snack-food outlets cramming the streets of **Chinatown**; most are much of a muchness, selling the same food in all-you-can-eat form. In fine weather, the casual little eating places on the ground floor of **Akarenga** (see page 251) are a good option.

RESTAURANTS

Bairan 梅蘭 133-10 Yamashita-chō ☎ 045 651 6695, ⓦ bairan.jp. Small, unpretentious restaurant tucked in the backstreets and known for its Bairan *yakisoba*, stir-fried noodles served like a sort of pie, crispy on the outside and with various varieties of juicy stuffing (from ¥940). Mon–Fri 11.30am–3pm & 5–10pm, Sat & Sun 11am–10pm.

Manchinrō 萬珍樓 153 Yamashita-chō ☎ 045 681 4004, ⓦ manchinro.com. This famous restaurant has been serving tasty Cantonese cuisine since 1892. Though prices are on the high side, the portions are generous; noodle and fried-rice dishes start at around ¥1600, lunch sets at ¥2400, and evening course menus at ¥5000. If these are beyond your budget, try the yummy steamed dumplings on sale from a hatch, from ¥300. Daily 11am–10pm.

Yamate Jūbankan 山手十番館 247 Yamate-chō ☎ 045 621 4466. Pleasant French restaurant in a pretty clapboard house opposite the Foreigners' Cemetery. The upstairs is on the formal side, with lunch like John Dory in butter sauce (¥1600) or beef tongue stew (¥2400), and expensive dinner sets (¥5000); the more casual ground floor offers desserts (¥750), and in July and August the restaurant runs a popular beer garden. Daily 11.30am–9pm.

CAFÉS AND TEAROOMS

★ **Café de la Presse** カフェードゥラプレス 2F Media Centre Building, 11 Nihon-dōri ☎ 045 222 3348. Viennese-style café in the corner of one of Yokohama's grand old buildings. Go for a coffee or tea (from ¥480), with a dessert such as macaroons or their utterly delectable crème brûlée (¥600). They also serve croques monsieur (¥800), and other sandwiches and light meals. Tues–Sun 10am–8pm.

Enokitei えの木てい 89-6 Yamate-chō ☎045 623 2288. Set in a venerable Yamate former residence, this cute English-style tearoom serves tea (¥600–700) and home-made cakes (¥380–620); get them with some dainty sandwiches in the full afternoon tea set. Tues–Fri 11am–7pm.

19

CLASSICAL DEPICTION OF SAMURAI AND GEISHA

Contexts

255 History

263 Books

266 Film

268 The arts, architecture and design

273 Japanese

281 Glossary

History

Although Tokyo's founding date is usually given as 1457, the year when Ōta Dōkan, a minor lord, built his modest castle on a bluff overlooking the Sumida-gawa, there have been people living on the Kantō plain since the Paleolithic period. Today's restless metropolis began life as a humble fishing village called Edo, meaning "river gate", a name granted in the twelfth century by Edo Shigenaga, a member of the Taira clan that held control of the Kantō district at the time.

The beginnings

The earliest archeological finds from the Tokyo area date back to the late Paleolithic period; the stone tools of ancient **hunter-gatherers**, who are believed to have arrived in Japan from Polynesia and mainland Asia, have been found at various sites to the west of today's city centre. The rationale behind their settling on the Kantō plain is clear, for it was, and remains, a strategically important spot at the nexus of sea, river and land routes. The centre of today's Tokyo, however, was under water for much of this time; as the land slowly rose due to tectonic shifts, the waters fell back, providing a boon to the Tokyoites of the time, since the resultant marshland provided an excellent source of food.

During the **Jōmon period** (10,000–3000 BC), the pottery for which Japan is now famed started to be produced in significant quantities, often employing distinctive "rope-cord" patterning. More elaborate techniques began to be used in the **Yayoi period** (300 BC–300 AD), when there were also major advances in wet-rice cultivation and the use of bronze and iron implements. Given the city's modern-day renown in the pottery field, it may come as a surprise to learn that Tokyo was actually nearer the end of the talent line: most advances can be sourced to China, from where they slowly trickled to western Japan (often via Korea), and then finally on to Tokyo and the north. The same can be said for Buddhism, which arrived from Sabi (now Buyeo), contemporary capital of the Korean kingdom of Baekje, around the mid-sixth century AD; and *kanji*, the Chinese characters that remain a hugely important component of Japan's writing system today.

Early dynasties

Tokyo was a mere bit-part player in Japan's early dynastic days. The **Soga clan** (592–645), based out west around Nara, were the first of Japan's non-imperial ruling dynasties; Asakusa's Sensō-ji, apparently built in 628 after local fishermen found a golden bodhisattva statue in their nets, was likely founded during these times. In 645 the **Nakatomi clan** staged a successful coup against the Soga; within the next year they had reorganized their nascent dynasty along a Tang Chinese system of land tenure and taxation (known as the Taika, or "great reforms"), with the area on which Tokyo now sits becoming part of Musashi province. It became customary to relocate the royal

10,000–3000 BC	628 AD	645	1180
Creation of earliest known pottery	Asakusa's Sensō-ji constructed	Nakatomi clan depose Soga in coup, and reform land tenure and taxation	First use of Tokyo's original name, Edo

palace after the death of each emperor, until Japan's first permanent capital, Nara, was founded in 710.

It wasn't long before the capital was on the move again, however; in 784 the Fujiwara court distanced itself from Nara's increasingly influential monks and priests by relocating to nearby Nagaoka, then to Heian (later known as Kyoto) in 794. The colourful Heian era came to a close with the Genpei wars of 1180–85; the victorious **Minamoto clan** chose to base themselves in Kamakura, just west of Tokyo. In fact, Tokyo's original name, **Edo**, meaning "river gate", can be traced back to the beginning of the war; it was first used by Shigenago Edo of the competing Taira clan, who had settled in the area.

The Kamakura and Muromachi eras

The leader of the Minamoto clan, Yoritomo, established his military-based Bakufu, or **"tent government"**, at **Kamakura**, styling himself Sei-i Tai Shogun, the "Barbarian-subduing Great General". Japan settled into a period of semi-feudalism, with peasants allowed tenure of land in return for service to their loyal lord. After Yoritomo's death in 1199, his loyal lieutenant Hōjō Tokimasa, in partnership with Yoritomo's widow Masako, took the helm, assuming the combined roles of military and civil governor, and ushering in the century-long era of the **Hōjō regents** – these regents, rather than the figurehead emperor or shogun, were the real power-holders during this time.

The Mongol invasions of the late thirteenth century – thwarted by typhoons, dubbed the kamikaze or "divine wind" by the Japanese of the time – contributed to the fall of the ineffectual Kamakura government, which in 1333 found itself roundly beaten by the forces of **Emperor Go-Daigo**. Kamakura's Bakufu soon dispatched the warrior **Ashikaga Takauji** to bring Go-Daigo to heel; the wily Takauji initially switched allegiance to the emperor but later turned against him, forcing Go-Daigo to retreat to the mountains of Yoshino. Takauji set up a rival emperor in Kyoto, and for sixty years Japan had two courts; they were reconciled in 1392, by which time the Ashikaga shogunate had established its headquarters in Kyoto's **Muromachi** district, from where they ruled for over two centuries.

In the meantime, things were quietly ticking along in Tokyo (then still named Edo), with its first castle erected in 1457 by Ōta Dōkan, a poet better known as **Ōta Sekenaga**, and now regarded as the founder of modern Tokyo; his battlements formed part of what is now the Higashi Gyoen, which abuts today's Imperial Palace, and it became the precursor to a small wave of nearby temples, shrines and mercantile complexes. Ōta himself came to a sticky end in 1486, killed in Sagami (now Kanagawa) after being falsely accused of traitorship. His death occurred during a period of national strife, with the **Ōnin wars** of 1467–77 effectively relieving the government of authority, and regional *daimyō* (feudal warlords) fighting for dominance – a pattern that continued for over a century.

Reunification

The civil wars ended with the reunification of Japan under a triumvirate of generals of outstanding ability. The first, Oda Nobunaga, achieved dominance of the Kyoto region; however, in 1582 he was betrayed and forced to commit ritual suicide. Toyotomi

1185	1333	1457	1467–77
Minamoto clan victorious in Genpei wars; base themselves in Kamakura	Kamakura government falls	Founding of Tokyo	Ōnin wars result in regional warlords fighting for dominance

Hideyoshi, who had risen from obscurity to become one of Nobunaga's most trusted generals, avenged his death, managing to outmanoeuvre all rivals with a shrewd mix of force and diplomacy. Success went to his head, however, and he embarked on costly excursions into Korea, each time stymied by far smaller forces and the armoured "turtle ships" of modern-day Korean hero General Yi Sun-shin.

In 1590 another ambitious warlord, **Tokugawa Ieyasu**, established his power base in Edo, far from the emperor in Kyoto. The same year, Hideyoshi gained control over the region by defeating the powerful Go-Hōjō family at nearby Odawara castle. Shortly before his death in 1598, Hideyoshi persuaded Ieyasu, now an ally after a period of circumspect confrontation, to support the succession of his son Hideyori. The trust was misplaced: after defeating the remaining western clans at the Battle of Sekigahara in 1600, Ieyasu seized power himself, reuniting the country and taking the title of **shogun** – effectively a military dictator. Though the emperor continued to hold court in Kyoto, Japan's real centre of power would henceforth lie in Edo, at this point still little more than a small huddle of buildings at the edge of the Hibiya inlet.

The Edo era

The **Tokugawa** dynasty set about creating a city befitting its new status, initiating massive construction projects – a trend which has continued to the present day. By 1640, Edo Castle was the most imposing in all Japan, and most probably the largest in the whole world – a sixteen-kilometre perimeter line of defences complete with a five-storey central keep, a double moat and a complex, spiralling network of canals. Drainage work also began on the surrounding marshes, where embankments were raised to protect the nascent city against flooding.

The shogun required his *daimyō* to split the year between their provincial holdings and Edo, where their families were kept as virtual hostages. Maintaining two households with two sets of retainers, travelling long distances and observing prescribed ceremonies on the way left them neither the time nor money to raise a serious threat.

In exchange for their loyalty, *daimyō* were granted prime land to the west of the castle, in the area known as **Yamanote**. Artisans, merchants and others at the bottom of the established order, meanwhile, were confined to **Shitamachi**, a low-lying, overcrowded region to the east. Though less distinct, this division between the "high" and "low" city (see page 77) is still apparent today.

Closed Japan

Though the *daimyō* had been cleverly kept in check, the shogun perceived another threat to state security: Christianity. Despite the fact that Ieyasu's advisers had included Englishman Will Adams (whose tale was fictionalized in the novel *Shogun*), heavy restrictions began to be placed on all foreigners residing in Japan; missionaries and Christian converts found themselves persecuted. A policy of national seclusion was introduced in 1639; by this time, an estimated 250,000 Japanese Christians had been executed, imprisoned or forced to apostatize. Thus began the period of *sakoku*, or the **"closed country"**, which lasted more or less continuously until 1853. The only exceptions to the edicts were Korean diplomats, and a handful of Dutch and Chinese traders allowed to operate out of Nagasaki, way out to the west.

1590	**1600**	**1639**	**1640**
Warlord Tokugawa Ieyasu establishes power base in Edo	Ieyasu reunites country, and declares himself shogun	Policy of national seclusion introduced; Christians persecuted	Completion of Edo Castle

FIRE OF THE LONG SLEEVES

Shitamachi's tightly packed streets of thatch and wood dwellings usually suffered worst in the great fires which broke out so frequently that they were dubbed *Edo no hana*, the "flowers of Edo". In January 1657, the **Fire of the Long Sleeves** – so named because it started at a temple where the long-sleeved kimono of women who had recently died were being burnt – laid waste to three-quarters of the district's buildings and killed an estimated 100,000 people. Subsequent precautions included earth firewalls, manned watchtowers and local firefighting teams, who were much revered for their acrobatic skills and bravery. The fires continued, however, and the life expectancy of an Edo building averaged a mere twenty years.

Edo rising

The long period of stability under the Tokugawa, interrupted only by a few peasant rebellions, brought steady economic development. Mid-eighteenth-century Edo was the world's largest city, with a population well over one million, of whom roughly half were squeezed into Shitamachi at an astonishing 70,000 people per square kilometre. Peace gave rise to an increasingly wealthy merchant class, and the arts flourished; in parallel with this ran a vigorous, often bawdy subculture where the pursuit of pleasure was taken to new extremes. In Shitamachi, the arbiters of fashion were the **Edo-ko**, the "children of Edo", with their earthy humour and delight in practical jokes. Inevitably, there was also a darker side to life and the *Edo-ko* knew their fair share of squalor, poverty and violence. Licensed brothels, euphemistically known as "pleasure quarters", in areas such as Shinjuku, flourished, and child prostitution was common.

The arrival of the Black Ships

During Japan's period of seclusion, a small number of Westerners managed to breach the barriers, among them Engelbert Kaempfer, a Dutchman who wrote the first European-language history of Japan in the late seventeenth century. Various British survey vessels and Russian envoys also visited Japan in the early nineteenth century, but the greatest pressure came from the US, whose trading and whaling routes passed to the south of the country. In 1853, Commodore Matthew Perry of the US Navy arrived in Shimoda – at the tip of the Izu peninsula, just west of Tokyo – with a small fleet of **"Black Ships"**, demanding that Japan open at least some of its ports to foreigners. Japan's ruling elite was thrown into turmoil – the shogunate was already fearful of foreign incursions following the British defeat of China in the Opium Wars. However, when the emperor demanded that the foreigners be rebuffed it quickly became clear that Japan's military was no longer up to the task.

American Townsend Harris managed to extract **concessions** in 1858, and similar treaties were soon concluded with other Western nations; certain ports were opened up (including Yokohama), while foreigners were given the right of residence and certain judicial rights in these enclaves. Opponents of such shameful appeasement by the shogunate took up the slogan "revere the emperor, expel the barbarians!"; less reactionary factions could see that Japan was in no state to do this, and that their only hope of remaining independent was to learn from the more powerful nations.

Edo's power was not only being weakened from outside Japan, but from inside as well. Evidence of a westward shift in power came in 1863, when the emperor ordered

1657	1684	1853	1858
Fire lays waste to most of Shitamachi	First sumo tournament held	Matthew Perry arrives with the "Black Ships"	Japan opens up to foreign trade

Shogun Iemochi to Kyoto to explain his conciliatory actions towards the West – the first visit of a shogun to the imperial capital since 1634. To add to the humiliation, Iemochi could only muster a mere 3000 retainers, compared with the 300,000 who had accompanied Ieyasu to Kyoto on the previous occasion.

In 1867 the fifteenth and final shogun, Tokugawa Yoshinobu, formally applied to the emperor to have imperial power restored. The shogunate was terminated, and in December of that year the **Imperial Restoration** was formally proclaimed and 15-year-old Mitsuhito acceded to the throne, ushering in a period dubbed Meiji, or **"enlightened rule"**.

The Meiji era

The first years of **Meiji rule** saw a wave of great changes take place. Far from following the shogunate in a fall from grace, Edo was cemented as the seat of national power; in 1869, the young emperor shifted his court from Kyoto to Edo, renaming it Tokyo, or the "eastern capital". Determined to modernize, Japan embraced the ideas and technologies of the West with startling enthusiasm. Brick buildings, electric lights, trams, trains and then cars all made their first appearance in Tokyo. Within a few decades the castle lost its outer gates and most of its grounds, canals were filled in or built over and the commercial focus shifted to Ginza, while Shitamachi's wealthier merchants decamped for the more desirable residential areas of Yamanote, leaving the low city to sink into slow decline.

Beneath its modern veneer, however, Tokyo remained largely a fragile city of wood. When the **Great Kantō Earthquake** struck at noon on September 1, 1923, half of Tokyo – by then a city of some two million – was destroyed, while 100,000 people lost their lives in the quake itself and in the blazes sparked by thousands of cooking-fires.

World War II and recovery

By the early 1930s Tokyo had rebuilt itself, but before long the city, like the rest of Japan, was gearing up for war. The first US bombs fell on Tokyo in April 1942, and, as the Allied forces drew closer, increasingly frequent raids reached a crescendo in March 1945. During three days of sustained **incendiary bombing** an estimated 100,000 people died, most of them on the night of March 9. The physical devastation surpassed even that of the Great Earthquake: Meiji-jingū, Sensō-ji and Edo Castle were all destroyed, and Shitamachi all but obliterated; from Hibiya it was possible to see clear across the 8km to Shinjuku.

From a prewar population of nearly seven million, Tokyo was reduced to around three million people in a state of near-starvation. Regeneration was fuelled by an influx of American dollars and food aid under the **Allied Occupation** led by General MacArthur. The liveliest sector of the economy during this period was the black market, first in Yūrakuchō and later in Ueno and Ikebukuro.

In 1950 the **Korean War** broke out, and central Tokyo underwent extensive redevelopment on the back of a manufacturing boom partly fuelled by the war, while immigrants flooded in from the provinces to fill the factories. Anti-American **demonstrations** occurred sporadically throughout the decade, and rumbled on into

1867	1869	1881	1923
Meiji restoration	Edo becomes imperial capital; renamed Tokyo ("eastern capital")	Small watch shop called Seikō opens in Ginza	Great Kantō Earthquake strikes, killing over 100,000

EDUCATION

"Efficient" is probably the stereotype most readily associated with Japan, and in a land where trains run to the second, you'll see plenty of supporting evidence during your stay. Efficiency, however, is not a word that can really be applied to the country's **educational system**: one of the most conservative elements of one of the world's most conservative countries, it has essentially remained unchanged for decades. For visitors, its problems will be most evident in the low levels of **English-speaking** ability: though all Japanese study the language for up to a decade, only a fraction are able to hold a simple conversation. With private language academies catering to a demand that the government has not been able to sate, this has been a boon to thousands upon thousands of **foreign teachers**, most of whom each cart a substantial chunk of their salary home at the end of their stay.

Then of course, there's the **pressure** on the students themselves. Days can be long, and even on Saturdays and Sundays you'll see plenty of kids walking around in school uniform. All students are required to attend after-school classes; most do sports of some kind, which is great for health, but some students clock up more than 36 hours per week doing extracurricular activities (baseball is said to be the most time-consuming). Though a majority of students go on to university, getting there is no walk in the park: those who want to go to Tokyo University or other high-end establishments have to sit full suites of independent tests (usually multiple-choice, with no room for discussion or debate). Pressure is thus magnified into a few precious hours, and results from previous years of schooling are often overshadowed. In Tokyo, and around the country, there exist lobby groups which demand wholesale change to the system; if change eventually arrives, it's likely to do so slowly.

the late 1960s (in 1968 the authorities closed Tokyo University for a year). Heavily armed riot police became a familiar sight on the streets, but the situation was never allowed to threaten the major event of the postwar period: on October 10, 1964, Emperor Hirohito opened the eighteenth **Olympic Games**. The first Olympics ever held in Asia, the Games marked Japan's return to economic health and to international respectability.

Boom and bust

Like the rest of the industrialized world, Japan suffered during the oil crisis of the 1970s, but by the following decade its economy was the envy of the world. The late 1980s **boom** saw land prices in Tokyo reach dizzying heights, matched by excesses of every conceivable sort – everything from gold-wrapped sushi to mink toilet-seat covers. Now referred to as the "bubble period", these days were characterized by fast living – the stereotype of salarymen throwing down tens of thousands of yen each night at champagne-and-girlie bars is not all that far off the truth.

Such heady optimism was reflected, too, in a series of ambitious **building projects**. Some came off, like the Metropolitan Government offices in Shinjuku and the Odaiba reclamation in Tokyo Bay, while others were left on the drawing board, among them the X-Seed 400, which remains the largest building ever designed in full: 4km high, larger than Mount Fuji and planned to house half a million.

By 1992, with the stock market rapidly sinking and businesses contracting, it was clear that the economic bubble had burst. This grim situation was compounded by

1942	1945	1964	1973	1979
First bombs fall in World War II	World War II ends; Japan under American occupation	Hosting of Olympic Games	First Family Mart convenience store opens	Walkman invented

revelations of deep-seated political corruption and by the **AUM Shinrikyō** terrorist group releasing deadly sarin gas on Tokyo commuter trains in 1995, leaving twelve dead and thousands injured.

Recession was officially announced in 1998, the same year a manual on how to commit suicide sold an incredible 1.1 million copies; over 30,000 people – the majority middle-aged men facing unemployment – killed themselves that year, followed by a record 33,000 in 1999. The new millennium brought glimmerings of **recovery** – hardly surprising after trillions of yen had been pumped into the economy through various government packages. But Tokyo would never quite be the same, and the blue-tarpaulin tent compounds of the **homeless** remain commonplace in the capital's parks.

To the present day

In 1999, the ultranationalistic **Ishihara Shintarō** was elected Tokyo's governor. Despite frequently going on record with racist and other intemperate remarks, Ishihara proved a popular figure with voters, winning two further mayoral elections.

Under Ishihara's stewardship, Tokyo joint-hosted a successful **2002 World Cup** and boosted itself as the crucible of Japan's "soft power" in areas such as anime, manga, pop music and fashion. Districts from Akihabara to Roppongi have undergone structural makeovers, the latest projects being a huge renovation of Tokyo station and its surrounding area, and the sprucing up of Oshiage around the Tokyo Skytree (see page 78). The city then went onto become the sole host of the **2019 World Cup**.

One of Ishihara's main aims was to make Tokyo the first Asian city to host the **Olympic Games** twice. The bid for 2016 failed, with the event going to Rio instead; after the Tokyo city reins had been handed over to former journalist **Inose Naoki** in

AFTER THE 'QUAKE

On 11 March, 2011, powerful tremors were felt throughout Tokyo. Foreign journalists sent the regular tweets and filed the regular reports about how their office had shaken; how things had fallen on the floor; how they'd had to evacuate their buildings. It quickly became clear that the situation was far more serious. Tokyo had merely been rattled by the fourth most powerful earthquake ever recorded, its epicentre further north, near the city of Sendai. While relatively few died in the **Tōhoku earthquake** itself, more than 16,000 perished as a result of the giant **tsunami** that inundated the country's eastern shore – helicopter images showed a sickening black wave sweeping across villages, roads and farmland, effortlessly swallowing anything and everything in its path. Substantial damage was suffered by the Fukushima Daiichi nuclear power plant, whose swamped reactors went into meltdown.

The tsunami displaced more than 300,000 people, many of whom were left without power and water for some time. Serious questions were asked about the government's failure to control the situation; it also emerged that details regarding leaks from the power plant had been covered up, and an exclusion zone remains in place around it today. Tokyo's tourism figures also took a tumble, though these have since rebounded: the capital is located a safe distance from the stricken power plant, and its buildings are designed to withstand the powerful earthquakes which will always remain a fact of life in Japan.

1981	Late 1980s	1992	1995
Mario makes first appearance in Donkey Kong	Boom-time in Tokyo: the "bubble years"	Bursting of economic bubble	Sarin attack on Tokyo subway

2012, the 2020 application proved successful, with Tokyo beating off competition from Madrid and Istanbul.

Tokyo was not physically hit too hard by the gigantic **Tōhoku earthquake** of 2011 (see page 261), though tens of thousands of its residents fled for the relative security of western Japan, and many never returned. Unemployment also spiked, but has since eased to just over 3 percent. There has also been better news of late regarding Japan's famously low birth rates, which a few years ago had dropped to 1.26 but have now risen to a marginally more nuclear 1.44. However, the looming problem of an ageing population remains one of the biggest challenges facing Tokyo, and Japan as a whole; countries expecting a similar timebomb to go off further down the line will be watching avidly.

2002	**2012**	**2019**	**2020**
Hosting of the Rugby World Cup (with Samoa)	Completion of Tokyo Skytree	Tokyo hosts the Rugby World Cup, the first time it is held solely in Asia	Tokyo hosts Olympic Games for the second time

Books

A byword for transformation, change and tradition – and even, on occasion, "the Orient" itself – it's no surprise that Tokyo is so well represented on the literary scene. In addition, the overseas popularity of Japanese fiction has ballooned in recent decades, with certain writers now household names abroad. The following publishers specialize in English-language books on Japan, as well as translations of Japanese works: Kodansha (⊕kodanshausa. com); Tuttle (⊕tuttlepublishing.com); Stone Bridge Press (⊕stonebridge. com); and Vertical (⊕vertical-inc.com). Note that Japanese authors listed below follow the Japanese convention of placing the family name first. Titles marked with the ★ symbol are particularly recommended.

HISTORY

Ian Buruma *Inventing Japan*. Focuses on the period 1853–1964, during which Japan went from a feudal, isolated state to a powerhouse of the modern world economy. Buruma's *The Wages of Guilt* also skilfully explains how and why Germany and Japan have come to terms so differently with their roles in World War II.

John Dower *Embracing Defeat: Japan in the Aftermath of World War II*. This Pulitzer Prize winner offers an erudite and clear appraisal of the impact of the American occu-pation on Japan. First-person accounts and snappy writing bring the book alive.

Stephen Mansfield *Tokyo: A Biography*. This summary of Tokyo's history may veer towards the bombastic, but it's a very decent rundown of what the city has been through over the years, from samurai days to the 2011 'quake, via World War II.

Bill O'Reilly *Killing the Rising Sun*. O'Reilly is not exactly a renowned Japan expert, but for this latest of his "Killing" series (which includes *Killing Jesus*, *Killing Patton* and *Killing Reagan*) he teamed up with Martin Dugard to create this very readable, if extremely one-sided, account of the main acts of World War II's Pacific Theater.

★ **Richard Lloyd Parry** *Ghosts of the Tsunami*. The most interesting account of the 2011 earthquake, the tsunami that soon followed, and the horrific aftermath – a thorough yet intimate account of a truly epic tragedy.

Edward Seidensticker *A History of Tokyo 1867–1989*. The most recent offering from this leading translator of ancient and modern Japanese literature tells the story of Tokyo from the Edo to the Showa periods, and makes for fascinating reading.

ARTS, CULTURE AND SOCIETY

★ **Jake Adelstein** *Tokyo Vice*. With forensic thoroughness and gallows humour Adelstein documents his unsentimental education in crime reporting for the *Yomiuri Shimbun*, Japan's top-selling newspaper. His main scoop is about three *yakuza* heavyweights who sneaked into the US, with FBI approval, to get liver transplants. A true-crime classic.

Edmund de Waal *The Hare with Amber Eyes: a Hidden Inheritance*. The tale of a family heirloom – some netsuke carvings found in his uncle's Tokyo apartment – written by one of Britain's most famous contemporary ceramicists.

Hector Garcia *A Geek in Japan*. A good read for newbie Japanophiles itching to learn more about manga, anime or the eponymous otaku (Japanese geeks); it also includes information about Zen, tea ceremonies and the like, even though they're a bit of a mismatch given the aim at a younger crowd, though the newest revision (published 2019) at least makes sure that the rest is up-to-date.

Alex Kerr *Dogs and Demons*. A scathing and thought-provoking attack on Japan's economic, environmental

and social policies of the past decades, by someone who first came to Japan as a child in the 1960s and has been fascinated by the country ever since. Also worth reading is his earlier book *Lost Japan*.

Gunji Masakatsu *Kabuki*. Excellent introduction to kabuki, if a little hard to track down these days, by one of the leading connoisseurs of Japanese drama, illustrated with copious annotated photos of the great actors and the most dramatic moments in kabuki theatre.

Shinzo Satomi *Sushi Chef Sukiyabashi Jiro*. The titular restaurant rocketed to fame after being featured in 2011 documentary *Jiro Dreams of Sushi*, culminating in a 2014 visit by Barack Obama. In this short book, star chef Ono Jiro talks about sushi, rather than dreaming of it, and his insights are quite absorbing. (Incidentally, Jiro's restaurant is not featured in this guide, since it's way too hard to get a reservation, but his son's place is; see page 165.)

Joan Stanley-Baker *Japanese Art*. Highly readable introduction to the broad range of Japan's artistic traditions

HARUKI MURAKAMI

One of Japan's most entertaining and translated contemporary writers, **Haruki Murakami** (ⓦharukimurakami.com) has been hailed as a postwar successor to the great novelists Mishima, Kawabata and Tanizaki, and talked of as a future Nobel laureate. Many of Murakami's books are set in Tokyo, drawing on his time studying at Waseda University in the early 1970s and running a jazz bar in Kokubunji, a place that became a haunt for literary types and, no doubt, provided inspiration for his jazz-bar-running hero in the bittersweet novella *South of the Border, West of the Sun*.

The de facto introduction to Murakami is *Norwegian Wood*, a book about the tender coming-of-age love of two students, which has sold over five million copies. The truly bizarre *A Wild Sheep Chase* and its follow-up *Dance Dance Dance* are funny but unsettling modern-day fables, dressed up as detective novels. Considered among his best works are *The Wind-Up Bird Chronicle*, a hefty yet dazzling cocktail of mystery, war reportage and philosophy, and the surreal *Kafka on the Shore*, a murder story in which cats talk to people and fish rain from the sky.

After Dark, set in the dead of Tokyo night, has all the usual Murakami trademark flourishes, from quirky characters to metaphysical speculation; while his mega-opus *1Q84*, a complex tale of cults and assassins set in 1984, unravels over three volumes totalling more than 1600 pages.

(though excluding theatre and music), tracing their development from prehistoric to modern times.

Robert Twigger *Angry White Pyjamas*. The subtitle "An Oxford poet trains with the Tokyo riot police" gives you the gist. Twigger provides an intense forensic account of the daily trials, humiliations and triumphs of becoming a master of aikido.

Robert Whiting *Tokyo Underworld*. This well-researched tale follows the ups and downs of Nick Zapapetti, a larger-than-life Italian-American who arrived with the occupying forces in 1945 and stayed on to become "the king of Roppongi" and Tokyo's Mafia boss. In the process, Whiting also charts the history of the *yakuza* in postwar Japan.

GUIDES AND REFERENCE BOOKS

Thomas F. Judge and Tomita Hiroyuki *Edo Craftsmen*. Beautifully produced portraits of some of the traditional craftsmen still working in the backstreets of Tokyo. A timely insight into a disappearing world.

Brian MacDuckston *Ramen at Home*. Now here's a challenge: this readable book may allow you to prove to yourself that good ramen doesn't only exist in restaurants. Good luck!

Ono Tadashi and Harris Salat *Japanese Soul Cooking*. Cookbook focusing on Japanese comfort food, such as

tempura, *tonkatsu*, curry, ramen and more.

Mark Robinson *Izakaya: The Japanese Pub Cookbook*. A beautifully illustrated celebration of some of the author's favourite Tokyo-based *izakaya*, with over sixty recipes for their rustic food.

Dominic Roskrow *Whisky Japan*. Japanese whisky is gaining an ever-better international reputation (one won the *Whisky Bible*'s prestigious annual award in 2013), and this handy guide will help you sort your Nikka Yoichi from your Yamazaki Single Malts.

JAPANESE FICTION

Kirino Natsuo *Out*. Four women working in a bentō factory just outside Tokyo discover that committing murder is both easier and much more complicated than they could ever have imagined, in this dark, superior thriller that mines a very dark seam of Japan's underbelly. Follow-up books are *Grotesque*, about the deaths of two Tokyo prostitutes, and *Real World*, a grim thriller about alienated Japanese teenagers.

Mishima Yukio *Spring Snow*. Novelist Mishima sealed his notoriety by committing ritual suicide after leading a failed military coup in 1970, leaving behind a highly respectable body of work, including *After the Banquet, Forbidden Colours* and *The Sea of Fertility. Spring Snow* is the most Tokyo-centric of his novels, part of it being set here in 1912.

★ **Murakami Haruki** *Norwegian Wood* and *After Dark*. Two Tokyo-based novels from the pen of one of Japan's most famous writers (see page 264).

★ **Murakami Ryū** *Coin Locker Babies* and *In the Miso Soup*. Murakami burst onto Japan's literary scene in the mid-1980s with *Almost Transparent Blue*, a disturbing tale of student life mixing reality and fantasy. *Coin Locker Babies* is his most ambitious work, spinning a revenger's tragedy about the lives of two boys dumped as babies in adjacent coin lockers, while *In the Miso Soup* is a superior thriller along the lines of *American Psycho*, set in Tokyo.

Various *The Book of Tokyo: a City in Short Fiction*. There are few translated anthologies of Japanese short stories, but this is an excellent series of Tokyo-centric shorts from

several acclaimed Japanese writers, including Banana Yoshimoto, Hideo Furukawa and Hiromi Kawakami.
Yu Miri *Tokyo Ueno Station*. Excellent novel from the pen of an inventive Korean-Japanese writer, telling the story of a homeless man who haunts Ueno Park after his death at the adjacent metro station.

TOKYO IN FOREIGN FICTION

★ **Alan Brown** *Audrey Hepburn's Neck*. Beneath this rib-tickling, acutely observed tale of a young guy from the sticks adrift in big-city Tokyo are several important themes, including the continuing impact of World War II and the confused relationships between the Japanese and *gaijin*.

William Gibson *Idoru*. Love in the age of the computer chip. Cyberpunk novelist Gibson's sci-fi vision of Tokyo's high-tech future – a world of non-intrusive DNA checks at airports and computerized pop icons (the *idoru* of the title) – rings disturbingly true. The hip thriller *Pattern Recognition* is also partly set in Tokyo.

★ **David Mitchell** *Ghostwritten* and *number9dream*. Mitchell made a splash with his debut *Ghostwritten*, a dazzling collection of interlocked short stories, a couple of which were set in Japan. *number9dream*, shortlisted for the Booker prize in 2001, conjures up a postmodern Japan of computer hackers, video games, gangsters and violence.

David Peace *Tokyo Year Zero* and *Occupied City*. The first two instalments in Peace's crime trilogy set in Tokyo immediately after the end of World War II. Never an easy read, Peace's novels nonetheless impress some with their attention to detail, complex plots and compelling characters.

Film

Dazzlingly colourful, fetchingly otherworldly and indisputably unique, Tokyo has proved an irresistible location and subject matter for film-makers – Japanese and foreign alike – down the ages. Films marked with the ★ symbol are particularly recommended.

Adrift in Tokyo (*Tenten*; Satoshi Miki; 2007). A debt-ridden law student and a loan shark heavy bond in this quirky comedy drama that sees the unlikely pair stroll across the city meeting a cast of oddball characters along the way.

★ **Akira** (Ōtomo Katsuhiro; 1988). Still the most Tokyo-centric major anime, this is set in a newly rebuilt Neo-Tokyo during the run-up to the fictional 2019 Olympics (funny, they'd have got the date spot on if they'd looked at the Olympic schedule properly).

Babel (Alejandro González Iñárritu; 2006). The talented Mexican director nails contemporary Tokyo. There's a particularly beautiful sequence filmed at Shibuya club *Womb*. Oscar-nominated Kikuchi Rinko as the mute Chieko and her father, played by veteran actor Yakusho Kōji, are both outstanding.

★ **The Garden of Words** (Makoto Shinkai; 2013). Exquisitely presented anime, mostly set in Shinjuku Gyoen (see page 133), telling the story of a school-skipping teen's fateful encounter with an older lady.

Godzilla (*Gojira*; Honda Ishirō; 1954). The whole world knows how Tokyo turns out in this classic, which sees the eponymous monster stomp his way through intricately constructed scale models of the city – much of it was filmed on the volcano-island of Ōshima.

House of Bamboo (Samuel Fuller; 1955). Released only a decade after the end of World War II, this American film isn't a great classic, but it acts as a time capsule of a let's-be-friends-again era, perhaps best exemplified by an inter-racial romance that far predates John and Yoko.

Ichi the Killer (*Koroshiya Ichi*; Miike Takashi; 2001). Stand by for graphic depictions of bodies sliced in half in this *yakuza* tale set in Kabukichō, as told by the *enfant terrible* of Japanese cinema. Not for the squeamish.

★ **Let's Go!** (Tanuma Yuichi; 1967). This early vehicle for actor Kayama Yūzō provides a lovely dollop of 1960s Japan. Not only does he solve crimes and get the girls, but he's a star football player, and also the singer-songwriter-guitarist of a popular band – take that, James Bond.

Like Someone in Love (Abbas Kiarostami; 2013). A great piece from the famed Iranian director, detailing the life of a young woman selling her body to pay her way through university.

Lost in Translation (Sofia Coppola; 2003). Memorable performances from Bill Murray and Scarlett Johansson in this stylish romantic drama set in and around Shinjuku's *Park Hyatt* hotel. Brilliantly captures what it's like to be a clueless *gaijin* adrift in Tokyo.

★ **Stray Dog** (*Nora Inu*; Kurosawa Akira; 1949). Not the most famous work from Japan's most famous director (who made his name with *Seven Samurai*, which begat *The Magnificent Seven*), but this gritty film noir is still up there with the best, following a cop as he chases a killer around sweaty summertime Tokyo.

Tampopo (Itami Jūzō; 1985). Tampopo, the proprietress of a noodle bar, is taught how to prepare the perfect ramen, in this comedy about Japan's gourmet boom. From the old woman squishing fruit in a supermarket to the gangster and his moll passing a raw egg sexily between their mouths, this is a film packed with memorable scenes.

Tokyo! (Michel Gondry, Bong Joon-ho & Leos Carax; 2009). Two French and one Korean director each provide their own distinctive takes on the shape-shifting megalopolis in this omnibus triptych.

Tokyo Godfathers (Kon Satoshi; 2003). This heart-warming Christmas fairy tale of redemption for three tramps and the baby they discover in the trash is pure anime magic.

Tokyo Sonata (Kurosawa Kiyoshi; 2008). When a father decides to keep it secret from his family that he's lost his job it has all kinds of repercussions in this bleak, satirical drama – a prize winner at Cannes – that's reflective of contemporary Japanese society.

★ **Tokyo Story** (*Tōkyō Monogatari*; Ozu Yasujirō; 1954). An elderly couple travel to Tokyo to visit their children and grandchildren. The only person who has any time for them is the widow of their son who was killed in the war. Ozu's themes of loneliness and the breakdown of tradition are grim, but his simple approach and the sincerity of the acting make the film a genuine classic.

Tokyo Tribe (Sion Sono; 2014). As with any other Sion Sono production, you're either going to love or hate this hip-hop *yakuza* opera. Just like *Tommy* or anything similar, the storyline is more incidental than the music, but some will find it a fun watch.

You Only Live Twice (Lewis Gilbert; 1967). A retro look at the city as Sean Connery, in his fifth outing as Bondo-san, grapples with arch-enemy Blofeld and sundry Japanese villains. Cool gadgets include a mini-helicopter in a suitcase (with rocket launchers, of course).

The arts, architecture and design

Tokyo isn't just the contemporary art capital of Japan – it has the biggest art scene of any Asian city (though Beijing is catching up fast). Innumerable galleries provide a window into a fascinating scene that's still relatively little known in the Western world – perhaps bar the manga comics lining the shelves of every convenience store. If the stage is more your thing, there are also plenty of local forms of performance to enjoy, from stylized nō to vibrant kabuki. The city offers a brilliant showcase of contemporary design, too. Concrete-and-glass buildings that double as enormous public sculptures or electronic art screens; fashions, consumer gadgets and household goods that could be – and often are – exhibits in galleries; striking blasts of elegant graphics and eye-grabbing visuals on practically every corner: all are part of the city's dazzling visual appeal.

Visual arts

Some of the oldest evidence of human habitation in Japan is artistic in nature: stylized **pottery** dating back millennia to the Jōmon period (see page 255) can be seen at a number of museums in Tokyo, as well as **ceramics** and **bells** from the Yayoi, who were based in what is now the Japanese capital from around 350 BC. Many of the traditional arts fostered in Japan since then can trace their lineage back to **China**, including Buddhist sculpture, oil paintings and even elements now thought of as quintessentially Japanese, including folding screens and calligraphy.

Shitamachi art

A more local aesthetic emerged from the seventeenth century with the burgeoning popularity of **ukiyo-e** woodblock prints and paintings. Some illustrated historical scenes and folk tales, and others flora and fauna, but perhaps most interesting for visitors to Tokyo are those that depict **Shitamachi** (Tokyo's old working-class quarter), giving an illuminating insight into the birth of sumo, kabuki and other gems spawned by the *hoi polloi* of yore. Whimsical views of **nature** were also popular: Mount Fuji's near-symmetrical cone became a regular *ukiyo-e* feature, and also made a guest appearance in Hokusai's *The Great Wave off Kanagawa*, created circa 1830 and still one of the most famous "Eastern" pictures in the West.

After the restoration

Hokusai's cracking tsunami-like wave did not, however, cause any ripples outside Japan for around thirty years; the country was, at the time, essentially closed to the wider world until the Meiji Restoration of 1868 (see page 259). After Japan's opening up, artists were foremost among those itching for knowledge of **Western culture**, and ideas and styles raced back and forth between Tokyo and Europe; Manet, Monet, van Gogh and Gauguin were among those who came to employ elements of "Japonisme" in their work. Almost inevitably, a chasm developed in Japanese art between European-influenced creators, and those determined to hang onto the traditional forms; with near-equal predictability, many in the latter school (known as **nihonga**) did eventually come to use things like shading and perspective in their work, while keeping things local in style.

To the modern day

This fusion was also evident in the work of the greatest artistic catalyst of recent years: **Murakami Takashi** – often referred to as Japan's own Andy Warhol – who rose to prominence in the 1990s. Famed for creating the "Superflat" genre, his blending of *nihonga* and Western-style pop art isn't to everyone's taste, but it suddenly made the wider world sit up and take notice of Japanese art again – and, perhaps more importantly, inspired a whole legion of local youngsters to give art a go. Also highly notable are the instantly recognisable, polka-dotted works – many now world-famous – of **Kusama Yayoi**, a contemporary of Warhol.

Talented artists who have cemented their reputations in recent years include **Chiho Aoshima**, a Superflat protege known for her fantastical urban landscapes (and, less interestingly, figures); **Chiharu Shiota**, a performance/installation artist who represented Japan at the 2015 Venice Biennale and then wowed Berlin Art Week the next year; **Makoto Aida**, who welds together manga, painting, video, sculpture, photography and more (find some of his work at the Museum of Contemporary Art; see page 102); **Jun Inoue**, a street artist who brings elements of ancient calligraphy to his graffiti; and **Tabaimo**, who created interesting video installations reflecting modern life, but has more recently focused on ghostly creations using a printing technique called monotyping. Notable art collectives include the occasionally controversial **Chim-Pom**, influenced by the aforementioned Makoto Aida; and the youthful **teamLAB**, a savvy business operation who were behind the creation of the phenomenally successful Mori Digital Art Museum (see page 104).

Manga

In Japan all types of cartoons, from comic strips to graphic novels to magazines, are known as **manga**, while animation is called **anime**. International reception of the medium can be clouded by the graphic sexual imagery and violence seen in some manga, compounded by the misconception that the subject matter is exclusively limited to sci-fi and fantasy. In reality, manga covers an enormous range of stories, from cooking to politics, and has many genres – for example, *manga-shi* (magazines) aimed at young people are split into *shōjo* (girls), *shōnen* (boys) and *seinen* (youth) categories.

The bestselling manga **magazine** is *Shūkan Shōnen Jump* (Ⓦviz.com/shonenjump. com), which once sold over six million copies a week – in these digital days it's down to a "mere" 1.7 million. Strips from this and other magazines are collected in **graphic-novel** style books (known as *tankōbon*), which come in several volumes. There are also *dōjinshi* – **amateur manga**, often with sexual themes, that are produced by fans. These works sometimes emulate the originals so faithfully that it's hard to tell them apart.

Performing arts

The traditional theatre arts of **nō**, **bunraku**, **kabuki** and **buyō** evolved in the context of broader cultural developments during different periods of Japan's history.

ART AROUND TOKYO

Tokyo has long boasted Asia's most vibrant art scene, and galleries in the city are listed throughout the Guide. These include **major venues** such as the National Art Center (see page 102), Mori Art Museum (see page 104) and the Museum of Contemporary Art (see page 84), but it's also fascinating to explore the city's many **commercial galleries**, make a few discoveries of your own and maybe even buy something. Ginza (see page 56) and Roppongi (see page 101) have the greatest concentrations of galleries.

The **Art Fair Tokyo** (Ⓦartfairtokyo.com) takes place each April, and brings together around one hundred galleries, with a strong focus on contemporary work. In between times, check out **Tokyo Art Beat** (Ⓦtokyoartbeat.com) for exhibition listings and interesting features on the city's art scene.

HUNTING DOWN THE STARCHITECTS

Andō Tadao Most of Andō's designs (especially his formative projects) were realized out west in his home region of Kansai, but the architect – famed for his less-is-more decorative aesthetic – has worked on a handful of buildings in Tokyo. As well as designing several ateliers in Shibuya, he landed a major Tokyo project with Omotesandō Hills (see page 120), before collaborating on Tokyo Midtown's 21_21 Design Sight gallery (see page 102) alongside fashion icon Issey Miyake, and product designers Fukasawa Naoto and Satoh Taku.

Kengo Kuma Although recently kept busy in the anything-goes architectural playground of Beijing, Kuma hailed from close to Tokyo, and some of his best work can be seen in the city, including the shrine at Akagi-jinja (see page 144), the acclaimed Nezu Museum (see page 120), the Suntory Museum of Art (see page 102) and Asakusa's quirky Culture and Sightseeing Centre (see page 74).

Tange Kenzō It's incredible how modern and daring Tange's iconic 1960s Yoyogi National Gymnasium (see page 122) and St Mary's Cathedral (see page 141) still look beside his late-career Tokyo Metropolitan Government Building (see page 129) and Fuji TV building (see page 94) – two structures that could have been ripped from the pages of a sci-fi manga. Although he died in 2005, the practice that Tange founded is also responsible for one of Tokyo's most recent "wow" structures: the cool, sleek **Mode Gakuen Cocoon Tower** (see page 130), duly dubbed the 2008 Skyscraper of the Year by the prestigious Emporis.

Frank Lloyd Wright Okay, so *Furanku Roido Raito* wasn't Japanese, but a clutch of his buildings live on in Tokyo, most pertinently the Myonichi-kan (see page 137). The *Imperial Hotel* that he designed so lovingly has been replaced with something more modern, but hints survive in the on-site *Old Imperial Bar* (see page 179).

Nō

The oldest – and most difficult to appreciate – type of Japanese theatre is **nō**. This form of masked drama has its roots in sacred Shinto dances, but was formalized six hundred years ago under the patronage of the Ashikaga shoguns and the aesthetic influence of Zen. The bare wooden stage with its painted backdrop, the actors' stylized robes and the fixed expressions of the finely crafted masks create an atmosphere that is both understated and refined. The dramatic contrasts of stillness and sudden rushes of movement, and of periods of silence punctuated by sound, conjure up the essence of the Zen aesthetic.

The comic **kyōgen** interludes in a nō programme provide light relief. As in the main drama, *kyōgen* performers are all male and assume a variety of roles, some of which are completely independent of the nō play, while others comment on the development of the main story. The language used is colloquial (though of sixteenth-century origin) and, compared with the esoteric poetry of nō, far more accessible to a contemporary audience.

Kabuki

Colourful, exuberant and full of larger-than-life characters, **kabuki** is a highly stylized theatrical form which delights in flamboyant gestures and elaborate costumes, make-up and staging effects. While the language may still be incomprehensible to foreigners, the plots themselves deal with easily understood, often tragic themes of love and betrayal.

Kabuki originated in the early 1600s as rather **risqué dances** performed by all-female troupes, but today kabuki actors are predominantly older men, some of whom specialize in performing female roles (*onnagata*). To learn more about kabuki, go to ⓦkabuki21.com and ⓦkabukiweb.net.

Bunraku

Japan's puppet theatre, **bunraku**, developed out of the *jōruri* storytelling of travelling minstrels, and was adapted to the stage in the early seventeenth century. Stylized **puppets**, one-half to one-third the size of humans, are worked by three operators, while a chanter tells the story to the accompaniment of *shamisen* (three-stringed guitar) music. The skill of the puppeteers – the result of lengthy apprenticeships – contributes to the high degree of **realism** in the performance, and the stylized movements can result in great drama. To learn more about *bunraku*, go to ⓦbunraku.or.jp.

Buyō
Classical Japanese dance is known as **buyō** and originates from the folk and ritual dances of ancient Japan. Dancers usually wear kimono, and as a result their graceful movements are slow and restricted.

Architecture
There has seldom been much of a grand plan to Tokyo's built environment, which has resulted in the city's cluttered, ad hoc look. However, the capital's great wealth and relative lack of planning restrictions have given architects almost unparalleled freedom to realize their wildest dreams. A fascinating time can be spent tracing the capital's modern evolution through its buildings, many designed by local luminaries. Japan has also provided more winners of the Pritzker Prize, the architecture world's most prestigious accolade, than any other nation – Tange Kenzō and Andō Tadao (see page 270, for more on these two), Maki Fumihiko, Sejima Kazuyo and Nishizawa Ryūe (of practice SANAA), Itō Toyō and Shigeru Ban, as well as the most recent Japanese recipient (2019), Arata Isozaki.

Ginza is a prime district to see cutting-edge architecture: **Itō Toyō**'s Mikimoto Ginza 2 building (see page 204) serves as a good example, as does the fantastic Hermes building. Ginza is also a local hub of **graphic design**, curated in a collection of small galleries (see page 56).

Recent developments have seen the city take a bit of a step back. Locals have been unimpressed by the ugly **Tokyo Skytree** – completed in 2011 along ostensibly "traditional" lines – and the boxy Shibuya Hikarie building which went up the following year. In 2013 protests followed the release of Iraqi-born Zaha Hadid's **2020 Olympic stadium** design (see page 123), and the government duly announced its replacement with a cheaper design by Kengo Kuma (see page 270).

Design
In Tokyo's **home furnishing** and **interior design** shops you can find iconic products such as Yanagi Sori's butterfly stool and cutlery collection, or Isamu Noguchi's paper lantern lamps, as well as new instant classics by rising local and overseas talents. Also acting as top design galleries are **"select shops"** (boutiques) such as *Cibone* in Aoyama (see page 208) and Do at the *Claska* hotel (see page 149), or the gift shop of the National Art Center, Tokyo (see page 102), all of which carry a meticulously curated range

---

DESIGNING THE FUTURE

To discover the absolute bleeding edge of Japanese design, time your trip to coincide with **Tokyo Design Week** (Oct/Nov), which has been going, and growing, since 1985. Aoyama, Roppongi and the outer grounds of Meiji Jingū are the focus for the annual whirlwind of events, exhibitions and installations that take place in giant tents and container crates as well as galleries and shops. Sampling the future is part of what TDW is all about, which makes for a lot of shows that tend toward the experimental rather than the commercial.

Even more anarchic and colourful are the biannual **Design Festa** events (May & Nov/Dec; see page 26). If you don't happen to be in town for one of them you can get a very good idea of the kinds of bizarre and beautiful things they can throw up by visiting the permanent **Design Festa Gallery** tucked away in Harajuku's backstreets (see page 120).

KINGS AND QUEENS OF THE CATWALK

Together with London and New York, Tokyo forms part of global fashion's holy trinity, acting as a magnet to clothing designers from all over Japan, many of whom have made their name here. Designers from overseas, too, often use Tokyo as an incubator or laboratory for their wilder ideas.

Nicola Formichetti Though he may not sound Japanese, Formichetti was born to a Japanese mother (and Italian father) and raised in Tokyo. He worked as fashion director for Uniqlo (see page 204), and has also been involved with Diesel and *Vogue*, plus as a personal stylist for Lady Gaga.

Jun Ashida Practical yet elegant, an incredible amount of attention goes into Ashida's designs, which have been worn by members of the royal family, as well as political leaders. His daughter Tae is also busily making a name for herself, and you can browse clothing from both designers at the Jun Ashida flagship store in Daikanyama (see page 204).

Yohji Yamamoto A big name since the 1970s, Yamamoto's designs (see page 205) tend to be timeless black-and-white numbers. He also designs clothing for major ballet companies, and sometimes even the sets themselves.

Rei Kawakubo A Tokyo native, Kawakubo was the driving force behind Comme des Garçons (see page 205), carving out a niche with designs that refused to kowtow to the general notions of body shape. Junya Watanabe, a one-time protégé, has also made it big.

Issey Miyake Still one of the big hitters after all these years, his flagship store in Aoyama (see page 205) has merely acted as the centre of a hub whose nodes have touched on museum exhibitions, theatre work and one of the world's best-selling perfume ranges.

of items, sometimes with displays highlighting the creators behind each product. If you're in the Tokyo Midtown area, you can browse an upscale branch of homeware and fashion emporium *Muji* (see page 207), as well as other contemporary Japan-focused interior design stores such as Design Hub (Ⓦdesignhub.jp).

Spare a moment also to admire the shopping environment itself. Some of the most eye-catching – and globally influential – **store designs** come courtesy of design agency Wonderwall (Ⓦwonder-wall.com). These include Bapexclusive in Aoyama (see page 204), with its sushi-inspired conveyor belt for sneakers, and recycled goods emporium Pass the Baton (see page 207). Other designers reference traditional design in creative new ways – witness the elegant gifts and packaging on display in the retail sections of tea and Japanese sweet café *Higashiya* (see page 176) and its offshoots, which are themselves beautifully designed spaces.

Japan publishes some of the world's most beautiful **design and culture magazines**, and they make for great primers on places you might want to see or things you might want to buy in Tokyo. Don't worry if your Japanese isn't up to scratch: popular titles like *Casa Brutus*, *Brutus*, *PEN* and *Real Design* tend to accentuate the visuals, while others such as *AXIS*, *+81* and *Kateigahō International* (available as a digital magazine at Ⓦint.kateigaho.com) are bilingual or fully English.

Lastly, the district of **Akihabara** deserves a special mention as an integral part of the city's contemporary design landscape; its stores are packed with the colourful output of Japan's manga, anime, toy and computer game industries.

Japanese

Picking up a few words of Japanese is not difficult. Pronunciation is simple and standard and there are few exceptions to the straightforward grammar rules. With just a little effort you should be able to read the words spelled out in *hiragana* and *katakana*, Japanese phonetic characters, even if you can't understand them. And any time spent learning Japanese will be amply rewarded by delighted locals, who'll always politely comment on your fine linguistic ability.

However, it takes a very great effort to master Japanese. The primary stumbling block is the thousands of **kanji** characters (Chinese ideograms) that need to be memorized, all of which have at least two pronunciations (often many, many more), depending on the sentence and their combination with other characters. Also tricky is the language's multiple levels of **politeness**, married with different sets of words used by men and women, as well as different **dialects** to deal with, involving whole new vocabularies.

Japanese characters

Japanese is written in a combination of three systems. To be able to read a newspaper, you'll need to know around two thousand *kanji*, much more difficult than it sounds, since what each one means varies with its context.

The easier writing systems to pick up are the phonetic syllabaries, **hiragana** and **katakana**. Both have 46 regular characters (see opposite) and can be learned within a couple of weeks. *Hiragana* is used for Japanese words, while *katakana*, with the squarer characters, is used mainly for "loan words" borrowed from other languages (especially English) and technical names. **Rōmaji** (see opposite), the roman script used to spell out Japanese words, is also used in advertisements and magazines.

The first five letters in *hiragana* and *katakana* (**a, i, u, e, o**) are the vowel sounds (see "Pronunciation", page 274). The remainder are a combination of a consonant and a vowel (eg **ka, ki, ku, ke, ko**), with the exception of **n**, the only consonant that exists on its own. While *hiragana* provides an exact phonetic reading of all Japanese words, *katakana* does not do the same for foreign loan words. Often words are abbreviated, hence "television" becomes *terebi* and "sexual harassment" *sekuhara*. Sometimes, they become almost unrecognizable, as with *kakutēru* (cocktail).

Traditionally, Japanese is written in vertical columns and read right to left. However, the Western way of writing from left to right, horizontally from top to bottom is increasingly common (though page-wise, books and magazines are usually read "backwards" from a Western perspective). In the media and on signs you'll see a mixture of the two ways of writing.

Grammar

In Japanese **verbs** do not change according to the person or number, so that *ikimasu* can mean "I go", "he/she/it goes", or "we/they go". **Pronouns** are usually omitted, since it's generally clear from the context who or what the speaker is referring to. There are no **definite articles**, and **nouns** stay the same whether they refer to singular or plural words.

Compared to English grammar, Japanese **sentences** are structured back to front. An English-speaker would say "I am going to Tokyo" which in Japanese would translate directly as "Tokyo to going". Placing the sound "*ka*" at the end of a verb indicates a **question**, hence *Tokyo e ikimasu-ka* means "Are you going to Tokyo?" There are also

HIRAGANA AND KATAKANA

Hiragana and *katakana* are two phonetic syllabaries represented by the characters shown below. *Katakana*, the squarer characters in the first table, are used for writing foreign "loan words". The rounder characters in the bottom table, *hiragana*, are used for Japanese words, in combination with, or as substitutes for, *kanji*.

KATAKANA

a ア	i イ	u ウ	e エ	o オ
ka カ	ki キ	ku ク	ke ケ	ko コ
sa サ	shi シ	su ス	se セ	so ソ
ta タ	chi チ	tsu ツ	te テ	to ト
na ナ	ni ニ	nu ヌ	ne ネ	no ノ
ha ハ	hi ヒ	fu フ	he ヘ	ho ホ
ma マ	mi ミ	mu ム	me メ	mo モ
ya ヤ		yu ユ		yo ヨ
ra ラ	ri リ	ru ル	re レ	ro ロ
wa ワ				wo ヲ
n ン				

HIRAGANA

a あ	i い	u う	e え	o お
ka か	ki き	ku く	ke け	ko こ
sa さ	shi し	su す	se せ	so そ
ta た	chi ち	tsu つ	te て	to と
na な	ni に	nu ぬ	ne ね	no の
ha は	hi ひ	fu ふ	he へ	ho ほ
ma ま	mi み	mu む	me め	mo も
ya や		yu ゆ		yo よ
ra ら	ri り	ru る	re れ	ro ろ
wa わ				wo を
n ん				

levels of **politeness** to contend with, which alter the way the verb is conjugated, and sometimes change the word entirely. Stick to the polite *-masu* form of verbs and you should be fine.

The Rough Guide Japanese Phrasebook includes essential phrases and expressions, and a dictionary section and menu reader.

Pronunciation

Japanese words in this book have been transliterated into the standard Hepburn system of romanization, called **rōmaji**. Pronunciation is as follows:

a as in m**a**d

i as in macar**o**ni, or **ee**

u as in y**ou**, or **oo**

e as in b**e**d; pronounced even at the end of a word

o as in n**o**t

ae as in the two separate sounds, **ah-eh**

ai as in Th**ai**

ei as in w**ei**ght

ie as in two separate sounds, **ee-eh**

ue as in two separate sounds, **oo-eh**

g, a hard sound as in **g**irl

s as in ma**s**s (never z)

y as in **y**et

A bar (macron) over a vowel or "ii" means that the vowel sound is twice as long as a vowel without a bar. Only where words are well known in English, such as Tokyo, Kyoto, judo and shogun, have we not used a bar to indicate long vowel sounds. Sometimes, vowel sounds are shortened or softened; for example, the verb *desu* sounds more like *dess* when pronounced, and *sukiyaki* like *skiyaki*. Some syllables are also softened or hardened by the addition of a small ° or " above the character; for example, **ka** (か) becomes **ga** (が) and **ba** (ば) becomes **pa** (ぱ). Likewise a smaller case ya, yu or yo following a character alters its sound, such as **kya** (きゃ) and **kyu** (きゅ). Lastly, double consonants (as in *kippu*, meaning ticket) require a momentary pause similar to a glottal stop; when you see "tch" (as in *matcha*, meaning powdered green tea) pronounce it as a double c.

Useful words and phrases

PERSONAL PRONOUNS

I Watashi 私

I (familiar, men only) Boku ぼく

You Anata あなた

You (familiar) Kimi きみ

He Kare 彼

She Kanojo 彼女

We Watashi-tachi 私たち

You (plural) Anata-tachi あなたたち

They (male/female) Karera/Kanojo-tachi 彼ら/彼女たち

They (objects) Sorera それら

BASIC COMMUNICATIONS

Yes Hai はい

No Lie/Chigaimasu いいえ/違います

OK Daijōbu/Ōkē 大丈夫/オーケー

Please (offering something) Dōzo どうぞ

Please (asking for something) Onegai shimasu お願いします

Excuse me Sumimasen/Shitsurei shimasu すみません/失礼します

I'm sorry Gomen nasai/Sumimasen ごめんなさい/すみません

Thanks (informal) Dōmo どうも

Thank you Arigatō ありがとう

Thank you very much Dōmo arigatō gozaimasu どうもありがとうございます

What? Nani? なに

When? Itsu? いつ

Where? Doko? どこ

Who? Dare? だれ

This Kore これ

That Sore それ

That (over there) Are あれ

How many? Ikutsu? いくつ

How much? Ikura? いくら

I want (x) (x) ga hoshii desu (x)が欲しいです

I don't want (x) (x) ga irimasen (x)がいりません

Is it possible …? … koto ga dekimasu ka … ことができますか

Is it …? … desu ka …ですか

Can you please help me? Tetsudatte kuremasen ka 手伝ってくれませんか

I can't speak Japanese Nihongo ga hanasemasen 日本語が話せません

I can't read Japanese Nihongo ga yomemasen 日本語が読めません

Can you speak English? Eigo ga dekimasu ka 英語ができますか

Is there someone who can interpret? Tsūyaku wa imasu ka 通訳はいますか

Could you please speak more slowly? Motto yukkuri hanashite kuremasen ka もっとゆっくり話してくれませんか

Could you say that again please? Mō ichido itte kuremasen ka もう一度言ってくれませんか

I understand/I see Wakarimasu/Naruhodo 分かります/なるほど

I don't understand Wakarimasen 分かりません

What does this mean? Kore wa dōiu imi desu ka これはどういう意味ですか

How do you say (x) in Japanese? Nihongo de (x) o nan-te iimasu ka 日本語で(x)を何て言いますか

What's this called? Kore wa nan-to iimasu ka これは何と言いますか

How do you pronounce this character? Kono kanji wa nan-te yomimasu ka この漢字は何て読みますか

Please write in English/Japanese Eigo/Nihongo de kaite kudasai 英語/日本語で書いてください

GREETINGS AND BASIC COURTESIES

Hello/Good day Konnichiwa 今日は

Good morning Ohayō gozaimasu おはようございます

Good evening Konbanwa 今晩は

Good night (when leaving) Osaki ni お先に

Good night (when going to bed) Oyasuminasai お休みなさい

How are you? O-genki desu ka お元気ですか

I'm fine Genki desu 元気です

I'm fine, thanks Okagesama de おかげさまで

How do you do/Nice to meet you Hajimemashite はじめまして

Don't mention it/you're welcome Dō itashimashite どういたしまして

I'm sorry Gomen nasai ごめんなさい

Just a minute please Chotto matte kudasai ちょっと待ってください

What's your name? Shitsurei desu ga o-namae wa 失礼ですがお名前は

My name is (x) Namae wa (x) desu 名前は(x)です

Goodbye Sayonara/Sayōnara さよなら/さようなら

Goodbye (informal) Dewa mata/Jā ne では又/じゃあね

CHITCHAT

Where are you from? O-kuni wa doko desu ka お国はどこですか

Britain Eikoku/Igirisu 英国/イギリス

Ireland Airurando アイルランド

America Amerika アメリカ

Australia Ōsutoraria オーストラリア

Canada Kanada カナダ

New Zealand Nyū Jiirando ニュージーランド

Japan Nihon 日本

How old are you? O-ikutsu desu ka おいくつですか

I am (x) years old (x) sai desu (x) 際です

Are you married? Kekkon shite imasu ka 結婚していますか

I am married/not married Kekkon shite imasu/imasen 結婚しています/いません

Do you like ...? ... suki desu ka 好きですか

I like ... suki desu …好きです

I don't like ... suki dewa arimasen …好きではありません

What's your job? O-shigoto wa nan desu ka お仕事は何ですか

I work for a company Kaishain desu 会社員です

I'm a tourist Kankō kyaku desu 観光客です

Really? (informal) Hontō 本当

It can't be helped (informal) Shikata ga nai (formal)/ Shō ga nai (informal) 仕方がない/しょうがない

NUMBERS, TIME AND DATES

There are special ways of **counting** different things in Japanese. The most common first translation is used when counting time and quantities and measurements, with added qualifiers such as minutes (*pun/fun*) or yen (*en*). The second translations are sometimes used for counting objects. From ten, there is only one set of numbers. For four, seven and nine, alternatives to the first translation are used in some circumstances.

Zero Zero/rei 0/零

One Ichi 一 Hitotsu ひとつ

Two Ni 二 Futatsu ふたつ

Three San 三 Mittsu みっつ

Four Yon/Shi 四 Yottsu よっつ

Five Go 五 Itsutsu いつつ

Six Roku 六 Muttsu むっつ

Seven Shichi/Nana 七 Nanatsu ななつ

Eight Hachi 八 Yattsu やっつ

Nine Kyū 九 Kokonotsu ここのつ

Ten Jū 十 Tō とう

Eleven Jū-ichi 十一

Twelve Jū-ni 十二

Twenty Ni-jū 二十

Twenty-one Ni-jū-ichi 二十一

Thirty San-jū 三十

One hundred Hyaku 百

Two hundred Ni-hyaku 二百

Thousand Sen 千

Ten thousand Ichi-man 一万

One hundred thousand Jū-man 十万

One million Hyaku-man 百万

One hundred million Ichi-oku 一億

TIME AND DATES

Now Ima 今

Today Kyō 今日

Morning Asa 朝

Evening Yūgata 夕方

Night Yoru/Ban 夜/晩

Tomorrow Ashita 明日

The day after tomorrow Asatte あさって

Yesterday Kinō 昨日

Week Shū 週

Month Getsu/Gatsu 月

Year Nen/Toshi 年

Monday Getsuyōbi 月曜日

Tuesday Kayōbi 火曜日

Wednesday Suiyōbi 水曜日

Thursday Mokuyōbi 木曜日

Friday Kin'yōbi 金曜日

Saturday Doyōbi 土曜日

Sunday Nichiyōbi 日曜日

What time is it? Ima nan-ji desu ka 今何時ですか

It's 10 o'clock Jū-ji desu 十時です

10.20 Jū-ji ni-juppun 十時二十分
10.30 Jū-ji han 十時半
10.50 Jū-ichi-ji juppun mae 十一時十分前

AM Gozen 午前
PM Gogo 午後

GETTING AROUND

Aeroplane Hikōki 飛行機
Airport Kūkō 空港
Bus Basu バス
Bus stop Basu tei バス停
Train Densha 電車
Station Eki 駅
Subway Chikatetsu 地下鉄
Ferry Ferii フェリー
Left-luggage office Ichiji azukarijo 一時預かり所
Coin locker Koin rokkā コインロッカー
Ticket Kippu 切符
Ticket office Kippu uriba 切符売り場
One-way Kata-michi 片道

Return Ōfuku 往復
Bicycle Jitensha 自転車
Taxi Takushii タクシー
Map Chizu 地図
Straight ahead Massugu まっすぐ
In front of Mae 前
Right Migi 右
Left Hidari 左
North Kita 北
South Minami 南
East Higashi 東
West Nishi 西

PLACES

Temple Otera/Odera/-ji/-in お寺/−寺/−院
Shrine Jinja/Jingū/-gū/-taisha 神社/神宮/−宮/−大社
Castle -jō 城
Park Kōen 公園
River Kawa/Gawa 川
Street Tōri/Dōri/Michi 通り/道
Bridge Hashi/Bashi 橋
Museum Hakubutsukan 博物館

Art gallery Bijutsukan 美術館
Garden Niwa/Teien/-en 庭/庭園/−園
Island Shima/-jima/-tō 島/−島
Hill Oka 丘
Mountain Yama/-san/-take 山/−山/−岳
Hot spring spa Onsen 温泉
Lake Mizu-umi/-ko 湖/−湖

ACCOMMODATION

Hotel Hoteru ホテル
Traditional-style inn Ryokan 旅館
Guesthouse Minshuku 民宿
Youth hostel Yūsu hosuteru ユースホステル
Single room Shinguru rūmu シングルルーム
Double room Daburu rūmu ダブルルーム
Twin room Tsuin rūmu ツインルーム
Dormitory Kyōdō/Ōbeya 共同/大部屋
Japanese-style room Washitsu 和室
Western-style room Yōshitsu 洋室
Western-style bed Beddo ベッド
Bath O-furo お風呂
Do you have any vacancies? Kūshitsu wa arimasu ka
空室はありますか
I'd like to make a reservation Yoyaku o shitai no desu
ga 予約をしたいのですが

I have a reservation Yoyaku shimashita 予約しました
I don't have a reservation Yoyaku shimasen deshita
予約しませんでした
How much is it per person? Hitori ikura desu ka
一人いくらですか
Does that include meals? Shokuji wa tsuite imasu ka
食事はついていますか
I would like to stay one night/two nights Hitoban/
Futaban tomaritai no desu ga
一晩/二晩泊まりたいのですが
I would like to see the room Heya o misete
kudasaimasen ka 部屋を見せてくださいませんか
Key Kagi 鍵
Passport Pasupōto パスポート

SHOPPING, MONEY AND BANKS

Shop Mise 店
How much is it? Kore wa ikura desu ka
これはいくらですか
It's too expensive Taka-sugimasu 高すぎます
Is there anything cheaper? Mō sukoshi yasui mono wa
arimasu ka もう少し安いものはありますか

Do you accept credit cards? Kurejitto kādo wa
tsukaemasu ka クレジットカードは使えますか
I'm just looking Miru dake desu 見るだけです
Foreign exchange Gaikoku-kawase
外国為替
Bank Ginkō 銀行

Travellers' cheque Toraberāzu chekku
トラベラーズチェック

Where is the nearest ATM? Ichiban chikai ATM wa doko desu ka 一番近いATMはどこですか

INTERNET, POST AND TELEPHONES

Internet Intānetto インターネット
Post office Yūbinkyoku 郵便局
Letter Tegami 手紙
Postcard Hagaki 葉書
Stamp Kitte 切手
Airmail Kōkūbin 航空便
Telephone Denwa 電話
International telephone call Kokusai-denwa
　国際電話

Reverse charge/collect call Korekuto-kōru
　コレクトコール
Telephone card Terefon kādo テレフォンカード
I would like to call (place) (place) e denwa o kaketai no desu (place) へ電話をかけたいのです
I would like to send a fax to (place) (place) e fakkusu shitai no desu (place) へファックスしたいのです
Telephone card Terefon kādo テレフォンカード

HEALTH

Hospital Byōin 病院
Pharmacy Yakkyoku 薬局
Medicine Kusuri 薬

Doctor Isha 医者
Dentist Haisha 歯医者
I'm ill Byōki desu 病気です

Food and drink

BASICS

Bar Nomiya 飲み屋
Standing-only bar Tachinomiya 立ちのみ屋
Café/coffee shop Kissaten 喫茶店
Cafeteria Shokudō 食堂
Pub Pabu パブ
Pub-style restaurant Izakaya 居酒屋
Restaurant Resutoran レストラン
Restaurant specializing in charcoal-grilled foods Robatayaki 炉端焼
Breakfast Asa-gohan 朝ご飯
Lunch Hiru-gohan 昼ご飯
Dinner Ban-gohan 晩ご飯
Boxed meal Bentō 弁当
Set meal Teishoku 定食

Daily special set meal Higawari-teishoku 日替り定食
Menu Menyū メニュー
Do you have an English menu? Eigo no menyū wa arimasu ka 英語のメニューはありますか
How much is that? Ikura desu ka いくらですか
I would like (a) … (a)… o onegai shimasu (a) をお願いします
May I have the bill? Okanjō o onegai shimasu お勘定をお願いします
I am a vegetarian Watashi wa bejitarian desu 私はベジタリアンです
Can I have it without meat? Niku nashi de onegai dekimasu ka 肉なしでお願いできますか

STAPLE FOODS

Bean curd tofu Tōfu 豆腐
Bread Pan パン
Butter Batā バター
Dried seaweed Nori のり
Egg Tamago 卵
Fermented soyabean paste Miso 味噌
Garlic Ninniku にんにく

Oil Abura 油
Pepper Koshō こしょう
Rice Gohan ご飯
Salt Shio 塩
Soy sauce Shōyu しょうゆ
Sugar Satō 砂糖

FRUITS AND VEGETABLES

Fruit Kudamono 果物
Apple Ringo りんご
Banana Banana バナナ
Grapefruit Gurēpufurūtsu グレープフルーツ
Grapes Budō ぶどう
Japanese plum Ume うめ

Lemon Remon レモン
Melon Meron メロン
Orange Orenji オレンジ
Peach Momo 桃
Pear Nashi なし
Persimmon Kaki 柿

Pineapple Painappuru パイナップル

Strawberry Ichigo いちご

Tangerine Mikan みかん

Watermelon Suika すいか

Vegetables Yasai 野菜

Salad Sarada サラダ

Aubergine Nasu なす

Beans Mame 豆

Beansprouts Moyashi もやし

Carrot Ninjin にんじん

Cauliflower Karifurawā カリフラワー

Green pepper Piiman ピーマン

Green horseradish Wasabi わさび

Leek Negi ねぎ

Mushroom Kinoko きのこ

Onion Tamanegi たまねぎ

Potato Poteto/Jagaimo ポテト/じゃがいも

Radish Daikon だいこん

Sweetcorn Kōn コーン

Tomato Tomato トマト

FISH AND SEAFOOD DISHES

Fish Sakana 魚

Shellfish Kai 貝

Raw fish Sashimi さしみ

Sushi Sushi 寿司

Serving of sushi rice with topping Nigiri-zushi
にぎり寿司

Sushi rolled in crisp seaweed Maki-zushi まき寿司

Bowl of sushi rice topped with fish, egg and
vegetables Chirashi-zushi ちらし寿司

Abalone Awabi あわび

Blowfish Fugu ふぐ

Cod Tara たら

Crab Kani かに

Eel Unagi うなぎ

Herring Nishin にしん

Horse mackerel Aji あじ

Lobster Ise-ebi 伊勢海老

Octopus Tako たこ

Oyster Kaki かき

Prawn Ebi えび

Sea bream Tai たい

Sea urchin Uni うに

Squid Ika いか

Tuna Maguro まぐろ

Yellowtail Buri ぶり

MEAT AND MEAT DISHES

Meat Niku 肉

Beef Gyūniku 牛肉

Chicken Toriniku 鶏肉

Lamb Ramu ラム

Pork Butaniku 豚肉

Breaded, deep-fried slice of pork Tonkatsu とんかつ

Chicken, other meat and vegetables grilled on
skewers Yakitori 焼き鳥

Skewers of food dipped in breadcrumbs and deep-
fried Kushiage 串揚げ

Stew including meat (or seafood), vegetables and
noodles Nabe 鍋

Thin beef slices cooked in broth Shabu-shabu
しゃぶしゃぶ

Thin beef slices braised in a sauce Sukiyaki すきやき

OTHER DISHES

Buddhist-style vegetarian cuisine Shōjin-ryōri 精進
料理

Chinese-style noodles Rāmen ラーメン

Chinese-style dumplings Gyōza ぎょうざ

Fried noodles Yakisoba/Yakiudon 焼そば/焼きうどん

Stewed chunks of vegetables and fish on skewers
Oden おでん

Thin buckwheat noodles Soba そば

Soba in a hot soup Kake-soba かけそば

Cold soba served with a dipping sauce Zaru-soba/
Mori-soba ざるそば/もりそば

Thick wheat noodles Udon うどん

Fried rice Chāhan チャーハン

Lightly battered seafood and vegetables Tempura
天ぷら

Meat, vegetable and fish cooked in soy sauce and
sweet sake Teriyaki 照り焼き

Mild curry served with rice Karē raisu
カレーライス

Octopus in balls of batter Takoyaki たこやき

Pounded rice cakes Mochii もち

Rice topped with fish, meat or vegetables Donburi
どんぶり

Rice triangles wrapped in crisp seaweed Onigiri
おにぎり

Savoury pancakes Okonomiyaki お好み焼き

Chinese food Chūka-ryōri/Chūgoku-ryōri
中華料理/中国料理

Japanese-style food Washoku 和食

Japanese haute cuisine Kaiseki-ryōri 懐石料理

Korean food Kankoku-ryōri 韓国料理

"No-nationality" food Mukokuseki-ryōri
無国籍料理

Western-style food Yōshoku 洋食

DRINKS

Beer Biiru ビール
Black tea Kōcha 紅茶
Coffee Kōhii コーヒー
Distilled liquor Shōchū 焼酎
Fruit juice Jūsu ジュース
Green tea Sencha 煎茶
Milk Miruku/Gyūnyū ミルク/牛乳

Oolong tea Ūron-cha ウーロン茶
Powdered green tea Matcha 抹茶
Sake (rice wine) Sake/Nihon-shu 酒/日本酒
Water Mizu 水
Whisky Uisukii ウイスキー
Whisky and water Mizu-wari 水割り
Wine Wain ワイン

Glossary

anime Animated movies or TV shows.

banzai Traditional cheer, meaning "10,000 years".

basho Sumo tournament.

bentō Food boxes.

bodhisattva Buddhist who has forsaken nirvana to work for the salvation of all humanity.

bunraku Puppet theatre.

-chō or **machi** Subdivision of the city, smaller than a -ku.

-chōme Area of the city consisting of a few blocks.

dai Big or great.

daimyō Feudal lords.

-dōri Main road.

Edo Pre-1868 name for Tokyo.

furo Traditional Japanese bath.

futon Bedding.

-gawa/kawa River.

gaijin/gaikokujin Foreigner.

geisha Traditional female entertainer accomplished in the arts.

geta Wooden sandals.

hanami Cherry-blossom viewing.

Heian Period when Japan was ruled from Heian-kyō, now Kyoto (794–1185).

izakaya Traditional bar, also serving food.

ji-biiru Beer produced in local microbreweries.

Jizō Buddhist protector of children, travellers and the dead.

JR Japan Railways.

kabuki Traditional theatre.

kaiseki Japanese haute cuisine.

kaiten-zushi Conveyor-belt sushi restaurant.

kampai "Cheers" when drinking.

kanji Japanese script derived from Chinese characters.

Kannon Buddhist Goddess of Mercy.

katakana Phonetic script used mainly for writing foreign words in Japanese.

kimono Literally "clothes" but usually referring to women's traditional dress.

kissaten Traditional, independent café.

kōban Local police box.

-kōen Park.

-ku Principal administrative division of the city, usually translated as "ward".

maid café A café where the waitresses are dressed in costumes and role play.

maiko apprentice geisha.

manga Comics.

matsuri Festival.

Meiji Period named after the Emperor Meiji (1868–1912).

mikoshi Portable shrine used in festivals.

minshuku Family-run lodge, similar to a bed and breakfast, cheaper than a ryokan.

mon Gate.

netsuke Small, intricately carved toggles for fastening the cords of cloth bags.

nō Traditional theatre.

noren Split curtain hanging in shop and restaurant doorways.

obi Wide sash worn with kimono.

okashi Japanese sweets.

omiyage Gift, souvenir.

onsen Hot spring, generally developed for bathing.

otaku Obsessive fan mainly of manga and anime but can refer to other things, too.

pachinko Vertical pinball machines.

rōnin Masterless samurai.

rotemburo Outdoor hot-spring bath.

ryokan Traditional Japanese inn.

ryōtei Restaurant serving *kaiseki*.

sabō Traditional teahouse.

sakura Cherry blossom.

samurai Warrior class who were retainers of the *daimyō*.

sentō Neighbourhood public bath.

shamisen Type of lute.

Shinkansen Bullet train.

Shinto Japan's indigenous animist religion.

Shitamachi Old working-class districts of east Tokyo.

shogun The military rulers of Japan before 1868.

shōji Paper-covered sliding screens used to divide rooms or cover windows.

soaplands Brothel.

soba-ya Noodle bar.

sumi-e Ink paintings.

sumo Japan's national sport, a form of heavyweight wrestling which evolved from ancient Shinto divination rites.

tansu Traditional chest of drawers.

tatami Rice-straw matting, the traditional covering for floors.

torii Gate to a Shinto shrine.

udon-ya Noodle bar.

ukiyo-e Colourful woodblock prints.

washi Japanese paper.

yakuza Professional criminal gangs.

yokochō Market-style area, often focusing on food shacks.

yukata Loose cotton dressing gown.

Small print and index

283 Small print

285 Index

292 Map symbols

293 City plan

A ROUGH GUIDE TO ROUGH GUIDES

Published in 1982, the first Rough Guide – to Greece – was a student scheme that became a publishing phenomenon. Mark Ellingham, a recent graduate in English from Bristol University, had been travelling in Greece the previous summer and couldn't find the right guidebook. With a small group of friends he wrote his own guide, combining a contemporary, journalistic style with a thoroughly practical approach to travellers' needs.

The immediate success of the book spawned a series that rapidly covered dozens of destinations. And, in addition to impecunious backpackers, Rough Guides soon acquired a much broader readership that relished the guides' wit and inquisitiveness as much as their enthusiastic, critical approach and value-for-money ethos. These days, Rough Guides include recommendations from budget to luxury and cover more than 120 destinations around the globe, from Amsterdam to Zanzibar, all regularly updated by our team of roaming writers.

Browse all our latest guides, read inspirational features and book your trip at **roughguides.com**.

Rough Guide credits

Editor: Aimee White
Author: Martin Zatko
Cartography: Ed Wright
Managing editor: Rachel Lawrence
Picture editor: Aude Vauconsant

Cover photo research: Aude Vauconsant
Senior DTP coordinator: Dan May
Head of DTP and Pre-Press: Rebeka Davies
Layout: Ruth Bradley

Publishing information

Eighth edition 2020

Distribution

UK, Ireland and Europe
Apa Publications (UK) Ltd; sales@roughguides.com
United States and Canada
Ingram Publisher Services; ips@ingramcontent.com
Australia and New Zealand
Woodslane; info@woodslane.com.au
Southeast Asia
Apa Publications (SN) Pte; sales@roughguides.com
Worldwide
Apa Publications (UK) Ltd; sales@roughguides.com
Special Sales, Content Licensing and CoPublishing
Rough Guides can be purchased in bulk quantities
at discounted prices. We can create special editions,
personalised jackets and corporate imprints tailored to
your needs. sales@roughguides.com.

roughguides.com
Printed in Poland by Interak
All rights reserved
© 2020 Apa Digital 2020 (CH) AG
License edition © Apa Publications Ltd UK
All rights reserved. No part of this publication may be
reproduced, stored in or introduced into a retrieval system,
or transmitted in any form, or by any means (electronic,
mechanical, photocopying, recording or otherwise) without
the prior written permission of the copyright owner.
A catalogue record for this book is available from the
British Library
The publishers and authors have done their best to
ensure the accuracy and currency of all the information
in **The Rough Guide to Tokyo**, however, they can accept
no responsibility for any loss, injury, or inconvenience
sustained by any traveller as a result of information or
advice contained in the guide.

Help us update

We've gone to a lot of effort to ensure that this edition of
The Rough Guide to Tokyo is accurate and up-to-date.
However, things change – places get "discovered", opening
hours are notoriously fickle, restaurants and rooms raise
prices or lower standards. If you feel we've got it wrong
or left something out, we'd like to know, and if you can
remember the address, the price, the hours, the phone
number, so much the better.

Please send your comments with the subject line
"Rough Guide Tokyo Update" to mail@uk.roughguides.
com. We'll credit all contributions and send a copy of the
next edition (or any other Rough Guide if you prefer) for
the very best emails.

Reader's update

Thanks to all the readers who have taken the time to write in with comments and suggestions (and apologies if we've
inadvertently omitted or misspelt anyone's name):
Eva Gunnarsson, Gary Foggo

Acknowledgements

Martin Zatko would like to thank all those who assisted him during his trip around Japan (or were simply able to hang out
and be great), including Keisuke Yamamoto and the Freshroom team, super-cool Swiss housemates Miri and Milos, Takako
and the team at the Tokyo Convention & Visitors Bureau, Ched for the part-time gig as a whisky and sashimi delivery
driver, Soyeon for the trip down memory lane in ever-convenient Nakameguro, the kombini dotted around Senkawa for
providing alcohol and snacks around the clock, and various seas and oceans for providing all the fish.

ABOUT THE AUTHOR

Martin Zatko has been in a state of almost continuous motion since 2002, wending his way
through 140-odd countries to date, and writing or contributing to almost fifty Rough Guides,
including various editions of Japan, Korea, China, Taiwan, Vietnam, Myanmar, India, Turkey,
Greece, Morocco and Fiji. Japan keeps drawing him back, and he one day hopes to hitch-hike
across the whole country (again).

Photo credits

(Key: T-top; C-centre; B-bottom; L-left; R-right)

Index

21_21 Design Sight 102
2020 Olympic stadium 271
3331 Arts Chiyoda 59

A

accommodation 145
Airbnb 155
capsule hotels 6, 153
essentials 146
hostels 154
long-term 156
love hotels 150
minshuku 152
room rates 147
ryokan 152
accommodation (by area) 146
Akasaka and Roppongi 100, 149, 155
Akihabara and around 148, 154
around Tokyo 222, 225, 229, 236, 246, 252
Asakusa and around 149, 152, 154
Bayside Tokyo 149
Ebisu, Meguro and the south 149, 153
Ginza and around 147, 154
Harajuku, Aoyama and Shibuya 150, 154, 155
Ikebukuro and around 151, 153, 155
Imperial Palace and around 147
Narita 154
Ryōgoku and Kiyosumi 155
Shinjuku and the west 151
Ueno and around 148, 152
addresses 23
adventure sports 225
Advertising Museum Tokyo 51
aikido 212
Airbnb 155
Ajinomoto Stadium 211
Akagi-jinja 144
Akasaka 96
Akasaka Detached Palace 100
Akihabara 58
Akihito, Emperor 43
Ameyokochō 69
amusement parks 143, 195, 227
Andō Tadao 270
animal cafés 173
anime 61, 198, 135, 134, 269
antiques 201
Aoyama 120
Aoyama Reien 122
apartments 156

Aqua Park 112
aquariums 79, 95, 112, 140
architecture 268, 270, 271
arrival 20
art 198, 268, 269
art galleries. See museums and galleries
Artizon Museum of Art 56
arts, the 191
Asakura Museum of Sculpture 72
Asakusa 73
Asakusa Hanayashiki 77
Asakusa-jinja 77
ATMs 36
Azabu-Jūban 104

B

Bakurochō 63
bars 179, 194
baseball 211
Baseball Hall of Fame and Museum 143
bathing 29, 105
Bayside Tokyo 86
beer 181
beer gardens 182
bicycles 23
bike rentals 65, 74
Black Ships 258
books 263
bookshops 200
Budōkan 45
bunraku 192, 270
buses 23, 90
bus terminal 21
butler cafés 173
buyō 271

C

cabaret bars 194
cafés 61, 158, 173
cameras, shopping for 201
capsule hotels 6, 153
9 Hours 154
Capsule Inn Komagome 154
Ginza Bay Hotel 154
Glansit Akihabara 154
Millennials Shibuya 154
cathedrals 62, 141
cherry blossom 26

Chichibu-Tama National Park 237
Chiharu Shiota 269
Chiho Aoshima 269
children, travelling with 30
Chinzan-sō 141
Chūshingura 113
Chūzenji-ko 223
cinemas 195
climate 8, 32
climbing 225, 228
clinics 34
clubs 186
comedy clubs 194
Conder, Josiah 62
consumption tax 36
Container Gallery 111
convenience stores 206
cookery courses 169
cosmetics 204
costs 31
crafts 198
Crafts Gallery 44
credit cards 36
crime 31
cruises 164
culture 27
currency 36
cycling 23

D

Daikanyama 110
dance 193, 271
debit cards 36
department stores 202
design 268, 271
Design Festa Gallery 120
disabilities, travellers with 38
drinking 179
drugs 31
Drum Museum 78
duty-free shopping 198
dynasties 255

E

earthquakes 31, 259, 261
eating 157
Ebisu 106
economy 260
Edo era 257

Edo Taito Traditional Crafts Center 77
Edo-Tokyo Museum 81
Edo-Tokyo Open Air Architectural Museum 135
education 260
electricity 32
electronics, shopping for 201
embassies 33
emergency numbers 31
emperors 43
employment 35
Enoshima 245
entertainment 191. *See also* nightlife
entry requirements 32
etiquette 27
    eating 158
exchange rates 36

F

fashion 115, 204, 272
ferries 74, 21, 24, 90
festivals and events 25
    at Meiji-jingū 118
    calendar 26
    Design Festa 271
    Festival/Tokyo 196
    Fuji Rock 189
    Hanami parties 26
    Hiwatarisai 237
    in Kamakura 238
    in Nikkō 219
    LGBTQ festivals 190
    Rainbow Reel 190, 196
    Rock in Japan 189
    Samba Carnival 76
    Sanja Matsuri 76
    Summer Sonic 189
    Tokyo Design Week 271
    Tokyo International Film Festival 196
    Tokyo Pride Parade 190
film 266
Fire of the Long Sleeves 258
fish market 89
flea markets 201
flights 19
    from Australia, New Zealand and South Africa 19
    from other Asian countries 19
    from the UK and Ireland 19
    from the US and Canada 19
    from within Japan 20
flower arranging 100
food and drink 160
    cookery courses 169
    on a budget 162

shopping for 206
vegetarian and vegan 168
football 211
footwear etiquette 29
Formichetti, Nicola 272
free Tokyo 32
Fujifilm Square 102
Fuji Five Lakes 225
    accommodation 229
    arrival and departure 228
    bars 230
    drinking 230
    eating 229
    Fujikyū Highland 227
    Fuji Sengen-jinja 227
    Itchiku Kubota Art Museum 228
    Kawaguchi-ko 227
    Mount Fuji 228
    restaurants 229
    Tenjō-zan 227
    Togawa-ke Jutaku 227
    tourist offices 229
    transport 229
Fuji, Mount 225, 228
Fuji TV Building 94
Fuji-Yoshida 227
Fukagawa Edo Museum 84
Fukagawa Fudō-dō 84

G

gaijin houses 156
galleries. See museums and galleries
game centres 6
games, shopping for 208
gardens. See parks and gardens
geisha 194
Ghibli Museum 135
gifts 28
Ginza 50, 54
Ginza Sony Park 54
glossary 281
go-karts 112
Golden Gai 6, 132
government building 97
Great Kantō Earthquake 259
greetings 28
Grutt Pass 30
gyms 213

H

Hachikō 125
Hakone 230
    accommodation 236
    arrival 236

Ashino-ko 232, 233, 234
bus terminal 236
eating 237
Gōra 232
Hakone Barrier 234
Hakone Museum of Art 232
Hakone Open-Air Museum 232
Hakone-Yumoto 230, 234
Lalique Museum Hakone 233
Miyanoshita 230
Moto-Hakone 234
onsen 233
Onshi-Hakone Kōen 234
Ōwakudani 232
Pola Museum of Art 233
tourist information 236
train station 236
travel passes 236
Hama Rikyū Onshi Teien 52
hanami 26
Hanazono-jinja 132
Haneda airport 21
Harajuku 114, 115
Hara Museum of Contemporary Art 112
Haruki Murakami 264
Hatakeyama Memorial Museum of Fine Art 112
health 34
Hibiya 49
Hie-jinja 97
Higashi Gyoen 43
Higashi-Shinjuku 130
hiking 241
Hillside Terrace 110
history 255
history timeline 255
holidays 37
homelessness 261
homeware shops 207
hospitality 28
hospitals 34
hostels 154
    1980 Hostel 154
    Anne Hostel 155
    Bunka Hostel 154
    Citan 154
    Imano Tokyo Ginza 154
    Kaisu 155
    Khaosan Tokyo Origami 154
    K's House Mount Fuji (Fuji Five Lakes) 229
    K's House Tokyo 155
    Michael's (Fuji Five Lakes) 229
    Mount Fuji huts 229
    Nikkō Park Lodge (Nikkō) 222
    Nikkorisō Backpackers (Nikkorisō Backpackers (Nikkō)) 222
    Nui Hostel & Bar Lounge 155
    Retrometro Backpackers 155

Sakura Hostel 155
Turntable Hostel 155
Unplan 155
WeBase Hostel (Kamakura) 246
Yokohama Central Hostel
  (Yokohama) 252
hotels 147. See also capsule
  hotels
Akihabara Washington 148
ANA InterContinental Tokyo 149
Andaz 149
Asakusa Central 149
b Roppongi 149
Caravan Tokyo 150
Century Southern Tower 151
Cerulean Tower Tōkyū Hotel 150
Chūzenji Kanaya Hotel (Yumoto) 225
Claska 149
Coco Grand Ueno Shinobazu 148
Conrad Tokyo 147
Daikoku-ya (Fuji Five Lakes) 229
Dormy Inn 150
Edit (Yokohama) 252
Four Seasons 147
Fuji-Hakone Guesthouse (Hakone)
  237
Fuji Lake (Fuji Five Lakes) 229
Fujiya (Hakone) 237
Glanz 149
Gracery Shinjuku 151
Granbell 150
Grand Hyatt Tokyo 149
Grand Nikkō 149
Graphy Nezu 148
Hakone Tent (Hakone) 237
Hanare 149
Hilltop 148
Hoshinoya 147
Hyatt Regency Hakone (Hakone)
  237
Imperial 49
Imperial Hotel 147
J-Mex 151
Juraku 148
Kadoya 151
Kaihinsō (Kamakura) 246
Kamakura Prince (Kamakura) 246
Keiō Plaza 151
Mandarin Oriental Tokyo 147
Metropolitan 151
Mitsui Garden Ginza 148
Moto-Hakone Guesthouse (Hakone)
  236
Muji Hotel 148
Navios Yokohama (Yokohama) 252
New Kamakura (Kamakura) 246
New Ōtani 100
Nikkō Kanaya (Nikkō) 222
Nikkō Senhime-Monogatari (Nikkō)
  222

Nohga 149
Ōkura 149
OMO5 151
Park Hyatt Tokyo 151
Peninsula 147
Prince Hakone (Hakone) 237
Ritz-Carlton 149
Royal Park Hotel (Yokohama) 252
Ryūmeikan Tokyo 148
Stay Nikkō (Nikkō) 222
Strings 150
Super Hotel Kabukichō 151
Sunnide Village (Fuji Five Lakes) 229
Sunroute Ginza 148
Tokyo Station 147
Tōkyū Stay Aoyama 150
Tōyoko Inn Takanawaguchi 150
Trunk 150
Turtle Inn Nikkō (Nikkō) 222
Two Way 151
Yuen Shinjuku 151
Zebra 151
hot springs 212, 251. See
  also onsen

I

Ichigaya 45
Ichigaya Kamegaoka
  Hachimangū 46
Idemitsu Museum of Arts 49
Ikebukuro 136
Imperial Hotel 49
Imperial Palace 40
insurance 34
interior design shops 207
Intermediatheque 48
internet 34
Ishihara Shintarō 261
Issey Miyake 272
itineraries 16
Itō Toyō 271
izakaya 179

J

Japan Folk Crafts Museum 125
Jingū Naien 118
Jōgai-shijō 89
Jōmon period 255
Joypolis 94
judo 212
Jun Ashida 272
Jun Inoue 269

K

K-1 212
kabuki 192, 270
Kabukichō 130
Kabukiza Theatre 54
Kagurazaka 144
Kamakura 238
  accommodation 246
  arrival and departure 245
  bars 247
  buses 246
  Daibutsu Hiking Course 241
  Daibutsu, the 244
  drinking 247
  eating 247
  Engaku-ji 240
  Enoshima 245
  Enoshima-jinja 245
  Hase 244
  Hase-dera 244
  hiking 241
  history 238, 256
  Hōkoku-ji 243
  Iwaya 245
  Jōchi-ji 241
  Kamakura-gū 243
  Kenchō-ji 242
  Kita-Kamakura 239
  Samuel Cocking Park 245
  Sugimoto-dera 243
  Ten'en Hiking Course 241
  Tōkei-ji 240
  tourist offices 246
  trains 246
  train station 246
  travel pass 246
  Tsurugaoka Hachiman-gū 242
  Zuisen-ji 244
Kanda Myōjin 59
karaoke 9
karate 212
Kasai Rinkai-kōen 94
kendo 213
Kengo Kuma 270
Kids' Tokyo 30
KidZania Tokyo 90
kimonos 78, 207, 208
Kitanomaru-kōen 44
Kitchenware Town 78
Kite Museum 56
Kiyomizu Kannon-dō 66
Kiyosumi 80, 82
Kiyosumi Teien 84
Kōenji 134
Koishikawa-Kōrakuen 143
Komagome 142
Komparu-yu bathhouse 54
Konica Minolta planetarium 79
Konnō Hachimangū 124

Koreatown 177
Kusama Yayoi 269
kyōgen 192, 270
Kyū Furukawa Gardens 142
Kyū Iwasaki-tei Gardens 69
Kyū Yoshidaya Sake-ten 72

L

language 273
laundry 34
left luggage 35
LGBTQ Tokyo 29, 190, 196
live music venues 188
living in Tokyo 35
Lloyd Wright, Frank 270
love hotels 150

M

magazines 25
maid cafés 173
mail 36
Makoto Aida 269
manga 198, 269
maps 36
    Akasaka and Roppongi 98
    Akihabara and around 60
    Around Tokyo 217
    Asakusa and around 75
    Bayside Tokyo 88
    Ebisu and the south 108
    Fuji Five Lakes 226
    Ginza and around 53
    Hakone 231
    Harajuku, Aoyama and Shibuya 116
    Ikebukuro 140
    Ikebukuro and the north 138
    Kamakura 239
    Nikkō 218
    Omotesando 119
    Ryōgoku and Kiyosumi 83
    Shibuya 124
    Shimokitazawa 134
    Shinjuku 128
    The Imperial Palace and around 42
    Tokyo 5
    Tokyo Subway 300
    Ueno and around 66
    Western Tokyo 133
    Yokohama 248
Maritime Science museum 92
markets 201
martial arts 212
Marunouchi 48
Masakado 44
media 25
meditation 240

meetings 28
Mega Web 91
Meguro 111
Meiji era 259
Meiji-jingū 118
Meiji Jingū Baseball Stadium 211
Meiji-jingū Outer Garden 122
Meiji Memorial Picture Gallery 122
Meiji Seimei-kan 48
Meiji University Museum 63
Mejirodai 141
Minakami 225
Minamoto clan 256
minshuku 152
Mitsubishi Ichigokan Museum 48
Mitsui Memorial Museum 57
Miyamoto Unosuke Store 78
mobile phones 37
Mode Gakuen Cocoon Tower 270
money 36
monjayaki 160
monorail 23, 90
Mori Art Museum 104
Mori Digital Art Museum 91
Mount Fuji 225, 228
Mount Sengen 232
Mount Takao 237
Murakami Takashi 269
Muromachi era 256
museums and galleries
    21_21 Design Sight 102
    3331 Arts Chiyoda 59
    Advertising Museum Tokyo 51
    Artizon Museum of Art 56
    Asakura Museum of Sculpture 72
    Baseball Hall of Fame and Museum 143
    commercial art galleries 56, 101
    Container Gallery 111
    Crafts Gallery 44
    Cup Noodle Museum (Yokohama) 251
    Design Festa Gallery 120
    Drum Museum 78
    Edo-Tokyo Museum 81
    Edo-Tokyo Open Air Architectural Museum 135
    Fujifilm Square 102
    Fukagawa Edo Museum 84
    Ghibli Museum 135
    Hakone Museum of Art (Hakone) 232
    Hakone Open-Air Museum (Hakone) 232
    Hara Museum of Contemporary Art 112

Hatakeyama Memorial Museum of Fine Art 112
Hikawa-maru Museum (Yokohama) 250
Hillside Gallery 110
Idemitsu Museum of Arts 49
Intermediatheque 48
Itchiku Kubota Art Museum (Fuji Five Lakes) 228
Japan Folk Crafts Museum 125
Kite Museum 56
Lalique Museum (Hakone) 233
Meiji Memorial Picture Gallery 122
Meiji University Museum 63
Miraikan 92
Mitsubishi Ichigokan Museum 48
Mitsui Memorial Museum 57
Mori Art Museum 104
Mori Digital Art Museum 91
Musée Tomo 101
Museum of Maritime Science 92
Museum of Yebisu Beer 107
National Art Center 102
National Museum of Emerging Science and Innovation 92
National Museum of Modern Art 44
National Museum of Nature and Science 68
National Museum of Western Art 68
Nezu Museum 120
NTT Intercommunication Centre 130
Okamoto Tarō Memorial Museum 120
Ōta Memorial Museum of Art 119
Pola Museum of Art (Hakone) 233
Railway History Exhibition Hall 52
Samurai Museum 132
SCAI The Bathhouse 72
Seiji Tōgō Memorial Sompo Japan Museum of Art 130
Shitamachi Museum 67
Shōwa-kan 45
Suginami Animation Museum 134
Sumida Hokusai Museum 82
Suntory Museum of Art 102
Sword Museum 82
Taro Nasu Gallery 63
Toguri Museum of Art 124
Tokyo Metropolitan Teien Art Museum 111
Tokyo Museum of Contemporary Art 84
Tokyo National Museum 68
Tokyo Photographic Art Museum 107
Tōshō-gū Museum of Art (Nikkō) 220
Yamatane Museum of Art 110
Yamate Museum (Yokohama) 249

Yokohama Museum of Art
  (Yokohama) 250
Yokohama Port Museum
  (Yokohama) 250
Yūshūkan 46
music, classical 195
music, Japanese traditional 189
music shops 200
Myonichi-kan 137

N

Nakagin Capsule Tower 52
Nakameguro 9, 110
Nakatomi clan 255
Namco Namja Town 141
Narita International Airport 20
Naruhito, Emperor 43
National Art Center 102
National Diet Building 97
National Museum of Emerging
  Science and Innovation 92
National Museum of Modern
  Art 44
National Museum of Nature and
  Science 68
National Museum of Western
  Art 68
National Park for Nature Study
  111
National Stadium 211
National Sumo Stadium 81, 213
newspapers 25
Nezu 70
Nezu-jinja 70
Nezu Museum 120
nightclubs 186
nightlife 178
Nihombashi 56
Nijūbashi 42
Nikkō 216
  accommodation 222
  arrival and departure 221
  bars 223
  drinking 223
  eating 222
  festivals 219
  Futarasan-jinja 220
  Ganman-ga-fuchi abyss 221
  Meiji-no-Yakata 221
  restaurants 222
  Rinnō-ji 216
  Shin-kyō 216
  Taiyūin Reibyō 220
  Tamozawa Imperial Villa 221
  Tōshō-gū 218
  Tōshō-gū Museum of Art 220
  tourist information 222
  travel passes 221

Yashio Onsen 221
Nikolai Cathedral 62
Nishi-Shinjuku 127
nō 192, 270
Nogi-jinja 102
nomiya 179
noodles 160, 230, 251
NTT Intercommunication Centre
  130

O

Nakagin Capsule Tower 52
Ochanomizu 62
Odaiba 90
Odaiba beach 94
oden 160
Ōedo Onsen Monogatari 92
Oguraya 72
Okamoto Tarō Memorial
  Museum 120
okonomiyaki 160
Olympic Games 210, 260, 261
  2020 Games 123
Omoide Yokochō 130
Omotesandō Hills 120
onsen
  Hakone Yuryō (Hakone) 233
  Ōedo Onsen Monogatari 92
  Onsen-ji (Yumoto) 224
  Somei Onsen Sakura 142
  Spa LaQua 143
  Takaragawa 225
  Tenoyu (Hakone) 233
  Tenzan Notemburo (Hakone) 233
  Yashio Onsen (Nikkō) 221
opening hours 37
opera 195
Origami Kaikan 61
Ōta Memorial Museum of Art
  119
Ōta Sekenaga 256

P

pachinko 132
Palette Town 91
Panasonic Center Tokyo 91
parks and gardens 8
  Chinzan-sō 141
  Hama Rikyū Onshi Teien 52
  Happōen 111
  Hibiya 49
  Higashi Gyoen 43
  Inokashira Park 135
  Jingū Naien 118
  Kasai Rinkai-kōen 94
  Kitanomaru-kōen 44
  Kiyosumi Teien 84

Koishikawa-Kōrakuen 143
Kyū Furukawa Gardens 142
Kyū Iwasaki-tei Gardens 69
Meiji-jingū Outer Garden 122
Meiji-no-Yakata (Nikkō) 221
National Park for Nature Study 111
palace grounds 41
Rikugi-en 142
Samuel Cocking Park (Kamakura)
  245
Shinjuku Gyoen 133
Shiokaze-kōen 94
Ueno Kōen 65
Yoyogi-kōen 119
passports 32
PechaKucha Night 187
performing arts 269
pharmacies 34
phones 37
planetarium 79
police 31
post offices 36
public holidays 37
puppet theatre 192, 270

R

rafting 225
Railway History Exhibition
  Hall 52
Rainbow Bridge 94
rainfall 8
ramen 160
Rei Kawakubo 272
restaurants 157
  banquet meals 165
  Korean 177
  lunch and dinner cruises 164
  Robot Restaurant 194
  vegetarian 168
  yokochō 171
restaurants (by area)
  Akasaka and Roppongi 165
  Akihabara and around 161
  around Tokyo 222
  Around Tokyo 229, 237, 247, 252
  Asakusa 163
  Bayside Tokyo 164
  Ebisu, Meguro and the south 166
  Ginza and around 161
  Harajuku, Aoyama and Shibuya 168
  Ikebukuro and the north 171
  Imperial Palace and around 159
  Ryōgoku and Kiyosumi 164
  Shinjuku and the west 170
  Ueno and around 162
rickshaw rides 74
Rikkyō University 137
Rikugi-en 142

Robot Restaurant 6, 194
robots 61
rōnin 113
Roppongi 96, 101
Roppongi Hills 104
rugby 213
running 213
Ryōgoku 80
ryokan 9, 152
  Akimoto 153
  Andon Ryokan 152
  Gōra Kadan (Hakone) 237
  Hakone Ginyu (Hakone) 237
  Hōmeikan Daimachi Bekkan 153
  Kimi Ryokan 153
  New Koyo 152
  Ryokan Kamogawa 153
  Ryokan Katsutarō 152
  Ryokan Sansuisō 153
  Ryokan Shigetsu 153
  Sawanoya 152
  Sukeroku-no-yado Sadachiyo 153
  Tokyo Ryokan 153
  Villa Sacra (Kamakura) 246

S

safety 31
Saitama Stadium 212
sake 9, 186
Sakura Tram Line 141
Samurai Museum 132
SCAI The Bathhouse 72
Sengaku-ji 113
Sengen, Mount 232
Senjōgahara marshland plateau 224
Sensō-ji 76
sexual harassment 31
Shibuya 6, 114, 123
Shibuya Hikarie building 123
Shimokitazawa 134
Shinagawa 112
Shinjuku 126
Shinjuku Park Tower 129
Shinjuku Station 129
Shinobazu Pond 65
Shiodome 51
Shiokaze-kōen 94
Shitamachi 77, 257
Shitamachi art 268
Shitamachi Museum 67
shōchū 186
shoes 29
shopping 197
Shōwa-kan 45
skiing 216
smoking 30, 38
snowboarding 216

Soga clan 255
Sōgetsu Foundation 100
Somei Onsen Sakura 142
Spa LaQua 143
sport 210
St Mary's Cathedral 141
Street Kart 112
studying in Tokyo 35
subway 21
Suginami Animation Museum 134
Suidōbashi 143
Sumida 78
Sumida aquarium 79
Sumida Hokusai Museum 82
Sumiyoshi-jinja 87
sumo 9, 81, 82, 213
Sunshine Aquarium 140
Sunshine City 140
Suntory Museum of Art 102
sushi 90, 160
Sword Museum 82

T

Tabaimo 269
tachinomiya 179
Takao, Mount 237
takarazuka 193
Take-no-yu 105
Tange Kenzō 270
Tanigawa-dake 225
Taro Nasu Gallery 63
Tarō, Okamoto 122, 123
tattoos 29
tax 36, 159
taxis 24
tea 176
tea ceremony 112
teahouses 158, 175
  Alley Lujiaoxiang 177
  Aoyama Flower Market 176
  Cha Ginza 175
  Enokitei (Yokohama) 253
  Ganchabō 176
  Higashiya Ginza 176
  Sabō Nonohana 176
  Saryō 177
  Suzukien 176
  Toraya 176
  Umezono 176
teamLAB 269
television 25
temperatures 8
tempura 160
theatres and concert halls 192, 195
theatre, traditional 192
theme parks 90, 95, 195

ticket agencies 192
time zone 38
tipping 28, 159
Toguri Museum of Art 124
Tōhoku earthquake 261
toilets 29
Tokugawa dynasty 257
Tokugawa Ieyasu 257
Tokyo Bay 94
Tokyo Big Sight 91
Tokyo City View 104
Tokyo Disney Resort 95
Tokyo Dome 211
Tokyo Dome City Attractions 143
Tokyo Marathon 213
Tokyo Metropolitan Government Building 129
Tokyo Metropolitan Gymnasium 122
Tokyo Metropolitan Teien Art Museum 111
Tokyo Midtown 102
Tokyo Museum of Contemporary Art 84
Tokyo National Museum 68
Tokyo Photographic Art Museum 107
Tokyo Sea Life Park 95
Tokyo Skytree 78, 271
Tokyo Tower 104
Tokyo University 69
Tomioka Hachiman-gū 85
Toranomon 100
Tōshō-gū 67
tourist information 38, 74, 127, 222, 229
tour operators 20, 24
tours 74, 24
Toyokawa Inari Tokyo Betsuin 100
Toyosu 89
Toyota 91
toy shops 208
trains 16, 22, 90
train stations 21
trams 141
transport passes 22
travel agents 20
travel cards 22
tsukemen 9
Tsukiji 87
Tsukiji Hongan-ji 87
Tsukudashima 87

U

Ueno 64
Ueno Kōen 65
Ueno Zoo 67

V

vegetarians 168
Venus Fort 92
video games 61, 91, 94
viewpoints 74, 51, 44, 79, 94,
    104, 94, 104, 129, 140, 227,
    234, 250
visas 32
volcanoes 31
volleyball 214
volunteer opportunities 33

W

Western Tokyo 133
whitewater rafting 225
Wholesale Fish Market 89
wi-fi 34
Wonder Wheel 91
words and phrases 275
working in Tokyo 33, 35
World War II 259

Y

Yamanote 257

Yamatane Museum of Art 110
Yanaka 70
Yanaka Cemetery 72
Yanaka Ginza 70
Yasukuni-jinja 45, 46
Yebisu Beer museum 107
Yebisu Garden Place 107
Yohji Yamamoto 272
yokochō 171
Yokohama 247
    accommodation 252
    arrival and departure 251
    buses 252
    cafés and tearooms 252
    Chinatown 249
    Cosmo Clock 21 251
    Cup Noodle Museum 251
    eating 252
    ferries 252
    harbour 250
    Hikawa-maru Museum 250
    history 249
    Kantei-byō 249
    Landmark Tower 250
    Manyō Club 251
    Minato Mirai 21 250
    Motomachi 249
    restaurants 252
    Shinkō island 251

sightseeing bus 252
sightseeing cruises 251
subway 252
tourist information centre 252
trains 252
transport 252
Yamate 249
Yamate Museum 249
Yokohama Foreign General
    Cemetery 249
Yokohama Museum of Art 250
Yokohama Port Museum 250
youth culture 115
Yoyogi-kōen 119
yukata 208
Yumoto 224
Yūrakuchō 49
Yushima Seidō 61
Yushima Tenjin 70
Yūshūkan 46

Z

Zazen 240
Zen Buddhism 240
Zōjō-ji 105
zoo 67

Map symbols

The symbols below are used on maps throughout the book

–––– ··	Provincial boundary	––– ––	Ferry	◆	Place of interest	♟	Museum
–––– ––	Chapter division boundary	–– –– ––	Path	P	Parking	▲	Mountain peak
▬▬▬	Motorway	▬▬▬▬	Tram	⊞	Hospital	❀	Ferris wheel
–––––	Road	⊰⊱	Bridge	E	Embassy	🦵	Waterfall
▬▬▬	Pedestrianized road	✈	Airport	⊙	Statue	◠◠	Onsen
══════	JR line	Ⓢ	Subway station	⊠	Gate	▬	Building
═══════	Shinkansen line	○	Rail stop	🌲	Pagoda	◯	Stadium
··············	Other rail line	⛴	Boat	♆	Shrine	🏠	Cemetery
––––––	Monorail	✉	Post office	⛩	Buddhist temple	⬚	Park
–– –– ––	Cable car	ⓘ	Tourist information				

Listings key

■ Accommodation

● Eating

■ Drinking/nightlife

● Shopping

City plan

The **city plan** on the pages that follow is divided as shown:

0   200

metres

N

National Sumo Stadium

Edo-Tokyo Museum

Ryōgoku

Ryōgoku Station

KEIYŌ-DŌRI

SHUTO EXPRESSWAY 7

YASUKUNI-DŌRI

EDO-DŌRI

KEIYŌ-DŌRI

Tokitsukaze-beya

RYŌGOKU

Kasugano-beya

Dewanoumi-beya

SHUTO EXPRESSWAY 7

SHUTO EXPRESSWAY 7

aro Nasu Gallery

(S) *Bakuroyokoyama*

Hamachō (S)

Morishita

SHIN-ŌHASHI-DŌRI

Studio Geisha Café

(S) *Kikukawa*

(S) *Ningyochō*

KIYOSUMI-DŌRI

MITSUME-DŌRI

MITSUME-DŌRI

(S) *Suitengumae*

Kiyosumi-shirakawa

KIYOSUMI

KIYOSU-BASHI-DŌRI

Sumida-gawa

Fukagawa Edo Museum

Kayabacho

Kiyosumi Teien

Museum of Contemporary Art

Kiba Park

KASAIBASHI DŌRI

Fukagawa Fudō-dō

Monzennakacho (S)

🏮 **Tomioka Hachiman-gū**

Botanical Garden

Kiba (S)

KIYOSUMI-DŌRI

Sumiyoshi-jinja

TSUKUDASHIMA

MONJA-DŌRI

KIYOSUMI-DŌRI

(S) *Tsukishima*

TOYOSU

Triton Square

Kidzania Tokyo

0   200
metres

N

Arakawaitehumae Station

Minami-senju Station

Minowabashi Station (Arakawa)

Minami-senju Station

MEIJI-DŌRI

Minowa

MEIJI-DŌRI

MEIJI-DŌRI

EGISHI

SHOWA-DŌRI

Iriya

KOTOTOI-DŌRI

Sumida-koen

Sumida-gawa

SHUTO EXPRESSWAY 6

EDO-DŌRI

UMAMICHI-DŌRI

KAPPABASHI-DŌGU-GAI

Edo Taito Traditional Crafts Center

KOTOTOI-DŌRI

Asakusa Hanayashiki

Senso-ji

Asakusa-jinja

ROKKU

Niten-mon

KOKUSAI-DŌRI

Rock-za

Asakusa Station (Tsukuba Express)

Asakusa Batting Stadium

MANMICHI-DŌRI

EDO-DŌRI

Rox Department Store

KAPPABASHI

Drum Museum

Jakotsu-yu

Asakusa Station

Water bus pier

Tokyo Skytree Station

Inaricho

KAMINARIMON-DŌRI

NAKAMISE-DŌRI

ASAKUSA

Asakusa

Asahi Beer Hall

Sumida Aquarium

Tokyo Skytree

IGASHIUENO

Tawaramachi

KOKUSAI-DŌRI

ASAKUSA-DŌRI

Asakusa

SHUTO EXPRESSWAY 6

AZUMA-BASHI

SUMIDA

ASAKUSA-DŌRI

MOTOASAKUSA

ASAKUSA-DŌRI

EDO-DŌRI

Honjo-azumabashi

SUGA-DŌRI

Shinokachimachi

KASUGA-DŌRI

Kuramae

MITSUME-DŌRI

Asakusa-DŌRI

KUMAME BASHI-DŌRI

Kuramae

KURAMAE BASHI-DŌRI

KURAMAE BASHI-DŌRI

KURAMAE BASHI-DŌRI

Asakushabashi Station

Asakushabashi

National Sumo Stadium

Edo-Tokyo Museum

Ryōgoku

TOKYO SUBWAY